*Early Modern Literature in History*
General Editors: Cedric C. Brown, Professor of English and Dean of the Faculty of Arts and Humanities, University of Reading; Andrew Hadfield, Professor of English, University of Sussex, Brighton

Advisory Board: Donna Hamilton, University of Maryland; Jean Howard, Columbia University; John Kerrigan, University of Cambridge; Richard McCoy, CUNY; Sharon Achinstein, University of Oxford

Within the period 1520–1740 this series discusses many kinds of writing, both within and outside the established canon. The volumes may employ different theoretical perspectives, but they share an historical awareness and an interest in seeing their texts in lively negotiation with their own and successive cultures.

*Titles include:*

Cedric C. Brown and Arthur F. Marotti (*editors*)
TEXTS AND CULTURAL CHANGE IN EARLY MODERN ENGLAND

Martin Butler (*editor*)
RE-PRESENTING BEN JONSON
Text, History, Performance

Jocelyn Catty
WRITING RAPE, WRITING WOMEN IN EARLY MODERN ENGLAND
Unbridled Speech

Dermot Cavanagh
LANGUAGE AND POLITICS IN THE SIXTEENTH-CENTURY HISTORY PLAY

Danielle Clarke and Elizabeth Clarke (*editors*)
'THIS DOUBLE VOICE'
Gendered Writing in Early Modern England

James Daybell (*editor*)
EARLY MODERN WOMEN'S LETTER-WRITING, 1450–1700

Jerome De Groot
ROYALIST IDENTITIES

John Dolan
POETIC OCCASION FROM MILTON TO WORDSWORTH

Henk Dragstra, Sheila Ottway and Helen Wilcox (*editors*)
BETRAYING OURSELVES
Forms of Self-Representation in Early Modern English Texts

Sarah M. Dunnigan
EROS AND POETRY AT THE COURTS OF MARY QUEEN OF SCOTS AND JAMES VI

Andrew Hadfield
SHAKESPEARE, SPENSER AND THE MATTER OF BRITAIN

William M. Hamlin
TRAGEDY AND SCEPTICISM IN SHAKESPEARE'S ENGLAND

Elizabeth Heale
AUTOBIOGRAPHY AND AUTHORSHIP IN RENAISSANCE VERSE
Chronicles of the Self

Pauline Kiernan
STAGING SHAKESPEARE AT THE NEW GLOBE

Ronald Knowles (editor)
SHAKESPEARE AND CARNIVAL
After Bakhtin

Anthony Miller
ROMAN TRIUMPHS AND EARLY MODERN ENGLISH CULTURE

Arthur F. Marotti (editor)
CATHOLICISM AND ANTI-CATHOLICISM IN EARLY MODERN
ENGLISH TEXTS

Jennifer Richards (editor)
EARLY MODERN CIVIL DISCOURSES

Sasha Roberts
READING SHAKESPEARE'S POEMS IN EARLY MODERN ENGLAND

Mark Thornton Burnett
CONSTRUCTING 'MONSTERS' IN SHAKESPEAREAN DRAMA AND EARLY
MODERN CULTURE

MASTERS AND SERVANTS IN ENGLISH RENAISSANCE DRAMA AND CULTURE
Authority and Obedience

The series Early Modern Literature in History is published in association with the Renaissance Texts Research Centre at the University of Reading.

Early Modern History: Society and Culture
Series Standing Order ISBN 0–333–71472–5
(outside North America only)

You can receive future titles in this series as they are published by placing a standing order. Please contact your bookseller or, in case of difficulty, write to us at the address below with your name and address, the title of the series and the ISBN quoted above.

Customer Services Department, Macmillan Distribution Ltd, Houndmills, Basingstoke, Hampshire RG21 6XS, England

# Tragedy and Scepticism in Shakespeare's England

William M. Hamlin
*Department of English*
*Washington State University*

First published 2005 by
PALGRAVE MACMILLAN
Houndmills, Basingstoke, Hampshire RG21 6XS and
175 Fifth Avenue, New York, N. Y. 10010
Companies and representatives throughout the world

PALGRAVE MACMILLAN is the global academic imprint of the Palgrave Macmillan division of St. Martin's Press, LLC and of Palgrave Macmillan Ltd. Macmillan® is a registered trademark in the United States, United Kingdom and other countries. Palgrave is a registered trademark in the European Union and other countries.

ISBN-13: 978–1–4039–4598–3 hardback
ISBN-10: 1–4039–4598–5    hardback

This book is printed on paper suitable for recycling and made from fully managed and sustained forest sources.

A catalogue record for this book is available from the British Library.

Library of Congress Cataloging-in-Publication Data
Hamlin, William M., 1957–
    Tragedy and scepticism in Shakespeare's England / William M. Hamlin.
        p. cm. – (Early modern literature in history)
    Includes bibliographical references and index.
    ISBN 1–4039–4598–5
        1. English drama (Tragedy)–History and criticism. 2. English drama–
Early modern and Elizabethan, 1500–1600–History and criticism. 3. English
drama–17th century–History and criticism. 4. Shakespeare, William,
1564–1616–Philosophy. 5. Shakespeare, William, 1564–1616–Tragedies.
6. Skepticim–History–16th century. 7. Skepticism–History–17th century.
8. Skepticism in literature. I. Title. II. Early modern literature in history
(Palgrave Macmillan (Firm))

PR658.T7H35 2005
822'.05120903–dc22                                                2004062851

10   9   8   7   6   5   4   3   2   1
14   13   12   11   10   09   08   07   06   05

Transferred to digital printing in 2006

*For my mother,*
*Florence Ruth Greathouse*

*and to the memory of my father,*
*William Carl Hamlin*

# Contents

# Acknowledgements

Generous grants from the British Academy, the Huntington Library and the Renaissance Society of America enabled me to spend many months pursuing my enquiries on both sides of the Atlantic. A year-long fellowship from the National Endowment for the Humanities gave me precious time during which I finished the preliminary draft of this book. Parts of my typescript, in various earlier forms, were delivered as papers at the Shakespeare Association of America, the World Shakespeare Congress, the Renaissance Society of America and the International Marlowe Conference; earlier sections of chapters were published in *Studies in English Literature, Comparative Drama, Montaigne Studies, Sixteenth Century Journal* and *Early Modern Literary Studies*. I thank the respective journal editors and conference organizers for extending me multiple opportunities to present my ideas over the past half-dozen years.

More fundamentally, however, I acknowledge with gratitude the collaborative spirit of an international community of librarians and students of early modern history, philosophy and literature. Colleagues, friends and people I may never meet have answered my queries, given thought to my hunches, read sections of my typescript and, more generally, taken the time to help me make this a better book than it might otherwise have been. I have profited immensely from conversation and correspondence with dozens of scholars, among them Julia Annas, Richmond Barbour, Ben Bertram, Tom Bishop, Victoria Burke, Alberto Cacicedo, Stuart Clark, John Cox, Bob Darcy, Gail Fine, Tom Flanigan, A. C. Hamilton, James Hankinson, Peter Holbrook, John Lee, Fritz Levy, Ian McAdam, Nick Moschovakis, Charles Nauert, Melissa Norton, Matt Prineas, Theodore Rabb, Roger Sale, Garrett Sullivan, Virginia Mason Vaughan, Russell Wahl, Jonathan Westphal, Frank Whigham and Charles Whitney. Elisabeth Leedham-Green at Cambridge University Library responded with wit and alacrity to scores of questions, and Stuart Adams introduced me to the rich literary holdings of the Middle Temple. I also learned enormously from the knowledge and able assistance of Muriel McCarthy at Archbishop Marsh's Library, Dublin; Sarah Bendall and Fiona Wilkes at Merton College, Oxford; William Hodges at the Bodleian; Tony Trowles at Westminster Abbey; Norma Potter at All Souls College, Oxford; Guy Holborn at Lincoln's

Inn; Laetitia Yeandle at the Folger Shakespeare Library; James Anthony at the Warburg Institute; Stuart Seanoir at Trinity College, Dublin; Matthew Phillips at Christ Church College, Oxford; Adrian Blunt at the Inner Temple; David Wykes and Brian Rackley at Dr Williams' Library; Roger Lovatt at Peterhouse, Cambridge; Suzanne Eward at Salisbury Cathedral; Gabriel Linehan at Lambeth Palace; Jill Cogen and Virginia Renner at the Huntington; Christine Butler and Sarah Newton at Corpus Christi College, Oxford; and Robert Smith, Frances Harris and Hilton Kelliher at the British Library.

I am grateful to the late William Elton for inviting me to write on scepticism in early modern England for his *Shakespearean International Yearbook*. I am equally indebted to Arthur Kinney, who encouraged and guided me in my edition of *The Sceptick* for *English Literary Renaissance*. Robert Ellrodt, Luciano Floridi, Drew Jones, Brian Vickers, Robert Pierce and Germaine Warkentin have been particularly steadfast correspondents during the years in which this book has taken shape, offering astute commentary and shrewd advice. Debbie Lee, Tim Steury, Nick Kiessling, John Snyder, Michael Hanly, David Fuller and Stan Linden have been the staunchest of friends. At Palgrave, Paula Kennedy has infinitely eased the latter stages of book production, and Andrew Hadfield and Cedric Brown have been the best of all possible series editors: fair-minded, judicious, quietly and steadily supportive. Finally, I thank Charles Frey, Verena Theile, Moti Feingold, Patrick Cheney, Richard Popkin and David Bevington, each of whom took an abiding interest in my project, read more of my typescript than I had any right to expect, and provided invaluable criticism and unflagging encouragement. I am profoundly in their debt.

To the members of my family – my wife, Theresa Jordan, and our sons, Michael and Christopher – I can say little that will not seem immediately inadequate. I will say none the less that, while it may not always have been apparent, I have been sustained and immeasurably heartened by their understanding, patience and indomitable good spirits.

# A Note on Citation, Quotation and Abbreviation

In an effort to keep my notes as brief as possible I have limited citations to surname and page number, adding cue-titles when necessary. Full citations can be found in the bibliography. For works cited frequently I rely on standard abbreviations, a list of which appears below. I have appended a separate list of journal abbreviations at the head of the bibliography.

*Advancement*: Francis Bacon, *Of the Proficience and Advancement of Learning*, in *Francis Bacon*, ed. Brian Vickers (Oxford, 1996), 120–299.

*Apology*: Michel de Montaigne, *An Apology for Raymond Sebond*, tr. M. A. Screech (Harmondsworth, 1987).

*BCI*: Elisabeth Leedham-Green, *Books in Cambridge Inventories*, 2 vols. (Cambridge, 1986).

*CLC*: David Shaw, ed., *The Cathedral Libraries Catalogue*, 2 vols. (London, 1998).

Cotgrave: Randle Cotgrave, *Dictionarie of the French and English Tongues* (London, 1611).

*CS*: Charles B. Schmitt, *Cicero Scepticus: A Study of the Influence of the Academica in the Renaissance* (The Hague, 1972).

*CWE*: *The Collected Works of Erasmus*, ed. James K. McConica, et al. (Toronto, 1974–).

*Essais*: Michel de Montaigne, *Les Essais*, ed. Pierre Villey, rev. V.-L. Saulnier, 3 vols. (Paris, 1992).

*Essays*: M. A. Screech, tr., *Montaigne: The Complete Essays* (Harmondsworth, 1991).

Florio: John Florio, tr., *The Essayes of Michael, Lord of Montaigne* (London, 1603; New York, 1933).

*HS*: Richard Popkin, *The History of Scepticism from Savonarola to Bayle* (Oxford, 2003).

*IMD*: Louis I. Bredvold, *The Intellectual Milieu of John Dryden* (Ann Arbor, 1934).

*KLG*: William R. Elton, *King Lear and the Gods* (San Marino, 1966).

*LP*: Diogenes Laertius, *The Life of Pyrrho*, in *Lives of Eminent Philosophers*, tr. R. D. Hicks, 2 vols. (London, 1925), 2:474–519.

*M*: Sextus Empiricus, *Against the Mathematicians* (*Adversus mathematicos*), tr. R. G. Bury (Cambridge, MA, 1933–49).

*PH*: Sextus Empiricus, *Outlines of Pyrrhonism* (*Pyrrhoniarum hypotyposeon*), tr. Julia Annas and Jonathan Barnes (Cambridge, 1994).

*PLRE*: Robert Fehrenbach and Elisabeth Leedham-Green, eds., *Private Libraries in Renaissance England* (Binghamton, 1992–).

*RP*: Brian Copenhaver and Charles Schmitt, *Renaissance Philosophy* (Oxford, 1992).

*Sceptick*: William Hamlin, ed., 'A Lost Translation Found? An Edition of *The Sceptick* (*c.* 1590) Based on Extant Manuscripts', *English Literary Renaissance*, 31:1 (2001), 34–51.

*SE*: Luciano Floridi, *Sextus Empiricus: The Transmission and Recovery of Pyrrhonism* (New York, 2002).

*SR*: Paul Kocher, *Science and Religion in Elizabethan England* (San Marino, 1953).

Tilley: Morris Palmer Tilley, *Dictionary of the Proverbs in England in the Sixteenth and Seventeenth Centuries* (Ann Arbor, 1950).

*WFB*: *The Works of Francis Bacon*, ed. James Spedding, Robert Ellis, and Douglas Heath, 14 vols. (London, 1857–74; Stuttgart, 1963).

Due to considerations of length I have been obliged to leave out many notes and bibliographic citations that I would otherwise have included; I have also truncated a number of quotations in the interests of concision. Readers may contact me with questions.

Because there are various available translations of such classical texts as Sextus Empiricus' *Outlines of Pyrrhonism,* Cicero's *Academica* and Diogenes Laertius' *Life of Pyrrho*, I normally cite passages not by page but by book and section number; readers using different translations may therefore find passages with relative ease. For the sake of convenience I treat the two parts of the *Academica* as a single work, distinguishing between the two only in my notes.

Montaigne and Bacon pose special problems. In the case of Bacon's *Advancement of Learning*, I quote from the 1996 Oxford edition prepared by Brian Vickers; otherwise I rely for the most part on the 14-volume *Works of Francis Bacon*, edited by James Spedding and Robert Ellis. For important Latin treatises not translated in the *Works* – specifically the *Temporis, Cogitata,* and *Redargutio* – I use Benjamin Farrington's English renditions from 1964.

Quotations in French from Montaigne's *Essays* are drawn from Pierre Villey's magisterial edition, revised and corrected by V.-L. Saulnier. Unless otherwise noted, quotations and titles in English derive from M. A. Screech's 1991 Penguin translation. Quotations from John Florio's Elizabethan version are always designated by the abbreviation 'Florio'.

As the twelfth chapter of Book Two of the *Essays* – the 'Apology for Raymond Sebond' – occupies one-sixth of the entire work and has often been printed as a separate volume, I refer to it herein as the *Apology*, italicizing it for readerly convenience.

With regard to titles and proper names I normally opt for English familiarity. Hence I use Peter Ramus rather than Pierre de la Ramée, *On the Nature of the Gods* rather than *De natura deorum*, *Essays* rather than *Essais*. Such a choice entails minor inconsistencies for which I take full responsibility.

All unattributed translations from Latin and French are my own.

# Introduction: Engaging Doubt

*Plato* hath loved this manner of Philosophying, Dialogue-wise in good earnest, that therby he might more decently place in sundry mouthes the diversity and variation of his owne conceits. Diversly to treat of matters is as good and better as to treat them conformably.

Montaigne, *Essays*

When I was a boy of eight or nine my parents gave me a microscope. For several months I spent a good deal of time preparing and examining slides. Most of what I looked at was unremarkable: flattened mosquitoes, dog saliva, egg yolk, blood. But what amazed me – what I still remember vividly – is that as I adjusted my focus on a given slide, or shifted the level of magnification, I brought utterly different worlds into view. It was like passing through adjacent but unrelated galaxies. With time, of course, the amazement wore off: I took for granted what had begun as a revelation. But when I think about it now, it still strikes me as extraordinary that an apparently perspicuous surface can harbour astonishing depths – that it may hold in suspension wildly disparate phenomena.

English Renaissance tragedy has something of this character. Indeed, one might say this of the period's drama more generally – the mingled drama of which Sir Philip Sidney disapproved – but in tragedy the mix of diverse elements is especially pronounced. I refer not only to the tonal shifts and infirm didactic purposes of 'mungrel tragi-comedy', but to a more basic tendency to juxtapose perspectives and to move in dialectical patterns that seldom yield synthetic resolutions.[1] English tragedy in the late Elizabethan and Jacobean years manifests contrariety with stunning vehemence, and one result is that its meditations can

1

seem disturbingly inconclusive. Anyone who has taught *Doctor Faustus* or *King Lear* knows this for a fact. Experiments more than demonstrations, plays such as these allow for an unfolding of story that works simultaneously as an exploration of idea. Topics tacit and explicit are examined from multiple angles, their constituent elements subsumed within a sceptical milieu where every perspective can be entertained and every utterance treated as provisional.

Of course, drama is inherently sceptical in some respects – certainly more so than most literary forms. Staging oppositional values through the speech and action of characters, its normal tendency is to eschew authorial pronouncement. Dialogue may in fact be destabilizing at its very core, since elements of uncertainty are introduced whenever the control of discourse shifts from one figure to another: all the preparation in the world cannot guarantee that a given speaker will inflect an interchange with the emphases he or she desires. Narrative shape, thematic elaboration and individual assertions of will are complicated by the intruding interiorities of drama, and, on the whole, plays tend to provoke thought and feeling rather than urge conclusions. To the extent, moreover, that they exploit discrepant levels of awareness, plays typically imply fascinating realms of doubt. One character remains ignorant of what another thinks or does; auditors are granted privileged access to intentions – or kept tantalizingly in the dark. Such tactics may be deployed in other genres too, but they lie at the heart of dramatic construction.

In tragedy, however, scepticism finds a particularly congenial environment, since questions of perception, knowledge, rashness and judgement already figure importantly in the genre. And in English Renaissance tragedy sceptical attitudes are absorbed to a remarkable degree. It is now widely recognized that scepticism flourished in western Europe during the sixteenth and seventeenth centuries: initially as a consequence of the philological habits of continental humanists, later because Reformation debates drew heavily on sceptical arguments regarding criteria for religious truth.[2] But in England, because Elizabethan developments in tragedy coincided with the belated arrival of many characteristic preoccupations of the Renaissance, literary material and socio-historical milieu offered equally promising terrain for the cultivation of sophisticated forms of doubt and enquiry. Moreover, since tragedy typically involves a complex calculus of self-awareness and ignorance, personal responsibility and external victimization, the models of mixed response on which it depends were aided by scepticism's rhetoric of opposed voices. Joel Altman has demonstrated that the humanist educational programme contributed formatively to the development of interludes and other theatrical modes in Tudor England, above all in preparing audiences to expect *disputatio in utramque partem* – the elaboration of the varied sides of any given question.[3] But in tragedy, and in serious drama more generally, the moral debates so fundamental to ancient scepticism found a perfect vehicle for continued exploration. Indeed, it might be said that the most searching moral philosophy of the age took place on the platform stages of London.

Both in antiquity and in early modern Europe, scepticism manifested itself in two basic configurations. Pyrrhonism, named after Pyrrho of Elis and carefully delineated in the treatises of Sextus Empiricus, suggested that we have inadequate grounds for claiming certain knowledge about anything; we should therefore suspend judgement on all matters where conflicting perceptions and opinions may be advanced. Academic scepticism, by contrast, argued that epistemological certainty is impossible to attain, and that we should rather seek to develop forms of probable knowledge based on the scrupulous study of appearances. Refined in the Platonic Academy during the third and second centuries BCE, Academic scepticism found theoretical formulation in the commentaries of Arcesilaus and Carneades, but its dissemination in Renaissance Europe depended primarily on its presentation by Cicero in the *Academica*, a dialogue that was widely read from the fifteenth century onward. Pyrrhonists, meanwhile, felt that the Academics had gone too far: the claim that nothing is certain – that 'everything is inapprehensible' – amounted in their view to a form of dogmatism, specifically a 'negative dogmatism' as compared to the positively dogmatic assertions of the Stoics and Epicureans.[4] Thus Pyrrhonists acquired a reputation as more thoroughgoing sceptics than those associated with Cicero and Academicism, and when Sextus' *Outlines of Pyrrhonism* and *Against the Mathematicians* were finally published in the mid-sixteenth century, they prompted reactions ranging from excited admiration to antagonistic contempt. Still, for a majority of Renaissance readers, the two traditions of scepticism were seen as fundamentally akin to one another in their common engagement with epistemological doubt and their shared emphasis on the radical situatedness of individual humans.

Excellent accounts of the reception of Pyrrhonian and Academic scepticism in Italy and France have been published by Charles Schmitt, Richard Popkin and Luciano Floridi, but until now no such account has existed for Tudor and Stuart Britain. This is largely because France and Italy are more obvious candidates for studies in this vein: England offers no Montaigne or Bruno. It does, however, offer Marlowe, Bacon, Shakespeare, Donne and a host of others, and because many of these writers rely to one degree or another on the assumptions and argumentative strategies of the sceptics, it is well worth investigating England's reception and literary appropriation of the ancient sceptical sources. This is what I do in the early chapters of this book. But since the reception of ideas is never pure – never unaffected by the processes of transmission – I also devote substantial attention to the more conspicuous ways in which the features of classical scepticism manifest themselves in the discursive habits of Elizabethan and Jacobean writing. I call these manifestations 'sceptical paradigms'. Just as the austere epistemological commentary of Sextus is coloured, for Montaigne, by the dialogues of Cicero and the doxographies of Diogenes Laertius, so the most distinctive tropes of Pyrrhonism are inflected, for Nashe, Donne and Ford, by their assimilation to English proverbial lore or their naturalization through the popular translations of Montaigne, Mornay and Charron. What begins as a sequence of ideas and elaborations becomes, inevitably, a palimpsest where specific intellectual contributions are subordinated to larger, more diffuse currents of thought. But despite such blending, indeed despite the progressive laicization of scepticism, certain features of the ancient outlook remain relatively constant, and others are nourished in their new historical moment: above all, the mode of ongoing enquiry whose genesis lies partly in the investigative or *zetetic* dimension of Pyrrhonism. I treat such matters in detail in chapter 4.

The range of meanings and valuations with which people endow the word 'scepticism' can itself constitute grounds for doubt. T. S. Eliot observed in his essay on Pascal that one kind of scepticism leads to questioning, another ends in denial and a third prompts religious faith and is integrated into belief systems that transcend it. More recently, Stephen Toulmin has argued that scepticism must be equated with tolerance, intellectual modesty and a civilized agreement to disagree; the sceptical attitudes of the humanists, he claims, were lost when Descartes and Newton promoted the quest for absolute certainty.[5] This is an exaggeration, since Toulmin peremptorily conscripts Erasmus and Montaigne to represent Renaissance humanism as a whole, but his emphasis on the sceptical acceptance of uncertainty none the less serves a salutary function – particularly given the predilection of detractors to characterize scepticism as defeatist or nihilistic. Other valuable definitions have been advanced by such scholars as William Elton, Jonathan Dollimore, Stanley Cavell, Graham Bradshaw and

Terence Cave, but I would like to suggest that the essence of scepticism as I treat it in this book is an irrepressible spirit of questioning: an abidingly critical attitude towards all dogmatic or doctrinaire positions conjoined with an implicit and unceasing defence of open-minded enquiry.[6] Scepticism provides an antidote for rash judgement and overconfident assertion, and it offers an epistemological basis for what the Pyrrhonists call *epochē*: the deliberate withholding of assent or dissent. It thus interrogates not only conclusions subject to rational doubt, but conclusions *generated* by such doubt, and to this extent it remains open to the possibility of transcendental reality or experience. Readers of Montaigne will recognize that my understanding of scepticism is closely related to that implied by the *Essays*, particularly by those chapters where Montaigne grapples simultaneously with the intimations of reason and the attractions of faith.

Unlike Stoicism, Epicureanism and other philosophical movements that reached maturity during the Hellenistic era, scepticism is less a school of thought than a temper of mind: a set of characteristic mental attitudes and practices. It offers no body of dogma; its most habitual targets are the dogmatic claims of others. But scepticism shares one major trait with its Hellenistic rivals. Like them, it was perceived in early modern Europe as part of an immense classical inheritance that also included Hellenic philosophy and the intellectual contributions of the pre-Socratics. Indeed, with the exception of Aristotelianism, whose pre-eminence was a function of its continuous development over many centuries, there was in the Renaissance no firmly established hierarchy among the philosophical movements of antiquity. Today, we regard Plato as an incomparably greater thinker than Sextus or Pyrrho, but Montaigne and his contemporaries drew no sharp line between the Hellenic and Hellenistic traditions – in fact, the latter were often studied more assiduously than the former inasmuch as they were understood to participate in the genre of wisdom literature.[7] And since humanist educational practice transformed classical texts even as it encountered them, narrowly philosophical ideas and arguments were often put to new uses and channelled into new modes and forms. To some extent this accounts for the catholicity of interest we find in writers like Bacon, Ralegh, Donne, Hall and Burton; the period did not recognize the strong disciplinary demarcations we typically acknowledge today. Still, Renaissance scepticism always retained its maverick identity. With the ability to induce judgemental vertigo, dislodging people from settled opinions and biases, it functioned as a discursive irritant and was readily available to anyone who sought to deploy its premises and tactics. Moreover, the spread of Pyrrhonism was a crucial factor in the development of a modern mentality. As Cave observes, scepticism functioned as an 'intellectual corrosive' which 'helped to undo institutional and ideological structures that had been in place for centuries, [making] possible the elaboration of new ones'.[8] It was, in short, a force of transition.

Among the most fundamental features of ancient scepticism was its suggestion that through a willing suspension of judgement people could attain *ataraxia* – cerebral tranquility, freedom from anxiety. According to Sextus, the painter Apelles was once so frustrated in his effort to depict the froth of a horse that he hurled a sponge at his canvas – and in so doing inadvertently produced the effect he desired. Similarly, writes Sextus, the ancient sceptics, finding themselves unable to resolve the antinomies of noumena and phenomena, suspended judgement on the matter, and immediately experienced a welcome sense of calm (*PH*, 1.28–9). In early modern Europe, however, and particularly in the writings of Montaigne, *ataraxia* underwent significant complication as a key sceptical topos. To be sure, Montaigne praises it warmly: it is that 'condition of a quiet and settled life, exempted from the agitations we receive by the opinion and knowledge we imagine to have of things; whence proceed immoderate desires, ambition, pride, rebellion, disobedience, and the greatest number of corporall evils'. But at the same time he is far from convinced that judgemental suspension necessarily induces 'ataraxie', and thus he subjects a basic sceptical assumption to continued sceptical scrutiny (Florio, 449, 563). This is typical of Montaigne, and it steers us back towards the realm of tragedy, since pride, desire, rebellion and similar 'evils' swirl at the heart of the genre. If uncertainty is calming, as the sceptics allege, then why is it so often a source of torment? If the characters in tragedy are afflicted with doubt, do their struggles towards resolution affirm or confute the standard sceptical premises? Does tragedy offer satisfactions, and, if so, how do they relate to sceptical calm? Are detachment and serenity equally desirable goals? How relevant is the Aristotelian theory of *catharsis* to the Pyrrhonian idea that anxieties may be purged by suspension of epistemic commitment? Both tragedy and scepticism are fascinated with failures of certainty, but the differences between their customary engagements with doubt produce a cognitive *frisson*, and this in turn emerges as a fundamental point of departure for the later chapters in this book.

Sextus must have been aware of the uneasy affinities between tragedy and the Pyrrhonism he espoused. He quotes Sophocles and

Euripides; he notes that tragic drama repeatedly stages the conflicting valuations placed by humans on that which they perceive (*PH*, 1.86). But he never explores these relations in depth, and in fairness we cannot expect him to have done so, any more than we can suppose that he could have begun to imagine the meanings of 'tragedy' as it came to be understood more than a millennium later in a far-flung place and culture. Still, Sextus would have appreciated the degree to which the flourishing of Elizabethan tragedy tacitly interrogated the generic descriptions promulgated by Aristotle and prescriptively endorsed by neoclassical orthodoxy. I suspect that he would have delighted in the formal indeterminacies of *Troilus and Cressida*. Thus I have no hesitation discussing several plays which lie outside the conventional bounds of 'tragedy': the term, indispensable though it is, perpetually risks the reification of that towards which it gestures, and one of my subsidiary goals is to shake loose the hardened associations that sometimes encrust the concept. Charles Schmitt once observed that 'dialogue of the sort written by Plato and Cicero, in allowing the various sides of an issue to be expounded, permits a more open approach to philosophy than either works of the sort written by Aristotle or the scholastic *quaestio*'.[9] I find that comparably open exploration is encouraged by the dialogic impulses of drama, and especially by the emphatic concern with collapse and catastrophe that draws plays within the domain of tragedy. Such plays' interests and discordant tendencies seem not only congenial to scepticism, but sceptical in themselves.

So I posit for the purposes of this book a provisional continuum between, on the one hand, literary and philosophical dialogue, and, on the other, tragedic drama. The formal dialogue was of course a favoured medium for the encouragement and sustenance of humanist readership, while the vast majority of plays have always been designed for the stage. But the common stress on *embodied* and *conflicting* voices suggests an alliance between dramatic expression and dialogic meditation that we devalue at our peril, particularly given the disciplinary interpenetrations that typify early modern writing. If the Renaissance dialogues of Erasmus, Bodin and Bruno hearken back to Plato's *Republic* and Cicero's *Academica*, the tragedies of Kyd, Marlowe and their successors participate in like-minded habits of polyphonic rumination.[10] And when Dryden writes that his *Essay of Dramatic Poesy* 'is a dialogue sustained by persons of several opinions, all of them left doubtful, to be determined by readers', his remarks resonate profoundly with the sense of intellectual irresolution we often feel at the close of a Jacobean tragedy.[11] This is not to deny that plays cultivate the emotional engagement of auditors to an extent never contemplated in critical dialogues, nor that they rely on intensely wrought language and carefully orchestrated depictions of dispute, choice and consequence. I merely stress that a fundamental commonality between tragedy and dialogic exploration is the tacit positing of an audience disinclined to reductive conclusion, unafraid of contradiction and ambiguity: an audience that searches not so much for definitive answers as for potent means to concentrate the mind and heart on basic, often painful questions.

Shakespeare and his fellow dramatists certainly had the potential to be sceptical without reading Montaigne, and Montaigne had the same potential without reading Sextus or Cicero. A century before *Hamlet* and *The Duchess of Malfi*, Thomas More had imagined a utopian realm where 'every man might cultivate the religion of his choice, and proselytize for it, provided that he did so modestly, rationally, and without bitterness toward others'.[12] This emphasis on toleration – an emphasis that jostles uneasily against More's later intolerance towards the followers of Luther and Tyndale – is consonant with the practical consequences of scepticism's detachment from dogmatic positions. And to be sure, the sixteenth century found many ways of exhibiting distrust of dogmatism; Erasmus, Castellio and Scot are only a few figures in a long line of Renaissance dissenters. But if sustained engagement with doubt was encouraged by widespread doctrinal dispute, it was further promoted by the translation and dissemination of the ancient sceptical treatises. And when such intellectual access was conjoined with the particular social anxieties of Britain at the end of Elizabeth's reign, the fusion of disparate uncertainties could not help but infiltrate literary imagination.[13] Even Spenser, among the least sceptical of poets, asks in *The Faerie Queene* why 'witlesse man [should] so much misweene, / That nothing is, but that which he hath seene'. So we should probably be unsurprised that it was England which produced the first vernacular translation of Sextus Empiricus: *The Sceptick*, which appeared around 1590. Marlowe and Shakespeare may never have seen the work, but its genesis within the same *fin de siècle* milieu that yielded *The Spanish Tragedy* and *Doctor Faustus* seems, in retrospect, virtually predictable. And its preoccupations, as I will argue, surface again in such varied plays as *Troilus and Cressida*, *The Changeling* and *The Tragedy of Mariam*.

Thus when Friar Bonaventura alludes, in *'Tis Pity She's a Whore*, to 'school-points' – topics for academic disputation – his meaning is not far removed from what Hamlet has in mind when he warns the visiting actors against obscuring, through misguided efforts at humour, 'some necessary question of the play'. If a modern scholar can speak of Bruno's London dialogues as 'bordering on drama in [their] clashes of opinion', we can certainly assimilate the interrogative energies of Elizabethan tragedy to the exploratory modes of early modern moral and metaphysical debate.[14] Indeed, these modes, steeped as they were in rhetorical culture and linked to habits such as the production of commonplace books, may well have predisposed audiences to contemplate dramatic performance through a template of argumentative development. And whether we refer narrowly to the examination of contemporary notions of providential supervision and divine justice, or more broadly to large-scale societal scrutiny of gender assumptions, sexual mores and concepts of the 'natural', we find that the modalities of enquiry promoted by ancient scepticism contribute to the power and efficacy of dramatic representation. In particular, we observe that various instrumentalizations of sceptical tropes and attitudes are appropriated within theatrical culture: propaedeutic scepticism, ocular modes of investigation, and the reinscription of doubt by desire are just a few of the forms in which Pyrrhonian and Academic ideas are transformed in the plays of Marlowe, Shakespeare and Cary. And since the very possibility of such transformation depends on the simultaneous intellectual probing of figures such as Montaigne, Bacon, Charron, Greville and Donne, I insist throughout this book on a studied avoidance of disciplinary segregation. Only this way can the discursive continuities to which I hope to draw attention come most clearly into view.

Regarding evidentiary concerns, I stress that, like Popkin, Schmitt and others, I concentrate on textual indications suggesting authentic intellectual connectedness with the sceptical traditions of antiquity. But I never demand that these indications demonstrate fully accurate representation or thoroughgoing comprehension of the relevant epistemological issues. Thus, for the purposes of my investigation, misunderstood or partially apprehended Pyrrhonism constitutes evidence of scepticism's reception in England, as do allusions to Pyrrho, Arcesilaus, Carneades, Sextus, 'Academike' philosophers and, depending on the context, pre-Socratic thinkers such as Protagoras, Empedocles, Anaxagoras or Democritus. Other forms of evidence include mockery of sceptical attitudes, sects or tropes, and misconstrual or misrepresentation of basic sceptical concepts such as contradiction (*anomalia*), equipollence (*isostheneia*), non-assertion (*aphasia*), suspension of judgement (*epochē*), inapprehensibility (*acatalepsia*) and unperturbedness (*ataraxia*). I propose, moreover, that forms of reciprocity habitually obtain between popular and philosophical scepticism: evidence of the latter often confirms the existence of the former, as well as providing one of the fundamental means by which the former is codified and perpetuated. And both owe their existence in late Renaissance Europe primarily to the period's unprecedented ideological controversies.

The evidentiary basis for such an understanding of scepticism in early modern England is thus diverse. It includes, beyond the kinds of textual data mentioned above, (1) lexical exploration in Tudor/Stuart dictionaries, compendia, thesauri and commonplace books; (2) investigation of proverbial wisdom regarding certainty and doubt; (3) consideration of *quaestiones* for academic disputation at sixteenth-century Oxford and Cambridge, and of rhetorical training in *pro et contra* débate more generally; (4) examination of the British dissemination of key sceptical sources (ancient and modern, sympathetic and critical) through translation, quotation and citation; (5) further examination of such dissemination through study of book and manuscript ownership and annotation, not only at university libraries, but at the Inns of Court, in cathedral and ecclesiastical collections, and in private bookstacks; (6) scrutiny of polemical works (moral, theological, astrological, demonological) which articulate, rebut or presuppose sceptical objections; (7) analysis of intellectual continuities between sceptical habits of thought and ecumenical challenges to early modern religious orthodoxy – challenges such as those posed by Socinian and Arminian critiques of the Reformed Church; and, finally, (8) study of synchronic and diachronic patterns of sceptical interrogation inferred from recurrent thought trajectories embedded within a heterogeneous body of English Renaissance writings: poetic, dramatic, devotional, historical, ethnological, pedagogical. My basic findings are twofold. First, scepticism derived from classical and contemporary sources was more widespread in early modern Britain than has been recognized by historians of philosophy, but not as unproblematically endorsed as has often been assumed by literary critics. Second, we must rely on a set of sceptical paradigms if we are to speak with authority and precision about sceptical habits of mind in Elizabethan and Jacobean literature. Writers are seldom systematic philosophers, and in their efforts to grasp the spirit they often neglect the letter. Accordingly, scepticism in Renaissance England was understood and appropriated in a range of distinct yet overlapping manners, and it is crucial for students seeking to explicate literary works within the matrices of social and intellectual history to take these configurations of reception into account.

In this monograph, then, chapter 1 summarizes the continental reception of Pyrrhonian and Academic scepticism from the humanist recovery of the manuscripts of Sextus until the later sixteenth century. Chapters 2 and 3 provide a 'thick description' of scepticism's reception in England from roughly 1570 through the Jacobean years and on to the founding of the Royal Society. Much of what I present here is based on the kinds of archival investigation to which I have just alluded, and among the central features are an account of *The Sceptick*, a survey of French discussions of scepticism whose circulation in England is readily demonstrable, and fresh treatments of Florio's rendition of Montaigne and Bacon's lifelong struggle with the challenges of epistemological doubt. Chapter 4 outlines the major paradigms of scepticism that become available to poets and playwrights as a consequence of scepticism's English reception; it offers, in effect, an inductively generated taxonomy of the literary appropriations of the sceptical tradition in early modern England. And chapters 5–12 treat individual plays by Marlowe, Kyd, Shakespeare, Marston, Cary, Webster, Middleton and Ford, examining them with the paradigms of scepticism's reception always in mind. Earlier students of drama and scepticism have tended to view individual characters as themselves sceptical in outlook: Rolf Soellner understands Troilus and Ulysses this way; William Elton presents Lear as an exemplar of thoroughgoing doubt.[15] My book, by contrast, isolates sceptical patterns in the larger fabric and dialogic structure of specific plays. Thus, in my chapter on *Faustus*, I argue that Marlowe's tragedy exploits the tensions and cognitive vexations of a high-stakes dialectic between desire and doubt. And regarding *'Tis Pity* I suggest that Ford's exploration of sexual transgression acquires part of its staggering power from deep structural participation in a culture's inchoate anxieties over criteria for moral judgement.

Many other plays could have found their way into this study. Indeed several lie just beneath the surface of my discussions: *Hamlet* in particular, but also *The Jew of Malta*, *Measure for Measure*, *King Lear* and *The Revenger's Tragedy*. Still, I trust that the plays I have chosen will serve my purposes. I make no claim to offer anything approaching a comprehensive view of English Renaissance tragedy, but only to provide sustained illumination of a crucial but often neglected aspect of the genre: an epistemological dimension that gestures towards issues of deep cultural concern. As social anxieties fused with religious and philosophical uncertainties in late Elizabethan Britain, the lineaments of scepticism revealed themselves in popular drama, and my book places their specifically tragic manifestations against an anatomy of early modern doubt. My readings are thus intended to function as a lens through which the vital but dispersed critical energies of English tragedy may come more sharply into focus. Important strata within diverse plays can thereby take on heightened significance, their contours growing more distinct in light of the discursive connections I draw to their intellectual environment. My hope, in the end, is that those who cherish the dramatic imaginings of Shakespeare and his fellows will find their satisfactions enhanced by this enquiry into tragedy's engagements with doubt.

# Part One

# The Reception of Ancient Scepticism in Elizabethan and Jacobean England

# 1
# The Continental Background

A: *Tu es mort o Pyrrhon?* P: *J'en doubte.* A: *Après la mort
Es tu doncques doubteux?* P: *Et je doubte plus fort.*

Pierre Le Loyer, Des Spectres

Sometime during the 1570s, at his hilltop château in southwestern
France, Michel de Montaigne wrote that 'Whoever seekes for anything,
commeth at last to this conclusion and saith that either he hath found
it, that it cannot be found, or that he is still in pursuit after it' (Florio,
448). When Montaigne's remarkable book of essays was subsequently
published in 1580, few of its readers would have known that this
particular idea had been lifted wholesale from the Hellenistic sceptic
Sextus Empiricus. Virtually all of them, however, would have seen that
Montaigne's sympathies lay principally with the active seekers, those
'still in pursuit'. And in John Florio's Elizabethan translation of the
*Essays*, English readers would have experienced the same response, for
Montaigne's impatience with dogmatic assertion readily transcends linguistic barriers. Thus it was, sixty years after the onset of Reformation
debate, that an idiosyncratic Frenchman living in rural retirement initi-
ated a curious and sustained engagement with the scepticism of antiquity – an engagement that not only shaped his life but helped to charge
the intellectual atmosphere of Europe during the late sixteenth and early
seventeenth centuries. Yet the story of how Montaigne came to read
Sextus, and how England came to read them both, begins much earlier.

   In quattrocento Italy, as Richard Popkin, Charles Schmitt and Luciano
Floridi have variously demonstrated, Greek manuscripts of Sextus' writings were known to many humanist intellectuals, among them Francesco Filelfo, Giovanni Aurispa, Marsilio Ficino and Giovanni Pico della
Mirandola. Latin manuscripts of Cicero's *Academica*, meanwhile, had

been available to Petrarch as early as 1344, and in the following century were read by Nicholas of Cusa, Lorenzo Valla and Rudolph Agricola, as well as by Ficino, Aurispa and Giovanni Pico, who were already familiar with Sextus. The humanist Filelfo, often credited with transporting manuscripts of Sextus to Italy from Constantinople, lent the works to Aurispa in 1441, and later in the century codices of Sextus were held in the Medici library, at the Vatican and in the Florentine Convent of San Marco. But even earlier, around 1433, Ambrogio Traversari had completed a Latin translation of Diogenes Laertius' *Lives of Eminent Philosophers*, and it was in Traversari's rendering of the *Life of Pyrrho* that the term 'scepticus' was introduced into early modern European thought.[1] Traversari's translation circulated widely in manuscript and was eventually published in 1472. Like Raymond Sebond's *Natural Theology* – also composed during the 1430s – it was destined to have a significant but utterly unanticipated impact on the Renaissance reception of ancient scepticism.

Still, it was the work of Sextus which, even more than that of Cicero and Laertius, introduced fifteenth- and sixteenth-century Europeans to the systematic presentation of epistemological scepticism.[2] By the late 1490s, Girolamo Savonarola had encountered Sextus in manuscript and was sufficiently impressed that he asked Florentine friends to translate the Greek into Latin. This seems never to have happened – probably due to his execution in 1498 – but as his biographer Gianfrancesco Pico della Mirandola notes, Savonarola 'loathed the ignorance of many people who boasted that they knew something'.[3] At the close of the fifteenth century, then, there was clear interest in the works of Sextus, at least in major Italian centres such as Florence, Venice and Rome. And it was not much later that intellectuals north of the Alps began to discuss the central issues of scepticism, even if their sources were limited at first to Plato, Aristotle, Cicero, Lucian, Galen, Laertius and Augustine.[4] By 1509 Erasmus had composed his *Praise of Folly*, the eponymous figure of which alleges that 'human affairs are so complex and obscure that nothing can be known of them for certain, as has been rightly stated by my Academicians, the least assuming of the philosophers'.[5] Erasmus also alludes to Lucian's *Icaromenippus*, which mentions Pyrrho and 'Academic suspense of judgment' in its ironic depiction of Zeus. Along with Thomas More, Erasmus had translated various Lucianic dialogues during his 1505–6 visit to England, and thus the mock encomium was eminently familiar to him.[6] Indeed, to the extent that Lucian's dialogues were used as school texts through much of Europe during the sixteenth century, such encomia became familiar to most scholars. Very likely Erasmus and More both knew Lucian's *Sale of Creeds*, which also addresses scepticism through its depiction of a slave, Pyrrhon, who is lampooned for his insistence that 'everything eludes my grasp' and for his claim, immediately after being sold, that he 'doubts' the existence of the transaction. The emphasis on appearances in Lucian's portrayal – Pyrrhon remarks that 'There does not appear to me to be anything' – suggests that Lucian is referring to the more radical scepticism of the Pyrrhonists rather than to the negative dogmatism of the New Academy. Thus, given Erasmus' evident knowledge of the latter form of scepticism, it is entirely possible that by the first decade of the sixteenth century he had been exposed to this crucial distinction among sceptical habits of thought.[7]

Erasmus also knew Galen's *The Best Kind of Teaching*, which he translated in 1526, and which was frequently reprinted before appearing in the Latin editions of Sextus by Henri Estienne (1562) and Gentian Hervet (1569). Attacking the first-century sceptic Favorinus of Arles and offering vehement critiques of Academic and Pyrrhonian doubt, Galen's work provides valuable information on both schools of thought; it was clearly known later in the century by Francisco Sanches, who relies on it in *That Nothing Is Known* (1581).[8] Galen also alludes to Pyrrhonism in other works, and in *My Own Books* he claims that as a young man 'I might well have fallen into a Pyrrhonian despair of knowledge, had I not had a firm grasp of geometry and arithmetic, in which subjects I excelled'.[9] The *a priori* certainties of mathematics, in short, kept Galen from endorsing Pyrrhonism. But to the extent that Galen's writings are also hostile to dogmatism, they resonate powerfully with the sixteenth-century revival of the anti-authoritarian attitudes of Cicero and Sextus. Over 600 editions of Galen were published in early modern Europe, and a partial consequence of this fact is that Renaissance medical treatises often comment on scepticism, even when it is remote from their primary concerns.[10]

Elsewhere beyond the Alps, the French humanist Guillaume Budé had recommended by 1514 that people pay more attention to the 'ephectici' so as to curb the rashness of their judgements.[11] And Henry Cornelius Agrippa had certainly encountered sceptical doctrines by 1515; in his *Address at Pavia* he lists the Peripatetics, Academics and Sceptics as the chief schools of philosophers, adding that he always shuns the last, 'among whom nothing is certain ... but all things indifferent'. Agrippa's delineation of three philosophical schools is reminiscent of that established at the outset of Sextus' *Outlines*; it suggests that he knew the central Pyrrhonian/Academic distinction by this date, a distinction which may have been commonplace, but which was not mentioned in Laertius' *Life of Pyrrho* or Cicero's *Academica*. Scholars generally concur, however, that Agrippa did *not* have access to Sextus' works. Charles Nauert asserts that Agrippa's sources included Ficino, Nicholas of Cusa, Jacques Lefèvre d'Etaples, John Colet and possibly Cicero and Galen, but probably not Sextus; Popkin finds 'no reference to Sextus' in Agrippa's later and more famous *Of the Vanitie and Uncertaintie of Artes and Sciences*, although he detects sections which 'may have been based on that source'.[12]

Indeed, Agrippa's *Vanitie* (1531) has convinced more than one scholar that its author knew Sextus' *Outlines*.[13] But while the book's allusions to 'Academikes', 'Pirronikes' and 'Academicke purginge' demonstrate that Agrippa understood the difference between those who claimed 'that nothinge might be affirmed' and those 'that affirmed nothinge', they probably derive from other sources. Nauert, in fact, claims that 'references to ancient sceptical authors, and expositions of their thought, were so numerous [by 1526] that Agrippa could hardly have avoided learning much about their viewpoints'.[14] Classified by Popkin as an instance of 'fundamentalist anti-intellectualism' rather than an authentic exploration of epistemological problems, Agrippa's book is perhaps more important for its wide dissemination of the 'vanity of learning' thesis than for its advancement of any genuinely philosophical arguments. Still, the book was immensely popular; its readers, besides Montaigne and the English translator James Sanford, included Sir Philip Sidney, Fulke Greville, Thomas Nashe, Giordano Bruno, John Rainolds and John Davies of Hereford, each of whom played a role in the British reception of ancient scepticism.[15]

Several years before Agrippa composed his *Vanitie*, Erasmus published his famous treatise *On Free Will* (1524), which criticizes the teachings of Luther by juxtaposing conflicting views of grace and freedom, much in the manner of the argumentation *in utramque partem* described in Cicero's *Academica* (1.45–6, 2.7–8). The work thereby advocates a sceptical justification for adhering to Catholicism, and indeed Erasmus concedes that 'I take so little pleasure in assertions that I gladly seek refuge in scepticism whenever this is allowed by the inviolable authority of Holy Scripture and the Church's decrees'.[16] Luther responded with *The Bondage of the Will*, a truculent attack which denounces Erasmus' opinions as 'trash' and maintains that Christians must delight in claims of certain knowledge:

> Let Sceptics and Academics keep away from us Christians, but let there be among us 'assertors' twice as unyielding as the Stoics ...

Permit us to be devoted to assertions and to delight in them, while you stick to your Sceptics and Academics till Christ calls you too. The Holy Spirit is no Sceptic, and it is not doubts or mere opinions that he has written on our hearts, but assertions more sure and certain than life itself.[17]

Luther's contempt for admissions of uncertainty was largely shared by his disciple Philip Melanchthon, though as an implementer of humanist curricula in German universities Melanchthon participated to some extent in the promotion of the moderate sceptical outlook characteristic of many humanists. In his frequently reprinted *Dialectics*, Melanchthon vehemently rejects nescience and probabilism, arguing that people 'must not listen to the Pyrrhonists or Academicians doing away with certainty and contending that everything is doubtful .... It is a crime to seek out tricks to slip away from statements which God wants us to embrace without doubting.'[18]

One of the ironies in the history of scepticism is that the Reformers' confidence that they knew at least some of God's desires was typically coupled with an emphasis on human depravity which, in many treatises, was viewed as entirely consonant with sceptical habits of mind. Conversely, the Reformers' critics – Erasmus as well as many Counter-Reformation thinkers – often used sceptical argumentation to preserve a view of God which implied confident understanding of his divinity and standard propensities, particularly with respect to rewarding or punishing humans. Erasmus' concern for human freedom, after all, is equally a concern for the character of God. Perhaps, as Montaigne suggests, humans of all religious persuasions experience genuine difficulty escaping anthropocentrism in their pronouncements on deity: 'We, in our ignorance, want to force God through human filters. All the raving errors this world possesses are bred from trying to squeeze onto human scales weights far beyond their capacity' (*Apology*, 101).

The references to scepticism in Luther and Melanchthon probably derive more directly from Cicero's *Academica* than from any other classical source. Initially printed in 1471 and thereafter becoming widely available, this work 'played a specific and well-documented role in the development of Renaissance thought'.[19] Still, the basic distinction between Academic and Pyrrhonian scepticism, never articulated by Cicero and often ignored or blurred by early modern thinkers, was none the less available through at least one other channel. The German scholar Johann Caesarius demonstrates in his *Dialectica* (1533) that the Academic habit of comparing opinions to determine which is the more probable may be distinguished from the Pyrrhonian reluctance to assent even to the idea of probability. And both tendencies differ markedly from the standard procedures of Stoics and Peripatetics, who believe themselves capable of attaining certainty. Caesarius derives this tripartite division from the preface to Ficino's *Of Pleasure* (1457) – and Ficino, as we have seen, was among the fifteenth-century Italians acquainted with Sextus' manuscripts.[20]

The most important pre-Montaignian student of Sextus, however, was Gianfrancesco Pico della Mirandola, nephew to the more famous Giovanni. Pico's *Examen vanitatis doctrinae gentium* (*The Weighing of Empty Pagan Learning Against Christian Teaching*, 1520), drew extensively on Sextus' writings in its attack on the schools of ancient philosophy – particularly Aristotelianism – and in its discrediting of all sources of knowledge apart from scripture. Popkin classifies the work as an early instance of 'Christian Pyrrhonism', and his phrase is apt in that it calls attention to differences between Pico's method and that of the Pyrrhonists, who would have subjected Christian revelation to the same scrutiny applied to any other form of authority. Pico, however, considered Christianity 'immune to sceptical infection because it does not depend on the dogmatic philosophies Sextus refuted'.[21] Popkin's phrase is also useful because it links Pico with Montaigne, Charron, Valencia and others in the fideistic tradition of employing sceptical argumentation to defend Christian revelation. Not surprisingly, Pico recoiled at being designated a 'sceptic' – a fact that goes far to suggest that quite early in the Renaissance reception of scepticism, epistemological doubt and dogmatic rejection of religious doctrine were not always sufficiently distinguished, and sometimes irresponsibly conflated.[22]

Pico's *Examen* was not widely read during the sixteenth and seventeenth centuries, but it was certainly known to the French humanist Jacques Lefèvre d'Etaples, to whom Pico sent a copy, as well as to several other writers who dealt explicitly with scepticism: Gentian Hervet, translator of Sextus' *Against the Mathematicians* (1569); Pierre Le Loyer, a spiritologist who mentions the book in his treatise *Des Spectres* (1586); Giovanni Bernardi, whose compendium of Platonic and Aristotelian philosophy (1599) relies on the *Examen* for Pyrrhonism's ten modes of doubt; and Montaigne. The Oxford scholar John Rainolds also read Pico; one of his lectures on Aristotle's *Rhetoric* bears a marginal note alluding to passages from the *Examen*. And John Dee had acquired a copy of the book no later than 1583.[23]

Between the publication of the *Examen* (1520) and the appearance of Henri Estienne's groundbreaking Latin translation of Sextus' *Outlines*

(1562), the reception of ancient scepticism was more strongly marked by attention to the doctrines of the New Academy – as presented in Cicero's *Academica* – than by examination of the works of Sextus. Still, evidence exists that Sextus was being read. Konrad Gesner mentions him (along with 'Pyrrhon') in his 1545 *Bibliotheca universalis*, drawing heavily on information derived from the *Suda* and claiming that manuscripts of the *Outlines* and *Against the Mathematicians* survive in Augsburg and Venice.[24] The same year, as Luciano Floridi has shown, the Spanish humanist Juan Paéz de Castro wrote that he had seen Sextus' *Outlines* in the library of Diego Hurtado de Mendoza. Shortly afterwards he decided to translate the book into Latin, a task that he completed in the early 1560s. Castro's correspondence reveals that he planned this rendition of Sextus 'several years before Estienne's edition, so that when the latter decided to publish his translation, his regard for Sextus was not a completely isolated case'.[25] Evidence for the broader truth of this claim is provided by the existence, at Oxford's Bodleian Library, of a Latin translation of part of *Against the Mathematicians* by the Englishman John Wolley, who undertook the project between 1553 and 1563. This translation, the first version in any language of that particular excerpt from Sextus, demonstrates that in Tudor England there was interest in the major sceptic of antiquity 'a generation before the flurry of activity around the lost English translation of about 1590'.[26] (It also demonstrates that a Greek manuscript of part or all of Sextus' treatise was held at Oxford during the middle of the century – a manuscript which now seems to have vanished.) Finally, it should be noted that the Italian literary critic Francesco Robortello, best known today as an early commentator on Aristotle's *Poetics*, referred to Sextus' *Outlines* in his *Annotations*, a work which illuminates key ideas in Cicero's *Academica*. Published in 1548, Robortello's book thus shows an awareness of Sextus' utility in clarifying aspects of ancient thought.[27]

But Robortello's very project – using Sextus to explicate Cicero – underlines Cicero's pre-eminence in the mid-sixteenth century both as a promoter of sceptical ideas and as a model for undermining philosophical certainty in the interest of suggesting standards of probable truth. And while the *Academica* is crucial in this regard, dialogues such as *On the Nature of the Gods* and the *Tusculan Disputations* also figure significantly. In 1509 Adriano Castellesi published *On True Philosophy*, a work of fideistic theology which attacked Ficinian Platonism and relied on anti-rational critiques derived from the *Academica*. According to Paul Kristeller, the Italian poet Mantuan also inclined towards Academic scepticism, granting only probability to all claims of knowledge besides Christian truth.[28] Indeed, Renaissance humanism, broadly conceived, has been characterized as fundamentally Ciceronian: 'Cicero's brand of skepticism', writes Thomas Sloane, 'is at the core of humanism ... In fact, calling it *Ciceronianism* or even *Academicism* might be preferable, considering the modern connotations of *skepticism*. For Cicero's position is not denial, nihilism, or atheism, but emotional and intellectual diffidence.'[29] One might counter that such diffidence seems more apt as a description of Pyrrhonian than Academic scepticism, particularly given the latter's portrayal by Sextus as a form of negative dogmatism. But if we stress as central to Academic scepticism *in utramque partem* disputation followed by an unwillingness to go beyond declaring one opinion as more plausible than another, Sloane's larger point remains compelling: Cicero unquestionably figures as a dominant force in the sixteenth century's intellectual agon.

Numerous commentaries on the *Academica* were published in the mid-to-late century, including those of Denys Lambin (1565–9) and Pedro de Valencia (1596). Criticism was voiced by Jacopo Sadoleto (1538) and Giulio Castellani (1558).[30] And, shortly after Calvin's execution of the Socinian Michael Servetus in 1553, the French humanist Sebastian Castellio pseudonymously issued his *De haereticis* (*On Heretics*, 1554), arguing that criteria for determining doctrinal unorthodoxy are far from evident, and that humans must exercise extreme caution before condemning anyone for heresy. Castellio, whose sources included Augustine and Erasmus, and who later wrote an even more sceptical treatise, *Of the Art of Doubting* (1561–2), was attacked almost instantly by Theodore de Beza, who claimed that heretics can be recognized without difficulty. Beza saw the scepticism of the New Academy lying just beneath the surface of Castellio's argument; like Melanchthon, he found no compatibility between doubt and Christian doctrine. Addressing Castellio directly at the close of his treatise, he asserted that 'it is right to restrain you and those like you, who try to introduce that sacrilegious and diabolical *acatalepsia* into the Church, as deadly enemies of the Christian religion'.[31]

Juan Luis Vives is yet another Renaissance humanist who seems to have been significantly influenced by Ciceronian scepticism, though his precise sources are difficult to identify. Vives spent time in England during the 1520s, was acquainted with Erasmus and More, and drew on the *Academica* as well as *Praise of Folly* in his *Introduction to Wisdom* (1524). He writes that 'our intellects, shackled in the prison of the body, lie oppressed in a great darkness of ignorance; the cutting edges of the mind are so dull that they cannot penetrate the surface of things' – a statement that may be profitably compared to Cicero's remark that 'no human intellect has sufficiently powerful sight to be able to penetrate the heavens'.[32] A few years later, in his massive treatise *On the Disciplines* (1531), Vives insists upon Cicero's *Academica* as required reading and challenges Aristotelian precepts: 'each person has different first principles: some are persuaded by what is only probable; others, like the Academicians, do not accept even what is most evident to the senses; others again, like the Epicureans, accept all sense perceptions'.[33] This is no endorsement of Academic scepticism, but it certainly counts as an instance of the marshalling of loosely sceptical arguments against sixteenth-century scholasticism. Later in the century, both Sanches and Rainolds rely on Vives in their critiques of Aristotle and his interpreters: Sanches in *That Nothing Is Known*, Rainolds in his lectures on Aristotle's *Rhetoric* (1572–8). Ben Jonson, too, draws significantly on Vives in various observations about language.[34]

Vives was a reader of Lucian, which links him to yet another classical source through which sceptical ideas were transmitted to early modern Europe. In *The Dream* (1521), Vives imitates Lucian's style in mocking Parisian sophists; like Erasmus and More, he found the irreverence of the Greek satirist a therapeutic antidote to the more tendentious and dogmatic aspects of intellectual discourse in his day.[35] But probably the most remarkable early modern revival of Lucianic satire lay in the works of Rabelais. As Mikhail Bakhtin, Lucien Febvre and others have noted, Lucian's works fundamentally influenced Rabelais; in *Tiers Livre* (1546), the sequel to *Gargantua* and *Pantagruel*, Rabelais evinces clear familiarity with Lucian's *Sale of Creeds* in his presentation of 'Pyrrhonism' through Trouillogan's debate with Panurge. Described as an 'ephectic' philosopher, Trouillogan talks with Panurge about the latter's desire to marry, and, through evasive and belligerent remarks, succeeds not in inducing *ataraxia*, but in arousing Panurge's ire. Witnessing the interchange, Gargantua observes that

> the most learned and prudent philosophers have [now] entered the think-tank and school of the Pyrrhonists, aporrhetics, skeptics, and ephectics. Praise be to the Lord! Truly from now on it will be possible to catch lions by the hair ... but never will such philosophers be caught by their words.[36]

This inventory of Pyrrhonian synonyms may indicate Rabelais' familiarity with another source text, Laertius' *Life of Pyrrho*, which mentions

'Aporetics, Sceptics, Ephectics, and even Zetetics' as names for philosophers whose practices include constant doubt, suspension of judgement and patient pursuit of truth.[37] In any event, sceptics come off only slightly better than Aristotelians in Rabelais's estimation. Later in *Tiers Livre*, Pantagruel ironically praises Judge Bridoye, mocking his naive faith in heavenly benevolence.[38] The strand of thought represented in this mockery – a view of scepticism scathingly critical of its inconclusiveness yet sympathetic to its premises regarding the rational frailty of humans and the bewildering contradictions among laws and opinions – is crucially important in the history of scepticism's early modern reception. It suggests that one of the principal means by which scepticism was assimilated into contemporary thought was through radically qualified acceptance: assent to its points of departure coupled with impatient rejection of its 'conclusions'.

Rabelais probably did not know the works of Sextus or Gianfrancesco Pico. But he may well have read Agrippa's *Vanitie* and was almost certainly acquainted with Cicero's *Academica*. Even Copernicus, whose primary interests lay far from doctrinal dispute, mentioned Cicero's treatise in a letter to Pope Paul III and relied on the work for information about Hicetas of Syracuse, who had argued that the earth was not stationary but in constant motion. Moreover, such mid-century figures as Reginald Pole and Pierre Bunel drew on elements of Academic scepticism in their presentation of fideistic theological positions.[39] Finally, various writers offered refutations of Academic scepticism, sometimes theological in nature, sometimes philosophical. In his dialogue *Phaedrus* (1538), Jacopo Sadoleto rejects Academic scepticism and the fideistic conclusions it sometimes prompts, stressing instead the rationalism of Plato and Aristotle. However, as Popkin observes, 'Sadoleto's answer to Academic skepticism is more a panegyric on the merits of ancient philosophy and human reason than an answer to the challenge. His faith in the capacities of rational thought does not seem based on any genuine analysis or answer to the arguments of the Academics'.[40]

A more substantial refutation was published in 1558 by Giulio Castellani, an Aristotelian who had read not only the *Academica* and *Life of Pyrrho*, but also Pico's *Examen* and Robortello's *Annotations*, thus indicating that he knew at least some of Sextus' arguments, if only at second hand. His book, *Against Cicero's Academica*, attempts to confute scepticism by defending the reliability of sense perception. It avers that Cicero creates a straw man in Lucullus: a more accurate presentation of the dogmatic eclecticism of Antiochus would be far less susceptible to the sceptical objections raised by Cicero. Unlike Sadoleto, Castellani did not see scepticism as a threat to religion, but rather to the hegemony of Peripatetic tradition. By the middle of the sixteenth century, then, scepticism could be and had been perceived as both compatible and wholly incompatible with Christian doctrine. Nor did the conflict of opinion divide itself neatly along Catholic and Protestant lines. In so far as it was accepted, scepticism 'was accepted by orthodox and unorthodox alike, by Protestants as well as Catholics ... there was no consensus of opinion among Renaissance thinkers in their attitude toward scepticism: some found it useful in promoting religious belief, others saw it as detrimental to every religious emotion'.[41]

Probably the most influential sixteenth-century use of Ciceronian scepticism lay in the works of the Parisian scholars Peter Ramus and Omer Talon in their attacks on scholastic dogmatism and their refashioning of Aristotelian logic. Paris had been the site of publication, in 1535, of the first discrete edition of the *Academica*, and while Academic scepticism, in and of itself seems not to have held great interest for Ramus and Talon, both men made use of sceptical arguments. Ramus, who taught philosophy for twenty years at the Collège Royal before dying a Protestant martyr in the St Bartholomew's Day Massacre (1572), speaks favourably of Academic philosophers – particularly as contrasted with Stoics and Epicureans – and he admires the conjunction of eloquence and philosophy which he believes manifested, above all, in the works of Cicero. Ramus also mentions Sextus in a work from 1565, though he appears to have known little about Sextus' contributions to the development of classical scepticism. He did, however, know Laertius' treatment of Pyrrhonism: in his *Remarks on Aristotle* (1548), later reprinted as *Lectures on Dialectic* (1569), he not only offers a short discussion of the 'aporetici, sceptici, ephectici, zetetici', but also presents a version of Laertius' epitome of the ten modes of doubt.[42]

Talon, whose main goal was always to promote Ramus' educational reforms, exhibits considerable interest in Cicero's *Academica*, editing the work for publication in 1548 and providing detailed commentary. This study, entitled *Academia* and expanded in 1550, places particular emphasis on the intellectual modesty of Academic sceptics and on the philosophical freedom their methods guarantee:

It is the proper and germane liberty of the Academics ... that in philosophy they submit to the laws and regulations of no man. It is also their modesty, for they introduce no proper judgment concerning uncertain things; their prudence as well, for by not asserting their own authority they compare the causes of things and bring out what might be said against any opinion; also their wisdom, for they devote themselves to the unique truth in all of life, and value this more than the testimony of all philosophers.

Moreover, Talon's *Academia* recommends *disputatio in utramque partem* as an ideal method for learning philosophy and, somewhat in the manner of Robortello, employs a second classical source to explicate a first – in this case, Laertius' *Life of Pyrrho*. Together, Ramus and Talon offer a vehement mid-sixteenth-century critique of dogmatic Aristotelianism, and while claims about a Parisian school of 'new Academics' are probably exaggerated, it is none the less evident that the Ramist critique, broadly construed, endorses the tolerance, reserve and dialogic openness of Ciceronian scepticism.[43]

But not all Parisian intellectuals were pleased with the Ramist programme. Pierre Galland defended Aristotelian scholasticism in 1551; his work, *Against the New Academician Peter Ramus*, virulently attacks the writings of both Ramus and Talon, condemning the perceived perversity of a philosophic stance that undermines all certainty.[44] Several years later Guy de Brués drafted a more interesting response to the Ramist controversy – interesting in part because it was composed in the vernacular. His *Dialogues Against the New Academicians* (1557) presents four interlocutors engaged in various conversations, one on epistemology and metaphysics, one on moral philosophy, and one on law. That Brués chose to compose his work in dialogue form, allowing sceptical positions to be advanced in detail by ostensible (if fictional) adherents, has led some interpreters to believe that he secretly advocated scepticism, even though he insists that his purpose is to protect people from corruption by the *nouveaux académiciens*, representing as they do a genuine danger 'to religion, to God's honour, to the power of our superiors, the authority of justice as well as to all sciences and disciplines'. It is also clear – at least on the surface – that the two anti-sceptical speakers, Ronsard and Nicot, adequately refute the arguments of their sceptical opponents, Baïf and Aubert. Still, if Brués does not endorse scepticism, he demonstrates sustained and lively interest in it; and his sources, besides the *Academica*, include Laertius' *Lives* and works by Galen, Plutarch, Pliny the Elder and Ramus. That Pyrrho and his followers ('Aporeticiens, Scepticiens, Ephecticiens, et zeteticiens') are explicitly condemned in Brués does not prevent Montaigne, twenty years later, from drawing on the *Dialogues* to fashion his own unique version of Pyrrhonism.[45]

The Ramist controversy held great interest for mid-century intellectuals, even if not all responses were as serious as those of Galland and Brués. Rabelais, in his *Quart Livre* (1552), depicts Jupiter in the following quandary: 'What shall we do with Ramus and Galland, who, swathed in their hangers-on, are stirring up this entire Academy of Paris? I'm in great perplexity about it and still haven't decided which way I should lean.'[46] And across the English Channel Ramus' works generated considerable enthusiasm. His *Dialecticae*, for instance, was translated by Roland Mackylmain as *The Logike of the Moste Excellent Philosopher P. Ramus Martyr* (1574). John Dee and John Rainolds both owned Ramus' books; Gabriel Harvey and Abraham Fraunce admired him (though Bacon called him a 'pestilent bookworm'); and, as educational historians have shown, Ramist influence at Cambridge was substantial from the late 1560s forward, with scholars such as Laurence Chaderton, William Temple and Alexander Richardson lecturing extensively on his works.[47]

This is not to say that by the third quarter of the sixteenth century the French fascination with ancient scepticism had passed with full force into England. Certainly Ramus, for all his anti-scholastic sentiment, cannot be viewed as an advocate of the epistemological positions of the New Academy or as a writer through whose works sceptical doctrines were widely disseminated. But when we reflect that, quite apart from the Sextus editions of Estienne and Hervet (which often traveled with surprising speed to England), Erasmus' translation of Lucian was issued in London in 1528, his *Apophthegms* and *Praise of Folly* were 'Englished' by Nicholas Udall (1542) and Thomas Chaloner (1549), Melanchthon's and Caesarius' *Dialectica* were frequently recommended as handbooks by Cambridge University statutes and Vives' *Wisdom* was translated by Richard Moryson in 1539 and frequently reprinted, it becomes increasingly clear that mid-century English intellectuals had contact, however indirectly, with sceptical ideas from antiquity. In the 1540s, according to Roger Ascham's *Scholemaster*, the Cambridge curriculum paid 'attention to the philosophical writings of Cicero', and while we can only surmise that this attention extended to the *Academica*, we know that Ascham grants Cicero considerable praise, mentioning him in conjunction with Ramus and Talon.[48] Meanwhile, in 1559, the Italian reformer Jacobus Acontius took refuge in London and, following the tradition of Erasmus and Castellio, defended religious toleration and freedom of conscience in *Satan's Stratagems*, dedicated to Queen Elizabeth and published in 1565. The same year, Thomas Cooper included 'Pyrrho' and 'Sextus' in the biographical appendix to his popular *Thesaurus*.[49] Finally, at Oxford some time around 1560, John Wolley of Merton College had access to a Greek manuscript of Sextus' *Against the Mathematicians*, and his Latin translation constitutes still further evidence that an interest in the recently recovered sceptical tradition was beginning to manifest itself in Tudor England.

# 2
# Crossed Opinions: The Elizabethan Years

Modest doubt is called the beacon of the wise.

*Troilus and Cressida*

A dozen years before Elizabeth acceded to the English throne, John Heywood's *Dialogue of Proverbs* (1546) offered the following couplet as an instance of common-sense scepticism regarding inductions about human character:

> Ye knowe what he hath been (quoth he) but ywis,
> Absence saieth playnely, ye knowe not what he is.

Half a century later, in *Hamlet*, Shakespeare gave Ophelia a strikingly similar speech: 'Lord, we know what we are, but know not what we may be' (4.5.42–3). It is thus evident that English proverbial wisdom in the sixteenth century could readily cast doubt on presumptions about human identity in a mutable world. The very fact that such doubt finds transmission through proverbial expression lends support to the idea that a lay scepticism pre-dated any manifestation of philosophical scepticism in early modern Britain. One is tempted to suggest that such fundamental doubt is ahistorical – that it appears under any circumstances, in any culture. And this may be true. What we see in late Elizabethan England, however, is that common-sense doubt quickly combines with the Socratic *Nihil scio*, lending proverbial scepticism a philosophic inflection. Thus Marston laces his plays with such remarks as 'I know I nothing know' and 'The more I learnt the more I learnt to doubt'.[1] English proverbs also hint, on occasion, at the perils of excessive doubt. The aphorism 'He that casts all doubts shall never be resolved' finds expression in works by John Lyly, Sir Philip Sidney and John Webster; *Hamlet* might be viewed as a literary monument to the idea. But on the whole it appears that self-conscious ignorance is more highly endorsed than scorn of conscious doubt. 'He that knows nothing doubts nothing' could serve as a motto for many of Montaigne's essays; indeed Randle Cotgrave, defining the noun *rien* in his French-English *Dictionarie* (1611), offers 'He that knowes nought of nothing doubts' as an apposite maxim.[2] Only fools, by this rule, eschew doubt. The wise, who are of course still ignorant, at least arrive at their ignorance consciously – and through a mature habit of 'casting' doubt. As Hippolito assures Vindice in *The Revenger's Tragedy*, 'It is not the least policy to be doubtful' (4.2.25).

We thus need no investigation of Renaissance scepticism to account for the endorsement of doubt in English proverbial wisdom. Nor do we need such a study to provide contextual background to a work like Reginald Scot's *Discoverie of Witchcraft* (1584), which deploys irony and mordant black humour in its exposé of fraud, credulity and supposed supernatural activity. As Sydney Anglo observes, Scot's book is 'uncompromisingly empirical, always eschewing a laborious and inconsistent explanation for any phenomenon when ... there is a more straightforward one'. But the straightforwardness of Scot's approach is in fact conditioned by considerable learning, and Anglo underlines this by comparing Scot's 'independent, anti-professional' argumentation to that of Montaigne.[3] Like Montaigne, Scot read widely; his *Discoverie* cites over 200 authorities, and while his list of 'forren authors' does not include Sextus, Laertius or Lucian, it mentions Cicero, Galen, Lucretius, Eusebius, Augustine, Erasmus, Agrippa and Jean Bodin, each of whom played a role in the transmission of ancient scepticism. Indeed Bodin, whose *On the Demon-Mania of Witches* (1580) was quickly translated into Latin, German and Italian, spends much of his preface distinguishing between 'Dogmatiques' and 'Sceptiques'.[4] While Scot, therefore, may not mention Pyrrhonism or employ arguments after the fashion of Sextus, he none the less must have known of scepticism as a prominent philosophical orientation and been at least marginally familiar with its customary epistemological stances.

It is indeed a mistake to assume that classical scepticism could not be disseminated in early modern Europe without Sextus' direct mediation. We have seen that Sanches' *That Nothing Is Known* was composed in apparent ignorance of the translations of Sextus, yet with clear knowledge of Cicero's *Academica*, Laertius' *Lives*, and various works by Galen and Vives.[5] Sanches was thus no Pyrrhonian, but his experiences as a physician and critic of Aristotelian authority still led him to profoundly sceptical conclusions. Similarly, Castellio's *On Heretics* and *The Art of Doubting* make no mention of Sextus or Pyrrhonism yet advance sceptical arguments regarding criteria for truth-claims and insist on the value of initial doubt. Scot, whose *Discoverie* is far from being rigorously philosophical, none the less demonstrates broad acquaintance with ancient and contemporary sources. And, if only because of his scrutiny of Bodin, he must have found his innate scepticism bolstered by the condemnation of Pyrrhonism in the Frenchman's prefatory diatribe:

> the Sceptics, seeing that nothing enters the soul without first being perceived by the senses, and seeing too that the senses deceive us, held that nothing can be known. For they said that if the maxim of Aristotle (borrowed from Plato) is true, that the intellectual soul is like a *carte blanche*, and if it is true as well that there is nothing in the soul that has not already passed through the senses, then it is impossible to know anything ... . One person finds hot what another finds cold, and the same person at different times renders different judgments about the same thing ... . The first who made this observation was Socrates, who claimed that he knew but one thing: that he knew nothing. And afterwards this sect underwent growth through the efforts of Arcesilaus, head of the Academy. Its adherents included Ariston, Pyrrho, Herillus, and, in our own memory, Cardinal Cusa, in his books concerning the doctrine of ignorance. And just as the first philosophers of whom I spoke called themselves Dogmatics, which is to say Doctors, these other philosophers called themselves Sceptics, or Ephectics, which is to say Doubters. They even preferred not to allege that they knew nothing – which is what Socrates had claimed – since in confessing that they knew they knew nothing, they simultaneously confessed that something could be known.[6]

Bodin's portrait of scepticism is not flattering, but his mockery is anything but conclusive as a refutation, and a staunchly anti-Catholic reader like Scot might well have been more repulsed by the dogmatic *Docteurs*, with whom Bodin finds common ground, than by the *Doubteurs* descended from Socrates.

## Continental drift

In any event, Scot encountered Bodin not in English but in Latin – and
in an edition that could at most have been three years old when he read
it. And these facts contribute to a pair of generalizations whose truth
cannot be too often stressed: (1) while continental works were routinely
translated into English, Elizabethan intellectuals were not dependent on
such translations; they often read these works either in Latin or in vernacular tongues, particularly French and Italian; and (2), continental
books could travel with astonishing speed to Britain. As Elisabeth
Leedham-Green has pointed out, the inventories of many Cambridge
booksellers show 'how swiftly [English] customers might lay their hands
on continental publications' (*BCI*, 1:485). With these truths in mind,
then, let us turn to a consideration of other continental works through
whose influence English readers could have been further exposed to
discussions and appropriations of ancient scepticism.

First and foremost, we have the Latin translations of Sextus' two major
treatises, *Outlines of Pyrrhonism* (1562) and *Against the Mathematicians*
(1569). The latter work, undertaken by the Counter-Reformation figure
Gentian Hervet, contains a reissue of the former, which was prepared by
Henri Estienne (and which, in turn, included Traversari's rendition of
Laertius' *Life of Pyrrho*). Both works offer prefaces by their translators.
Estienne's is a brief narrative explaining how he came across a Greek
manuscript of Sextus, found its critique of dogmatism not only informa-
tive but intellectually restorative, and consequently underwent a 'sceptical metamorphosis'.[7] Hervet's, by contrast, constitutes a serious and
polemical introduction, arguing that Sextus' depiction of endless philosophical controversy instils humility, prompting readers to accept
Christian revelation on faith and to reject the theological novelties of
Calvin and the fashionable doubting of *nouveaux académiciens*.[8] We will
never know precisely how many copies of the Estienne and Hervet translations circulated in early modern England, but it is safe to say that there
were more than those I have so far been able to document. Thus the following list, while by no means exhaustive, constitutes a representative
sampling of the British dissemination of the printed Sextus translations
from 1562 until roughly 1625:

1  A copy of the 1562 Estienne octavo acquired in the year of its
   publication by William Wykeham, MA candidate at King's College,
   Cambridge. Wykeham later became Bishop of Lincoln and of
   Winchester.[9]

2 A copy of the 1569 Hervet edition owned by Andrew Perne, Master of Peterhouse, Cambridge. Perne (d. 1589) probably acquired the book during the 1570s.

3 A copy of 1569 in the inventory of an anonymous Cambridge bookseller who died around 1588.[10]

4 A copy of 1569 in the University Library at Cambridge. Entering the collection no later than 1583, the book was probably donated by Nicholas Bacon (father of Francis) before his death in 1579.[11]

5 A copy of 1569 owned by James Montagu, Master of Sidney Sussex College, Cambridge, during the 1590s, and later one of the translators of the King James Bible. Probably acquired in the late 1580s, this copy was held for centuries at Sidney Sussex, but is now lost.[12]

6 A copy of 1562 owned by Edmund Guest, Bishop of Salisbury during the 1570s, and bequeathed to Salisbury Cathedral Library at his death in 1577.

7 A copy of 1562 acquired in 1588 by Samuel Burton, student at Christ Church, Oxford. In 1599 Burton gave the book to James Weston of the Inner Temple; ultimately, it entered the library of Seth Ward, Bishop of Salisbury, who donated it to the Cathedral Library at his death in 1689.[13]

8 A copy of 1562 signed in 1590 by Thomas Saunderson, student at Broadgates Hall, Oxford. The book was given to Thomas Grantham of Christ Church College, who also signed and dated it: '1590 Hoc me donauit'. Both men later studied at Lincoln's Inn, and Saunderson may be the 'Thomas Sanderson' who helped to translate the King James Bible. The book was eventually acquired by the Warburg Institute.[14]

9 A copy of 1562 purchased for the library of Merton College, Oxford, by Thomas Savile at the Frankfurt Book Fair in 1591, and recorded that year in the college register.[15]

10 A copy of 1562 owned by William Camden, Ben Jonson's teacher at Westminster School. Camden gave the book to Robert Cotton at his death in 1623; eventually it found its way back to the library of Westminster Abbey.[16]

11 A copy of 1569 owned by John Rainolds, fellow of Corpus Christi College, Oxford; the book was bequeathed at Rainolds' death (1607) to John Bancroft of Christ Church, tutor to Robert Burton and later Bishop of Oxford.[17]

12 A copy of 1569 owned by Nathaniel Torporley. Educated at Oxford, Torporley served as amanuensis to the French mathematician François Viète, and subsequently became associated with

Thomas Harriot and Henry Percy, ninth Earl of Northumberland. At his death (1632) Torporley bequeathed his books to Sion College; they are now held at Lambeth Palace Library.[18]

13  A copy of 1569 donated in 1601 to Oxford's recently-established Bodleian Library by Alice Chamberlaine, widow of Robert Chamberlaine of Shirburne.[19]

14  A copy of 1562 acquired by the Bodleian between 1605 and 1620, and catalogued in that interim by Thomas James.[20]

15  A copy of 1562 owned by Charles Blount, Earl of Devonshire. Blount studied at Oxford and the Middle Temple, bequeathing the book to John Selden at his death (1606); Selden in turn left it to the Bodleian (1654).[21]

16  A copy of 1569 forming part of John Dee's large library no later than September 1583. Previously owned by the Catholic controversialist Nicholas Sanders, the book was ultimately acquired by the Royal College of Physicians.[22]

17  A copy of 1562 owned by Anthony Higgin, Dean of Ripon during the Jacobean years, and probably acquired in the late-sixteenth century, as Higgin was known to collect books from his Cambridge days (1570–83) forward. The volume passed into the library of Ripon Cathedral at Higgin's death (1624).[23]

18  A copy of 1569 inscribed by 'Thomas Jennings', probably the poet and Catholic sympathizer Thomas Jennings (or Jenye) who played a role in the Northern Rebellion (1569) and spent time during the 1560s/1570s in France and Italy.[24]

19  A copy of 1569 held in the Staffordshire library of William Paget, and recorded in the 1617 manuscript catalogue of the Paget library.[25]

20  and 21 Copies of 1562 and 1569 in the library of the Norfolk gentleman Thomas Knyvett, who studied law at London's Middle Temple in the 1560s and died in 1618.[26]

22  A copy of 1569 at the Middle Temple, forming part of an extensive collection of books amassed during the late Tudor years. Its donation signature, 'Tobias Matthew Joani Dalabero', likely refers to John Delaber[e], who entered the Temple in 1576 and died as a senior barrister in 1607.[27]

We also know that during this period many English cathedrals came to possess copies of either the 1562 *Sextus* or the 1621 *Opera* (the *editio principes*), though we can seldom say precisely when these copies were acquired.[28] The 1569 and 1621 editions, moreover, surface relatively early in other secular and ecclesiastical collections. Copies of all three books were held in the Penshurst library of Philip Sidney's nephew, the second Earl of Leicester.[29] Copies of 1621 were held in the Royal Library at St. James' Palace and in the library at Petworth, where Henry Percy, the 'Wizard Earl', spent much of his life.[30] Another copy of 1621 was donated to the Bodleian about four years after its publication, a copy owned first by Henry Savile and then by William Sidley Miles.[31] Thus academic, legal, aristocratic and ecclesiastical collections all took an interest in Sextus, and his printed writings were known to clerics, theologians, historians, lawyers, translators and gentlemen scholars. Nor does my list include the various Sextus manuscripts extant at the time in Britain: those owned, for instance, by Henry Savile and Isaac Vossius, or the partial English translation of the *Outlines* entitled *The Sceptick* (c. 1590), copies of which belonged to Sir Walter Ralegh, Archbishop James Ussher and, later, Bishop Edward Stillingfleet.[32] Louis Bredvold may exaggerate matters when he writes that in seventeenth-century England 'almost every scholar had read Sextus', but if Pedro de Valencia could claim in 1596 that virtually everyone had *access* to Latin versions of Sextus, it seems fair to assume that a significant number of Elizabethans and Jacobeans could be included in this estimate – certainly more than has previously been assumed.[33]

Marlowe, for instance, quotes from *Against the Mathematicians* in *Doctor Faustus*, and a dozen years later John Chamber paraphrases from the same work in his *Treatise Against Judicial Astrologie* (1601), a sceptical exposé of divination.[34] In the intervening decade, Spenser, Donne, Richard Thomson and William Cornwallis all show familiarity with Sextus. Cornwallis turns the arch-sceptic into a dogmatist when he claims in his *Essayes* (1600–1) that he is 'not of *Emperycus*' minde, who holdes the qualities of thinges to bee more in number then our senses'. Derived from Sextus' discussion of the third mode of doubt (*PH*, 1.94–9), the idea that the five senses may be inadequate to the task of complete perception also finds expression in Montaigne, whom Cornwallis seems to have read in John Florio's as yet unpublished translation. Elsewhere, however, Cornwallis demonstrates a more accurate understanding of Sextus, as when he terms himself 'halfe a *Pyrrhonian* concerning these Terrene businesses, in my opinion holding opinion the mother of joy and Sorrow'.[35]

As for Spenser, his *View of the Present State of Ireland* likely derives the name 'Eudoxus' from Sextus' *Outlines* (*PH*, 1.152), where Eudoxus of Cnidos is discussed. Thomson, a biblical scholar trained at Cambridge and later one of the translators of the Authorized Version, writes in

1594 to Isaac Casaubon in France, asking to borrow the manuscript of Sextus' *Outlines* which Casaubon's father-in-law, Henri Estienne, had used for his 1562 translation, and upon which Casaubon himself had drawn for notes to his edition of Diogenes Laertius.[36] The request implies prior knowledge of the book and perhaps suggests a desire on Thomson's part to produce an edition or translation. Donne, too, seems to evince knowledge of Sextus in the 1590s. *Paradox 3*, probably composed during his 1591–4 tenure at London's Inns of Court, asserts that 'the Sceptique which doubts all is more contentious then eyther the Dogmatique which affirmes, or Academique which denyes'. Donne thus knew the conventional tripartite distinction between Pyrrhonists, Academics and Dogmatists, and this suggests that he had access to Sextus' *Outlines* (where the distinction is originally presented), to Montaigne's *Essays* (where it is repeated) or perhaps to *The Sceptick*.[37] The portrayal of Phrygius in *Satire 3* (1595) likewise prompts speculation that Donne had scepticism in mind. 'Careless Phrygius' is presented as a man who abhors all religions 'because all cannot be good'; he eschews religion entirely since some churches are impure.[38] This is not a standard Pyrrhonian thought trajectory, and Donne presumably knew it given his remark about 'the Sceptique which doubts all'. But ancient scepticism manifested itself in many distorted guises during the Renaissance, and the syndrome of false generalization – the 'Troilus paradigm' – was among the most prevalent forms in which early modern writers appropriated and deployed the tropes of the sceptical inheritance.

## Du Bartas, Primaudaye, Mornay, Le Loyer

So much, then, for direct Elizabethan acquaintance with the works of Sextus. And this is not even to mention Christopher Heydon's vitriolic condemnation of Chamber's *Treatise* in his *Defence of Judiciall Astrologie* (1603), which asserts that Sextus was a 'Sceptick Philosopher, which sect doubting of all things and affirming nothing, did neither trust their owne eies nor eares'.[39] Nor have I yet discussed the English translation of Sextus mentioned by Thomas Nashe, the anonymous treatise *The Sceptick*, relevant writings by Bacon, Joseph Mede's 'Pyrrhonian crisis' or Florio's rendition of Montaigne. I will return in due course to each of these contributions to scepticism's English reception. But for the present I wish to pursue my consideration of other continental works by means of which English readers could have gained additional acquaintance with ancient scepticism.

During the mid-1570s, two French Protestants composed works which rapidly attracted attention in England. The first was Guillaume du Bartas, whose collection of poems, *La Muse Chrestienne*, included a piece entitled *La Triomphe de la Foi*. Translated in 1592 by Joshua Sylvester, this poem presents Christianity's vanquishing of various philosophical sects:

> There moorns in vaine, *Pirrhon Plistarchus* sonne,
> That (fond) beleeves not what his eares doo heare,
> Eies see, nose smels, toong tasts, & hands do beare.
>
> (sig. C2r)

Bartas presumably derives the claim that Pyrrho was '*Plistarchus* sonne' from the opening of Laertius' *Life of Pyrrho*, a work readily available to him. As for the mocking litany of Pyrrhonian attitudes towards sense-deception, Bartas clearly distorts matters, transforming terminal doubt about the reliability of sense-data into dogmatic disbelief. And he is not alone. John Davies of Hereford, almost certainly relying on the same translation by Sylvester, concludes in his *Mirum in Modum* (1602) that

> *Pirrhon, Plutarchus* Sonne, would not believe,
> What his Eyes, Eares, Nose, Tongue, and hands did know,
> His *Sences* he imagin'd might deceive,
> And therefore did conclude, they still did so.
>
> (*Works*, 1:27)

A more probable conclusion is that Davies and Bartas distort the scepticism of Pyrrho. But this is not the first time such distortions circulate – nor the last.

Further indications that Pyrrhonism occupied Bartas' mind lie in his epic poem *La Semaine, ou Création du Monde*, which Sylvester translated piecemeal through the 1590s. Discussing Original Sin, Bartas claims that prior to the Fall, Socrates would have experienced no impulse to 'suppose / That *nought he knowes, save this, that nought he knowes*'. But in the postlapsarian state, 'even light Pirrhons wavering fantasies / Reave him the skill his un-skill to agnize'. In other words, Pyrrho's hesitations merely amount, in a fallen world, to further confirmation of humanity's 'un-skill'. But Bartas misrepresents Pyrrho in characterizing him as unable to 'agnize' his own frailty. Indeed, it is precisely this emphasis on humanity's seeming inability to make intellectual progress that attracts Montaigne and others to scepticism – and that facilitates the association between ignorance and Original Sin that underlies Christian Pyrrhonism. Scepticism is thus invoked once again only to be maligned. Still, Sylvester offers an essentially accurate biographical comment on Pyrrho in his 1605 edition of Bartas' *Devine Weekes*: he was 'a philosopher alwayes doubtfull of all thinges, yea even of those subject to our sences'.[40] In one and the same work we thus find utterly incompatible presentations of the philosophical views of scepticism's eponymous figure.

The second French writer of the 1570s whose works contributed to the dissemination of sceptical ideas in England is Pierre de la Primaudaye, whose compendious and popular *French Academie* was published in multiple editions from 1577 forward. In Part One of this work, translated in 1586, Primaudaye praises the 'Academiks' above the 'Peripatetiks' and 'Stoiks' on the grounds that they 'taught that our true good consisted in the tranquillitie of the soule, void of all perturbations' (48). Primaudaye is concerned here with the Platonic Academy and its descendants, not with strict Pyrrhonism, and later comments underscore his belief in a eudaemonistic knowledge that 'will teach us to know ourselves and our dutie, whereby we shall be led to that happie end, which we seeke for' (160). But Primaudaye is conscious of the attractions of doubt, and his attention to epistemological distinctions in the *Second Part of the Academie* shows that he seeks to quash scepticism even while endorsing 'Academicall' attitudes. He defines 'doubt' as 'a neuter judgement, hanging betweene consent and his contrary, inclining neither to one side nor the other'. He goes on to stress differences 'betwixte beleefe, opinion, doubting, and incredulitie':

> Incredulitie is contrary to beleefe; it goeth farther then doubting, which concludeth nothing on either side, as both beleefe and opinion do, but incredulitie concludeth contrarie to them both. It giveth no consent, as beleefe and opinion doe, but taketh the cleane contrary: therefore it may well be called dissent, as being opposite to that consent that is in beleefe ... . For a man to knowe himself to be ignorant, is a goodlie science ... Therefore Socrates was greatly commended by the ancients. (185–8)

Primaudaye, in short, distinguishes between doubt and dogmatic 'incredulitie' on the grounds of consent. And while he goes on to excoriate 'Epicures and Atheists', he none the less endorses preliminary doubt as a valuable habit and avoids equating doubters with non-believers (527). The two parts of his *Academie* were widely read in Britain, and many Elizabethans might have found his anatomy of doubt useful in understanding the range of cognitive positions between consent and dissent.

The next continental work of major significance to England's reception of scepticism is Philippe du Plessis-Mornay's *De la Verité de la religion chrestienne* (1581). A liberal Huguenot whose 'mind had been formed in the Erasmian tradition', Mornay served Henri de Navarre prior to his Catholic conversion and consistently advocated peace during the French religious wars. He was also a friend of Sidney's, and indeed it was Sidney who, along with Arthur Golding, rendered Mornay's treatise into English, calling it *A Woorke concerning the trewnesse of the Christian Religion* (1587). Published after Sidney's death, this popular translation was reissued several times. Many contemporaries appear to have read it closely, among them Florio, Fulke Greville, Sir John Davies and, later, members of the Great Tew circle such as Lucius Cary, William Chillingworth, Thomas Hobbes and John Earle.[41]

Mornay does not seem to have studied Sextus, but his references to Cicero, Plutarch, Galen, Laertius and Augustine, combined with his allusions to 'Academikes both old and new', strongly suggest an awareness of classical scepticism.[42] This suggestion is confirmed when he observes that, in antiquity,

> there were in deede a kinde of Philosophers called Scepticks (that is to say Dowters) which did rather suspend their Judgement concerning the Godhead, then call it in question. But it ought to suffize us, that they be the selfsame which deny al Sciences, yea even those which consist in Demonstration; and which professe themselves to doubt of the things which they see and feele; in so much that they doubt whether they themselves have any beeing or no. But yet for all that, let us see after what maner these kind of people doe reason against the thing which the world preacheth, which Nations worship, and which wise men wonder at; these folke say at a worde for all, how shall wee beleeve there is a God, sith we see him not?
> (12)

Mornay's blend of accuracy and gross misrepresentation is maddening. On the one hand, he characterizes 'Scepticks' with reasonable precision as 'Dowters' who 'suspend their Judgement'. But almost immediately he stipulates a narrowed scope for this suspension, limiting it to 'the Godhead'. He implies, moreover, that sceptics are dogmatic deniers with respect to 'Sciences', and that their argument against God's existence amounts merely to what we might call the doubting Thomas topos – that we demand 'ocular proof', withholding belief until we see. Once again, we have an instance of distorted depiction: a suggestion that an author understands fundamental Pyrrhonian attitudes, but warps their portrayal to render them innocuous.

After the fashion of countless early modern religious tracts, Mornay's book repeatedly entertains objections to previously articulated positions; many of these are sceptical in nature. To the view that the soul is immortal, Mornay presents a critic alleging that 'the Soule dyeth with the body, bycause the Soule and the body are but one thing'. He then refutes his critic: 'This argument is all one with theirs, which denyed that there is any God, bycause they sawe him not. But by his dooings thou mayst perceyve that there is a God: discerne lykewise by the dooings of thy soule, that thou haste a Soule' (247–8). The reference to atheism, combined with the reductive presentation of the atheists' supposed deduction, indicates that Mornay again has 'Scepticks' in mind. And this indication is reinforced by Mornay's subsequent attempt – lifted from Calvin – to defend inferences from effects back to causes. Just as 'thou beleevest there is a Sunne, even when thou art in a Dongeon, because his beames are shed in at the windowes', so by God's actions 'thou mayst perceyve there is a God' (12, 248). Richard Popkin has argued that a characteristic Protestant response to the late sixteenth-century alliance of Pyrrhonism and Catholicism was a defence of reason and sense-perception, somewhat in the Aristotelian tradition.[43] Traces of this response are evident in Mornay, who deploys dubious forms of inferential reasoning as though they are entirely invulnerable to empirical, let alone logical, objection. Mornay also asks his 'despisers' to 'suspend their judgement in things they understand not', demonstrating that even as he responds to sceptical objections, he resorts to standard tactics of sceptical argumentation (475). Indeed, he acknowledges the value of open-minded enquiry when he writes that 'foresetled opinions doo bring in bondage the reason of them that have best wits; wheras notwithstanding, it belongeth not to the will to overrrule the wit, but to the wit to guide the will' (sig. ***iir). Mornay's position *vis-à-vis* scepticism is thus complex: like most early modern Christians, Protestant or Catholic, he sees radical Pyrrhonian attitudes as misguided, even laughable, but he is simultaneously conscious of the potency of sceptical objections. The time he devotes to rejecting, ridiculing and (occasionally) deploying them suggests the extent to which they coloured his outlook as a religious polemicist.

Yet another French writer whose consideration of scepticism infiltrated England is the spiritologist Pierre Le Loyer, whose *Des Spectres* (1586) was partly translated by the barrister Zachary Jones as *A treatise of specters* (1605). Loyer knew Pico's *Examen* and also appears to have studied Laertius' *Lives*, Lucian's dialogues, apologetics by Eusebius, Augustine and Lactantius, and probably Sextus' *Outlines*.[44] Like Christopher Heydon, who blasts John Chamber for taking arguments against astrology from a 'Sceptick', Loyer mocks the Pyrrhonians. But the seriousness with which he does so, combined with his reliance on sceptical premises, undermines his refutation:

> Others there have beene, who have referred all that which is spoken of the vision of Spirites, unto the naturall and perpetuall deprava- tion of the humane senses. Such were the Sceptikes and Aporreticks, who were followers of the Philosopher Pirrhon: as also the second and third Academie, who held that the senses, were they never so sound, could not imagine anything but falsely. (sig. Gv)

In other words, sceptics explain allegations about supernatural intervention as fantasies attributable to perceptual depravity. And because Loyer agrees that sense-perception is unreliable, it is no surprise that his principal mode of distancing himself from doubters lies in distorting their habitual responses to sense-deception.

A foretaste of this distortion is provided by the sixth chapter of Book One, entitled 'Of the opinions of Pirrhon, the Sceptiques, and the Aporretiques, and what they alleadge to shew, that the humane senses, and the imaginative power of man, are false' (49r). From this we see that Pyrrhonian suspension of judgement will metamor- phose, in Loyer's account, into a dogmatic claim about the falsity of perception and imagination. Somewhat later, Loyer elaborates his view:

> If the Sceptiques had not so earnestly maintained the falsenesse and uncertaintie of our knowledge, by meane of the senses ... their opinion had not bin rejected by all learned men: neither had they bin so hardie as to conclude, that nothing could be knowne in certaine. For howsoever the senses may somtimes be deceived, yet ought not therefore to be inferred any generall conclusion; that our senses being sound and entire, may be deceived; or if the senses be deceived, that therefore the fantasie of a wise man should be corrupted. (88v–89r)

The verbs here are all-important: 'maintained', 'inferred', 'conclude'. And even if we allow that Loyer, like many contemporaries, blurs the distinction between Academicism and Pyrrhonism, we see that his refutation involves a further misrepresentation: it implies that sceptics induce a 'generall conclusion' about human proneness to sense-deception, then apply this conclusion to new cases. Yet according to Sextus, Pyrrhonists are more modest, never arguing for general truths but simply alleging that conflicting sense-data prompt suspension of judgement (*PH*, 1.8). It is possible, of course, that despite references to 'Pirrhoniens' and 'Sextus Philosophe', Loyer had not read the *Outlines*; certainly, it is more difficult to attain a thorough understanding of Pyrrhonism from its second-hand representations by Laertius, Eusebius and Gianfrancesco Pico. But it seems unlikely that a French intellectual writing a quarter-century after the publication of Estienne's translation would ignore the main authority on scepticism while actively refuting him. More probable is that Loyer resorted to facile distortion as a pre-emptive offensive tactic. If the 'Sceptiques', after all, are 'semblable a noz Atheistes', we have progressed no further than when we identify agnosticism with dogmatic unbelief. It is thus mildly ironic that Loyer, near the end of his book, refers to his opponents as 'Dogmatistes': those, in short, who deny *or* doubt the existence of diabolical spirits.[45]

## Taking stock

By the late 1580s, not only were the treatises of Sextus readily available in Latin, but summaries, elaborations and refutations of scepticism had appeared in many continental publications.[46] Henri Estienne had relied on Sextus in his Greek *Thesaurus* and in *Virtutum encomia*, a widely disseminated commonplace book. Joseph Scaliger drew on *Against the Mathematicians* as a source of critical authority; Matthew Devaris assumed wide familiarity with Sextus, quoting him several times in his 1588 Greek grammar; and late sixteenth-century augmentations of Erasmus' *Adagia* sometimes included commentaries on Pyrrhonism.[47] In 1578, an English translation of Lambert Daneau's *Wonderfull Woorkmanship of the World* appeared, and while this dialogue ultimately maintained that anyone despising reason and sense-perception 'despiseth the gifts of GOD', it argued too that 'mans reason is many times, and his senses most times deceived' (4r, 13v). Bodin, by around 1588, had completed his *Colloquium Heptaplomeres*, a vast dialogue with seven interlocutors, one of them a philosophical sceptic. Notwithstanding the instances of Mornay and Daneau, many of these works had yet to be translated into English: Bodin's books were not so translated until centuries later. But it is difficult to imagine that Elizabethans interested in philosophical and theological debates would not have been exposed by this time to the terminology and argumentative commonplaces of scepticism. Various additional bits of evidence substantiate this view.

The Oxford-trained John Rider, for instance, includes the word 'Sceptica' in his *Bibliotheca Scholastica* (1589), a Latin dictionary; he defines it as 'A sect of philosophers so named for the fact that it continually seeks and never finds'. But well before Rider confers legitimacy on this term, the sceptical lexicon and fragments of Pyrrhonian lore begin to manifest themselves in English writing. As early as 1549, the word 'sceptical' appears in an English printed book.[48] In 1568 – a year *before* Hervet's translation of *Against the Mathematicians* – both Lewis Evans and Edmond Tilney demonstrate acquaintance with Pyrrhonism. Evans, a logician and recusant Catholic, asserts in his *Abridgement of Logique* that attention to the processes of reasoning will enable readers to 'conceyve the certaintie of things': for 'what is so to be hated, as the wallowing in the foule myre of ignoraunce: What therein is so to be abhorred as the opinion of Pyrro, or [the] judgement of the Academikes, who doe alleage all things to be uncertaine & doubtfull' (C6v–C7r). And Tilney, later the Master of the Revels, writes in his *Flower of Friendship* that he desires from Queen Elizabeth an acceptance of his work 'no otherwise, than that [of] Noble *Alexander* of *Macedon*, who greatly esteemed the poor Poeme, given him by the Philosopher *Pirrho*' (100). This remark suggests that Tilney was familiar with Sextus' *Adversus grammaticos*, which states that Pyrrho was rewarded with thousands of gold coins for a poem he offered Alexander (*M*, 1.282). As for Evans, the inaccurate conflation of 'the opinion of Pyrro' with the 'judgement of the Academikes' is a familiar feature of scepticism's early modern reception. Gesner, for instance, merges 'Sceptici' with 'Academici' in his *Bibliotheca*, and in all likelihood Evans has in mind the negative dogmatism of Cicero's *Academica* as he paints scepticism not merely as folly but as rebellion against God.

In 1575 the Scottish scholar George Buchanan uses the adjective 'skeptik' in private correspondence: 'I can not tak you', he tells Thomas Randolph, 'for ane *Stoik philosopher*, havinge ane head inexpugnable with the frenetyk tormentis of Jalozie or ane cairless skeptik hart that taks cuccaldris as thyng indifferent' (57). The remark indicates that Buchanan's impression of scepticism is most strongly coloured by its characterization as an attitude of indifference. Warmly praised by Montaigne, Buchanan was a Protestant humanist who spent time in France during the mid-sixteenth century and later served as tutor to Scotland's James VI. Montaigne was his pupil at Bordeaux's Collège de Guyenne in the 1540s, and while it is unlikely that Buchanan found exposure to scepticism at that time, perhaps during his later tenure in Paris he became familiar with Pyrrhonian ideas as presented by Sextus or Laertius. In any case, his 'skeptik' appears to be the first instance of the word's use in English.

The same year saw the publication of George Gascoigne's closet drama *The Glass of Government*, a 'tragicall Comedie' which chastises ancient philosophers for defending 'propositions [that] seeme most rediculous & estranged from reason; *Anaxagoras* decided that snow was black and yet was accompted a philosopher of gravitie & judgement'. Despite this praise of reason, however, Gascoigne also displays interest in the 'vanity of learning' topos. In his *Droomme of Doomes Day* (1576) he follows the standard Socratic line in pronouncing that there is 'scarcely anything' humans can comprehend, 'unlesse perchaunce that is perfectly knowne, that nothing is perfectly knowne'.[49] Another evocation of Socrates and Anaxagoras appears in Stephen Gosson's romance *The Ephemerides of Phialo* (1579), a didactic piece of euphuism. As so often with Elizabethan considerations of 'Academikes', Gosson's discussion involves a vexed combination of admiration and disgust:

Sith thou hast likened me to Socrates, whose *Nihil scio* is confirmed by Arcesilas, Zeno, Empedocles, Anaxagoras, and the whole rabble of them which taught us to wander in the darke, giving no credit to the senses, but doubting continually whether Snowe were white, or the Crowe black; I might ripp up that controversie of the Academikes and the Peripatetikes, and shew thee by reason, that I knowe nothing, to drive thee off from the thinge which thou longest to heare ... . Therefore acknowledging myself to be made of a Soule, and of a bodie, the one derived from Heaven, the fountaine of Knowledge, the other from Earth, the seate of ignoraunce, I am driven to confesse that I neither knowe all thinges, which belongeth to GOD, nor am ignoraunte in all thinges, which is proper to Beastes; but am perfecte in some thinges, and unskilfull in others, which life is onely peculiar to man. This doctrine is taught by Aristotle, layde open by Tully, and soundely discoursed by Lactantius. (1:9v–10r)

Gosson, then, takes an intermediate position. He derides the sceptical excesses of the 'rabble' and intimates that radical doubt is untenable: even if we wish to 'dote' we will be brought back, involuntarily, to our senses. But at the same time he endorses a view of limited ignorance. The allusion to 'Tully' is noteworthy, since Cicero's *Academica* mentions Arcesilaus, Zeno, Socrates, Anaxagoras and Empedocles in quick succession, suggesting a possible genealogy of Academic scepticism (1.44–5). It seems probable, then, that Gosson had read at least this section of Cicero, and therefore understood the basic positions of the sceptics of the later Academy. And since we know that Gosson spent 1572–6 at Corpus Christi, Oxford, where John Rainolds was lecturing on Aristotle's *Rhetoric* and frequently drawing on the *Academica*, such a supposition seems all the more likely.

Soon after the appearance of Gosson's *Ephemerides*, John Lyly published his first play, *Campaspe* (1584). Indebted to Cicero's *On the Nature of the Gods* and Laertius' *Lives*, this work includes several pseudo-philosophical dialogues, one of which depicts Anaxarchus telling Plato, Chrysippus and other luminaries that in an imminent disputation he will 'take part with Aristotle that there is *Natura naturans*, and yet not God' (1.3.54–5).[50] The reasons for Anaxarchus' self-styled alignment with Aristotle are not entirely clear, but as a 'naturalist' and reputed friend of Pyrrho he belongs, *ipso facto*, to the sceptical persuasion. So too do the 'Efettici', 'Pirroni' and 'sceptici' mentioned in Giordano Bruno's mid-1580s dialogues, composed and published in London. Bruno, who seems to have had contact with figures such as Sidney, Greville, Bacon, Florio and Harriot, was no sceptic himself, as remarks in his *Ash Wednesday Supper* (1584) suggest: 'Pyrrhonists have another method: professing that it is not possible to know anything, they are always asking questions and looking without ever finding.' Yet elsewhere – and despite his idiosyncracies as a philosopher – Bruno evinces sympathy for sceptical positions. In his *Cabal of the Horse Pegasus* (1585), Saulino aligns himself with Socrates in asserting that our most significant knowledge is that nothing can be known. And in *The Triple Minimum* (1591), Bruno argues that

> He who desires to philosophize will first doubt all things, refusing to assume any position in a debate before having heard contrasting points of view, and after having considered the arguments for and against he will judge and take up his position not on the basis of

hearsay or according to the opinion of the majority or their age, merits, or prestige, but according to the persuasiveness of an organic doctrine which adheres to reality as well as to a truth which is comprehensive according to the light of reason.

The emphasis on 'organic doctrine' and 'the light of reason' is clearly non-Pyrrhonian, but Bruno's advocacy of preliminary scepticism in philosophical enquiry has curious affinities with Bacon's characteristic response, fifteen years later, to the challenges posed by epistemological doubt.[51]

By the late 1580s, Marlowe must have acquired some sort of familiarity with Sextus, as his reference to *On kai me on* almost certainly demonstrates. Around the same time, another writer with Cambridge connections shows acquaintance with scepticism, if not specifically with Sextus. This is Abraham Fraunce, whose *Lawiers Logike* and *Arcadian Rhetorike* (both 1588) championed Ramus and Talon. Writing in the former book on 'the severall kindes of Argumentes', Fraunce informs us that

there is great controversie among the auncient Philosophers, concerning [science and opinion]: some mayntayne onely Science, others holde with opinion onely. Heraclitus called opinion the falling sicknesse, for that thereby men many times fell headlong into erronious conceiptes. In like maner, the Stoikes held for one of their Paradoxes, that a wise man never judgeth according to opinion. On the other side Anaxarchus was of this opinion, that all mans judgment was but opinion, and that his understanding coulde perfitly understand nothing, which the Pyrrhonians taught after him, and the new Academikes. (sig. Cr)

Fraunce goes on to note that Plato and Aristotle 'declared that man is capable both of Science and certayne knowledge'. And he shares their view. But it is clear that Fraunce's 'eight yeares labour at Cambridge' left his mind well stocked not only with quotations from ancient and modern poets – the *Rhetorike* is laced with passages from Virgil, Cicero, Erasmus, Bartas, Sidney and Spenser – but with scattered knowledge of classical philosophy, including the pre-Socratics.[52] And if, like so many contemporaries, Fraunce conflates Pyrrhonism and Academicism, he none the less implies that sceptical habits of thought must be taken seriously, if not ultimately endorsed.

## The three universities

When we consider that (1) Spenser studied at Cambridge's Pembroke College (1569–76); (2) Fraunce and Nashe both lived at St John's (1575–83; 1582–8); (3) Marlowe studied at Corpus Christi, earning degrees in 1584 and 1587; (4) Richard Thomson took degrees at Clare Hall in 1584 and 1591; (5) William Wykeham, at King's, acquired a copy of Estienne's Sextus in 1562; (6) Joseph Hall studied at Emmanuel from 1589 onward; (7) a copy of the 1569 Sextus was held in the main library no later than 1583; and (8) additional copies of 1569 were owned by Andrew Perne (Master of Peterhouse, 1554–89) and James Montagu (Master of Sidney Sussex in the 1590s), it seems evident that Cambridge students could be, and occasionally were, exposed to the epistemological concerns raised by classical sceptics. This supposition is further borne out by the appearance, in 1585, of a philosophical treatise by Andrew Willet, a student of Perne's at Peterhouse. Composed in Latin, Willet's *Questions Concerning the Nature and Powers of the Soul* includes a chapter which asks 'Whether anything is comprehended with a certain mind?'[53] Willet concludes that 'Nothing can be truly known or perceived without distortion', going so far as to find Socrates 'worthy of rebuke, who claimed that he knew only this – that he knew nothing' (163). Such a pronouncement sounds uncannily akin to the Pyrrhonian view that Academic scepticism amounts to a form of negative dogmatism – a view that Willet could just as easily have encountered in Perne's copy of Sextus (*PH*, 1.226) as in Cicero's *Academica* (1.45). And while Willet makes no references to Sextus or Pyrrhonism, he alludes to the Academics and to pre-Socratics like Empedocles and Anaxagoras, his Latin vocabulary suggesting permeation by sceptical modes of enquiry.[54]

It was not only at Cambridge, however, that Elizabethan intellectuals might be introduced to sceptical epistemology. We have seen that Oxford's Merton College purchased a copy of the 1562 Sextus in 1591, that students at Christ Church were reading Sextus in the 1580s and 1590s, and that even earlier – between 1553 and 1563 – a portion of Sextus' *Adversus logicos* had been translated into Latin by John Wolley, again at Merton. Some years later, in 1569, John Rainolds completed his BA at Corpus Christi by delivering orations in response to three questions, one of which was 'Do the senses deceive?' And in the following decade Rainolds returned to epistemological concerns in his lectures on Aristotle's *Rhetoric*, referring frequently to 'Academic philosophers' and citing such sources as Cicero's *Academica* and Pico's

*Examen.*[55] Hence when Charles Schmitt claims that Oxford's academic disputations during the 1580s–1590s involved 'a strikingly large number of epistemological *quaestiones* which seem to reflect a sceptical threat', his view is supported by additional evidence from the 1570s. And while it might be an exaggeration to speak of a 'threat' since, as Schmitt acknowledges, scepticism has never been 'the philosophical position of the many' and could not be 'institutionalized', it none the less seems reasonable to conclude that scepticism was perceived, at both Oxford and Cambridge, as an intellectual orientation with which students needed to reckon, and about which they were therefore expected to possess some degree of familiarity.[56]

But there was a third corner to the 'golden triangle' of Elizabethan education: London, and especially its four Inns of Court with their associated Inns of Chancery. And it was in London, particularly around the beginning of the 1590s, that still further interest in ancient scepticism seems to have taken hold. We know that Donne, who studied at Thavie's and Lincoln's Inns (1591–4), was fully cognizant of the distinction Sextus draws between Pyrrhonists, Academics and Dogmatists. We know, too, that Fraunce spent time at Gray's Inn (1583–8) and that many other Elizabethan writers – Marston, Bacon, Ralegh, Lodge, Greville, Beaumont, Ford and very likely Webster and Tourneur – were associated with one or another of the Inns during the 1590s and early 1600s.[57] Marston, who occupied chambers at the Middle Temple from 1595 to 1606, chastises a fictional interlocutor in his *Scourge of Villanie* (1598): 'Fye *Gallus*, what, a skeptick *Pyrrhomist?*'[58] And the same institution, which held a copy of the 1569 Sextus, was also home to Sir John Davies, who studied and practised there from 1588, demonstrating significant interest in sceptical issues in his *Nosce Teipsum* (1599). Shakespeare, too, had connections with the Middle Temple, though of course he was never a member: *Twelfth Night* was staged there in 1602, and, if William Elton is correct, *Troilus and Cressida* may have been conceived for performance there or at another Inn.[59] And while Nashe, who seems to have moved from Cambridge to London by 1588, does not have connections with the law schools, it may none the less be the case that it was an indirect consequence of their presence – their wealth, libraries, disputations and general concentration of literary activity – that enabled Nashe to speak, in his 1591 preface to Sidney's *Astrophil and Stella*, of a version of Sextus 'latelie translated into English, for the benefit of unlearned writers'.[60] This translation, long regarded as a lost document of the Renaissance, is remarkable for having existed at all: it was the first rendering into any vernacular tongue of a philosopher now considered one of the most important Hellenistic thinkers.

## The 'lost translation' and *The Sceptick*

Several inferences about the Sextus translation may be made on the basis of Nashe's remark, on his subsequent quotations from the work, and on Samuel Rowlands' similar reliance in *Greene's Ghost Haunting Conycatchers* (1602). First, the translation's very existence implies the prior presence, presumably in London, of a non-English version of Sextus, most likely Estienne's 1562 rendition of the *Outlines*, also available in Hervet's 1569 compendium. Second, Nashe's adverb 'latelie' suggests that the translation cannot date from much earlier than 1590. Third, due to the source attribution of Ronald McKerrow in his magisterial edition of Nashe, we can deduce that the translation included, at the minimum, a substantial portion of the chapter in the *Outlines* where Sextus presents the ten modes of doubt (*PH*, 1.35–163). It must have included, for example, Sextus' discussion of the perceptive and ratiocinative capacities of the dog, since a speech in *Summer's Last Will and Testament* (1592) relies on that discussion, as does a portion of Rowlands' tract. It also contained other sections from the same chapter, as passages from *Pierce Penniless* (1592) and *The Unfortunate Traveller* (1594) clearly indicate.[61] In short, the translation very likely incorporated the bulk of Book One, chapter 14 of the *Outlines* – and probably not much more, for if it had, Nashe presumably would have referred to other sections as well.

McKerrow's discussion of the Sextus translation does not allude to the anonymous treatise *The Sceptick*, often attributed to Ralegh. But it is crucial to note that this short tract, whose date of composition is unknown, bears an important relation to the questions posed by Nashe's reliance on Sextus. First published in 1651, and preserved in four manuscript versions whose discrepancies suggest a complex history of textual transmission, *The Sceptick* is a loose translation of Book One, chapter 14 of Sextus' *Outlines*. It spans, in other words, precisely the same portion of the work from which all the allusions in Nashe and Rowlands are drawn. And while S. E. Sprott has argued that *The Sceptick* derives from the Sextus translation to which Nashe alludes, my own collation of the four manuscripts suggests rather that *The Sceptick* and the 'lost' translation are in essence one and the same work. More precisely, the English translation of Sextus to which Nashe alludes is simply an earlier manuscript copy of *The Sceptick* than any of

the four now extant. Apart from a small number of textual discrepancies whose existence may be imputed to scribal error, the version of
*The Sceptick* that Nashe and Rowlands quote was in all essential attributes the same version of this curious and pioneering work that we still
possess today: the first vernacular translation of the most important
classical account of Pyrrhonism.

How can we know this? The argument is complex – too detailed to
rehearse completely here – and I have presented much of it elsewhere
in the introduction to my edition of *The Sceptick*.[62] Suffice it to say that
my claim derives from two closely related strands of argumentation.
First, evidence generated by collating *The Sceptick*'s four manuscripts
and its 1651 printed text points to the one-time existence of at least
four additional manuscripts which we must now presume lost. The
range of textual variation among the surviving versions makes it plausible to suppose that a similar range existed among the copies no
longer extant. To posit, therefore, that the 'ur-text' of *The Sceptick* – the
work's initial incarnation – contained several brief passages absent
from the Harleian manuscript (the fullest surviving version), is scarcely
earthshaking, particularly when versions such as 1651 and the Dublin
manuscript differ from Harleian more than Harleian differs from this
reconstructed 'ur-text', and each of these passages falls within the
limits of Sextus' *Outlines* covered by Harleian and, indeed, by all extant
versions of *The Sceptick*. No evidence suggests that the 'lost' translation,
if it existed, exceeded the bounds of *The Sceptick* in its coverage of
Sextus.

Second, McKerrow's theory weakens severely when *The Sceptick* is
taken into account. The only way to preserve it is to hypothesize that
*The Sceptick* derives not from Estienne's Latin but from an exuberant
English translation of Sextus, and that its author then painstakingly
deletes virtually all non-Sextian additions that subsequently appear in
Nashe and Rowlands. The implausibility of this hypothesis is self-
evident, as is the corresponding unlikelihood of a translation that
strives to preserve Sextus' sober tone and careful distinctions while
simultaneously indulging in jokes and topical similes. More obvious, to
my mind, is that both Nashe and Rowlands worked from a serious
translation of Sextus that, while not identical to *The Sceptick* we now
possess, was none the less in all essential attributes the same text, cov-
ering the same portion of the *Outlines*, though not yet reduced in
length through the vagaries of scribal transmission. In numerous
instances, after all, Nashe and Rowlands reproduce multiple-word
phrasings from *The Sceptick*. And of Nashe's 27 borrowings from Sextus,

25 find verbatim or near-verbatim parallels in *The Sceptick*, while the remaining two constitute examples that add nothing to Sextus' point and that a scribe may be excused for omitting. Most importantly, no evidence from *The Sceptick* may be adduced to suggest that it derives from an earlier English translation of Sextus that, as McKerrow's theory necessitates, was exceptionally faithful yet frequently embellished with topical allusions and witty figures of speech. And since we possess *The Sceptick* and can account for the verbal evidence in Nashe and Rowlands without positing a separate translation of the *Outlines*, the time has come to cease alluding to two distinct Elizabethan renditions of Sextus. We must speak, rather, of an earlier and slightly fuller version of *The Sceptick* – a version based on Estienne's Latin and prepared, as Nashe suggests, around 1590.

Why does this matter? Apart from its truth value – assuming that it *is* true – why is it significant that *The Sceptick* is the 'lost' translation of Sextus? It is significant in the first place because it demonstrates that there was an English audience for Sextus in the late sixteenth century. Intellectuals could have read Sextus in Latin had they wished, but *The Sceptick*'s existence shows that someone thought Sextus – at least *part* of Sextus – was important enough to be rendered into English and thus available to non-Latinists. That there were a minimum of eight manuscript copies of the treatise further reinforces the sense that Elizabethans wanted to read about Pyrrhonism. In particular, they were interested in the section of the *Outlines* where the ten modes of doubt are presented. These modes constitute a veritable arsenal of sceptical argumentation, and the very fact that they were selected for translation underscores the extent to which they were perceived as a core component of the *Outlines*. We must not forget that Pico devoted considerable space to elaborating these modes in his *Examen*, that Ramus summarized them, and that Giovanni Bernardi presented them yet again in his encyclopaedia of Platonic and Aristotelian philosophy.[63] When writers like Nashe gained access to *The Sceptick*, they were thus positioned to combine its treatment of the modes with other fragments about scepticism they might have gleaned from Cicero, Laertius, Agrippa, Erasmus and Montaigne, not to mention the refutations of sceptical thought surfacing in Mornay, Bodin, Loyer and other figures. Sextus' modes of doubt were viewed as central to the activity of the sceptic, and therefore central to an understanding of sceptical epistemology.

Second, *The Sceptick*'s probable date of composition, 1590, forces us to adjust our sense of the impact on English intellectual culture of the

Renaissance revival of scepticism. There is no question that scepticism made a bigger splash in France and Italy; we know that Montaigne, Bodin, Loyer and others were reading Sextus in the 1570s. But allegations that interest in Sextus' writings spread rather slowly in early modern England probably need revision.[64] Donne, as we have seen, evinces likely familiarity with *The Sceptick* and thus with Sextus when he writes that sceptics doubt everything and are 'more contentious' than other sects. And if, besides Donne, Nashe, Rowlands and Ralegh, we add to our list Marlowe, Bacon, Cornwallis, Harriot, Marston, Wolley, Willet, Fraunce, Thomson, Chamber, Heydon, Davies of Hereford, Greville, Hall and Joseph Mede, it looks as though familiarity with Sextus in late sixteenth- and early seventeenth-century Britain was not so rare after all. At least ten copies of the 1562 and 1569 editions of Sextus were held in private, ecclesiastical or university libraries in London, Oxford, Cambridge and Salisbury in or before 1590; in 1591 Thomas Savile was purchasing printed and manuscript copies of Sextus at the Frankfurt Book Fair; and by 1601 at least eleven additional printed copies of Sextus were held in Britain. These are not large numbers, but as absolute minimums they point to larger numbers, and in any case it takes only one copy of a work to serve as the source of a translation.

Third, and most interestingly, *The Sceptick* makes occasional additions to Sextus, giving voice to a home-grown and common-sense scepticism that pre-dates widespread familiarity with Montaigne and finds sanction and respectability through its association with the ideas of a classical philosopher. As I have stressed, *The Sceptick*'s translator was fundamentally serious in his intentions, and his alterations to Sextus, whether additions or omissions, always preserve the spirit and tone of the original. But the translator had ideas of his own – particularly regarding animal intelligence – and on two occasions his ideas emerge vividly. In one instance, when Sextus is discussing the ability of non-human creatures to communicate with one another, *The Sceptick*'s translator illustrates the point by adding two sentences about birds:

> Do not birds by one kind of speech call their young ones, and by another cause them to hide themselves? Do they not by their several voices express their several passions of joy, of grief, of fear, in such manner that their fellows understand them? (47)

And in a second instance, when Sextus argues that humans have no business privileging their perceptions over those of animals, the translator augments Sextus' point using language surprising in its vehemence:

> Why should I presume to prefer my conceit and imagination in affirming that a thing is thus or thus in its own nature, because it seemeth to me to be so, before the conceit of other living creatures, who may as well think it to be otherwise in its own nature, because it appeareth otherwise to them than it doth to me? These are living creatures as well as I, why then should I condemn their conceit and fantasy concerning any thing more than they may mine? They may be in the truth and I in error, as well as I in the truth and they err. (45)

Perhaps this belabours Sextus' claim; certainly it contributes nothing not implicit in the original. But at the same time the translator's words offer a sense of lived experience, of sympathy, even outrage, at the common spectacle of human presumption towards non-human beings. I find it an attractive voice, almost Montaignian in quality (e.g. Florio, 382–3), and I think we hear it because Sextus gives it legitimacy and an occasion for expression.

The significance of *The Sceptick* thus lies principally in its capacity not merely to transmit ancient ideas, but to attract and channel currents of scepticism that existed in Britain towards the close of the sixteenth century. A glance at Nashe or Donne demonstrates that such scepticism was familiar to some Elizabethans, and we may plausibly infer that there were many others. *The Sceptick* appeared in English not only because Sextus was seen as important, not only because he was talked about on the Continent, not only because he was championed by Montaigne, but also because the English, too, had their doubts.

As for *The Sceptick*'s authorship, the jury is still out. The work has conventionally been attributed to Ralegh, primarily on the strength of the authorial ascription in the 1651 edition, secondarily because a manuscript copy was found among genuine Ralegh papers. Sprott leans in the direction of Ralegh's authorship, and he has been joined by others: Christopher Hill asserts that 'It was through Ralegh that much of the most advanced continental thought was popularized in England – Machiavelli, Bodin, scepticism'.[65] But Pierre Lefranc has argued that since none of the surviving *Sceptick* manuscripts bears any indication that Ralegh composed the treatise, we must consider the attribution dubious.[66] My own view is that attributing authorship to *The Sceptick* is far less important than ascertaining its date and degree of circulation.

Given the evidence we possess, it is probably best to suspend judgement on the question of who composed the piece – or, more accurately, who *adapted* it from Estienne's translation of Sextus. We may never possess sufficient evidence to trace the authorship and provenance of *The Sceptick*, let alone specify its exact relation to other contemporary works, but the very complexity of the textual problem suggests the extent to which Elizabethan intellectuals were intrigued and irritated, provoked and disturbed, by the issues raised in Sextus' *Outlines*.

## Bacon: part one

Francis Bacon perfectly exemplifies this mingled response. Associated with Gray's Inn for almost fifty years after his stint at Cambridge (1573–5) and his subsequent travels in France (1576–9), Bacon first emerges in the history of scepticism's reception on precisely 17 November 1595 with his *Of Love and Self-Love*, a 'device' staged for the 37th anniversary of Elizabeth's accession. In this courtly entertainment, Bacon presents a Knight who rejects the suggestion of a Hermit that he embrace a life of contemplation:

> You [Father] that pretend to truth and knowledge, how are you assured that you adore not vain chimeras? that in your high prospect, when you think men wander up and down, that they stand not indeed still in their place, and it is some cloud between you and them which moveth, or else the dazzling of your own eyes?[67]

As Geoffrey Bullough notes, this rejection exhibits 'a trace of scepticism' not unlike that in *The Sceptick*.[68] More specifically, its emphasis on sense-deception resembles that of Sextus in his fourth and fifth modes of doubt (*PH*, 1.100–23), modes which deal with the mutability of appearances according to shifts in circumstance and orientation. Indeed, though we have no conclusive evidence that Bacon read Sextus – or, for that matter, *The Sceptick* – we may assume that a man of his learning would have been familiar with the argumentative strategies of the Pyrrhonians. Certainly by 1597 he had read the refutation of Cicero in Augustine's *Contra Academicos*, for his fragmentary *Colours of Good and Evil* paraphrases a significant portion of the treatise (*WFB*, 7:78; *Academicos*, 3.15–16). Bacon's choice, moreover, to use the word 'Essayes' as the title of his collection of prose meditations strongly suggests that he knew Montaigne's remarkable book – and probably had read it in French.

But Bacon's first explicit reference to Pyrrho and scepticism does not occur until around 1603, when his *Masculine Birth of Time* was composed. This work, anticipating the later 'Idols of the Mind' section of *The New Organon* (1620), argues that the mind requires preparatory discipline before it can expand beyond its 'deplorably narrow' limits and extend its 'dominion over the universe'. Accompanying this optimistic programme is an alternately bemused and strident denunciation of numerous thinkers – Aristotle, Aquinas and Ramus among others – who serve as representatives of the classical, medieval and humanist traditions. In the midst of this polemic Bacon pauses to touch on scepticism: 'I even find entertainment in Pyrrho and the Academics, though they waver from one side to the other like an orator speaking from a boat ... other philosophers follow straight after their idols, [but] these fellows are led round in circles, which is more diverting.'[69] Presumably, the 'idols' of the sceptics are mainly those Bacon later refers to as Idols of the Cave and Theatre, which centre on the peculiarities of individual humans and the attachments they form to specific subjects and dogmas. No doubt Bacon misrepresents the sceptics by implying that they, too, are dogmatic. But in this, as in his conflation of Pyrrho with the Academics, he does no more than many of his contemporaries have done. Bacon finds the wavering of the sceptics amusing, and though he believes it possible – through close observation, empirical reasoning, collective enterprise and 'true induction' – to ascertain the truth about things-in-themselves, he none the less prefers the indecisiveness of Pyrrhonians to the confidence of other sects. Indeed, as one biographer writes, Bacon 'practised and recommended the virtues of sustained doubt as Pyrrhonians did ... he forcefully admits to going part of the way with sceptics'.[70]

Another work contemporary with the *Masculine Birth* corroborates this. As we read in *Valerius Terminus* (1603), the opinion of 'the second school of the Academics and the sect of Pyrrho' is 'well to be allowed', although these 'considerers' who 'denied comprehension' should, in Bacon's view, have gone on to 'build better' after overthrowing their opponents' dogmas (*WFB*, 3:244). The metaphor of razing and reconstructing illustrates that Bacon's prevailing intellectual attitude, even as early as 1603, is hopeful and positivistic; he therefore cannot endorse scepticism, though like Giordano Bruno he respects the position of preliminary doubt. For Bacon, even the Idols of the Tribe can be mitigated, if not overcome: these include proneness to abstraction, 'incompetency of the senses' and other vexing features of cognition (*WFB*, 4:59). For Montaigne, by contrast, such problems are insuperable: 'Things external to [the soul] may have their own weight and dimension: but within us, she gives them such measures as she wills.' It is scarcely surprising, then, that while Bacon finds sceptics mildly risible, Montaigne broadens the source of amusement: 'Our own specific property is to be equally laughable and able to laugh' (*Essays*, 338–40).

## Fin de siècle

I will discuss Bacon again in chapter 3, for it is during the Jacobean years that he fully articulates his response to epistemological scepticism. But at present I wish to return to the last decade of the sixteenth century and the opening years of the seventeenth, for it is then, with ever-increasing frequency, that scepticism enters the lexicon of English poets and intellectuals. Allusions to 'Academicks' appear in Marston's *Satyres* (1598) and Richard Broughton's *Resolution of Religion* (1603); allusions to Arcesilaus and Carneades in Robert Parry's *Moderatus* (1595) and Joseph Hall's *Virgidemiae* (1598). Greene's *Friar Bacon and Friar Bungay* (1590) speaks of 'strange doubts' (1.2.26); and the word 'libertine' is employed repeatedly, surfacing in Edward Guilpin's *Skialethia* (1598), Jonson's *Poetaster* (1601), Davies of Hereford's *Mirum in Modum* (1602) and of course *Hamlet* ('a puffed and reckless libertine'). In 1599 Thomas Morton publishes his *Treatise of the Nature of God*, a dialogue between a religious doubter and his monitor; in 1600 John Norden's *Vicissitudo Rerum* appears, one of the best-known commentaries on the world's mutability and progressive decay; and the same year Marston's tragedy *Antonio's Revenge* launches a scathing attack on the vanity of learning (4.1.1–60).[71]

By 1598 the Catholic scholar-priest Thomas Wright had completed *The Passions of the Mind*, first published in 1601. Within this popular exposition of Renaissance psychology we find an extensive list of apparently insoluble 'Problems concerning the substance of our Souls', concluding with Wright's inference of 'our extreme Ignorance'.[72] Similar problems worry Marston's Lampatho, a malcontent who laments his fruitless years as a student:

> I was a scholar: seven useful springs
> Did I deflower in quotations

> Of cross'd opinions 'bout the soul of man;
> The more I learnt the more I learnt to doubt.
> (*What You Will*, 2.2.151–4)

1601 also saw the composition of Donne's unfinished satire *The Progress of the Soul*, which alleges that 'There's nothing simply good, nor ill alone ... The only measure is, and judge, opinion'.[73] Hamlet's claim that 'there is nothing either good or bad, but thinking makes it so' springs to mind as an analogue to Donne's remark, as does Nashe's comment that 'opinion (as *Sextus Empiricus* affirmeth) gives the name of good or ill to everything'. All three assertions may derive, as Nashe's quotation suggests, from the 'ur-text' of *The Sceptick* – or perhaps from Montaigne, or even from Laertius' *Life of Pyrrho*, which proffers the following lugubrious discussion:

> There is nothing good or bad by nature, for if there is anything good or bad by nature, it must be good or bad for all persons alike, just as snow is cold to all. But there is no good or bad which is such to all persons; therefore there is no such thing as good or bad by nature.[74]

In short, we cannot ascertain the precise genealogy of the idea, though we can recognize its startling sychronicity at the turn of the seventeenth century. What seems indisputable, however, is that the notion of 'opinion' as a significantly influential force in determinations of 'good' and 'ill' cannot be dismissed. The idea finds expression across a wide range of genres and purposes, and its appearance in John Beaumont's mock-heroic *Metamorphosis of Tabacco* (1602) merely confirms the point:

> The lumpish *Stoicks*, which did thus decree,
> A mortall man might without passion bee,
> Had they once cast their carelesse eyes on this,
> Would soone have showne what humane nature is:
> The *Epicureans*, whose chiefe good was plac't
> In earthly pleasures vaine voluptuous tast,
> Had our *Tabacco* in their daies been found,
> Had built their frame on a more likely ground.
> *Pyrrho* that held all by opinion stood,
> Would have affirm'd this were by nature good.
> (Ev–E2v)

If Pyrrho, according to Beaumont, endorsed this view of opinion, so too do the adherents of 'the darke doctrine of poperie' – at least according to more than a few late sixteenth-century Calvinists who publish treatises against Catholicism. One such writer is the Puritan divine Thomas Wilcox, whose *Discourse Touching the Doctrine of Doubting* (1598) deserves attention because its author, as supervisor of the third edition of Mornay's *Woorke* (1604), was undoubtedly familiar with Mornay's discussion of 'Scepticks'. Wilcox characterizes the 'doctrine of doubting' as a Catholic injunction for 'all men to doubt of their justification and salvation' (4), and he devotes his book to the refutation of this tenet. According to Wilcox, spiritual doubt is a function either of our necessary depravity as humans or else the deliberate malice of Satan. Doubting 'cannot choose but be evill'; it is a vice that must be combated by faith in God's word, whose truth is guaranteed by the grace which the faithful 'receive from God and feele in themselves' (147, 80). Hence spiritual certainty is possible; its criterion is the inner persuasion proceeding from grace.[75] Doubting is therefore sinful, and prolonged doubting a sign of reprobation:

> where there is doubting concerning Gods grace, the forgivenes of sinnes, the hope of everlasting life &c. there cannot be peace of conscience, but terrours and distrustfulnesse, ... because as there is in the godly, through the love of God toward them in Jesus Christ, an increase & proceeding from faith to faith: so is there in the wicked by reason of their owne sinne and Satans malice against them, a proceeding from one iniquity to another. (220–1)

It might be objected that since Wilcox's book deals solely with spiritual doubt, epistemological scepticism is unlikely to have played a role in its genesis. And to the best of my knowledge Wilcox makes no mention of Pyrrhonism, nor does he allude to Sextus. But he knows about 'Scepticks' from his study of Mornay, and he also discusses commonplaces of sceptical argumentation which powerfully suggest that he has the polemical strategies of Catholic Pyrrhonists in mind. Writing that his adversaries urge that 'men must beware of rash entring into that reverend misterie of predestination' (98–9), he demonstrates that he regards the allegation of 'rash presumption' – what Charron calls 'precipitation of judgement' – as worthy of confutation.[76] Still more significantly, he dwells on the concept of *epochē*, though he does not use the word. Quoting Luke's injunction to 'aske not what ye shall eate or what ye shall drinke, neither hang ye in suspense' (12:29), he then explicates the passage:

> it is as if he should say, be not of a suspended or doubtfull heart. For it is metaphoricall, & borrowed from things that hang in the aire, which are so uncertaine that no man knoweth whether they will fall or hang there still. Even so they that are carefull for this worldly life have wavering & doubtful mindes, swaying sometimes this way & sometimes that, neither they themselves nor other men knowing what will become of them, or which way they will fall. (186)

The 'wavering' that for Bacon is mildly amusing, and for Bartas worthy of ridicule, is for Wilcox a sign of feeble faith. And while it is true that even Montaigne, the most famous representative of the 'marriage' of Christianity and scepticism, practises suspension of judgement less frequently than is often supposed, it is none the less the case that he and other post-Reformation Catholics often view *epochē* as a necessary phase in the cognitive progression from awareness of contrariety to assent to scripture.[77] Wilcox, by contrast, sees no place for judgemental suspension in religious affairs, viewing it as sinful by definition. It will either be eradicated by faith – in which case the believer is granted further confirmation of grace – or it will fester, thereby proving reprobation.

The harsh Calvinist logic of Wilcox's treatise is nowhere in evidence in Sir John Davies' philosophical poem, *Nosce Teipsum* (1599). Like Wilcox, Davies knew Mornay's *Woorke*, but unlike Wilcox he had read Montaigne, almost certainly in the original French. The poem, indeed, feels strongly Montaignian – or Montaignian with a hint of Donne – in its favourable references to Socrates and Democritus and its emphasis on ignorance as a consequence of Original Sin.[78] 'What can we know?' asks Davies,

> or what can we discerne?
> When *Error* chokes the windowes of the mind;
> The diverse formes of things how can we learne,
> That have bene ever from our birth-day blind?

Davies then quotes Cicero's *Academica*, as Montaigne so often does, and in meditating on the Delphic exhortation to 'Know Thyself' he offers a trenchant critique of the soul's tendency towards dogmatic stasis:

> why should we the busie Soule beleeve,
> When boldly she concludes of that, and this?

When of her selfe she can no judgement geve,
Now how, nor whence, nor where, nor what, she is?

There are, in short, serious grounds for doubt, and while Davies does not pursue at length this sceptical line of thought, he shares Montaigne's distrust of the arrogance – even hubris – of the habitual propensities of 'our curious braine' (57–60, 83–8).

But Davies' portrayal of the human condition is not unrelentingly bleak. Some hope remains, and it lies in suffering: '*Afflictions* lookes ... Teach us to *know our selves*, beyond all bookes' (149–51). Suffering is providential; it prompts self-recognition, which serves in turn as the ground for accurate observation of the world. Davies' premise is thus quite simple: without self-knowledge, all other knowledge is useless. But with self-knowledge – particularly with the recognition that a human is 'a *proud* and yet a *wretched* thing' (180) – the rest of learning can be placed in proper perspective. *Nosce Teipsum* thus embodies the 'vanity of learning' thesis, though it in no way constitutes a thorough-going exploration of scepticism along Pyrrhonian or Academic lines. As Paul Kocher writes, its discussion of immortality is couched in 'orthodox Neo-Aristotelian terms'; the poem, if severed 'from its skeptical introduction, could serve as an average treatise on Elizabethan episte-mology'.[79] But the poem is *not* so severed, and Kocher fails to note that its suspicion of worldly dogmatism is consonant with the sixteenth-century revival of scepticism. Hence, to the extent that this con-sonance depends on familiarity with Montaigne, Cicero and, perhaps indirectly, Sextus, *Nosce Teipsum* offers further illustration of a standard paradigm of early modern Britain's appropriation of ancient sceptical thought.

## Florio's Montaigne

Familiarity with Montaigne: we have now seen such familiarity in Davies, Bacon and Donne, and we will see it too in works by Marston, Jonson, Webster, Cary, Burton, Ford and Chillingworth. We know as well that the Stationers' Register in 1595 records an English version of Montaigne by Edward Aggas, a version that has not survived.[80] Half a decade later the Register lists another rendering, this one by the Oxford-trained lexicographer John Florio, a member, like Shakespeare, of the circle surrounding the Earl of Southampton. And while Florio's translation does not appear in print until 1603, evidence exists that it circulated in manuscript during the interim. William Cornwallis writes in 1600 that Montaigne is 'most excellent, whom though I have not [seen] in his Originall, yet divers peeces I have seen translated' (42). The following year Robert Johnson borrows the title *Essaies* for his volume of prose compositions; Bacon had done the same in 1597.[81] And Shakespeare too appears to be reading Montaigne, as editors of *Hamlet* have long conjectured: Harold Jenkins concludes that 'of the ideas which Shakespeare so lavishly bestowed on Hamlet, a few at least were prompted by his recent reading in Florio's Montaigne'.[82] Hence there is ample support for Jonson's claim in *Volpone* that 'Montagnié' is the continental author from whom English writers most often 'deign to steal' (3.4.89–90). And the theft occurs even before Florio's translation is printed.

But what in fact does familiarity with Montaigne – or with Florio's Montaigne – amount to among writers in Shakespeare's England? At the most superficial level it amounts to verbal borrowing – a habit from which Florio himself is not exempt. As Frances Yates has shown, Florio draws on imagery from Montaigne in his *Worlde of Wordes* (1598), an Italian-English dictionary. He was thus presumably at work on the translation by then, relying primarily on the 1595 posthumous edition of the *Essais*, though referring occasionally to other versions, particularly that of 1588.[83] As a consequence, modern students must check Florio against critical editions of the original text, for he often adds to Montaigne's thoughts, sometimes needlessly elaborating them, sometimes inflecting them with his own opinions or misunderstandings. The title 'Des senteurs' becomes 'Of Smels and Odors'; the 'erreurs de Wiclef' are reduced to 'Wickliffs opinions' (12); and the mordantly ironic conclusion of 'Des cannibales' – 'Tout cela ne vas pas trop mal: mais quoy, ils ne portent point de haut de chausses' – metamorphoses into the lethargic and flaccid 'All that is not verie ill; but what of that? They weare no kinde of breeches nor hosen' (171). Still, Florio redeems himself for every pleonastic blunder. Who does not delight in 'botcherly-patchcotes' for 'ravaudeurs', 'dastardly meacocke' for 'poltron' (955, 295)? Certainly Shakespeare relished Florio's vocabulary; in *Lear* he probably derived such words as 'goatish', 'disnatured', 'sectary', 'marble-hearted', 'sophisticated' and 'handy-dandy' from the now published *Essays*. And he may well have encountered three other terms that Florio introduced into English, terms specifically derived from the sceptical lexicon: 'Pyrrhonisme', 'Ataraxie' and 'Pyrrhonize' (449–53, 516–22).[84]

All three appear in the *Apology for Raymond Sebond*, Montaigne's longest chapter. Despite its size, however, the *Apology* is not truly anomalous: its engagement with source-texts and its expression of sceptical ideas reveal its commonality with other essays. Like the early chapter on opinion (1:14), it relies on information drawn from Laertius' *Life of Pyrrho*. And like the late essays 'On vanity' and 'On experience' it draws heavily on Cicero's *Academica*, which Montaigne must have reread with great intensity in the years between 1588 and his death in 1592. More generally, we observe throughout the *Essays* – and not merely in the *Apology* – an authorial tendency to return time and again to a fundamental constellation of ideas and discursive tactics which may be loosely characterized as 'sceptical', though it includes cognitive moves which constitute significant abandonments of the two basic models of scepticism that Montaigne had encountered in Sextus, Cicero and other sources. Indeed, it may not be an exaggeration to say that Montaigne misunderstands or misrepresents ancient scepticism in profoundly influential ways. Elizabethan and Jacobean familiarity with Montaigne, then, amounts not only to verbal borrowing, but also, and more importantly, to acquaintance with certain charismatic, highly idiosyncratic thought trajectories that manifest themselves repeatedly in the *Essays*.

One of the most prominent elements in this Montaignian constellation is the habit of contrasting diverse opinions, much in the Pyrrhonian manner of delineating opposed beliefs or appearances (*PH*, 1.31–4). 'There is law sufficient to speake every where, both *pro* and *contra*', writes Montaigne as early as 1572, and he never relinquishes this view (242). Indeed, the technique of opposition comes naturally to him, often serving a heuristic function. The chapter entitled 'A custom of the Isle of Cea' is a tissue of arguments and *exempla* for and against suicide; the *Apology* rehearses contradictory views on topics ranging from metempsychosis to female beauty. Part of the point is species-condemnatory: 'Nothing may be spoken so absurdly, but that it is spoken by some of the Philosophers' (490). But part of it is salutary. As we learn in 'On educating children', the tutor's job is not to pronounce, but to expose the pupil to a range of opinion: 'different lawes and fantasticall customes teach us to judge rightly of ours, and instruct our judgement to acknowledge his imperfections, which is no easie apprentiship' (120).

It is in fact an immensely difficult apprenticeship, and even Montaigne sometimes fails to put its lessons into practice. None the less, no writer in early modern Europe is better able to withhold judgement and remain 'doubtfull'. Montaigne is quite familiar with the Pyrrhonian concept of *epochē*: he defines it as an 'absolute surceasing and

suspence of judgement' (451). And in chapters ranging from 'On cannibals' to 'On experience' he models the behaviour for readers.
Regarding witchcraft, he avers that 'I am of opinion that we uphold
our judgement, as wel to reject as to receive' (932). And with respect to
standards of civility, he relates that

> I have seene men brought by sea from distant countries, whose
> language, because we could in no wise understand, and that their
> fashions, their countenance, and their clothes did altogether differ
> from ours; who of us did not deeme them brutish and savage? ...
> Whatsoever seemeth strange unto us, and we understand not, we
> blame and condemne. (413–14)

Here the judgemental suspension is implicit, conveyed through
trenchant irony and the interrogative mood. In classic Pyrrhonian
fashion Montaigne questions the existence of a standard of truth by
which judgements of any sort may be formed (*PH*, 1.114–17). The
vulgar view – that the unfamiliar is by definition inferior – receives a
sound mocking. Humans, after all, 'are borne to quest and seeke
after truth ... The world is but a Schoole of inquisition.' Yet precisely
here, in the conviction that truth, *pace* Democritus, is not 'hidden'
in an 'abisse' but 'elevated in the infinite height of divine knowledge', Montaigne abandons the Pyrrhonian trajectory he has so
assiduously followed (838).[85] And it is an abandonment that belies
his assertion elsewhere that he is afflicted with 'irresolution': a
'blemish' and 'incommodious defect'. He claims that he 'can main-
taine an opinion, but not make choise of it', that he 'cannot resolve
in matters of doubtfulnesse' (592). But he *does* so resolve – and
perhaps more often than he is aware.

This resolution takes two forms. Of these the former is nowhere
better illustrated than in 'On cannibals', where Montaigne offers the
following commentary:

> I finde there is nothing in that nation, that is either barbarous or
> savage, unlesse men call that barbarisme which is not common to
> them. As indeed, we have no other ayme of truth and reason, than
> the example and *Idea* of the opinions and customes of the countrie
> we live in. There is ever perfect religion, perfect policie, perfect and
> compleat use of all things. They are even savage, as we call those
> fruits wilde, which nature of her selfe, and of her ordinarie progresse
> hath produced: whereas indeed they are those which our selves

have altered by our artificiall devices, and diverted from their common order, we should rather terme savage. (163)

Montaigne follows a Pyrrhonian trajectory here only to reach a non-Pyrrhonian conclusion. When he mocks his countrymen's knee-jerk judgement of Tupinamba inferiority, he is sceptical in a way that Sextus could not but admire: he avoids the assumption of any criteria of judgement, in fact tacitly questioning the existence of such criteria. But when he introduces the wild fruit analogy, he subtly *assumes* a criterion – a criterion based on simplicity, purity and original natural-ness. This in turn allows him to reach a conclusion of New World supe-riority. It is not a conclusion to which he long adheres, and for this reason commentaries emphasizing Montaigne's 'primitivism' or 'noble savagism' are often overstated; still, it is unquestionably a departure from what Florio dubs 'the true Phyrrhonisme' (451). Nor is it the only such a departure in 'On cannibals'. A later passage, often overlooked by critics, condemns the 'barbarous horror' of certain Tupi practices, then offers a general denouncement of warfare, treachery and cruelty: 'We may then well call [the Tupinamba] barbarous, in regard of reasons rules, but not in respect of us that exceed them in all kinde of bar-barisme' (166–7). Reason becomes the criterion for judgement, and by reason's 'rules' the inhabitants of both the Old World and the New fall short of ideal standards of conduct.[86]

The introduction of reason as a judgemental criterion in 'On cannibals' strikes many readers as peculiar – particularly those who recall the *Apology*'s definition of reason as that 'shew of discourses, which every man deviseth or forgeth in himselfe' (509), not to mention its condemna-tion of the faculty for 'topsi-turving the visage of all things, according to her inconstant vanity and vaine inconstancy' (525). Indeed, Montaigne's dual attitude towards reason constitutes one of the fundamental contra-dictions of his book, a contradiction only intensified by its manifestation not merely between different sections but within specific chapters. But if the assumption of reason as a valid criterion terminates the Pyrrhonian tendencies in 'On cannibals', the excoriation of reason in the *Apology* like-wise results in non-Pyrrhonian conclusions. Most notoriously, it results in the fideistic leap that Montaigne reinscribes as sceptical quietude.[87] Sextus could never have endorsed a consideration of diverse opinion that concludes with the following thought:

[C]ustomes and conceipts differing from mine, doe not so much dislike me, as instruct me; and at what time I compare them together, they doe not so much puffe me up with pride, as humble me with lowlinesse. And each other choyce, except that which commeth from the expresse hand of God, seemeth to me a choyce of small consequence. (461)

This begins well enough, from a Pyrrhonian perspective, but the movement from humility to divinely directed choice again involves the covert introduction of a criterion, this time one that remains utterly inviolable. Much like Gianfrancesco Pico, whose *Examen* portrays Christian revelation as immune to sceptical scrutiny, Montaigne sees Church and Scripture as inhabiting an ontological niche entirely distinct from that occupied by dogmatic philosophical pronouncement: God's ordinance is 'incapable of doubt or alteration' (279).

Moreover, Montaigne understands his subscription to Christianity as an instance of Pyrrhonian conformity (*PH*, 1.16–24). 'There is nothing in mans invention' that exceeds the scepticism of Pyrrho in terms of intrinsic 'likelyhood' and 'profit':

[It] representeth man bare and naked, acknowledging his naturall weaknesse, apt to receive from above some strange power, disfurnished of all humane knowledge, and so much the more fitte to harbour divine understanding, disannulling his judgement, so he may give more place unto faith: Neither misbeleeving nor establishing any doctrine or opinion repugnant unto common lawes and observances ... It is a white sheet prepared to take from the finger of God what form soever it shall please him to imprint therin. (452)

This, then, is the second and more powerful form of Montaignian resolution. It constitutes an abandonment of Pyrrhonism in a double sense: first, because it locates Christian revelation beyond the reach of sceptical objection; second, because it reconceives Christian subscription as Pyrrhonian conformity. Had Montaigne been an adherent of 'true Phyrrhonisme', he would have conformed to Roman Catholicism without affirming that it represented truth. Had he been a true Pyrrhonist, he could never have been a fideist, using the imbecility of reason to justify a leap of faith.

But it is by no means clear that Montaigne could have been a true Pyrrhonist. It is by no means clear that anyone can – or that the term is even coherent. From the vantage point of four centuries we see that Montaigne's inability to subject his faith in God and Rome to sceptical interrogation constitutes a blind spot in his application of the

Pyrrhonian programme. But who can deny that similar blind spots might cloud the project of any *nouveau pyrrhonien*? What is most important to take away from Montaigne's Pyrrhonian experimentation is the idea that being a sceptic – in early modern Europe or at any other time – necessarily involves participation in a complex calculus of deployments and partial deployments of sceptical theory. In Montaigne's case, it involves not only the demonstration of clear understanding of Pyrrhonian ideas, but also sympathetic *mis*understanding; not only impeccable application of Pyrrhonist tactics, but strategic appropriation, distortion and transformation of those tactics. Montaigne writes that 'There is no man that doth not discover in himselfe a peculiar forme of his, a swaying forme [*forme maistresse*], which wrestleth against the institution, and against passions which are contrary to him' (731). And this conviction figures profoundly in his practice of scepticism. His entire project would have foundered had he not represented his thoughts as they in fact occurred to him (602). What we see, time and again, is a process of negotiation between Montaigne's own natural tendencies and the guidance provided by his encounters with Sextus, Cicero and other authorities both ancient and modern.

Consider, for instance, Montaigne's attitude to the investigative dimensions of scepticism. We have seen that he calls the world 'a Schoole of inquisition'; elsewhere he remarks that his task is 'not to establish the truth, but to find it out' (273). He repeatedly stresses that Pyrrhonists 'are still seeking after truth': they 'use their reason to enquire and to debate, not to stay and choose'; their habit 'is ever to waver, to doubt and enquire' (448–51). In short, Montaigne powerfully emphasizes the continuing search for truth, the component of the sceptical persuasion that Sextus identifies as *zetetic* (*PH*, 1.7). Yet he does this in concert with (1) his conviction that Church and Scripture provide valid criteria for truth, and (2) his awareness of Sextus' stress on *ataraxia* and on the 'constitutive principle' of scepticism: 'to every account an equal account is opposed' (*PH*, 1.8–30). An isolated reading of Sextus, in other words, might easily yield the conclusion that since an opposing account may always be juxtaposed against whatever is affirmed, suspension of judgement and subsequent *ataraxia* are inevitable; this in turn suggests that Sextus' characterization of scepticism as *zetetic* must be subordinated to the overwhelming impression he leaves that certain knowledge will not be attained. But Montaigne refuses to subordinate the one to the other. The search continues. Even after Montaigne has introduced faith into the discussion, scepticism remains alive; the two coexist. To be sure, Montaigne demarcates the legitimate realm for sceptical doubt as that lying outside the resolutions offered by 'the authoritie of Gods divine will'. But the region is vast and the potential to inquire and debate virtually limitless. For a man who 'love[s] to contest and discourse' (834), it is scarcely surprising that Montaigne so thoroughly reinforces Sextus' point about ongoing investigation. Montaigne's desire to continue the conversation is a central feature of his *forme maistresse*, and this facet of his scepticism relies on a conflation of ancient theory and personal predilection.

Or consider the relation between Montaigne's distaste for rash assertion and his pervasive commentary on presumption. Yet another element in the Montaignian constellation, this relation beautifully illustrates the negotiation between *institution* and *forme maistresse*. As early as 1572–4, Montaigne points to the perils of despising 'what we conceive not' and quite moderately expresses his impatience with dogmatism by arguing that 'reason hath taught me that resolutely to condemne a thing for false is to assume unto himselfe to have the limits of God's will, and the power of our common mother Nature, tied to his sleeve: And there is no greater folly in the world, than to reduce them to the measure of our capacitie' (141–3).[88] And as late as 1587–8 he returns to the same theme: 'Affirmation and selfe-conceit are manifest signes of foolishnesse' (973). The tenor of these remarks is fundamentally consonant with Sextus' discussion of non-assertion (*aphasia*) and dogmatic rashness (*propeteia*) in the *Outlines* (*PH*, 1.186–93).

But it is only a short step from describing the inherent problems of assertion to condemning the human propensities that lead to it. And we have no full appreciation of Montaigne if we do not recognize that he often takes this step. That delightful aside in 'On the lame' – 'I love these words and phrases which moderate the temerity of our propositions: *It may be*: *Peradventure*: *I thinke*, and such like' – is inseparably tied to the adjacent claim that 'I am drawn to hate likely things, when men goe about to set them downe as infallible' (932). Assertion and dogmatism, for Montaigne, are signs of depravity, ignorance, presumption. Indeed, they are proof (485). In the 'filth and mire of the worlde', humans exercise their intrinsic inanity: 'Is it possible to imagine anything so ridiculous as this wretched creature, which is not so much as master of himselfe, subject to offences of all things, and yet dareth call himselfe Master and Emperour of the Universe?' Presumption, argues Montaigne, is 'our originall infirmitie' (396–9). And while such a claim resonates profoundly with Christian doctrine and Original Sin, it simultaneously constitutes a blatant instance of the very tendency towards assertion that Montaigne attempts to explain. We have, in short, self-indictment. But whether Montaigne is conscious of the contradiction at any particular point, he is unquestionably aware of contradiction as a general fact about himself and others. 'Our owne condition is as ridiculous as risible'; we are 'as much to be laught at, as able to laugh' (263). Indeed, for Montaigne, self-recognition is a redemptive and providential gift. As Erasmus had written eighty years earlier, at the outset of the same tumultuous century, the truly wise person 'reflects that since he is mortal himself, he shouldn't want to be wiser than befits a mortal, but cast his lot in with the rest of the human race and blunder along in good company' (*CWE*, 27:103). This is the folly to which Erasmus grants his highest praise.

The final element in the Montaignian constellation – and a further example of the negotiation of self and education – is the blurring of boundaries between Pyrrhonian and Academic doubt. There is no question that Montaigne knew the difference: his presentation of the tripartite division of philosophers ('*Dogmatists*', '*Academikes*' and '*Sceptikes*, or *Epechistes*') comes directly from the opening of Sextus' *Outlines*, and his critique of Academic probabilism further confirms his familiarity with the distinction (448–9, 506–7).[89] Yet like many early modern intellectuals, Montaigne was not insistent on separating Pyrrhonism from Academicism. The *Apology* is laced with post-1588 additions drawn from the *Academica*. Many are inserted into that crucial early section where ancient scepticism is introduced: where *epochē*, *ataraxia* and the technique of opposition are defined, where the 'sceptical phrases' are set forth, and where Pyrrhonian conformity is summarized (447–53). Yet the effect is not one of dissonance. Nor need we conclude that because the *Academica* 'revealed to Montaigne many different sceptical arguments', he was thereby prompted to 'abandon the negative and destructive scepticism of Sextus for the more positive and pragmatic scepticism of Socrates and the Old Academy'.[90] Rather, we see a conflation that demonstrates Montaigne's greater interest in the broad unifying characteristics of sceptical thought than in the differentiations among competing schools. Montaigne is not a systematic philosopher; to be so would be to risk the very presumption against which he so often rails. Chastising Academicism as negatively dogmatic, for instance, never occurs to him, even though he is familiar with Sextus' characterization to that effect (*PH*, 1.220–35). The intellectual affinities between Socrates and Pyrrho are more significant than any differences: 'Of three generall Sects of Philosophie, two make expresse profession of doubt and ignorance' (452).

It is entirely appropriate, then, to speak of a Montaignian 'synthesis' of Academic and Pyrrhonian scepticism.[91] What we must recognize, however, is that the Montaignian synthesis is itself a deployment of scepticism, a facet of Montaigne's encounter with source-texts that becomes part of the constellation of ideas and tactics which 'familiarity with Montaigne' ultimately comprises. The synthesis, in short, is a sceptical paradigm. And if on close inspection it appears unrigorous or philosophically incoherent, this is of small consequence to Montaigne. What attracts him to both the Pyrrhonian and Academic outlooks is their common utility in combating intolerance, closed-mindedness, and dogmatic pronouncement. 'A man were better bend towards doubt', he writes, 'than encline towards certaintie ... When al is done, it is an overvaluing of ones conjectures, by them to cause a man to be burned alive' (934–5).

Indeed, Montaigne's own tendency to assertion lies always in the interest of demonstrating human limitation. 'Mans eyes cannot perceive things, but by the formes of his knowledge': an inevitable assimilationism lies embedded in perception and ratiocination (480). Yet while Montaigne, earlier in the *Apology*, criticizes anthropomorphic imaginings as hubristic and prideful, he recognizes how difficult they are to avoid. What we have, then, is a dogmatic claim about the homocentric puniness of humanity: it is our fate that we make gods only in our image. And such a claim is more in keeping with Academic than with Pyrrhonian scepticism. Still, Montaigne prefers to assert this than to suspend judgement on the matter. Probably, if questioned, he would have argued that the difficulty lies in language itself: that certain forms of affirmation purge themselves even as they take linguistic shape, that propositions concerned with doubt evacuate themselves 'as Rewbarbe doeth, which scowres ill humours away, and therewith is carried away himselfe'. After all, Montaigne formulated the question *Que sçay-je?* precisely to deflect the allegation that one has the Pyrrhonists 'by the throat' when they say 'I doubt' (472) – an allegation implicit in Augustine's 'Si fallor, sum' and later deployed by Descartes.[92] In any case, of paramount importance is that Montaigne's adoption of Platonic terminology – the 'formes' of knowledge – again points to a strict abandonment of sceptical thought-trajectories even in the process of illustrating the virtues of a sceptical outlook. Montaigne's 'Christian Pyrrhonism' is an adaptation, an eclectic hybrid, a convenient and syncretic deployment of certain strands of ancient and modern thought. It is a refashioned Pyrrhonism, depicting a fortunate impasse; it stresses not only perpetual but providential doubt: 'Oh God, what bond or duetie is it, that we owe not to our Creators benignitie, in that he hath beene pleased to enfranchize our beliefe from vagabondizing and arbitrary devolutions, and fixt it upon the eternall Base of his holy word?' (523). Still, virtually all the fundamental Pyrrhonian ideas and arguments remain present in the Montaignian constellation, suspended in multiple discursive arrangements and available for subsequent recombination in countless permutations. And this is what familiarity with Montaignian scepticism ultimately encompasses for Elizabethan and Jacobean writers. It is familiarity with scepticism not in its ideal 'forme' but in its imperfect worldly deployments. It is familiarity, in short, with sceptical paradigms – paradigms that 'participate', as Socrates might say, in a pure Form of scepticism, but that in fact are only distorted manifestations of that Form. Yet given their human generation, what else could they be, Montaigne would ask. *Que sçay-je?*

## 1603

Elizabeth's death marks a watershed year in the history of England's reception of scepticism. Not only does Florio's Montaigne appear in print, but works of theological controversy speak in increasingly overt terms of sceptics, of Pyrrho, of Sextus. As Scot's *Discoverie of Witchcraft* (1584) gives way to Nashe's *Terrors of the Night* (1594) – the one exhibiting no acquaintance with formal scepticism, the other composed by a writer clearly conscious of Sextus' ideas – so, by 1603, works by such polemicists as Chamber, Heydon and Samuel Harsnett show explicit familiarity with elements of the sceptical lexicon and with aspects of Sextus' epistemology. We thus witness a gradual fusion of common-sense scepticism with its philosophically grounded counterpart. And the quick association of conscious doubt with things Socratic and with French intellectual activity suggests that there was a predisposition to establish such connections once the ideas and vocabulary had become available. Moreover, writers of all sorts exhibit a sensitivity to epistemological questions, distinctions and anxieties which I believe to be a crucial feature of the age, and which we, as students of Britain's history and literature, ignore at our risk. Perhaps it is true, as Paul Kocher observes, that 'Only in a relatively small but illustrious group of lay intellectuals did classical skepticism have real force', but I maintain that scepticism in a less narrowly defined sense had far-reaching consequences during the period.[93] Its tendency to prompt repeated refutations implies that it was a force to be reckoned with, and while attraction to sceptical attitudes is vulnerable to many objections, it aligns itself none the less with a sense of intellectual humility, an interest in free expression and open-minded enquiry, and a powerful distaste for dogmatic authority, intolerance, and persecution. The continental tradition of scepticism extending from Erasmus to Montaigne had adherents in early modern England as well, and in the years following 1603 this becomes ever more clear.

# 3
# Seeming Knowledge: The Jacobean Years and Beyond

> They say miracles are past, and we have our philosophical persons to make modern and familiar things supernatural and causeless. Hence is it that we make trifles of terrors, ensconcing ourselves into seeming knowledge when we should submit ourselves to an unknown fear.
>
> *All's Well That Ends Well*

Characterizing the first half of England's turbulent seventeenth century, Douglas Bush writes in 1945 that 'from Donne to Dryden thoughtful men ask "What do I know?" Sharing the critical spirit, yet conscious of its destructive results, they seek standing-ground more firm than that which served their fathers.' Bush goes on to list many of the questions regarding judgemental criteria and legitimate authority that troubled seventeenth-century intellectuals, focusing in particular on the moral, theological and political realms. But while he speaks of the 'melancholy' and 'Jacobean pessimism' so familiarly associated with the early Stuart years, he cautions against thinking exclusively in such terms. He thus questions longstanding stereotypes and complicates the narrative of the Elizabethan/Jacobean transition, in the process emphasizing many historical and ideological continuities.[1] I wish to do much the same as I discuss the British reception of ancient scepticism in the period from the publication of Florio's Montaigne to the death of James and the last flourishing of Jacobean tragedy.

Bush claims that Montaigne was widely read in the early seventeenth century; Louis Bredvold adds that by the time Dryden was a young man 'every reader of any pretensions to cultivation knew Montaigne and Charron intimately, and almost every scholar had read Sextus'.[2] Certainly Jonson and Marston were reading Montaigne shortly after Florio's translation appeared: Jonson owned a copy of the book, and Marston drew on it heavily as he composed *The Dutch Courtesan*. Donne, too, seems to have known Montaigne, and like Bacon may have read him in French before 1603; Bredvold goes so far as to claim that he was the earliest of the seventeenth-century 'religious Pyrrhonists in England', having studied 'scepticism in Sextus and probably in Montaigne, and cultivated Augustine as his favorite religious teacher'.[3] Bacon alludes explicitly to Montaigne in his *Essays* and, later, in *De Dignitate et Augmentis Scientiarum* (1623); Middleton, probable author of *The Revenger's Tragedy*, borrows from the essayist around 1606, as does Webster in *The White Devil* and *The Duchess of Malfi*; and Shakespeare famously lifts a passage from Florio's rendition of 'On cannibals' as he drafts *The Tempest* – and probably draws from 'On cruelty' too. Even Randle Cotgrave's French-English *Dictionarie* (1611) shows unmistakable indebtedness to Montaigne in offering definitions of such words as 'Ataraxie' and 'Ephectique': a 'Sceptique', for instance, is 'One that is ever seeking, and never finds; the fortune of a Pyrrhonian'.[4] Thus Jonson does not exaggerate when he alludes in *Volpone* to the popularity of 'Montagnié' among English writers.

## Charron, Lipsius, Lancre

But for all his importance, Montaigne is only one of many continental figures through whose works the ideas and practices of scepticism are channelled into Britain. Another is the priest and moral philosopher Pierre Charron, who met Montaigne in the 1580s and later systematized many of his sceptical attitudes. Of Charron's writings, two in particular are relevant here: a treatise from 1593 entitled *Les trois verités*, and the better known *De la sagesse* (1601, 1604), translated by Samson Lennard as *Of Wisdome* and published no later than 1608.[5] *Verités* attacks Jews, Calvinists and other 'heretics', showing an acquaintance with Sextus but little patience for sceptics. Identifying three types of atheists, Charron characterizes the second as those who neither affirm nor deny God's existence; rather, 'like Academics and Pyrrhonians who profess perpetual doubt, they belong to no party, since, as they say, truth cannot be discovered; there are arguments and appearances on all sides' (19). The position of terminal agnosticism is thus assimilated to the category of 'atheism', and Charron conflates Academic and Pyrrhonian sects, finding them united in a doctrinaire conviction of humanity's inability to find truth.

Charron's *Wisdome*, by contrast, treats scepticism in more detail and relies extensively on Montaigne. Characterized as 'the most important Renaissance treatise on wisdom' and as 'an encyclopedia of moral and political philosophy', the book was immensely popular, acquiring substantial notoriety in the debate over the *libertins érudits*.[6] More sympathetic than *Verités* to sceptical habits of mind, *Wisdome* argues that the search for truth requires extraordinary patience and that the 'putting off' of judgement must be founded on several 'celebrated' propositions:

> that there is nothing certaine, that we know nothing, that there is nothing in nature but doubt, nothing certaine but incertaintie ... that we do nothing but search, enquire, and grope after appearances ... that veritie is not a thing of our owne invention, and when it yeelds itselfe into our hands, we have nothing in ourselves whereby we may assure ourselves of it ... That all things have two handles and two visages, and there is reason for all, and there is not any that hath not his contrarie.

In short, inquirers after truth follow the practice of those philosophers 'who have made profession of ignorance, doubting, searching' (237–8). Wisdom, for Charron, is not knowledge but intellectual freedom conjoined with moral integrity – the former involving an inquisitive and tolerant scepticism, the latter based on Stoic adherence to the law of nature (234–7).[7] But precisely here, by introducing Stoic theory, Charron qualifies the scepticism he elsewhere propounds. Indeed, his confidence in the ability of 'universall reason' to aid humans in recognizing absolute moral values stands in contradiction to his praise for the attitude that nothing is certain. Still, Charron's partial embrace of scepticism is hardly new; its lineaments, though idiosyncratic, constitute a familiar paradigm of scepticism's early modern reception.

Like Montaigne, Charron knows the differences between Pyrrhonism and Academicism, but like Montaigne he blurs them. A reluctance to pronounce and affirm, for example, 'is very neere the disorder [*ataraxie*] of the *Pyrhonians*, the neutralitie and indifference of the *Academicks*' (247). Charron also isolates Christian revelation from sceptical enquiry, insisting that we err if we think we have liberty to judge 'verities which have bin revealed to us, which we are to receive simplie with all humilitie' (231). One result is that the sceptical tendency to 'renounce all opinions and beleefs' is perfectly consonant with the Christian practice Charron recommends: 'An *Academicke* or *Pyrrhonian* was never hereticke, they are things opposite' (242). Finally, and again like his mentor, Charron stresses scepticism's *zetetic* dimension – its emphasis on 'the search of the truth' (231–8).[8] Montaigne accentuates this feature of Pyrrhonism much more than Sextus, so it is clear that Charron takes his cue from the *Essays*, and probably from such chapters as 'On prayer' and 'The art of conversation' as well as the *Apology*.

But Charron also differs importantly from Montaigne. In several respects his scepticism is less subtle, as for instance in his motto, *Je ne sçay*, which contrasts markedly with Montaigne's interrogative *Que sçay-je?* – the latter conceived precisely to avoid the problems invited by the former.[9] Additionally, Charron embraces a form of probabilism. Discussing burial versus cremation, he argues that while he himself is content to follow the European custom of interring corpses, he judges the 'ancient manner' of burning them 'more noble' (234) – a judgement which relies on an uninterrogated criterion to determine that one cultural habit is more admirable than another.[10] Montaigne occasionally resorts to this sort of judgement, but his sense of the relativity of custom and value is typically more acute than Charron's. What is perhaps most interesting, however, is that Charron conceives of scepticism in distinctly instrumental terms. The 'precipitation of judgement' he condemns and the 'suspence' of belief he commends are both temporary, both subordinate to a weighing of 'the reasons and counter-reasons on all parts' fundamental to a project whose ultimate goal is to 'worke out the truth' (169, 242, 230). Armed with his assumption of the Stoic criterion of natural reason, Charron is confident that truth may almost always be worked out. And in this respect he shares less with Montaigne than with Bacon, who may have read *Wisdome* but never mentions its author, and who indeed has little else in common with him.

Before discussing Bacon, however, I wish to continue my survey of other continental writers whose works, directly or in translation, contributed to scepticism's dissemination in Jacobean England. I have already treated relevant writings by Bartas, Mornay, Loyer and Isaac Casaubon; by 1605, new or reprinted English versions of their works had appeared in London.[11] Casaubon's 1593 edition of Laertius, with copious references to Sextus' *Outlines*, Cicero's *Academica* and the *Suda*, would have been increasingly available in Britain during the first decade of James' reign. Scholars might also find discussions of Pyrrhonism in such philosophical works as Marsilio Cagnati's *Variorum observationum* (1587), Johann Frisius' *Bibliotheca Philosophorum* (1592), Jacopo Mazzoni's *Comparatione Platonis & Aristotelis* (1597) and Israel Spach's *Nomenclatur* (1598). Readers following astronomical debates would have known that Christoph Clavius attacked sceptical critics of Ptolemaic geocentrism in his commentary on Sacro Bosco's *Of the Spheres*. The Copernican Johannes Kepler, meanwhile, defended astronomy against those who, in the 'Pyrrhonian manner', held everything uncertain.[12]

Less likely to have come to the attention of English readers would have been the *Essay Sceptique* (*c.* 1603) of Jean-Pierre Camus, a disciple of Montaigne and later a Catholic bishop. Self-characterized as 'fresh from the shop of Sextus', Camus was only nineteen when he wrote his treatise and, as Popkin notes, later found its tone embarrassing.[13] Still, the work displays the appeal of Christian Pyrrhonism at the outset of the seventeenth century, and it was certainly familiar to later figures such as Bayle. Equally cognizant of Sextus, but making quite different use of his writings, was the Belgian classicist Justus Lipsius. Much admired by Montaigne, Lipsius established his reputation as an editor of Tacitus before composing the works for which he is now chiefly remembered: *On Constancy* (1584), the *Politics* (1589) and the *Digest of Stoic Philosophy* (1604). In the last of these, Lipsius makes frequent recourse to sceptical texts from antiquity as he argues that Stoicism is philosophy's most useful accommodation to Christianity. Part of Lipsius' reason for relying on such texts is that they provide crucial evidence about Stoic views; Sextus and Cicero have always been doxographic treasuries. But to the extent that Lipsius repeats Sextus' division of philosophers into three groups ('Dogmaticam, Academicam, Scepticam') and also relies on discussions of *epochē* and *ataraxia* in clarifying the Stoic ideal of *apatheia* (freedom from passion), he demonstrates that ancient sceptical analyses of epistemology and ethics are useful to current constructions of Christianity.[14] Lipsius is no sceptic; his Christian Stoicism is genuine. But in his consolidated understanding of scepticism – derived not only from the *Outlines* and *Academica*, but also from *Against the Mathematicians*, the *Life of Pyrrho*, Plutarch's *Against Colotes* and Eusebius' *Evangelical Preparation* – he illustrates how thoroughly an early seventeenth-century scholar could synthesize the major classical accounts of the movement.

I have discussed the partial English translation of Loyer's *Treatise of Spectres*, a book that misrepresents the arguments of Pyrrhonism even while demonstrating how lively and useful they are. Another French work in this vein is Pierre de Lancre's *Inconstancy of All Things* (1607). Married to a grand-niece of Montaigne, Lancre had read the *Essays* of his famous in-law but does not appear to have been much influenced by them; indeed, the demonological writings of Loyer and Bodin seem to have left a far stronger impression.[15] And while Lancre's critique of scepticism is by no means as vehement as that of Loyer – it begins by frankly acknowledging the frailty of sense-perception – it none the less exhibits Aristotelian confidence about the human potential for knowing. Lancre's book has rarely been discussed, and never translated into English, so I quote from it at some length:

> To understand the folly that derives from corrupt opinion, it is worth mentioning these Academics who have left us so many uncertain opinions, and then to see if human understanding can remain firm without the ministration of the senses. The old and new schools of the Academics had great asserters of their opinions. Lucullus belonged to the old school; Cicero belonged to the new ... he was thus among the number of the Sceptics – the sect of Ariston, Pyrrho, and Herillus – who were right in many ways to maintain that nothing is certain but uncertainty ... . The Sceptics also held that the uncertainty of our judgement derives from the imperfection of our senses. But they went too far, subsuming all things beneath the generalization of incertitude, and saying that all the senses are deceptive – even to the extent that ideas that come to us through their channels are equally dubious and false. For the Sceptics, nothing that could be understood was certain. But here is what is notoriously false in their proposition: since they know that nothing can be known, as a consequence something *can* be known, for to affirm that one cannot affirm anything is a kind of affirmation. Moreover, even though our senses are for the most part deceptive, and many things uncertain because incapable of being represented to us except through the false mirror of the senses' imperfection, is it therefore necessary to claim that *all* things are uncertain? Consider that many things are conveyed to us not by means of the eyes, ears, or any exterior sense. Consider that the most important mysteries – those of our health and of all that lies in faith and belief – would not cease to remain certain and confirmed within us, even if our exterior senses failed. Consider that the eyes of the understanding are clear precisely because they are *not* corporeal. The consequence of this is that the understanding, despite sense-corruption, is able to reason, to distinguish truth from falsity, and to contemplate. Hence from the corruption of the senses it does not follow that the soul is likewise corrupt. (394–6)

The first thing to note is that Lancre's commentary responds principally to scepticism as presented by Cicero. It is not clear that Lancre has read Sextus, but evident that the *Academica* and *Tusculan Disputations* figure among his sources; the latter lists the same three philosophers as leaders of schools that 'have disappeared without trace' (5.85). Lancre's subsequent remarks constitute a digest of common rebuttals of scepticism, focusing in particular on over-generalizations about ignorance and on the way sceptics contradict themselves by asserting that nothing can be known. The latter criticism ignores the careful qualifications that Sextus and Montaigne make as they discuss sceptical assertion. The former, however, marks an interesting departure in counter-scepticism inasmuch as it concedes the frailty of the senses while maintaining that the understanding can function accurately without them. I will not discuss the coherence or sustainability of Lancre's position, nor deal with its possible relation to Descartes' later confidence in rational processes, but only note that in its agreement with one of scepticism's major premises it shares important traits with many writings of the period that attempt to answer sceptical arguments not with derision but through negotiation, taking their challenges seriously while countering their more extreme consequences.

The most obvious indication of scepticism's ongoing significance to intellectual life in this period is the publication, in 1621, of Sextus' *Opera quae extant*. Prepared by Jacob and Peter Chouet, this volume contained Greek texts of the *Outlines* and *Against the Mathematicians* as well as the Latin translations by Estienne and Hervet. A sense of the book's impact in Britain may be suggested by the fact that no later than 1624 the Bodleian had acquired a copy; eventually, no fewer than fifteen Oxford colleges did the same. But as I have stressed earlier, we cannot look solely at acquisitions of Sextus in gauging the emergent British interest in scepticism's revival. Lancre's *Inconstancy*, for instance, was acquired by the Bodleian in the year of its publication (1607); Charron's *Sagesse* surfaced there five years after its initial issue; a reprint of Loyer's *Spectres* was also added in 1607; and editions of Montaigne's *Essais*, Valencia's *Academica* and Chamber's *Treatise* were all held by 1605 or earlier. And this is just at the Bodleian, which had also acquired copies of the 1562 and 1569 Sextus editions, as well as Pico's *Examen* and Agrippa's *Vanitie*.[16] Elsewhere in England, John Lumley owned a copy of Sanches' *That Nothing Is Known* by 1609; Thomas Knyvett possessed the Estienne and Hervet editions of Sextus by 1618; and London's Middle Temple, sometime during the century, came to hold both a 1606 imprint of Charron's *Sagesse* and a copy of

Lennard's translation.[17] Ownership of books does not entail knowledge of their contents, but it normally suggests some degree of familiarity with their aims and purposes, and certainly we know that students like William Chillingworth, encountering Sextus at Oxford around 1618, was profoundly struck by what he read. But even non-academic readers had the potential for exposure to dilutions of sceptical thought. Richard Norwood offers the following commentary about a programme of reading he undertook in 1612: 'I [then] read Agrippa of the *Vanity of Sciences*, whereby whether I received more good or hurt I know not, for I began to understand the nature of learning and the bounds of arts, and that there was no such excellency in learning that a man should make it his *summum bonum*.'[18] Norwood's encounter with a vehement exposition of the vanity of learning was not, of course, an encounter with rigorous epistemological scepticism. But it certainly exposed him to serious doubt about the validity of knowledge – or 'seeming knowledge', as Lafeu puts it in *All's Well*. And Norwood's experience cannot have been unique.

## Cambridge connections

We have seen that during the later sixteenth century Cambridge scholars such as Andrew Perne, Richard Thomson, Andrew Willet and Abraham Fraunce were acquainted with sceptical debates and sometimes owned copies of Sextus. We have seen too that Cambridge-educated writers like Marlowe, Nashe and Spenser drew variously on the works of Sextus. It thus comes as no surprise that this trend grew increasingly strong as the new century unfolded. In 1603 Samuel Harsnett (BA, Pembroke Hall, 1584) published his *Declaration of Egregious Popish Impostures*, a work that Shakespeare discovered soon after its appearance, drawing on it for devils' names in *King Lear*. Arguing that exorcism is merely a scripted performance, Harsnett poses many '*Quaeres*' which he answers with varying degrees of sarcasm:

> If the Sceptick will demaund whence the Pope and his consistory doe borrow that divine power to consecrate water, candle, potions, etc., and to put into them such a scorching flame as shal turne them into scorpions to sting the devil and fire him out, as men smoke a Foxe out of his burrow: ... This is a saucie question and deserves to be aunswered with scorne. But because wee wil give reason of all that proceeds from that sacred head, wel may his *holines* and his Chapter doe as much as *S. Peter* did.

As Richard Strier notes, a careful reading of the *Declaration* makes it abundantly clear that the 'Sceptick' is 'a positive figure for Harsnett'.[19]

Another Cambridge graduate, Joseph Hall, published his satirical *Virgidemiae* in 1598, alluding several times to Arcesilaus, founder of the Middle Academy and chief architect of Academic scepticism. Hall was acutely conscious of the fallibility of sense-perception and reason, an attitude consonant with his early Calvinist sympathies but at odds with aspects of his Christian Stoicism: just as our senses 'are deceived by distances to think the stars beamy and sparkling ... so doth our understanding err in divine things: it thinks it knows God when it is but an idol of fancy'. Not that Hall is a sceptic, of course; his Theophrastan character 'Of the Distrustfull' (1608) lays to rest any suspicion of his adherence to strictly conceived Pyrrhonism. The 'distrustfull man' finds nothing certain 'but what he sees'; in spiritual matters, 'God must leave a pawne with him, or seeke some other Creditor'. Suspecting everything and everybody, he 'is a Scepticke, and dare hardly give credit to his senses, which he hath often arraigned of false intelligence'.[20] For the moderate Hall, scepticism can clearly be carried too far.

This impression is reinforced by Hall's dystopian satire *Mundus alter et idem*, translated by John Healey as *The Discovery of a New World* (*c.* 1609). In this work, Hall's Cambridge-educated narrator Mercurius describes a voyage to 'Terre Australis', a world turned upside-down where vices are virtues and where good sense and moderation are supplanted by zeal. Indebted to Lucian as well as to Erasmus and More, Hall alternates in this work between mockery of worldly pretensions and serious attacks on targets such as the Roman Church and the Spanish Inquisition. Among the comic episodes is Mercurius' sojourn at the 'Academy of Dudosa'. Here he finds two colleges, one of doubters (*Scepticorum*) and one of innovators (*Novatorum*). Describing the former as '*Skeptikes*, who deny that there is any trust to bee given to the sence', Mercurius adds that 'they are such absolute suspenders, that they dare not for their eares decree any thing positively, no not this, that they ought to hold al things in suspence' (87). Unlike some of his contemporaries, Hall demonstrates a relatively accurate understanding of Pyrrhonism, stressing the 'absolute' nature of its judgemental suspension even to the extent of noting its reluctance to affirm the desirability of suspension itself. But in the interests of rendering radical doubt absurd, Hall also alleges that sceptics 'deny' we can trust the senses, a claim that contradicts the principle of *epochē*. Healey, meanwhile, feels obliged to add a marginal note to his rendition, defining

'Skeptikes' as 'exact inquirers of all things' and citing Gellius' *Attic Nights* as his source (87). It is perhaps significant that Hall, in the Latin *Mundus*, exhibits no equivalent pressure for explanation. But Healey quickly adopts the new vocabulary: in the second imprint of *Discovery*, he chastises 'divers inquisitive Sceptiques' who have unjustly censured Hall in hostile 'misconstructions' of the satire, failing to respect the virtues of 'that Reverend man' (145).

Despite his criticism, then, it is evident that Hall understands Pyrrhonism. The same may be said of Hall's younger contemporary, the biblical scholar Joseph Mede. Matriculating at Christ's College in 1602, Mede underwent a sceptical *crise* soon after his arrival. In the words of his editor John Worthington, Mede found that, upon commencing serious philosophical study,

> he was for some time disquieted with Scepticisme, that troublesome disease of the Pyrrhonian School of old. For lighting upon a Book in a neighbor-Scholar's Chamber (whether it were Sextus Empiricus, or some other upon the same Subject, is not now remembered), he began upon perusal of it to move strange Questions to himself, and even to doubt whether the whole Frame of things, as it appears to us, were any more then a mere Phantasm.

For Worthington, and perhaps for Mede, Pyrrhonism is dangerous in part because it can lure and entrap the youthful. It can even lead to external world scepticism, an extreme form of doubt not normally associated with Sextus and usually thought to have been first expressed by Descartes.[21]

What we do not know, however, is the degree to which the very entertainment of radical doubt may have pushed Mede in the trajectory he subsequently followed as a religious scholar and devout Christian. Certainly, we know that in his later years as a tutor at Christ's, where his pupils included John Milton and Henry More, he required students to report in detail on their endeavours: 'The first question which he us'd to propound to every one was, *Quid dubitas?* What Doubts have you met in your studies to day? For he supposed that to doubt nothing and to understand nothing were verifiable alike.' Mede thus tolerated no scholars who were not – at least at first – doubtful. But doubts existed to be resolved. Thus when Popkin writes that Mede's case 'shows how Pyrrhonism was triumphing over accepted views at the outset of the seventeenth century', we see a touch of exaggeration, though I agree that Mede is far from alone in his exposure to epistemological scepticism.[22] Mede's experience represents one more instance of English accommodation to Pyrrhonism: a concession of its intellectual vitality united with confidence that its queries may none the less be resolved.

Other writers with Cambridge connections include Christopher Heydon (BA, Peterhouse, 1579) and Fulke Greville, whose *Treatie of Humane Learning* (c. 1605) I discuss below in relation to Bacon's *Advancement of Learning*. But there are more: Thomas Tomkis, for instance, who earned his BA at Trinity and subsequently became a fellow. Tomkis's comedy *Lingua* (1607) demonstrates keen interest in early modern understandings of sense-perception, at one point presenting the characters Visus and Auditus debating the relative virtues of vision and hearing. The result is that Common Sense, their judge, declares: 'I am almost a Scepticke in this matter, scarce knowing which way the ballance of the cause will decline' (H3v). Or Godfrey Goodman, Tomkis's younger contemporary at Trinity, who had studied under William Camden at Westminster School and later published *The Fall of Man* (1616), a book stressing the progressive decay of the world and the consequent need for humans to contemplate an unchanging God. Or the physician Helkiah Crooke, educated at St John's in the mid-1590s, whose *Mikrokosmographia* (1615) claims that even 'the most irresolute Scepticke cannot but acknowledge' that the chest and belly are 'principall Organs', as Aristotle had maintained centuries earlier.[23]

One of the most telling indications of the interest in scepticism at Cambridge is the appearance, around 1605, of an act verse praising Pyrrhonian *epochē*. Act verses were briefly argued theses composed in Latin and printed for candidates planning to participate in academic disputations as part of their progress towards degrees. The *Short-Title Catalogue* lists over 200 such verses surviving from Cambridge in the years 1580–1640. One of them, *Scepticorum Epochē, est retinenda* (STC, 4474.109), may be rendered in prose as follows:

*On the Epochē, or Holding-Back, of the Sceptics*
A gullible old man believes in earnest whatever his guest (his pimp or host, his son or whore) makes up. At three words he flies into a rage; enraged, three words calm him down. The mind is like that man. Deceitful perception fawns on it, tricking it by taste, by smell, by hearing, sight, and touch, entangling it within the uncertain appearances of things.

What would you know? And from what source know it? From its causes? But the disagreement is vexing over what kind of and how many origins should be attributed to things. From perception? But the air and sea declare this a fraud: the sun smaller than a bushel of corn, the oar 'bent' beneath the ocean's surface. And still we hesitate to doubt doubt itself?

But innate intelligence, you will say, is a lofty thing. I say it is too, but not for you alone. One error cajoles this man, another that, a third cajoles me.

In the midst of these questions, while your mind is tossed on the billows of error, I have a safe haven, since 'I don't know' settles each and all. Hence the Stagirite's complaint faulting reason's scale that tips now this way, now that, and faulting the depths of a mind for which the very same reason will overturn tomorrow what it successfully argued yesterday.

To me, therefore, the sceptic is wiser than other men. In the midst of such great doubts let him cry out everywhere, *Epochē!*[24]

We do not know who composed this verse, but it could have been a scholar such as Mede, or perhaps Tomkis or Andrew Willet, each of whom was in residence at Cambridge during the first decade of the seventeenth century. In any case, the piece demonstrates literary as well as philosophical sensibilities. Drawing on the stock-character tradition of Roman comedy, the poem amusingly likens the human proneness to sense-deception to the volatile credulity of an old man. It then touches on common sceptical arguments regarding causal knowledge, perception, and rational frailty (*PH*, 1.180–6). Finally, it broaches the Pyrrhonian *epochē* and offers 'I don't know' as humanity's wisest solution to the onslaught of doubt. Like La Mothe Le Vayer's later paean – 'O precious *Epochē*! O sure and agreeable mental retreat!' – the praise may strike modern ears as excessive.[25] To seventeenth-century readers, however, it would have been a familiar refrain. And while its presence in this verse is, by definition, provisional rather than doctrinaire, there is no question that by this date in England the arguments of scepticism were regarded as basic components of intellectual debate.

## Bacon: part two

If 1605 was indeed the year in which *Scepticorum Epochē* was published, it also marked the appearance of one of the monuments of early modern scientific thought: Bacon's *Of the Proficience and Advancement of Learning*. Later vastly expanded, this study of contemporary knowledge and enquiry is central to any account of seventeenth-century intellectual history. Along with the prefatory materials to the unfinished *Instauratio Magna*, the aphorisms of *The New Organon* (1620), and various shorter works including *Cogitata et visa* (1607), *Redargutio philosophiarum* (1608), the *Ladder of the Intellect* (1620–6) and the essay 'Of Truth' (1625), it aids us immensely in tracing Bacon's complex and evolving encounter with the scepticism of antiquity.

That Bacon feels obliged to position himself *vis-à-vis* scepticism is clear. And while historians of philosophy have paid scant attention to this aspect of his work, Bacon's responses to the sceptical challenge are crucially significant both as evidence of scepticism's dissemination in Britain and as indications of a principal means of opposing it that emerges in Europe after the heyday of Montaigne and Charron.[26] Indeed, Bacon's familiarity with Montaigne is indisputable: his writings indicate clear knowledge of some chapters and probable acquaintance with others. He also appears to have drawn on Charron in the *Advancement*, and his allusion to 'discoursing wits' may target Francisco Sanches.[27] But while references to Cicero's *Academica*, Laertius' *Life of Pyrrho* and Agrippa's *Vanitie* are scarce – and references to Sextus nonexistent, apart from a possible allusion to Heraclitus – this in itself can be taken as evidence that by the time Bacon was fully engaged in philosophical writing, from about 1603 forward, the arguments and commonplaces of scepticism required no introduction.[28]

Consideration of doubt is never far from the centre of Bacon's attention. In the *Advancement* he explains that attending to doubt serves two 'excellent' functions:

> the one, that it saveth philosophy from errors and falsehoods; when that which is not fully appearing is not collected into assertion, whereby error might draw error, but reserved in doubt: the other, that the entry of doubts are as so many suckers or spunges as to draw use of knowledge; insomuch as that which, if doubts had not preceded, a man should never have advised but passed over without note, by the suggestion and solicitation of doubts is made to be attended. (203)

Doubt can also be excessive, and Bacon cautions against over-cultivating it; in the *Organon* he even construes the cherishing of doubt as a sceptical dogma (*WFB*, 4:68–75). But a constant theme for Bacon is that 'impatience of doubt' is an error, as is 'haste to assertion' without 'mature suspension of judgement'. Doubt is thus foundational: 'if a man will begin with certainties, he shall end in doubts; but if he will be content to begin with doubts, he shall end in certainties' (*Advancement*, 147). All this amounts to agreement with the sceptical critique of precipitous judgement as well as to partial endorsement of Pyrrhonian *epochē*. I stress that the endorsement is partial, since Bacon believes that most doubts admit of ultimate resolution. But given a choice between Peripatetic pronouncement and sceptical indecision, Bacon favours the latter. As he writes in *The Wisdom of the Ancients* (1609), Empedocles and Democritus, though they complain that 'truth is drowned in deep wells', are none the less 'more to be approved than the school of Aristotle so dogmatical' (*WFB*, 6:749). Similarly, while Bacon discourages the excessive cultivation of oppositions, he advocates a limited balancing of opinions: it 'turn[s] back the first offers and conceits of the mind' (*Advancement*, 164). Several of the basic sceptical attitudes, in short, are entirely congenial to Bacon.

As for consideration of sense-data and the operations of the intellect, here too Bacon exhibits interesting affinities with the traditions of scepticism, as well as important departures. And his relations to Descartes in this regard are intriguing. Like sceptics ancient and modern, Bacon often acknowledges the problems of perception; discussing the 'Idols of the Tribe', he notes the characteristic 'incompetency and deceptions of the senses' (*WFB*, 4:58). Still, such frailties may be overcome. As he states in the *Advancement* when introducing the scepticism of the New Academy, 'here was their chief error: they charged the deceit upon the Senses; which in my judgement are very sufficient to certify and report truth, though not always immediately, yet by comparison, by help of instruments, and other like assistance' (222). Sense-perception in itself may be highly unreliable, but when conjoined with certain 'helps' it can no longer be despised. Indeed, as Bacon stresses in the *Instauratio*, the intellect 'is far more prone to error than the sense' (*WFB*, 4:27, 4:111–12). And here, in privileging perception over ratiocination, Bacon differs significantly from Descartes, his younger contemporary and fellow opponent of scepticism.

In keeping with mainstream Christian doctrine, Bacon dwells frequently on the 'frailty of man' subsequent to the Fall. Readily allowing that humans are 'full of savage and unreclaimed desires', he goes on to introduce the mental fallacies he later terms 'idols', arguing that it is impossible to divorce ourselves from them because 'they are inseparable from our nature' (*Advancement*, 150–4, 227–8). The human mind is an 'enchanted glass', a 'false mirror' that 'distorts the natures of things by mingling its own' with them (*WFB*, 4:54). But just as the senses may be improved by 'helps', the intellect may to some extent be delivered from its weaknesses and 'reduced' to its proper condition (*Advancement*, 227). The most interesting way to effect this deliverance lies in Bacon's theory of scientific induction.[29] He makes no claim that a correct inductive method will eliminate the 'Idols of the Tribe', but he argues repeatedly that such a method will prevent conclusions from being 'overhastily abstracted from facts' (*WFB*, 4:24). He also demands that the enumerative induction of Aristotle be replaced by an eliminative induction which actively seeks contradictory instances (*Advancement*, 221; *WFB*, 4:24–6). Only then can we avoid the mistake of flying 'to the most general conclusions' (*WFB*, 4:111). An eschewing of precipitous judgement is thus foregrounded again, this time within the more specific context of logic and inductive method.

Inseparable from Bacon's treatment of induction is his emphasis on patient enquiry. Of the two ways of 'discovering truth', the correct approach 'derives axioms from the senses and particulars, rising by a gradual and unbroken ascent, so that it arrives at the most general axioms last'. Such a process demands restraint, scrupulous care and unstinting commitment to an ideal of ongoing investigation. 'Inquiry of truth', after all, is a 'sovereign good of human nature' (*WFB*, 4:50, 6:378). And Bacon is at pains to stress that the 'inquisition of nature' has too often been construed as forbidden. Dogmatic philosophers in particular have been 'effective in quenching inquiry' in direct proportion to the degree to which they have been 'successful in inducing belief'. One of Bacon's professed aims in the *Instauratio* is to redress this tendency by presenting 'examples of inquiry and invention' according to his method – examples intended to spur the investigative spirit of like-minded searchers (*WFB*, 4:20, 4:39). Bacon also praises the efforts of such pre-Socratic philosophers as Heraclitus, Anaxagoras, Empedocles and Democritus. Characterizing them as men who 'devoted themselves to the search for truth', he finds that they provide superior models for scientific investigation than their more famous successors – Aristotle, Zeno, Epicurus – who founded schools and promoted fixed systems of belief.[30] In short, Bacon places considerable stress on the *zetetic* mode of scepticism: that dimension of the sceptical outlook subordinating *acatalepsia* to unceasing enquiry, and crucially important to Montaigne and Charron (*PH*, 1.7; *Academica*, 2.127–8; *Contra Academicos*, 1.5–11). The stress, moreover, grows stronger towards Bacon's later years; it is more evident in the *Instauratio* and *Organon* than in the *Advancement*. And while it seems likely that Bacon customarily associated scepticism with intellectual lassitude rather than with vigorous questioning, it remains the case that an important paradigm of scepticism's early modern reception involved greater emphasis on continuing investigation than on despair of knowledge.

How well, then, did Bacon know the ancient and early modern sceptical traditions? And how well positioned was he to be conversant with conventional distinctions between scepticism's Pyrrhonian and Academic strains? We have seen that Bacon read Montaigne and was probably familiar with Charron. Nor is there any question that he studied Laertius and knew the *Life of Pyrrho*. Quotations from Cicero's *Academica* imply his awareness of its contents, an implication reinforced by the repeated treatment of *acatalepsia* at this stage in his intellectual development (*Advancement*, 222). Other works by Cicero, particularly *On the Nature of the Gods* and the *Tusculan Disputations*, also likely contributed to Bacon's understanding of scepticism's history; Cicero's remark in the *Disputations* about the sects of Pyrrho, Aristo and Herillus having 'disappeared without trace' (5.85) may be echoed in *De Dignitate* when Bacon alludes to 'that exploded school of Pyrrho and Herillus' (*WFB*, 5:9). As for Sextus, while scholars have plausibly proposed the *Outlines* and *Against the Mathematicians* as sources for passages in the *Advancement*, evidence for direct acquaintance seems weaker than in the cases of Laertius and Cicero.[31] Indeed, had Bacon read Sextus carefully, it would have been difficult for him to conflate the Pyrrhonians and Academics as readily as he does.

What is particularly odd is that Bacon knows a difference exists. Or he does by the time he writes the *Organon*: aphorism 67 of Book One contrasts the New Academy with the sect of Pyrrho, claiming that the former offers a 'fairer seeming way'. Its adherents argue that their position does not 'destroy all investigation, like Pyrrho and his Refrainers', but allows 'some things to be followed as probable', though none to be maintained as true (*WFB*, 4:69). Yet elsewhere Bacon merges the groups that Sextus so carefully distinguishes. In *Valerius Terminus*, he refers collectively to 'the second school of Academics and the sect of Pyrrho' as 'considerers that denied comprehension'. He adds in the *Instauratio* that no one need be alarmed at the provisional 'suspension of judgement' he advocates, since it is practised not by one who maintains that 'nothing can be known' but by one who believes that knowledge must be obtained 'in a certain course and way'. We should therefore beware premature assertion, for even those philosophers who maintained the impossibility of knowing anything 'were not inferior to those which took upon them to pronounce' (*WFB*, 3:244, 4:32).[32]

The heart of the problem, I believe, lies in Bacon's understanding of *acatalepsia*. He defines the term as the 'denial of the capacity of the mind to comprehend truth' (*WFB*, 4:111), and, following Cicero, associates it with the later Platonic Academy, which 'made a cult of the incomprehensibility of nature and condemned mankind to eternal darkness' (*Refutation*, 127). As we have seen, however, Bacon also hopes to rescue Academics from the charge that they destroy all investigation; this applies, in his view, only to more radical sceptics – the Pyrrhonists. And given one understanding of *acatalepsia*, this makes perfect sense, for a denial of the mind's capacity to comprehend truth is not a denial of its capacity to know anything; a science of appearances and probabilities might remain possible. This, after all, is the gist of the *Advancement*'s discussion of *acatalepsia*:

> it was not without cause that so many excellent philosophers became Sceptics and Academics, and denied any certainty of knowledge or comprehension, and held opinion that the knowledge of man extended only to appearances and probabilities ... in the latter Academy, which Cicero embraced, this opinion also of *acatalepsia* (I doubt) was not held sincerely ... . But assuredly many scattered in both Academies did hold it in subtilty and integrity. (222)

Here *acatalepsia* is presented with relative sympathy; criticism is levelled only against those Academics who espoused the doctrine insincerely. But Bacon's discussions elsewhere transform *acatalepsia* into something more extreme: an assertion 'that absolutely nothing can be known', a denial 'that certainty [can] be attained' (*WFB*, 4:39, 4:53). Bacon thus departs from the sharper classical senses of the term – Cicero understands it as an inability to grasp, Sextus as the 'inapprehensibility' of truth – and he appears to do this in the interests of condemning a full-scale despair of knowledge.[33] He thereby casts his own optimism in a brighter light. But he also caricatures the outlook of the Pyrrhonists, who, if Sextus may be taken at his word, hold no dogmas at all – including the dogma that nothing can be known. Instead, they suspend judgement on this and all other questions (*PH*, 1.1–4, 1.226–8). If the crucial distinction lies, in Kantian terms, between phenomenal and noumenal knowledge, then Bacon oscillates between the two, and it is mildly ironic that someone so conscious of linguistic problems should be the victim of an 'Idol of the Marketplace'.

Bacon's customary opinion of sceptics then, especially in his later works, is that they dogmatically assert that nothing can be known. They condemn humanity to darkness through this capitulation, and their despair of finding truth accordingly prevents them from pursuing any course of 'severe inquisition'. The capitulation itself is presented as a dogma, as are the sceptics' recommendations that we question the reliability of sense-data and suspend judgement on doubtful matters. So Bacon hoists the sceptics with their own petard; they represent the converse of the dogmatists they condemn, extending epistemological 'intemperance' in the opposite direction as they manifest an excessive tendency to withhold assent (*WFB*, 4:68–9). Bacon prefers an intermediate position, 'between the presumption of pronouncing on everything, and the despair of comprehending anything', and he alludes to the pre-Socratics in this regard (*WFB*, 4:39). But precisely here his depiction of the sceptics begins to lose focus, since elsewhere he links them closely with such pre-Socratics as Empedocles and Democritus. More generally, however, Bacon's condemnation of scepticism rests on the twin supports of mischaracterization and conflicting emphasis. I have already discussed the latter in treating Bacon's inconsistent account of *acatalepsia*. As for the former, Bacon not only states that *acatalepsia* is affirmed by sceptics as a dogma, but he ignores the *zetetic* dimension of Pyrrhonism and he misleadingly depicts sceptical suspension of judgement as necessarily permanent. 'Ignores' may, of course, be the wrong word if, as I suspect, Bacon did not study Sextus' *Outlines*. Had he done so, he would have been less inclined to harden Pyrrhonian tendencies into fixed doctrines. On the other hand, while Sextus never rules out the possibility that truth may be found, his emphasis in the *Outlines* lies more on refraining than on actively searching. What is crucial is that the two not be seen as mutually exclusive, for to the extent that Sextus is willing to present Pyrrhonists as both *zetetic* (investigative) and *ephectic* (suspensive), to the same extent he is unwilling to rule out either tendency.

Probably, then, Bacon did not read Sextus. Evidence points more clearly towards Cicero, Laertius, and Montaigne as his sources for ancient scepticism. But these, like all sources, are problematic inasmuch as they colour their information with their own points of view. And Bacon is no different. At one level he grows increasingly hostile towards scepticism as his philosophical outlook matures: *De Dignitate* defends sense-perception against sceptical attack more vigorously than does the *Advancement* (222, 247; *WFB*, 4:412, 5:9); the *Ladder of the Intellect* radically misrepresents sceptics in depicting them as 'asserting the absolute ... incompetency of the human intellect'.[34] At the same time Bacon cannot forget his indebtedness to sceptical habits of doubt. Elsewhere in the *Ladder*, for instance, he writes that it would be 'difficult to find fault with those who affirm that "nothing is known" had they tempered the rigour of their decision by a softening explanation'. He denounces scepticism as 'preposterous', yet adds that 'if there be any fellowship between the ancients and ourselves, it is principally as connected with this species of philosophy', for scepticism stresses 'the varying nature of the senses, the weakness of human judgment, and the propriety of withholding assent'. Indeed, Bacon is 'not at all ashamed' of this fellowship, for if we add to the 'aggregate' those who, like various pre-Socratics, exhibit sceptical tendencies, the resulting group comprises the 'most profound of the ancient thinkers, with whom no modern need blush to be associated' (519).[35]

Hence the 'mature suspension of judgement' that Bacon praises from first to last is indelibly associated with ancient scepticism. And while he goes on to transform judgemental suspension into an instrument for the discovery of truth, such characteristic Baconian maxims as 'the sinews of wisdom are slowness of belief and distrust' betray a sense in which their author acknowledges that his path and that of the sceptics have for a time been virtually identical (*Advancement*, 273). Bacon also notes that the reasons people become sceptics are 'not to be despised' (*WFB*, 4:39); he admires their seriousness, their consciousness of the obstacles to knowing, their frustration with received authority and overconfident assertion. It is thus inaccurate to claim that Bacon 'never took the skeptical challenge to knowledge seriously'.[36] I think, rather, that Bacon was continually aware of the challenge, but aware of it in diluted form, perhaps through ignorance of Sextus, perhaps through wilful misconstruction. Those aspects he respected he emphasized, and those he scorned he evaded through exaggeration and misrepresentation. Bacon failed to respond fully to scepticism, not because he dismissed it but because he allowed himself to understand it as less potent a force than it seemed to many contemporaries.

It is therefore curious that Marin Mersenne, an architect of the mitigated scepticism that emerged in France during the 1620s, saw Bacon as imitating the Pyrrhonists in his protests against Aristotelianism and other systems of thought. And while Popkin overstates matters in suggesting that Bacon employs 'stock arguments from the sceptical tradition' in attacking scholasticism, it is true that Bacon encourages the adoption of 'a temporary scepticism until all the procedures of the *Organon* can be successfully employed'. Capitalizing on the instrumentality of doubt and judgemental suspension is one of the basic elements in Bacon's programme; he repeatedly demonstrates that he understands this move as having its genesis, though not its fulfilment, in the scepticism of antiquity. But in the twin suggestions that sceptical suspension is necessarily permanent and that the negative dogma of *acatalepsia* is maintained by Academics and Pyrrhonists alike, Bacon simplifies the sceptical tradition and highlights his own departures from it. Moreover, even if Bacon does not know Sextus, ample evidence exists that readers in early seventeenth-century Britain could be exposed – in their own language – to the Pyrrhonian outlook: 'The Sceptick doth neither affirm nor deny any position, but doubteth of it, and opposeth his reasons against that which is affirmed or denied to justify his not consenting.'[37] There is no assertion here of the inapprehensibility of truth, but rather a statement of method and customary habit. By conflating the Academic and Pyrrhonian traditions and presenting scepticism as a defeatest theory of knowledge, Bacon fails to do justice to sceptical epistemology. And it is a failure all the more striking given Bacon's dependence on the very habits of deliberate questioning and patient exploration that were always part of the sceptical outlook and that became ever more central in its post-Montaignian manifestations.

## Collateral indications

Bacon's optimism attracted many admirers in later seventeenth-century Britain, but when the *Advancement* was published, there were still strong currents of thought, some inflected by scepticism, that prevented a significant portion of Bacon's readership from embracing his confidence. One such reader was the courtier-poet Fulke Greville. Author of the closet drama *Mustapha*, with its famous Chorus Sacerdotum (once described as 'the most penetrating attack on the Christian concept of the good God before *Lear* and the plays of Webster'), Greville seems to have read Bacon's *Advancement* in manuscript, since his philosophical poem *A Treatie of Humane Learning* (*c.* 1605) shows acquaintance with the work. He alludes to the 'vaine Idols of humanity'; he stresses that desire and affection profoundly influence human understanding; and he argues that '*Sciences* from *Nature* should be drawne, / As *Arts* from *practise*, never out of Bookes'.[38] But whereas Bacon cites human frailties to show how they can be overcome with method and technological innovation, Greville finds them fundamentally insuperable, stressing instead their contribution to the 'declination' of the world. Guided by constant reference to Original Sin and humanity's 'naturall Defects', he prizes obedience, humility and the avoidance of vain learning and curiosity. And because he stresses the weaknesses of perception and reason, it is little surprise that several critics have traced his ideas to Pyrrho and Sextus.[39]

This genealogy may be accurate. But such a claim as 'men know no truth at all' suggests a scepticism more general and more pessimistic than that likely generated by familiarity with Sextus. Greville's sceptical outlook is unique: resolutely bleak, even for a Calvinist; more deductive than inductive, given its impetus from meditation on the Fall; yet mildly Baconian in its practicality. Paul Kocher has claimed that Greville's *Treatie* offers a 'skepticism Christianized, but Christianized in a way that neither Catholicism nor Protestantism approved, since both theologies assigned no such drastic consequences to Original Sin'; no other poem from the period 'was based on a skepticism so profound, consistent, and thoroughly reasoned'.[40] I would add only that Greville's intense pessimism, while not itself sceptical in any strict sense, depends on a kind of mental saturation in the constituent elements of classical and early modern scepticism. I think too that this saturation required collective as well as individual mediation; Greville's perspective, however unique, was not achieved in isolation. And such an achievement, in all likelihood, became possible in Britain only a decade or two before Greville completed his poem.

John Davies of Hereford was another poet familiar with commonplaces of ancient scepticism, though his attitudes were more moderate than those of Greville. Like Bartas, and with information probably derived from Gesner's *Bibliotheca*, he offers a distorted snapshot of Pyrrhonism in *Mirum in Modum* (1602). And the following year, in the verse treatise *Microcosmos*, he relies explicitly on Agrippa's *Vanitie* for his opening gambit. Ever since the Fall, he writes:

> the state of things is so unstay'd
> That *humane wisedome* stands it wotts not howe;
> Unsure in all; for *Judgment's* oft betrai'd
> In that which *proofe* before had well assai'd.

Glossing the word 'proofe', Davies quotes the 1569 translation of Agrippa: 'knowledge hath its beginning of the senses, which are often deceiv'd. Therefore all sciences which are ... rooted in the senses are uncertaine.'[41] Like Greville, though with less intensity, Davies locates the genesis of scepticism in the consequences of the Fall. Prior to that disastrous moment, 'proofe' had been successfully 'assai'd' by humans.

Because Davies was the tutor of Elizabeth Cary, future author of *The Tragedy of Mariam,* and because Cary herself read Montaigne and Bacon, one wonders whether Davies' mild scepticism impinged on Cary's consciousness and, if so, whether it emerged in contrast to the more inductive and thoroughgoing scepticism of Montaigne. This is a question we cannot answer, but at the very least we can say that Cary, and others like her, not only had the potential for exposure to scepticism, but in many instances must have encountered it directly, in both reading and conversation. Cary's fellow playwright George Chapman was undoubtedly familiar with the movement. In *Bussy D'Ambois* (1604) he describes a duel between his hero and the king's courtiers:

> you could see no fear of death, for life;
> Nor love of life, for death: but in their brows
> Pyrrho's Opinion in great letters shone,
> That life and death in all respects are one.
> (2.1.49–52)

Probably derived from Montaigne, this allusion shows, if nothing else, how easily the ideas of scepticism and Stoicism can intermingle in the mind of an imaginative reader.[42] But more accurate appropriations of ancient scepticism also abound in the period. I have mentioned John Chamber's reliance on Sextus in his *Treatise* against astrology, a reliance for which he is furiously rebuked by Christopher Heydon. But in his unpublished *Confutation of Astrologicall Daemonologie* (1603–4), a lengthy rejoinder to Heydon, Chamber continues to cite Sextus among his authorities. In one intriguing passage he unites Hellenistic and early Christian perspectives in lampooning Heydon's enthusiasm for divination:

> Whereas Basill reckneth diverse impedimentes of the true knowledge of the birthe time in which he agreeth with that learned philosopher Sixtus Empericus, to those two profound philosophers [Heydon] opposeth the wisdome of his watche, as yf the waye by the watche were not as deceatfull as anye, beinge altogether subiect to the chaunge of weather, the spring, etc. (159r; cp. 226v)

Basil of Caesarea might have been astounded to see his name linked with that of Sextus, but in their common doubts about the predictive value of astrology, Chamber found them powerful allies. Heydon, for his part, is best known today for his appearance as a figure of ludicrous learning in Jonson's epigram 'On the Famous Voyage'.

If 1604 saw the completion of Chamber's *Confutation* and the production of Chapman's *Bussy*, it was also an important year in London publishing. The third English edition of Mornay's *Woorke* appeared, as did the expanded version of Wright's *Passions of the Mind*. Still more interesting was a slim quarto entitled *The Tragicall History of D. Faustus*. I have discussed Mornay already, and I will treat Marlowe's tragedy in due course, but here I would like to comment briefly on Wright, whose study of the emotions is generally considered the most wide-ranging of the psychological treatises produced in England before Robert Burton's *Anatomy of Melancholy*.

Born in 1561, Wright hailed from York, where his family were staunch Roman Catholics. Educated at Douai, Rheims and Rome, Wright was ordained in 1586 and subsequently taught moral theology at Louvain and other universities. He returned to England in 1595, hoping to aid the Catholic cause, but his political naïveté proved a liability, and he spent much of his time under house arrest. He did, however, complete the *Passions* in 1597 and published it under his own name in 1601, its contents being deemed inoffensive with respect to religious matters. Indebted to Aquinas' discussion of the emotions in the *Summa Theologica*, but also conversant with Aristotle's *Ethics*, Cicero's *Tusculan Disputations*, Laertius' *Lives* and scores of other ancient and early modern works, Wright's book treats not only the essences and effects of the emotions, but the means of controlling and mobilizing them. It thus offers physiological, moral and rhetorical analysis, and in this respect moves beyond such earlier treatises as Primaudaye's *French Academie* and Timothy Bright's *Treatise of Melancholie*. Its popularity, moreover, is evidenced by its reissue in 1604, with further reprints in 1621 and 1630.

Wright never mentions Pyrrhonism, but textual indications suggest that sceptical doubt figured significantly among his concerns.[43] I have alluded to Wright's list of problems concerning the soul (303–9); he also deals at length with the question of whether and to what extent we can 'behold the secrets of the heart' by examining 'the windows of the face' (109). This is a matter of paramount interest to Jacobean dramatists, and Wright's response is instructive. By and large, he claims, we may 'attain unto the knowledge' of our fellow humans' passions, though 'not by philosophical demonstrations, but only by natural conjectures and probabilities' (165). More specifically,

> As the faces of those which look into waters shine unto them, so the hearts of men are manifest unto the wise; not that they can exactly understand the hearts, which be inscrutable and open only unto God, but that by conjectures they may aim well at them; for as he which beholdeth his face in the water doth not discern it

exactly but rather a shadow than a face, so he that by external physiognomy will divine what lieth hidden in the heart may rather conceive an image of that affection than a perfect knowledge. (109)

Wright's contention that we can have probable knowledge of human interiors may be assimilated to the epistemological orientation of Academic scepticism. Likewise, his discussion of the ways in which 'the imagination putteth green spectacles before the eyes of our wit' (128) strongly resembles Sextus' treatment of the sixth mode of Pyrrhonian doubt: the medium of transmission typically distorts that which is transmitted to the mind (*PH*, 1.124–8). Without being overtly sceptical, Wright's habitual attitudes to the understanding of emotions are none the less tempered by a healthy leavening of doubt.

That the hermeneutics of face-reading were important to Wright's readers is attested to by Ben Jonson's dedicatory sonnet for the 1604 edition. Historians have long conjectured that Wright converted Jonson to Catholicism in 1598, and literary scholars have argued that Wright's book influenced Jonson's understanding of dramatic character.[44] But even if these suppositions are untrue, it is clear that Jonson admires Wright's treatise: he praises its author for presenting 'Each subtlest Passion, with her source and spring', and he argues that if Wright's readers, after studying his descriptions,

> languish in suspense –
> To judge which Passion's false and which is true –
> Between the doubtful sway of Reason and sense,
> 'Tis not your fault if they shall sense prefer,
> Being told there Reason cannot, Sense may err.
> (86)

Jonson refers here to an early chapter of the *Passions* where Wright explains that emotions are more likely to ally themselves with corporeal than cerebral impulses (94–6). But it is intriguing that he adopts the vocabulary of scepticism – 'suspense', 'doubtful sway', judgement between false and true – in characterizing the reader who attempts self-analysis using Wright's account. And though Jonson, to the best of my knowledge, makes no explicit allusions to the sceptical tradition this early in his career, he later assigns the following speech to Ambler in his comedy *The Devil is an Ass* (1616): 'He hopes to make one o' these *Scipticks* o' me / (I thinke I name 'hem right) and do's not fly me' (5.2.40–1).

Another Catholic who shows acquaintance with the ancient sceptical inheritance is the priest Thomas Fitzherbert, whose *Treatise Concerning Policy and Religion* was published at Douai in 1606. Achieving considerable reputation among English Catholics of the period, Fitzherbert's book is much concerned to refute Luther and Calvin, condemning them as heretical sectarians. And though Fitzherbert is not discussed by Popkin, his fideistic argument – that awareness of human frailty is the best preparation for Christian evangelization – fits well with Popkin's analysis of the appropriation of scepticism by Catholic controversialists. Relying on Cicero's *Academica*, Fitzherbert makes his case:

> the wisest Philosophers did so well consider, that many of them affirmed that nothing in this world can certainly be knowne, by reason of the error in mans senses, imbecilitie of their wites, and the obscurity of truth; of which opinion were Socrates, Plato, Democritus, Anaxagoras, Empedocles, and all the new Academicks; in so much that Socrates was judged by the Oracle, to be the wisest man then living, because he was wont to say, *I know only this, that I know nothing*; whereto Arcesilaus added that not so much as that could be knowne. (*Treatise*, 6)

Frequent references to Augustine complement this argument, and the implication is that any rational defence of sectarian religious profession is suspect by definition. Interesting too is Fitzherbert's genealogy of Academic scepticism. Like Bacon, he follows Cicero in tracing its origins to the pre-Socratics, and in so doing he confers a form of historical legitimacy to the fundamentally anti-rational nature of his defence of the Roman Church.[45]

I have intimated from the outset of this book that certain literary-critical assessments of Elizabethan and Jacobean scepticism have tended towards exaggeration. My own argument, by contrast, has been not that epistemological scepticism emerged full-fledged during the 1580s and 1590s but that various sceptical paradigms developed by fits and starts as the period wore on. Still, by the end of the first decade of the seventeenth century, it is fair to say that we witness a 'growing Jacobean scepticism', even if Irving Ribner stretches the point by adding that 'the spirit of scepticism' was 'as much a part of the Renaissance as Christian humanism'.[46] I would say, rather, that scepticism increasingly tempered humanist optimism. And by the time *Lear*, *Mariam* and *The Revenger's Tragedy* are written we begin to detect a second generation of sceptical awareness in Britain: writers allude not only to ideas derived from the major sources but also to discussions of those ideas in contemporary debates. George Hakewill relies variously on Charron, Bodin and Primaudaye in his *Vanitie of the Eye* (1608), a book maintaining that vision is often deceptive – indeed a principal channel for imposture and disappointment. As Hakewill claims, '*Charron*, [following] the Stoicks and Academicks, hold[s] this sense rather to hinder then further true and sound knowledge'.[47] And Hakewill's older contemporary, Thomas Harriot, had certainly pondered elements of Pyrrhonism, for manuscript notes show him wrestling with foundational sceptical questions. Several ancient philosophers, he writes, 'denied all knowledge ... . And Aristarchus ... sayd he knew not as many as that; & Pyrho with [h]is followers ... called Scepticks ... will not affirme or deny any knowledge to be true or false but do still doubte, yet ... they make their knowledge certayne to doubt assuredly'.[48] In other words, Pyrrhonists assume at least one certainty, since they tacitly affirm that any knowledge claim may be doubted. Thus Harriot, like others at the time, attempts to catch the sceptics out on the grounds of philosophical inconsistency. Descartes will later do the same with his *cogito*.

Less rigorous than Harriot, but like Hakewill alert to contemporary epistemological conversation, are such writers as Ralegh, Richard Brathwaite and Robert Burton. Ralegh owned a manuscript of *The Sceptick* and may have been involved in translating it from Estienne's Latin edition of Sextus. He was associated with both Harriot and Henry Percy, ninth Earl of Northumberland, and his library also included Agrippa's *Vanitie*, Loyer's *Treatise* and Montaigne's *Essays*. In 1592 Robert Parsons accused him of sponsoring a 'school of atheism', and two years later he was interrogated for unorthodoxy, one of the questions being, 'Whom do you know, or have heard, that have argued or spoken against, or as doubting, the being of any God?'[49] Not surprisingly, scholars have claimed that the allegations against Ralegh prove little except that contemporary definitions of 'atheism' could be very broad. It is worth noting, however, that the above-quoted question suggests a distinction between doubting and denying that is crucial to understanding scepticism's early modern reception. And Ralegh continues to engage matters of doubt. His *History of the World* (1614) repeatedly challenges Aristotelian authority and stresses the ubiquity of conflicting accounts: '*For saith Charron in his Booke of wisdome*, every humane proposition hath equall authoritie, if reason make not the difference, *the rest being but the fables of principles'* (72). Christopher Hill may overstate matters in arguing that 'Ralegh's scepticism of the possibility of arriving at historical truth made him cling to Biblical certainties', but there seems no question that Ralegh was acutely conscious of the problems in achieving historical veracity through the examination of evidence whose truth-value was inherently subject to doubt.[50]

As for Brathwaite, the crucial point to stress is that his acquaintance with sceptical ideas, while genuine, is thoroughly derivative. In his *Essaies upon the Five Senses* (1620) he mentions 'Athenagoras of Argus, who never felt any paine, when stung by a Scorpion' (27); this is an allusion to a passage from Sextus (*PH*, 1.82), but Brathwaite probably discovers it either in *The Sceptick* or in Nashe's *Christ's Tears*.[51] Brathwaite also knows the word 'scepticke', using it in his *Strappado for the Divell* (1615), where it carries relatively positive connotations. If people 'were dispos'd as they should be',

> Then might our Satyre mixe his inke with gall,
> But with his mixture do no hurt at all.
> Then might our scepticke give his judgement free,
> Yet do small harme to mens integritie.
>
> (28)

A 'scepticke', for Brathwaite, is a free-speaking social critic – someone like Malevole in Marston's *Malcontent* – and there seems a tacit acknowledgement that a well-adjusted society will encourage such critics even as it takes their barbs in stride.

Passing his entire adult life at Oxford's Christ Church College, Robert Burton serves admirably as a concluding figure to this portion of my chapter because his reading was so vast and his range of borrowing so delightfully unpredictable. Like Montaigne, Burton found affinities between himself and the 'laughing philosopher' Democritus, and his general attitude in *The Anatomy of Melancholy* (1621) is 'one of excited and amused scepticism'.[52] Writing of judicial astrology, he alludes even-handedly to its opponents and defenders before advancing a lukewarm compromise: the stars 'doe incline, but not compell; no necessity at all: and so gently incline, that a wise man may resist them' (1:199). Even when Burton's opinions are firmer, they tend to be hedged with conflicting authority to such an extent that readers may feel cautioned against adopting them. Discussing atheism, he presents the sceptical case so fairly that his subsequent commendation of

Mornay, Grotius and other Christian apologists seems lost in after-thought:

> These Atheisticall spirits professe religion, but *timide & haesitanter*, tempted thereunto out of that horrible consideration of diversity of Religions, which are and have been in the world ... whence they inferre, that if there be so many religious sects and denied by the rest, why may they not be all false? or why should this or that be preferred before the rest? The Scepticks urge this and amongst others it is the conclusion of *Sextus Empericus lib. 8. advers. Mathematicos*, after many philosophicall arguments and reasons *pro* and *con* that there are Gods, and againe that there are no Gods, he so concludes, *cum tot inter se pugnent, &c. Una tantum potest esse vera*, as *Tully* likewise disputes. (3:399)

As we have seen, in 1601 the Bodleian had acquired Hervet's 1569 translation of Sextus, and it was in this volume that Burton encountered the above-mentioned arguments regarding the existence of gods.[53] But Burton was too eclectic to rely overmuch on any source: Agrippa and Vives, Montaigne and Charron are all given voice, but so are Petronius, Chaucer and Rabelais, not to mention Hall (*Mundus*) and Wright (*Passions*). The proliferation of opinion so often cited by Sextus as grounds for judgemental suspension serves as a structuring principle in Burton's book. But the irony is that the same book presents the views of Sextus as just one further set of opinions.

## Donne at last

An exact contemporary of Burton's, John Donne is his opposite in almost every other respect. Passionate and acute rather than mild and expansive, Donne's writings evoke an inward realm of intensely meditated experience. But like Burton, Donne was deeply read, and like Bacon his encounters with classical scepticism spanned the Elizabethan and Jacobean years. Indeed, by the early 1590s Donne was already familiar with the conventional distinction between 'Sceptique', 'Academique' and 'Dogmatique' – a fact that makes Bacon's failure to mention this distinction seem all the more strange. And in a sermon delivered thirty years later, Donne again notes the crucial differences.[54] The conflation of Academic and Pyrrhonian scepticism so common in this period was not a temptation for Donne: he knew how Sextus separated the schools, and he evidently found the separation worth preserving.

Donne had also read Laertius. He alludes to the *Life of Pyrrho* in his *Essays in Divinity*, mining it for a depiction of 'the quarelsome contending of *Sextus*' (27–8; *LP*, 9.61). Donne finds the Pyrrhonists wrongheaded, but at the same time understands the allure of their arguments better than most of his contemporaries. In a sermon from 1618 he draws out parallels between doubting philosophers and doubting Christians:

> Those Sceptique philosophers, that doubted of all, though they affirmed nothing, yet they denied nothing either, but they saw no reason in the opinions of others. Those Sceptique Christians, that doubt whether God have any particular providence ... that conform themselves outwardly with us, because that may be true, that we profess, for any thing they know, there may be a Christ ... these men, if they come to Church, think themselves safe enough, but they are deceived.[55]

Unlike many of the earlier Christian apologists I have discussed, Donne knows too well the powerful attractions of doubt: its apparent reasonableness, its provision of safe non-committal, its ability to pass for orthodoxy. But for Donne, there are truths beyond doubt, and scepticism masked by conformity is an offense in the eyes of God.

What, however, of the period between Donne's discovery of scepticism and his later years at St Paul's? Many of his *Songs and Sonnets* were composed during this interim, as were most of the *Holy Sonnets* and the two *Anniversaries*. Critics routinely speak of the scepticism embodied in these poems. Rosalie Colie observes that *Negative Love* ends in 'a libertine paradox of unknowing'; John Carey argues that *Confined Love* attacks monogamy 'from the viewpoint of unbridled naturalism', casting doubt on social institutions ostensibly sanctioned by reason. Reason, indeed, often proves weak or untrue for Donne, and when, in *The Will*, his poetic persona bequeaths his 'doubtfulness' to Aristotelian 'schoolmen', there seems little question that the speaker's frustration with complacent dogmatism is in fact Donne's own. We thus witness Donne's partial alignment with sceptics, as we do earlier in *Satire 3*, where Donne incorporates elements of classical scepticism even as he adapts them to his own purposes.[56] The most significant of these adaptations is the instrumentalization of doubt. Donne's claim that 'in strange way / To stand inquiring right, is not to stray' certainly evokes scepticism (especially the *zetetic* mode) in its emphasis on active questioning. But when coupled with the prior imperative to 'Seek true religion', the claim presupposes an ultimate arrival at truth. Much like Bacon, Donne advocates an end-driven deployment of doubt, and this of course is non-Pyrrhonian. But it is a sceptical paradigm none the less, and indeed the distinction was becoming commonplace: by 1614 the Arminian scholar Gerhard Vossius, writing to Hugo Grotius, carefully separated permanent suspension of judgement ('Scepticam ac Pyrrhoniam') from temporary suspension viewed as a means of finding truth. The force of his distinction lies precisely in its suggestion of partial rather than absolute commitment to the principle of doubt.[57]

Of all Donne's writings, the two *Anniversaries* (1611–12) have probably occasioned the greatest attention to the early modern revival of scepticism. The notorious claim that 'new philosophy calls all in doubt' has been endlessly quoted as evidence of the perceived breakdown of traditional understandings and values. It is worth remarking, however, that the assault of which Donne speaks is not the assault of doubt, but rather of new forms of dogma. While Donne laments what he perceives as a devastating loss of coherence and an onset of cosmic uncertainty, he attributes the change not to habits of doubt but to novel expressions of confidence. It is no co-incidence, after all, that Galileo's *Starry Messenger*, with its news of sunspots and moons orbiting Jupiter, was published just a year before the *Anatomy of the World*. Donne follows the ancient sceptics in finding grounds for doubt in conflicting accounts of reality, but he leaves their path in construing this doubt not as therapeutic but as anguishing and corrosive.

Or, to be more precise, anguishing until understood as providential. For the death of Elizabeth Drury allows humanity to be 'succoured' with a 'perplexed doubt, / Whether the world did lose, or gain' (*Anatomy*, 14–15). Doubt can thus serve a nurturing function, and indeed Donne reminds us that 'there's a kind of world remaining still' (67). True, it is a world undergoing progressive decay; like Hamlet's Denmark it is 'Quite out of joint' (192). Our minds are replete with 'corruptions', and we even 'make heaven come to us' by corralling the mysteries of faith within the pale of our own paltry understandings (330, 282). As Montaigne had observed, 'What can be more vain than trying to make guesses about God from human analogies?' (*Apology*, 81). But despite all this Donne assures us that the 'twilight' of Elizabeth's memory remains, creating a new world from the 'carcase' of the old (74–7). Hence a limited optimism is embedded within Donne's prevailing pessimism, and 'perplexed doubt' has been crucial to its discovery.

But the focus of this optimism must be confined to the human soul. As we read in lines germane to one of Jacobean tragedy's dominant moods, 'Our blushing red, which used in cheeks to spread, / Is inward sunk, and only our souls are red' (357–8). Hope and conscience remain, but their sphere is limited, their external signs readily manipulable. Donne will not go even as far as Wright in allowing for probable knowledge of others' interiors, though he concurs that the soul looks 'through spectacles': 'When wilt thou shake off this pedantery, / Of being taught by sense, and fantasy?' (*Progress*, 291–3). Indeed, it is in the second of the *Anniversaries* that this examination of the soul's desperate circumscription finds full development. Donne asks, 'Poor soul, in this thy flesh what dost thou know?' (254), and his answer is that it knows virtually nothing. Not quite nothing, I should add, for Donne does not align his view with the *acatalepsia* of the Academics, though his opinion cannot be severed from scepticism more generally. Some 'matters of fact' may be known: 'unconcerning things' like 'What Caesar did' and 'what Cicero said'. But self-knowledge is typically so impoverished among humans that it amounts almost to no knowledge at all. And regarding external matters,

> We see in authors, too stiff to recant,
> A hundred controversies of an ant ... .
> Why grass is green, or why our blood is red,
> Are mysteries which none have reached unto.
>                                             (255–89)

We have many opinions, but scarcely any knowledge, and the knowledge we have concerns matters not worth knowing. Altogether a sorry state of affairs.

But Donne's hope remains, for the soul in itself 'carries no desire to know, nor sense'; it is indifferent as to whether 'th' air's middle region be intense' (191–2). It knows what Donne knows, and what Donne wants *us* to know: that 'In heaven thou straight know'st all'. What does not concern us we 'straight forget' (299–300). Our hope, then, lies in superimposing such untainted souls upon souls thoroughly infected by fleshly sin. This, according to the poem's hyperbole, is the example set by Elizabeth Drury – and this the 'new world' offered by contemplation of her death. Writing of the *Anniversaries*, Colie concludes that 'The world's variety and change frighten [Donne], alarm him into a Skeptical questioning of men's Stoical security, and stir him to understand variety, change, and contradiction'.[58] Doubt, for

Donne, is providential; however much it draws us through anguished scrutiny – of both self and world – it leads in the end to clarification, humility, acceptance. And while this final state is no more the undiluted *ataraxia* of Pyrrhonism than is Donne's earlier doubting the deliberate technique of opposition, it still partakes of the sceptical tradition and is not exclusively derivative from meditation on Original Sin. Donne's scepticism in the *Anniversaries* is thus both Christian and classical: the former more than the latter, especially in its Augustinian stress on depravity, but the composite whole none the less configured in patterns that would have seemed familiar to Cicero or Sextus. The emphases on questioning, on withholding judgement in the face of contrariety, on pursuing truth despite such withholding, and above all on doubting 'wisely' – each finds grounding in the scepticism of antiquity. Precisely because Donne understands the Academic and Pyrrhonian traditions so well, he embraces and rejects their outlooks in a fashion uniquely his own.

## Arminians and Socinians

In 1594, around the time Donne was composing *Satire 3*, Richard Thomson sought to borrow Isaac Casaubon's manuscript of Sextus' *Outlines*. Because Thomson was associated with anti-Calvinist circles at Cambridge and was an acquaintance of the Dutch theologian Jacobus Arminius, his interest in Sextus raises questions about possible relations between scepticism and Arminianism, which I define here as the rejection of absolute predestination coupled with an espousal of free will. Indeed, Nicholas Tyacke has written that 'Arminianism can plausibly be understood as part of a more widespread philosophical scepticism, engendered by way of reaction to the dogmatic certainties of the sixteenth-century Reformation'.[59]

At Cambridge Thomson would have known the divinity professors William Barrett and Peter Baro, whose virulent dispute with William Perkins and other Calvinist dons resulted in Barrett's recantation and Baro's dismissal.[60] He would also have been familiar with the sentiments of such anti-Calvinists as Harsnett, John Overall and Lancelot Andrewes. Overall, in fact, gave Grotius a copy of Thomson's anti-Calvinist tract *De amissione et intercisione gratiae* (1616), which was drafted in the 1590s and argued that not even God's Elect were invulnerable to a fall from grace. Grotius himself, friend to Casaubon and Gerhard Vossius, supported Oldenbarnevelt's policy of toleration for the Dutch Remonstrants; among his books is a *Disquisitio* that lays out differences between Arminianism and the heresies associated with ancient Pelagians. This is not the place to treat the controversies between pro- and anti-Calvinist factions within the Church of England, but it is clear that the Arminians' hostility to strict determinism found an eager hearing among many British intellectuals. Harriot was fascinated by the topic, judging from books he purchased in 1618, and so, too, was his benefactor Northumberland, who offered patronage to the outspoken Arminian Richard Montagu. Elizabeth Cary discussed Arminianism with Montagu prior to her Catholic conversion in 1626; Edward Herbert of Cherbury found the movement intriguing in so far as it coincided with his own anti-predestinarian views; and, later in the century, John Milton famously wrote that Adam and Eve, expelled from Paradise, still possessed the freedom to add 'deeds' to their 'knowledge answerable': deeds of faith, virtue and love, all conducive to a 'paradise within ... happier far'.[61]

From the perspective of international politics, Calvinist hegemony within the English Church slowly declined in the 1590s, partly as a consequence of such events as the execution of Mary Stuart and the defeat of the Spanish Armada. A decreased sense of Catholic danger at home also contributed to this decline, though there were breaks in the trend such as the Gunpowder Plot of 1605. In short, from the late 1590s forward – and despite the still-dominant Calvinism of the Church – there was increasing scope for a less unified Protestant front, and Arminianism constituted one of the more attractive theological alternatives. The main intersection between Arminianism and scepticism, as Tyacke suggests, lies in a shared sense of combating dogmatic pronouncement regarding matters open to doubt. But recent scholarship also demonstrates that by 1638, in anti-Arminian tracts by Robert Baillie and other Scottish ministers, sceptical 'Acatalepsie' was introduced into theological polemic as an attempt to discredit the opponents of Calvinism.[62] We thus witness, in essence, a revisiting of the foundational debate between Erasmus and Luther a century earlier.

And if Erasmus figures prominently as a precursor of Arminian theology, he looms even more largely as a symbolic forebear of the Socinian tradition in post-Reformation Europe. The writings of this tradition's founder, the Polish reformer Faustus Socinus, are of course central to the movement, but its intellectual genealogy may be traced from Erasmus through Castellio and Acontius, and eventually on to Mornay, Hooker and Grotius. In the strictest sense Socinianism involved a rejection of the Trinity, hence a denial of Christ's divinity. Its unitarianism was perceived by many as a revival of the ancient Arian heresy; indeed unitarianism was the crime for which Servetus had been executed by Calvin. But few Europeans charged with Socinian sympathies went this far. An 'acknowledgement of the rights of reason in religion' was rather the primary meaning of the term for thinkers with Socinian leanings.[63] Among these thinkers in England were William Chillingworth and Lucius Cary; Cary's sister Lucy notes that her brother was 'opened' to new avenues of religious reflection upon 'meeting a book of Socinus', and John Aubrey claims that he was 'the first Socinian in England'. Chillingworth, meanwhile, who 'delighted in Sextus Empeiricus', was accused in 1636 of being 'a downright Socinian'. And so too, of course, was Chillingworth's godfather, Archbishop Laud.[64]

Rigid Protestants and Catholics alike saw Socinianism as a threat – a 'deviation to the extreme left' – and its tolerant, pacifist tendencies were anathema to polities animated by Calvinist or by Counter-Reformation orthodoxy. The ecumenical outlook of a book like Edwin Sandys' *Relation of the State of Religion* (1605), for example, was effectively condemned by the book's *de facto* suppression in the wake of the Gunpowder Plot, even though Grotius, Chillingworth and others admired it. They also admired Castellio's *On Heretics* (1554), which denounced the execution of Servetus, and Acontius' *Stratagemata Satanae* (1565), which developed Castellio's arguments supporting freedom of religious belief. According to Chillingworth, Castellio was an 'Academicall Protestant', by which he meant, in essence, a liberal – a theologian open to doubt.[65] Indeed openness to doubt was a hallmark of the general sort of thinking labelled Socinian.

Very much in the Erasmian tradition of impatience with intractably dogmatic positions, Socinians were drawn to the positive functions of scepticism: questioning authority, entertaining multiple viewpoints, restraining premature assent, pursuing the investigation. By and large, of course, they were not Pyrrhonists – certainly not in any strict sense. For while doubting understood as a therapeutic activity is consonant with ancient sceptical practice, doubting seen to exemplify the virtues of reason takes on a character foreign to the Pyrrhonian outlook, since Pyrrhonism always recognizes that reason can deceive, lead to contradictions, and instill false confidence. Chillingworth and Cary would have known this, as would Vossius and Grotius; they were all familiar with Sextus – not to mention Montaigne and Charron – and they would have been conscious of departures from more fully-fledged forms of scepticism. But at the same time a milder scepticism was their constant ally. As Charles Larmore has written, the strategy of Grotius was to accept that aspect of sceptical theory 'which suffices to refute the dogmatist, but then show how rational inquiry can still be fruit-ful'.[66] And while the mitigated scepticism of Chillingworth and others in the Great Tew circle has been extensively studied, it is worth remarking that Chillingworth's theory of progressive levels of assent and certainty – expounded in his *Religion of Protestants* – derives in part from Grotius' *Truth of the Christian Religion* (1624), and never disputes the standard Pyrrhonian suspicion that epistemological certainty is unattainable.[67] Probable truths and qualified assurances, however, may indeed be ascertained, and in this respect Chillingworth, like Grotius and Vossius before him, departs from thoroughgoing scepticism. Vossius' distinction between temporary and absolute suspension of judgement, though in fact a distortion of Sextus' Pyrrhonism, none the less serves as a useful indication of the way in which more radical scep-tical paradigms could be perceived – even by sympathetic thinkers – as primarily destructive in character. Thus the Socinian outlook, with its adoption of instrumental doubt and its faith in reason's utility in reli-gious matters, may be understood as constructively appropriating certain aspects of ancient scepticism while staunchly eschewing others. And both Socinianism and Arminianism cultivate an idea of religious toleration that has deep roots in the fundamental sceptical emphasis on the way in which the ubiquitous fact of conflicting belief should engender humility and an ongoing reluctance to judge.

## Mitigations, refutations, perpetuations

Among Chillingworth's friends at Oxford was John Earle, fellow of Merton College and later Bishop of Salisbury. Earle's *Microcosmography* (1628), a collection of Theophrastan characters, includes a sketch enti-tled 'A Sceptic in Religion' which usefully illustrates why radical Pyrrhonism was often lampooned in intellectual circles. Such a sceptic is 'one that hangs in the balance with all sorts of opinions', failing to achieve resolution because 'out of his belief of everything … he fully believes nothing'. This is blatant misrepresentation, of course, but we must allow that Earle's imperative is wit more than accuracy. Still, Earle gets things mostly right when he adds that the sceptic 'finds reason in all opinions, truth in none … he uses the land's Religion because it is next him, and … hammers much upon our opinion's uncertainty'. Not surprisingly, Earle is particularly concerned with the sceptic's relation to established belief, taking umbrage at his willingness to listen to Catholics and Puritans alike: 'His conscience interposes itself betwixt duellers, and whilst it would part both, is by both wounded.' Having thus intimated the sceptic's pacifist impulse, Earle continues by alluding both to Socinus and to Arminius' successor Conrad Vorstius, whose opinions pique the sceptic afresh. Above all, however, the sceptic 'hates authority as the tyrant of reason … and yet that many are not persuaded with reason shall authorise his doubt. In sum, his whole life is a question, and his salvation a greater, which death only concludes, and then he is resolved' (74–6).

Much more than Joseph Hall's character 'Of the Distrustfull', Earle's depiction shows sympathy for several sceptical predilections, not to mention recognition that sustained doubt finds grounding in open-minded attention to contemporary debates. Unlike Hall's sceptic, Earle's is an avid reader, and if Earle faults him for timidity, he weakens his case by categorically asserting the Church of England's superiority to rival Christian polities. And this, far from being a cogent rebuttal of scepticism, is simply grist to the mill. Earle also says the sceptic 'agrees with none worse than himself' – an allegation that Montaigne, for one, would take as a compliment. And while the sketch ends with good-natured mockery, even here Earle's portrayal remains double-edged. To say that a person's 'whole life is a question' is surely to render praise, if that person has diligently searched but failed to discover truth. Thus Earle gently ridicules scepticism, but only by presupposing with equally gentle confidence the truth of precisely that which the sceptic doubts.

One of the ways in which the seventeenth-century reception of scepticism has most frequently been described relies on a broad distinction between scepticism in 'destructive' and 'constructive' forms.[68] This distinction has limitations, since Pyrrhonism is by no means best understood as fundamentally nihilistic. But if we accept, for the moment, the taxonomy of seventeenth-century refutations of scepticism provided by Popkin, we find that the destructive/constructive opposition serves a useful purpose. Popkin writes that rebuttals to scepticism come in three basic forms:

(1) refutations based on principles of Aristotelian philosophy; (2) refutations that admit the full force and validity of Pyrrhonian arguments and then attempt to mitigate the effects of total scepticism; (3) refutations that attempt to construct a new system of philosophy in order to meet the sceptical challenge.[69]

Following Popkin's scheme, I suggest that the first and third forms of refutation see scepticism as fundamentally 'destructive' in character and thus in need of definitive rejection. The second form, however, finds Pyrrhonian arguments sufficiently powerful that it seeks, one way or another, to incorporate them into a mitigated or 'constructive' scepticism that can yield provisional, if not indubitable, knowledge. Chillingworth's meditations on religious certainty fall into this expansive category, as do the writings of Grotius and the philosophical treatises of Mersenne and Gassendi. Since Popkin and others have treated these figures in detail, I will say little about them here, stressing only that while they generally agree that knowledge of the underlying nature of things appears to be unattainable, knowledge of appearances is unquestionably available.[70] Advocacy of a new science of appearances is thus one of Mersenne's objectives in *La verité des sciences* (1625), which suggests that we may still have forms of knowledge even though we cannot have the levels of assurance for knowledge that dogmatic philosophers would like to think we do. And Gassendi, initially attracted to thoroughgoing Pyrrhonism, gradually accepts Mersenne's objections to Sextus, eventually going beyond them in his *Syntagma philosophicum* (1655), where he argues for probable truths about the nature of things-in-themselves as he presents a form of Epicurean atomism.[71]

Mitigated sceptics in Britain include such figures as Joseph Glanvill and John Wilkins, both members of the Royal Society.[72] Glanvill, who may have relied on Thomas Stanley's 1659 *Summary of Scepticism* – a complete English rendition of Sextus' *Outlines* – writes in his *Vanity of Dogmatizing* (1661) that '*Confidence* in uncertainties is the greatest enemy to what is certain; and were I a *Sceptick*, I'de plead for *Dogmatizing*: For the way to bring men to stick to *nothing*, is confidently to perswade them to swallow *all things*' (sig. A3). He also praises Charron, stating that he 'cannot quarrel with his *Motto*: in a sense *Je ne scay* is a justifiable *Scepticism*' (234). It is beyond the scope of my study to treat Glanvill in detail, let alone to examine related writings by such figures as Wilkins, John Tillotson or Robert Boyle. Suffice it to say that from the 1640s onward British intellectuals entertain forms of mitigated scepticism on a regular basis, and perhaps only with the publication, a century later, of Hume's *Enquiry Concerning Human Understanding* does a collective sense emerge that philosophy may agree to a considerable extent with Pyrrhonian premises, while still moving substantially beyond them.[73]

In the meantime, repudiations of scepticism falling within Popkin's third category – rebuttals grounded in 'new systems of philosophy' and purporting to yield truths not only about appearances but about the intrinsic nature of reality – continued to emerge on the Continent and in Britain. I have discussed one of these systems, that of Bacon, in some detail. And because commentaries on another, the rational philosophy of Descartes, are abundant, I will say little about Cartesianism here. Rather, I wish to turn back briefly to the 1620s – the early years of Armininian and Socinian thinking in England – and consider the once famous treatise *De Veritate* by Edward Herbert of Cherbury, older brother of the poet George. Like Bacon, Herbert viewed scepticism as fundamentally destructive, describing it as one of two philosophical outlooks requiring annihilation in order for fruitful enquiry to flourish. The other was Aristotelianism, particularly in its scholastic manifestations. As Herbert writes,

> there has always existed a perverse class of professors who expounded with equal zeal and confidence both these doctrines: that we can know everything, and that we can know nothing. The latter group says that truth lies hidden in a well, that we know one thing only, namely that we know nothing ... The former party, on the other hand, maintain with remarkable daring that the principles of the Universe can be deduced from the principles of thought, in spite of the fact that these refer only to us. They proclaim, with unaccountable disregard for truth, that there is nothing which is not open to their understanding. (76)[74]

Given these allegations, it is mildly ironic that Herbert's own philosophy of truth is accompanied by the claim that his elaborate set of heuristic questions, the *Zetetica*, will enable readers to 'achieve complete certainty in all points of definition, classification, and inference' (282). Indeed, Herbert often exhibits the same zeal which he condemns in sceptics and dogmatic philosophers. But there is still no question that he is an original and independent thinker.

A friend to both Donne and Jonson, Herbert matriculated at New College, Oxford, in 1595 and studied there for several years, though like many gentlemen he never took a degree. In 1608 he travelled to France, where he met Isaac Casaubon and was entertained at the court of Henri IV. A decade later he was appointed English ambassador to Paris, and it was during his five-year tenure that he composed *De Veritate*, publishing it in 1624 at the urging of Grotius and the French Arminian Daniel Tilenus. The book's appeal to Arminian sympathizers perhaps lay more in its advocacy of free will than in its epistemological disquisitions, but it none the less gained the attention of philosophers.

Mersenne is believed to have translated it into French in 1639; Descartes and Gassendi both read it with interest; and Locke famously disputed its claims in his *Essay Concerning Human Understanding* (1690).

Like many thinkers of his time, Herbert sought, or claimed that he sought, a *via media* between excessive doubt and overconfident certainty: 'I hold neither that we can know everything, nor that we can know nothing; but I think there are some things which can be known' (78). These 'things', as we subsequently learn, are truths not merely about appearances but about ultimate realities lying behind them. Herbert thus abandons the path of the mitigated sceptics and, like Bacon (whose writings he ignores), concentrates instead on the exposition of a complex method of ascertaining indubitable truths. He also takes issue with the *nouveaux pyrrhoniens* – Montaigne, Charron, La Mothe Le Vayer and others – dismissing their fideism as premature despair of rational potential. Inclining 'to that school which taught that it was impossible to know anything', they 'prefer faith to reason' and thus 'pass judgement on the facts before the case is argued' (76).[75] Such remarks undoubtedly contributed to Herbert's reputation in the eighteenth century as a theological rationalist – indeed, as a founder of deism.

Herbert's elaborate method of discovering truth lies at the heart of *De Veritate*, serving to substantiate his declaration that 'truth exists' despite the protestations of 'imbeciles and sceptics' (83). Right away, therefore, Herbert creates a problem for himself, since he asserts, without demonstration, the existence of truth, then promises to show how it can be found. His solution is familiar: the positing of 'Common Notions', innate truths whose veridical status passes unquestioned by normal humans, and whose existence is providential (86–9, 105–7, 126–7). The criterion of these Common Notions' validity is universal consent, which may in turn be ascertained through empirical investigation (119–21). Herbert thus satisfies, at least on the surface, the sceptical demand for a criterion of truth which requires no further justification. But as Popkin shows, both Gassendi and Descartes rejected Herbert's theory, finding its answer to the *crise pyrrhonienne* 'open to sceptical objections at almost every level'.[76]

The most obvious level is where Herbert argues for the possibility of absolute conformity between appearances and reality. Acknowledging that perception is fallible – though less so than reason (232) – Herbert devises a scheme whereby external realities, provided they meet certain conditions for proper perceptual apprehension, become known to the intellect through their correspondence with the appearances by which they manifest themselves to inner perception (86–102). The guarantee of the veracity of this correspondence lies in the Common Notions. A multitude of sceptical challenges might be posed to such a theory, and Descartes – himself entirely sympathetic to the refutation of scepticism – finds Herbert's system wholly inadequate in the face of such challenges.[77] Thus Herbert's *Veritate*, despite its originality, is decidedly less convincing as a proposal for truth-acquisition than either Bacon's inductive and empirical methods or Descartes' rationalism. Bacon's awareness of sceptical problems, while not as fully developed as it might have been, none the less enables him to avoid many of the pitfalls unwittingly created by Herbert. And Descartes effectively out-Pyrrhonizes the Pyrrhonists through his supposition of a *malin génie* and subsequent development of the *cogito*. This is not the place to comment on the adequacy of the Cartesian rebuttal of scepticism; I merely wish to reiterate the paradoxical fact that the understanding of scepticism as an essentially destructive force, however much it misrepresents the Pyrrhonism outlined by Sextus and appropriated by Montaigne, none the less underlies and partly motivates the development of such positive theories of knowledge as those proposed by Bacon, Herbert and Descartes.

A final word on Herbert. *Veritate* devotes considerable space to a heuristic scheme called the *Zetetica*: a 'number of questions which can be asked by discursive reason' and by means of which anyone can 'compose whole volumes on any subject' (240–1). Reminiscent of other sets of categories or *topoi* in western philosophy, the *Zetetica* seem rather Aristotelian in character – and ironically so, given Herbert's antipathy to Peripatetic traditions. It is difficult to know whether Herbert intended his *Zetetica* to allude to the *zetetic* mode of scepticism stressed not only by Sextus but also, more vehemently, by Montaigne and Charron.[78] Certainly, the nature of the questioning is different, since for Herbert it is finite: once one has posed and answered all the *Zetetica*, nothing further may be learned (240–4). But on a broader level Herbert's interest in sustained investigation is very much of a piece with the *zetetic* paradigm of scepticism's early modern reception. We should not forget that Lucius Cary is described as presenting himself in religious debates as 'rather an inquirer than an absolute defender of anything'. And later, in Stanley's rendition of Sextus, the point is again stressed: 'The *Sceptick* Institution is called also *Zetetick* (*Inquisitive*) from the act of enquiring' (7). Herbert had died before Stanley's translation appeared, but there is no question that he knew Sextus; his *Pagan Religion* alludes explicitly to passages in *Against the Mathematicians*.[79] Like Chamber, Burton and others, Herbert relied on Sextus for information about antiquity, and while his own intellectual tendencies were decidedly anti-sceptical, he may have absorbed more of Sextus' inquisitive and oppositional outlook than he would consciously have acknowledged.

Herbert had many readers but few followers; in this he differs enormously from Bacon and Descartes. One of the few was Charles Blount, translator of Spinoza and, with John Toland and Matthew Tindal, among the earliest avowed deists in England. But on the whole Herbert's views, with their combination of naïveté and dogmatic zeal, never garnered significant support. Indeed, Locke permanently shut the door on Herbert's theory of Common Notions by arguing that even if 'there were certain truths wherein all mankind agreed, it would not prove them innate, if there can be any other way shown how men may come to that universal agreement in the things they do consent in, which I presume may be done'.[80] And while Locke was by no means a thoroughgoing sceptic (though he occasionally expressed respect for sceptical views), his distaste for such theories as that of innate ideas participates significantly in the widespread European retreat from epistemologies promising vast reaches of indubitable knowledge. The Royal Society, for instance, is praised by Dryden for its 'modest inquisitions', and Thomas Sprat, its first historian, admits that 'to this fault of *Sceptical doubting*, the *Royal Society* may perhaps be suspected to be a little too much inclin'd'.[81] Robert Boyle in particular may have been the Society's least dogmatic member. Having undergone a sceptical *crise* during the 1640s, and having also studied Sextus, he later felt the need to insist, in his *Sceptical Chymist* (1661), that he was 'far from being one of that sect', though he sometimes had occasion 'to discourse like a Sceptick'. Other members, no doubt, also discoursed in that fashion from time to time – Glanvill, Tillotson and Wilkins, for instance – and while they certainly repudiated *acatalepsia*, they embraced the more general sceptical view that we must always embark on inquiries by acknowledging the potential deceptiveness of our intellectual faculties.[82]

Such acknowledgement was also crucial to Pascal and Bayle. Pascal, whose deep familiarity with Montaigne is matched by his frustration with the essayist's buoyant tone, agrees with his predecessor that reason leads only so far. But whereas Montaigne's fideism coexists with ongoing doubt, Pascal's is more decisive: the advent of faith is the vanquishing of doubt. Scepticism is thus reduced to a necessary but prefatory gambit; its value is only instrumental.[83] As for Bayle, perhaps the most remarkable aspect of his Pyrrhonism is its very extremity. Writing at the close of a century that had witnessed the anti-sceptical onslaughts of Bacon, Descartes and Leibniz, he none the less scourged reason relentlessly in his *Dictionnaire*, insisting on our rational incapacity 'to make sense either of the principles of nature or [those] on which God has created the world'. Not surprisingly, Bayle was also an opponent of Socinianism, condemning the 'heresy' of theologians who defended reason as the rule of faith. At times he even expressed an extreme historical scepticism, suspending judgement, for instance, on the question of whether Bruno had in fact been burned at Rome a century earlier. Hence when Descartes writes that 'We must not think the sect of sceptics long extinct', he is not merely correct but prescient. The sect, he continues, 'flourishes today as much as ever, and nearly all who think they have some ability beyond the rest of mankind, finding nothing that satisfies them in the common philosophy, and seeing no other truth, take refuge in scepticism'.[84]

But what strikes Descartes as an indefensible refuge strikes others as a sane and salutary haven; few are as willing as he to suppose that reason can yield truths immune to doubt. Sir Thomas Browne speaks for many when he writes in *Religio Medici* (1643) that while 'our junior endeavors may stile us Peripateticks, Stoicks, or Academicks, yet I perceive the wisest heads prove at last, almost all Scepticks, and stand like *Janus* in the field of knowledge'. Hobbes too undergoes a long negotiation with sceptical epistemology, and Dryden famously describes his own temperament as one of 'natural Diffidence and Scepticism'.[85] It may be, of course, that sceptical leanings come more easily to those unwilling or unable to confront the problems of knowledge as vigorously as Descartes and Bacon; clearly Descartes sees Pyrrhonian irresolution as a failure of attention, a capitulation to sloth. But by the same token few thinkers are likely to concentrate with Cartesian intensity on epistemological issues divorced from the broader concerns of social life. As a consequence, theologians, moral philosophers, poets and dramatists resort throughout the seventeenth century to aspects of scepticism without feeling obliged to embrace it completely. They create and elaborate new sceptical paradigms, and if they fail to inspect the interiors of Pyrrhonism as closely as they might, this makes little difference in the long run, since the ancient ideas survive none the less through their very resuscitation in evolving historical milieux. Religious polemicists of diverse orientations – Arminians like John Hales, Puritans like Richard Baxter, moderate Anglicans like Edward Stillingfleet – repeatedly display sceptical affiliations.[86] John Goodwin provides an especially intriguing case. A republican who offers spiritual support to the imprisoned King Charles, a Calvinist who prepares the first English rendition of Acontius (*Satan's Stratagems*, 1648), he baffles many of his contemporaries, and none more so than the obstreperous Thomas Edwards. In *Gangraena* (1646), Edwards furiously exposes his confusion, fulminating against Goodwin as 'a monstrous sectary, a compound of Socinianism, Arminianism, antinomianism, independency, popery, yea, and of scepticism' (1:156).

But if the sceptical inheritance of antiquity is evident in seventeenth-century religious controversy, and if it surfaces as well in the writings of educational reformers like Comenius and Hartlib or Cambridge Platonists like More and Cudworth, what about its less elite manifestations?[87] Historians have shown that 'plebeian materialist scepticism' existed in Britain long before its overt appearances in the 1640s and later. A. G. Dickens asserts that anti-clericalism in the early sixteenth century merged to some degree with popular 'tavern-unbelief' – and that separating the latter from 'positive Lollardy and Protestantism' is not always easy. Keith Thomas adds that 'there was plenty of scope in sixteenth- and seventeenth-century England for a wide degree of religious heterodoxy', surmising that 'many thought what they dared not say'.[88] Still, doubts about miracles, providence, transubstantiation and other doctrinal points must be distinguished from the more purely philosophical doubting on which I have concentrated. Nor can such lay scepticism be supposed to have emerged only with the Reformation. On the other hand, popular and philosophical doubt cross paths on an increasingly frequent basis, above all due to their shared interest in questions of religious belief. Thus, while we can assume that common-sense doubt about spiritual matters pre-dates Renaissance epistemological doubt, this very fact helps explain why the Reformation's disputes so quickly promote the revival of sustained philosophical scepticism. The self-conscious deployments of doubt in Montaigne, Sanches and others are just as much products of the sixteenth century's ideological turbulence as are such popular phenomena as questioning the soul's immortality or the confessional's efficacy. The relations between the two are reciprocal; evidence of the former often confirms the existence of the latter, as well as providing one of the fundamental means by which the latter is codified and perpetuated. Each legitimates the other.

# Paradigms

Still, in the end, the case for the wide dissemination of sceptical ideas rests principally on evidence other than vocabulary, book ownership, citation or the topics for academic debate. All these have their place, and all are useful indicators – but none in itself is sufficient. The best evidence is that which is the most inaccessible: the inward thoughts of ordinary people. To the extent, however, that these thoughts are both shaped and reflected by contemporary literary works – especially dramatic works composed for the popular stage – the study of such literature may yield highly suggestive inferences. Scholars have long believed that Elizabethan and Jacobean drama exposes deep currents of scepticism in the culture of its origins; *Measure for Measure* and *Bartholomew Fair* have been characterized as 'profoundly subversive' plays, and comparable claims have been made for *Faustus*, *Lear*, and *The Duchess of Malfi*.[89] The problem is that the genesis and nature of such scepticism have seldom been examined – a problem I hope to redress.

Hence my argument centres on sceptical paradigms. The more that popular and philosophical scepticism intersect, the more they generate characteristic paradigms of reception: recognizable assumptions, attitudes and trajectories of interrogation. Deployed by poets and dramatists, these are received by readers and auditors, and they constitute the most genuine vocabulary of Renaissance scepticism, a vocabulary of investigation and judgement. It is in the light of these paradigms that I hope we can newly consider and assess such claims as Donne's – that 'new philosophy calls all in doubt' – or meditate on the enigmatic play-worlds of *Faustus* and *Mariam*, *Troilus and Cressida* and *'Tis Pity She's a Whore*. Shakespeare's Lafeu remarks that 'philosophical persons' now make 'modern and familiar things supernatural and causeless'. But Lafeu's attitude is itself philosophical – and strongly aligned with a tradition of uncertainty, wonder and humility that Montaigne, for one, would have found entirely congenial. A scepticism that relegates miracles to the past, making 'trifles of terrors' through the generation of 'seeming knowledge', is ultimately inseparable from the scepticism voiced by Lafeu. Both cast doubt; both depend on vulnerable acts of faith. Their structures are alike if their habitual resting places differ. And their inquisitive analyses of social interaction, however much inflected by contemporary historical conditions, simultaneously participate in the time-worn patterns of an ancient philosophical scepticism whose power, utility and charisma were consistently acknowledged by the most thoughtful and creative minds of early modern England.

# Part Two

# Fools of Nature: Scepticism and Tragedy

# 4
# Literary Adaptation: Sceptical Paradigms, Sceptical Values

> The wisest heads prove at last, almost all Scepticks, and stand like Janus in the field of knowledge.
>
> *Religio Medici*

Above all else, the lesson of chapters 2 and 3 is that the reception of ancient scepticism in Renaissance England, especially the literary reception, may be characterized more as distortion than as precise reflection, more as tendentious appropriation than as dispassionate representation. And this is scarcely surprising. It would have been remarkable had the writers of early modern Britain taken up the epistemological debates of Sextus and Cicero without altering their terms and balances. Still, as I trust my survey has shown, the concerns of classical scepticism were by no means unfamiliar to English intellectuals, even if specific manifestations of these concerns were coloured by contemporary social questions. Nor was lay scepticism entirely severed from its philosophically elaborated counterpart. On the contrary, the two became increasingly interlaced as the period wore on, and in no realm is this more apparent than in that of literary production. We find in many literary texts, even those decidedly non-sceptical in general tenor, various constellations of sceptical ideas and attitudes that inflect and are inflected by scripture, proverbial wisdom, contemporary politics and Reformation debate. The locus of interest, then, lies in literary recombinations: the adaptations, deformations and deployments of scepticism – in short, with sceptical paradigms.

Richard Popkin has argued that the 'sceptical crisis' of the early seventeenth century manifested itself particularly in three arenas: those of theological dispute, humanist learning and emergent scientific discourse. He adds that Montaigne's *Apology* deals to a greater or lesser degree with all three. I believe these claims are accurate, but I would suggest that the revival of scepticism reveals itself as well in popular literature, especially in plays for the popular stage. Such literary works do not, of course, explore the problems raised by epistemological scepticism in systematic fashion or in philosophic detail. But they none the less register sceptical concerns. As Louis Bredvold has written in his study of Dryden's intellectual environment, strict Pyrrhonism was not the form in which ancient scepticism most engaged early modern writers. Rather, scepticism took many looser shapes and often merged with the anti-rationalism of St Paul and various patristic writers, especially Augustine.[1] But at the same time, a work such as *The Sceptick* demonstrates that strictly conceived scepticism did indeed interest some Elizabethans and Jacobeans; Nashe, Thomson, Ralegh, Harriot and Donne may be numbered among them. Hence it is probably best to think of the early modern paradigms of scepticism as constituting a broad range of manifestations: from those with a fairly narrow philosophical focus to those combined with other influences and currents of thought.

What, then, are these paradigms? How is ancient scepticism understood – and misunderstood – in imaginative writing of the English Renaissance? How does it revive itself in new temporal and ideological contexts, and to what purposes is it applied? What are the patterns of doubt and habits of enquiry that most clearly mark its revival? What sceptical values, if any, emerge from its paradigms of appropriation and deployment? And how, more particularly, does scepticism intersect with dramatic tragedy? How does familiarity with early modern sceptical paradigms help us better understand and evaluate the complex amalgam of intellectual and emotional power for which English Renaissance tragedy is deservedly famous?

These are the questions I wish to address. I will begin by outlining what I see as the basic *kinds* of scepticism available to early modern thinkers. I will then examine and illustrate the major paradigms of scepticism observable in English literary works from the period, particularly dramatic works. Finally, I will turn to the sceptical values inherent in or emerging from these literary paradigms.

Probably the best place to start is with scepticism as conjoined with Original Sin. The Christian consensus regarding postlapsarian human frailty finds particular emphasis in the Augustinian tradition, which is exhaustively appropriated by Reformation theology. Claims about human ignorance, presumption and depravity are readily assimilated into the theological systems of Luther and Calvin. This is not to say that early modern Protestants with a strong Augustinian orientation are somehow inclined to philosophical scepticism; often quite the opposite is true. But the Augustinian emphasis on human infirmity none the less overlaps with ancient scepticism's pervasive doubt about the reliability of the body's sense organs and the mind's ratiocination.[2] Greville's *Treatie of Humane Learning* offers an excellent example: alluding frequently to the Fall, the poem grounds itself in Christian orthodoxy while simultaneously elaborating fragments of epistemological scepticism very likely derived, ultimately, from Sextus.

Related to this conjunction of scepticism and Christianity is the long tradition of Christian anti-rationalism. With roots in Ecclesiastes and in Paul's injunction to beware vain philosophy, this tradition finds Renaissance manifestation in Gianfrancesco Pico, Agrippa, Erasmus and Montaigne. As Bredvold observes, the warnings of Solomon and the Church Fathers against 'the vanity of worldly knowledge might lead pious Christian apologists to a respectful reading of Sextus'.[3] And while Erasmus and Montaigne may seem less than consistently pious, certainly Montaigne's successor La Mothe Le Vayer exemplifies this strand of scepticism's reception when he writes that 'Nothing the sceptics have argued against the pride of Dogmatists weighs so heavily as what [Paul] wrote to the Corinthians, warning them that it is necessary to be foolish according to the world in order to be wise according to God'. By this logic, Pyrrhonism's extended genealogy comprehends the Pauline epistles. As for Agrippa, Popkin goes so far as to term his basic attitude 'fundamentalist anti-intellectualism'.[4] Such a claim would be extreme with respect to Erasmus or Montaigne, but both writers, in varying ways, share an outlook in which pure intellectuality is subordinated to other human potentials. Thus once again scepticism presents itself as a convenient ally, if not a natural consequence, of Christian devotion.

Moving away from specifically Christian intersections with sceptical tradition, I find a third major form of early modern doubt in those habits of thought variously termed 'popular', 'plebeian' or 'materialist' scepticism. Keith Thomas, A. G. Dickens, Christopher Hill and others have treated such habits of thought in detail – particularly as applied to religious observance and doctrine – so I will say little about them here.[5] I will note, however, that common-sense doubts regarding ghosts, witches, dream visions or astrological prediction also figure significantly as instances of popular scepticism. Such doubts require no grounding in epistemological scepticism, and indeed are likely to surface in any culture, at any time. But to the extent that they often combine with more developed expressions of scepticism – as in the critiques of judicial astrology offered by Agrippa or John Chamber – they suggest that continuities with philosophical traditions of antiquity may be readily activated among limited but influential sectors of a given population. Put another way, while Reginald Scot does not cite Sextus in his *Discoverie of Witchcraft*, he none the less would have found Sextus' arguments congenial to his purposes, and might well have listed him in his index of 'forren authors' had his reading taken different directions.

Genuine epistemological scepticism, whether it develops (as in Montaigne and Charron) from direct acquaintance with Sextus, Cicero and other authorities, or (as in Sanches, Greville, and Donne) more circuitously, may be distinguished from common-sense doubt by a number of obvious features. Among these are discussions of the problems of sense-perception and ratiocination, explorations of criteria for judgement, and praise of doubt, non-assertion and suspension of epistemic commitment. At the same time, however, additional aspects of ancient scepticism may present themselves in isolated or distorted forms. The Academic concept of *acatalepsia* – that nothing can be known with certainty – is one such aspect, and manifests itself regularly in early modern literary and philosophical discourse. Another is the strict understanding of doubt as the withholding of both assent *and* dissent; Donne, for instance, is quite insistent about this. Finally, we have an assortment of minor motifs. These include a concern with making arguments about the relative probability of differing claims or theories, and an understanding of philosophy as comprehending three basic kinds of practice: dogmatic, negatively dogmatic and sceptical. Indeed, the very concept of negative dogmatism derives from Sextus and was partly adopted by Montaigne (*PH*, 1.226; *Apology*, 67–9). Coming from Sextus as well are various sub-meditations within the more general category of sense-data discussion: the idea that dream perception may be indistinguishable from waking perception; the suspicion that humans lack perceptive faculties which, if possessed, might yield a different understanding of the world; and the theory that sense organs, through their normal functioning, may distort what they present to the mind, so that sense mediation intrinsically alters its objects (*PH*, 1.96–104, 1.126–8, 2.55–6). All these epistemological considerations constitute aspects of ancient scepticism, and all may be found, with varied degrees of frequency and precision, in the early modern discursive realms that serve as the focus of this study (e.g. *Apology*, 171–84).

The last broad form of scepticism commonly available to Renaissance thinkers is an applied form: scepticism about the practice of standard human activities like writing history or wielding political power. To some extent a form of common-sense doubt, applied scepticism is typically allied with a modicum of specialized learning – learning that may include but need not necessarily involve acquaintance with ancient sources. No one insists that Machiavelli read Sextus or inclined towards Pyrrhonism, yet his studies of political morality have often been characterized as profoundly sceptical of earlier ideals of governance. Justus Lipsius, writing at the end of the same century in which *The Prince* appeared, asserts that people 'rage too much against Machiavell'; in matters of 'publike profit' rulers must often 'play the foxe' – especially when 'having to deale with a foxe'. The Tacitean exposé of imperial Rome, so popular in the late sixteenth century, thus combines with the attitude of detachment implicitly promoted by scepticism, and together the two encourage an analysis of 'policy', or *realpolitik*, which in turn surfaces in many contemporary literary works. By the same token, scepticism about the ascertainment of historical truth often merges with doubts about current historiography, so that Sidney, for instance, can write that historians for the most part rely merely on 'other histories, whose greatest authorities are built upon the notable foundation of hearsay'.[6] Donne seconds this idea when he wryly considers the difficulties in knowing even 'unconcerning things, matters of fact; / How others on our stage their parts did act' (*Progress of the Soul*, 287–8). Whether Sidney or Donne knew Sextus' commentary on historiographical practice (*M*, 1.248–69) is ultimately less germane than the plain fact that both men express reservations about the reliability of historical accounts. In Italy, Francesco Patrizi and Paolo Sarpi do the same, though they also work towards refining conventional approaches to the evaluation of historical evidence.[7] Few thinkers in the period are genuine historical Pyrrhonists, but many apply a healthy dose of scepticism to the methods and conclusions of their historiographical predecessors. And, as I have suggested, applied scepticism surfaces in other arenas as well: in matters of education, or in the investigation of nature and the interpretation of cultural and religious difference. Montaigne comes quickly to mind as an exemplar of such doubt. But he was far from alone.

These, then, are the basic kinds of scepticism that in my view were available to early modern Europeans. I stress that only one of them is genuinely philosophical in character, though all have the potential for philosophic elaboration. And I add that what is nowadays called 'religious scepticism', or atheism and its variants, was certainly a possible outcome of common-sense doubt – but not, in fact, a commonly disseminated conclusion. Many scholars have noted this, and while I will not turn here to the extensive debate over Renaissance unbelief, I wish to observe that it is crucial to distinguish not only between what was unthinkable and what was unprintable, but also between what was thinkable and what was thought. In other words, while early modern Europeans were perfectly capable of imagining that God does not exist or that providential supervision is a useful myth, they were certainly *not* capable of disseminating such views with impunity. More importantly, few of them would have been able to entertain such views for extended periods due to the psychic pressures of a vast infrastructure of cultural traditions, beliefs and institutions that supported and were reinforced by doctrinal authority. Doubt, in short, though likely to arise, was more likely to remain its agnostic self than to harden into cynicism or denial.[8]

And this very fact – that doubt could be entertained *as doubt* without metamorphosing into other cognitive configurations – is important to everything that follows regarding sceptical paradigms. Early modern literary texts frequently exhibit extraordinary sensitivity to epistemological questions, distinctions and anxieties. They may not immerse themselves in the philosophical technicalities of scepticism, but they routinely display sharp discrimination among closely related states of mind – between suspicion and conviction, between assurance and belief. As the Provost remarks to the Duke in *Measure for Measure*, only under Angelo's scrutiny has Barnardine's guilt come to 'an undoubtful proof' (4.2.127) – a remark suggesting that proof accompanied by doubt has also been a cognitive possibility in Vincentio's Vienna. Epistemological sensitivity is a distinguishing feature of many Renaissance texts, especially dramatic texts. And understanding doubt not as denial but as thoughtful uncertainty is the fundamental starting place for any consideration of the literary paradigms of early modern scepticism.

(1) The first of these paradigms is that which develops from a collective sense of human weakness and mental frailty. Such frailty may be explicitly accounted for by reference to the Fall, or it may simply be taken as an experientially verified induction. Either way, it generates extensive literary treatment and serves an animating function in many Renaissance plays. In comedies it is often invoked as an explanatory principle. *Twelfth Night*'s Viola exclaims that she hates ingratitude more than 'any taint of vice whose strong corruption / Inhabits our

frail blood' (3.4.321–2); in *The Merchant of Venice*, Lorenzo discourses on the music of the spheres, regretfully adding that 'whilst this muddy vesture of decay / Doth grossly close [our souls], we cannot hear it' (5.1.63–4). In tragedies, by contrast, human weakness is less overtly embraced, but still widely acknowledged. Hamlet reminds Horatio that there are 'more things in heaven and earth' than are 'dreamt of' in philosophy (1.5.168–9); Gloucester laments that while 'the wisdom of Nature can reason it thus and thus, yet nature finds itself scourged by the sequent effects' (*Lear*, 1.2.104–6); and Ferdinand, in *The Duchess of Malfi*, observes that reason's 'imperfect light' allows us 'to foresee / What we can least prevent' (3.2.77–9). Tragic exploitation of this motif thus capitalizes on the disparities and consequent ironies between what humans know or think they can explain and what they do not know and cannot control.[9]

Montaigne is interesting in this regard. He stresses human frailty incessantly yet rarely yokes it with Original Sin. 'Is not Man a wretched creature?' he asks. We should pay more attention to 'our ignorance and weakness'; we should remember that inconstancy is 'the most blatant defect of our nature' (*Essays*, 225, 202, 373). Indeed, the rejection of Stoic truisms so characteristic of Montaigne's middle and later essays partly accounts for the minor role that Christian doctrine plays in his elucidation of human infirmity.[10] It is not that the explanation is false; it is superfluous. One glance at the world, as Democritus would have confirmed, reveals not only that our folly is laughable, but that our wisdom is too (928). Hence Montaigne's habitual emphasis on weakness merges almost imperceptibly with an ongoing mockery of intellectual arrogance. And this, in turn, is echoed in English Renaissance drama. Above all it appears in the fascination with the 'be and seem' topos: the obsessive concern with potentially deceptive exteriors, the critique of the presumption that we know a thing when we know only how it seems.[11] 'If circumstances lead me', boasts Polonius, 'I will / Find where truth is hid, though it were hid indeed / Within the centre' (2.2.157–9). But truth, in the end, proves well beyond Polonius' grasp.

That Sidney can speak of the 'cloudy knowledge of mankind' is due not only to a general sense of humanity's limited comprehension, but to a more specific sense of its rational and perceptual frailty (*Defence*, 235). I will treat these features of cognition more fully below, but I mention them here because of their centrality to virtually all the paradigms of scepticism's literary reception. When Milton, in *Paradise Lost*, alludes to the 'senses dark' (3.188), he has no need to elaborate his claim with instances of postlapsarian deception; his assertion's assumed validity obviates all demand for illustration. But, as with Montaigne, an inductive rather than deductive conclusion of cognitive frailty repeatedly surfaces in early modern considerations of human potential, and when it does, recourse to the ancient sceptical battery is almost automatic. We encounter such recourse, or something very close to it, in Davies' *Nosce Teipsum*, Greville's *Treatie* and Wright's *Passions*, and it is present too in Agrippa and Mornay.[12] Agrippa's distrust of human mental capacity – his sense that the intellect is eternally suspect – is a particularly apt illustration, since the nature of Agrippa's acquaintance with sceptical sources seems terminally unclear. But Bacon, too, serves well as an example. It is true that his faith in sense-data is surprisingly high, especially compared to that of many contemporaries. At the same time, his recognition that humans have pre-logical biases is formidably strong, and, as Mersenne observed, appears to imitate or derive from the classic Pyrrhonian arguments.[13] Characterizing these biases as 'Idols of the Mind' is novel and effective, but Bacon's understanding of cerebral circumscription has a lengthy pre-history.

A final aspect of this paradigm of scepticism's reception is the literary fascination with secret or forbidden knowledge. Related to mockery of the idea that truth may be fully ascertained, this concern differs from such mockery in its insistence that certain truths should never be sought. These things may be knowable – or they may not – but humans have no business looking into them. Bacon, acutely aware of this concern, labours to distinguish between potential objects of study, arguing that we must separate 'knowledge of nature and universality' from 'the proud knowledge of good and evil' (*Advancement*, 123–5). He accepts revealed knowledge with respect to human action in the moral sphere, but believes that humans are free to explore the natural world and God's works therein, declaring that the mind's intrinsic capacity, once liberated from the stranglehold of the Idols, is impressive and indeed equal to substantial familiarity with 'second causes' (*WFB*, 3:596, 4:20). But Bacon's optimism is unusual. When Volumnia, in *Coriolanus*, alludes to 'mysteries which heaven / Will not have earth to know' (4.2.37–8), she speaks for a tremendous number of Shakespeare's contemporaries. Greville urges that we 'not overbuild our states, / In searching secrets of the Deity', but 'measure first our own Humanity' (190). And Milton's Raphael explains to Adam that there exists a body of knowledge which God has concealed from humans: 'Solicit not thy thoughts with matters hid'; 'be lowly wise' (8.167–73). Forbidden knowledge thus emerges as a foil to proper sublunary concerns. At times it takes on a Medusa-like aspect, ominously threatening those who, like Marlowe's Faustus or Ford's Giovanni, persist in investigating that which should be left alone. Erasmus notes that there are many topics 'better let go than pursued', many subjects 'on which to doubt is more healthy than to lay down the law'.[14] The very progression here from forbidden knowledge to judgemental suspension illuminates the deep connection in Erasmus' mind between a general sense of human mental limitation and a more specific activation of ancient sceptical tropes.

(2) Less amorphous than the first paradigm is a second which grows from an awareness of the blatant fact of conflicting judgements and appearances. A paradigm of opposition or contrariety, this amalgam of consciousness and literary deployment appears with striking frequency in early modern texts. As Montaigne writes, 'there is no proposition which is not subject to debate ... [this] proves that our natural judgment does not grasp very clearly even what it does grasp, since my judgment cannot bring a fellow man's judgment to accept it' (*Apology*, 141). Or, as Richard II observes in his prison cell, 'no thought is contented'; all are 'intermixed / With scruples, and do set the faith itself / Against the faith' (5.5.11–14). Robert Pierce, in a study of Shakespeare and the modes of Pyrrhonian doubt, suggests that conflicting perception and judgement is 'perhaps the most common argument for scepticism', and he shows how Shakespeare depicts such conflict, especially in *Julius Caesar* and *Hamlet*.[15] But the paradigm of opposition comprehends not only clashing views within a group, but also, and more dramatically, within an individual. 'This is and is not Cressid', exclaims an anguished Troilus (5.2.153), and Hamlet, revealing more to Rosencrantz and Guildenstern than they understand, calls the world both 'goodly frame' and 'sterile promontory' (2.2.289–90). Perhaps more than anyone else in the period, Montaigne exemplifies this habit of mind: 'I may happen to contradict myself but, as Demades said, I never contradict truth' (*Essays*, 908). And it is no great step from this paradigm of opposing judgement to the theory of 'double truth' associated with Averroës and Pomponazzi.[16] The idea of the simultaneous veracity and falsity of a given claim – or, more precisely, of a claim's variable truth-status relative to a particular conceptual outlook – is a philosophically elaborated version of the paradigm of opposition. The coincidence of contraries necessarily prompts doubt.

If the fact of opposed perception and judgement is frequently remarked, the potential for such opposition to combat dogmatic pronouncement is frequently exploited. Again Montaigne is pivotal, for his interest in conflicting opinion often passes from bemused contemplation to intentional deployment. Pondering the education of boys, he cautions against privileging any system of thought: 'Let the principles of Aristotle not be principles any more than those of the Stoics or Epicureans. Let this diversity of judgements be set before [the child]; if he can, he will make a choice: if he cannot then he will remain in doubt. Only fools have made up their minds and are certain' (*Essays*, 170). In effect, Montaigne recommends staging opposition as a pedagogical tactic. And it is a tactic that he also employs with his readers. But what has gone largely unnoticed is that purposeful depiction of difference – of alternative ways of ordering human experience – glides easily between the bounds of personal essay and stage play. What Montaigne achieves in 'On cannibals', remarkable though it is, is not fundamentally different from what Shakespeare sometimes achieves in drama: at critical moments in *The Merchant of Venice*, in the debates of *Troilus and Cressida*, in the colliding worlds of *Antony and Cleopatra*. Steven Mullaney has written extensively about the 'rehearsal' of alterity on the Renaissance stage, and I merely add that such rehearsal not only evokes but often merges with the ancient sceptical emphasis on displaying oppositions in the interest of countering dogmatism.[17]

(3) Closely related to the paradigm of opposition is an abiding fascination with the moment of *skepsis*, or judgemental suspension, which is prompted involuntarily by confusing or incompatible appearances. In *All's Well* the Countess refers to the possibility of Helena's love for Bertram as something 'which hung so tott'ring in the balance that I could neither believe nor misdoubt' (1.3.107–9). Here the Pyrrhonian ethos is almost uncannily evoked, but conventional sceptical awareness is also manifest in Banquo's interrogation of the Weird Sisters: 'I'th' name of truth, / Are ye fantastical or that indeed / Which outwardly ye show?' (1.3.50–2). And in *The Tempest*, Gonzalo muses on the seeming presence of Prospero: 'Whether this be / Or be not, I'll not swear' (5.1.124–5).[18] In most dramatic instances, of course, such crises of doubt are quickly resolved: Helena *does* love Bertram; Prospero *is* alive. But sometimes the crisis is interestingly exploited, as when Faustus, confronted with a bloody inscription on his arm, claims that his 'senses are deceived; here's nothing writ'. Doubt becomes denial, only to reverse itself an instant later: 'I see it plain. Here in this place is writ / '*Homo, fuge!*' Yet shall not Faustus fly' (2.1.79–81).[19]

As with the paradigm of opposition, here too we often see a movement from involuntary withholding of judgement to conscious, willing *epochē*. Regarding allegations of miracles, for instance, Montaigne writes that it is wise 'to suspend our judgement, neither believing nor rejecting' (*Essays*, 1165). And he defines *epochē*, the 'sacramental' word of Pyrrhonism, as 'I hold and stir not' (Florio, 451).[20] But Montaigne's restraint – his ability to remain in doubt without hankering for commitment – is remarkable. As we have seen in Gerhard Vossius' distinction between temporary and permanent suspension of judgement, Pyrrhonian agnosticism acquires a generally negative reputation by the early seventeenth century. Charron more often than not conceives of doubt in distinctly instrumental terms; Bacon values doubt mainly as a tool in the service of truth-acquisition. As Hector argues in *Troilus*, 'modest doubt' is 'the tent that searches / To th' bottom of the worst' (2.2.15–17), and a metaphorical understanding of doubt as painful surgical probing is indeed common in Jacobean drama. Cautious and prudential, such doubt at least promises to open our minds to the extent of our misery, if not to explain it. But even before this gloomy instrumentalizing, doubt's value as a step in the direction of truth is often stressed in early modern texts. In Spenser's *Faerie Queene*, after Satyrane informs Paridell of Florimell's death, Paridell responds first by enquiring into the evidentiary basis of the claim and then by vowing to abstain temporarily from belief: 'Yet will I not forsake my forward way, / Till triall doe more certaine truth bewray' (3.8.48–50). And Donne urges his readers to 'doubt wisely', for truth lies at the summit of a great hill: 'he that will / Reach her, about must, and about must go'.[21] Instrumental doubt entails ongoing enquiry, and, as we will see, this latter aspect of scepticism finds intriguing elaboration in a substantial number of early modern writings.

(4) Paridell's response to Satyrane also suggests another and far less philosophical strand of scepticism. What might be called the 'doubting Thomas' paradigm capitalizes on the comparatively shallow conviction that seeing is believing, that eyewitness affirmation resolves matters of dubious allegation. It thus eschews all sense of the potential unreliability of perception, and indeed is less intrinsically sophisticated than many forms of common-sense doubt. None the less it remains a sceptical paradigm because of the frequency with which it appears and, more importantly, the degree to which its successful exploitation depends upon an audience's prior acceptance of human perceptual frailty. When the Emperor demands visual proof of Faustus' magic, he justifies his request by revealing a desire that his eyes 'may be witnesses to confirm what [his] ears have heard' (A.4.1.6–8). Only slightly less naive than Othello's demand for 'ocular proof', this appeal to specular authority is ultimately based on the same unfounded assumption that allows Claudio, in *Much Ado*, to be convinced of Hero's disloyalty.[22] 'If

you dare not trust that you see,' says Don John, 'confess not that you know' (3.2.100–1). And the play spirals suddenly towards tragedy.

The popular prominence of the seeing-is-believing topos finds visual expression in Caravaggio's famous portrait of the apostle Thomas. Depicting the saint with his finger inserted deeply into the wound on Christ's torso, Caravaggio highlights the grotesque quality of Thomas's desire for sensory confirmation.[23] But such desires – alternately absurd, shallow and irrelevant – also condition a good deal of rhetorical calculation in early modern writing, for instance in travel narratives. Richard Hakluyt notes in his *Principal Navigations* (1589–90) that he has been 'ravished in beholding' many curiosities acquired on sea voyages, and the force of his claim lies precisely in its assumed power to dissipate readerly disbelief regarding the accounts presented in his book. Indeed, as François Hartog argues in his study of Herodotus' 'rhetoric of otherness', eyewitness allegation serves as a major guarantor of veracity, even if the potential for deception or misrepresentation is simultaneously transparent.[24] Hamlet's impulse to reprove Horatio thus strikes audiences as entirely sympathetic, even though Horatio himself has earlier remarked that 'I might not this believe / Without the sensible and true avouch / Of mine own eyes' (1.1.54–6). A too quick readiness to assume the full comprehensibility of a given set of phenomena is always reprovable, as Montaigne would be the first to acknowledge.[25] And though the level of complexity is higher, the same fundamental dynamic is activated when Thersites asks whether Troilus will 'swagger himself out on's own eyes' (5.2.142). As audience members we may laugh at this line – we know that Cressida has passed the point of no return – but at the same time Thersites' question cannot dispel the power of Troilus' lament:

> there is a credence in my heart,
> An esperance so obstinately strong,
> That doth invert th'attest of eyes and ears,
> As if those organs had deceptious functions,
> Created only to calumniate.
> Was Cressid here?
>
> (5.2.126–31)

The very activation of the language and ideas of scepticism underlies Troilus' sense that such a facile summing-up as that of Thersites does not and cannot lay to rest the uncertainties so agonizingly conjured earlier in the scene.

(5) More deeply considered than the doubting Thomas paradigm, but essentially a variant of the same set of concerns, is the scepticism revolving specifically around the untrustworthiness of sense-data. This of course is intimately related to the first paradigm I have outlined – that dealing more generally with human frailty – and it is quite often explicitly associated with humanity's postlapsarian condition. But I wish briefly to return to it here, particularly as it coalesces with early modern England's almost obsessive interest in the fault-lines between being and seeming. Katharine Maus has discussed George Hakewill's anecdote about a man's apparent discovery that his neighbour is committing bestiality with a mare – only to find, moments later, that the same neighbour is sound asleep in his bed. As Maus writes, the moral of this story is that the eyes cannot be trusted, although Hakewill ultimately 'seems less interested in the abstract philosophical problem – the possibility that *all* sense impressions might be deceptive – than in the practical difficulties attendant upon the fact that *some* sense impressions are deceptive'.[26] The same shift – from abstract concern to pragmatic response – is repeatedly evident in Renaissance drama. In a speech painfully germane to Posthumous' early behaviour in *Cymbeline*, Imogen observes that 'Our very eyes / Are sometimes like our judgements, blind' (4.2.303–4).[27] And Prospero, late in *The Tempest*, remarks that Antonio and Sebastian 'scarce think / Their eyes do offices of truth' – a suspicion comically seconded by Trinculo, who wonders 'if these be true spies which I wear in my head' (5.1.157–8, 5.1.262).

But nowhere is the misleading potential of sense-data more emphatically foreground than in what I call the 'be and seem' topos, the almost ubiquitous anxiety regarding gaps between external representation and internal truth. A feeling for the complexity of contemporary response to this problem may be suggested by Montaigne's conflicting observations. He marvels at how difficult it is 'to protect oneself from an enemy who is hidden behind the face of the most dutiful friend we have, or to know the inner thoughts of those who surround us'. Yet elsewhere he stresses the frequency with which 'compelling facial movements bear witness to thoughts which we were keeping secret, betraying us to those who are with us' (*Essays*, 145, 115). On the whole, Montaigne inclines to the point of view of *Macbeth*'s Duncan, who claims that 'There's no art / To find the mind's construction in the face' (1.4.11–12).[28] He condemns judgements based on external appearances as 'unbelievably unreliable', adding that 'Others never see you: they surmise about you from uncertain conjectures; they do not see your nature so much as your artifice' (711, 911). And indeed it is artifice that particularly worries Hamlet in his speech on 'the trappings and the suits of woe' (1.2.76–86). Cognizant that interiors and exteriors routinely diverge, Hamlet is less concerned with intentional deception than with the startling supposition that authentic surfaces may *never* be possible. Because he has 'that within which passeth show', he speculates that no combination of 'forms, moods, shows of grief' can ever denote him truly. At the same time, artificial displays of sorrow can clearly function to mislead, and it is Gertrude's implication that he may be employing such tactics that he finds so insulting. Hamlet's exterior, in this case at least, is deceptive not because of but despite his intentions.

We thus feel the enormous attraction of Othello's desire that 'men should be what they seem' (3.3.131), although we know, as Iago and Hamlet know, that since men are *not* we must exercise perpetual vigilance. 'Craft against vice I must apply,' concludes Vincentio in *Measure for Measure* (3.1.497). And a character like *The Faerie Queene*'s Una, who 'did seeme such, as she was' (1.12.8), appears almost ludicrously improbable in the play-worlds to which we grow accustomed through reading Shakespeare and his contemporaries. As *The Sceptick* reminds us, 'I may tell what the outward object seemeth to me, but what it seemeth to other creatures, or whether it be indeed that which it seemeth to me or to any other of them, I know not' (47). To profess to know, and especially to profess unshakable confidence in that knowledge, is the mental predilection lying at the base of the next sceptical paradigm.

(6) The critique of dogmatic pronouncement – of precipitous judgement, intellectual arrogance and credulity in varying forms – is one of the paradigms most closely tied to the ancient sources. *Propeteia*, or rash assertion, is frequently discussed by Sextus (*PH*, 1.20, 2.17–21), and Cicero elaborates the proposition that 'a man must always restrain his rashness' (*Academica*, 1.44–6). Montaigne and Bacon, despite vast differences, both maintain that humans must curb their readiness to pronounce: 'Assertion and stubbornness are express signs of stupidity,' writes the former; the latter stresses that one of the 'peccant humours' of humanity is 'an impatience of doubt, and haste to assertion without due suspension of judgement' (*Essays*, 1220; *Advancement*, 144–7). Overhasty conclusion is frequently staged in Shakespeare – in *Much Ado*, *Othello*, *Lear*, *The Winter's Tale*, *Cymbeline* – but it is also a paramount concern in such diverse plays as *Faustus* and *Mariam*, its epistemic violence presaging a literal counterpart. As

an indicator of explicit awareness of this problem we may cite such instances of judgemental caution as those exhibited by Malcolm upon testing Macduff (4.3.120–1), or by Imogen as she reacts to Iachimo's scandalous allegations about Posthumous:

> If this be true –
> As I have such a heart that both mine ears
> Must not in haste abuse – if it be true,
> How should I be revenged?
>
> (1.6.130–3)

We may think, too, of overt ridicule of the rush to judgement, as in the mockery afforded by *Hamlet* of Polonius' varied diagnoses of the prince.

One of the major forms in which 'hideous rashness' appears in Renaissance drama lies in the syndrome of false generalization. Familiar from Lear's misogynistic rants and Hamlet's brutal treatment of Ophelia, this motif derives power not only from hyperbole's synechdochal relation with madness, but also from an audience's collective recoil in the face of illicit inference.[29] When the disguised Vindice successfully persuades his mother to assist in the prostitution of his sister, his scene-concluding tirade on female depravity contributes crucially to our sense of his mixed audacity and villainy (*Revenger's Tragedy*, 2.1.245–53). Similarly, Mendoza's remark to Pietro in *The Malcontent*, 'I hate all women for 't' (1.7.38), indicts both speaker and listener. I have earlier referred to this generalizing habit as the 'Troilus paradigm', thinking particularly of Troilus' desperate effort not 'to square the general sex / By Cressid's rule' (5.2.138–9), but the tendency manifests itself well beyond the vituperative condemnation of women. *The Changeling*'s Tomazo, for instance, reasons that because he is ignorant of the identity of his brother's murderer, he 'must think all men villains' (5.2.6).[30] And Donne's portrayal of Phrygius depends for its success on readerly recognition that Phrygius' logic is hopelessly flawed. That some churches are impure cannot justify abhorrence of all churches any more than all poetry may be detested because some poems are trite.

Another common manner in which dogmatism is attacked occurs in the interrogation of claims of supernatural causation. In *The Comedy of Errors*, Ephesian sorcery is broached by Antipholus of Syracuse as a likely explanation for the bizarre encounter he has had with his supposed servant Dromio: 'They say this town is full of cozenage, / As nimble jugglers that deceive the eye, / Dark-working sorcerers that change the mind' (1.2.97–9). But the audience knows better, and invocations of preternatural influence are consequently lampooned. Richard Strier has written about this aspect of scepticism in Shakespeare, concentrating on *Lear* and *A Midsummer Night's Dream* as well as *Errors*. His argument is that Shakespeare routinely secularizes attitudes or impulses that can be (and often are) understood as transcendental or providential. Such secularization, he suggests, amounts to a form of scepticism, specifically 'skepticism about supernatural intervention and causation – one of the many sets of attitudes the Renaissance termed "atheism"'.[31] But when Strier argues that it is 'impossible' to read *Errors* as anything but 'totally skeptical' about witchcraft, exorcism and demonic possession, his terminology undergoes a denotative slippage. I do not quarrel with his non-transcendental reading of *Errors*, but rather with the idea that 'total' scepticism amounts to casting doubt in the service of definitive conclusion. I propose, rather, that total scepticism deploys doubt not only towards credulous assumptions but towards rational attempts to dismiss them. As Montaigne writes, to deem something impossible 'is to be rashly presumptuous, boasting that we know the limits of the possible' (*Essays*, 202). And while such a remark raises the old question of whether one can live one's Pyrrhonism, it also suggests that we must not too hastily equate scepticism with sustained ratiocination.

This is a vexed and difficult matter, one that bears more generally on all the paradigms I outline. What I wish to emphasize here is that it is reductive to align Renaissance scepticism exclusively with displays of rational doubt or with thoroughly anti-rational habits of mind. Both are aspects of scepticism, but neither can serve as its be-all and end-all. We may say that Antigonus is a sceptic when he claims that 'Dreams are toys' (3.3.38), and we may think the same about Lady Macbeth when she tells her husband that Banquo's ghost is merely the 'painting of [his] fear': 'When all's done / You look but on a stool' (3.4.60–7). But the plays in which these lines occur insistently place such remarks in ironic perspective. Macbeth himself speaks of 'the pauser, reason' as the respectable impulse that was overrun by 'violent love' when he slaughtered Duncan's grooms (2.3.107–8). And while this is a stipulative and self-serving definition, its plausibility to Macbeth's listeners is indicative of its importance to our understanding of the early modern dynamic between reason and doubt. Macbeth presents reason as intrinsically cautious and wary of precipitation; delay and deliberation are privileged over ineluctable movement towards truth. And Montaigne's example is instructive in this regard. As soon as scepticism becomes exclusively equated with rational doubt, it hardens into a form of overconfidence. The humility of always imagining that something might have escaped reason's scrutiny – that there might be forces at work on whose operations reason has no purchase – is consistently kept alive in the *Essays*. This is why Montaigne's attitude towards reason is difficult to characterize, and why he can maintain a hostile stance towards rational theorizing while exhibiting sympathy towards reasoning in local, practical contexts. He approves of sceptics, he implies, because 'they use their reason for inquiry and debate but never to make choices' (*Apology*, 72).

If we turn to Sextus we find that while strict Pyrrhonism distrusts reason (*PH*, 1.20), it also relies tacitly on the rational view that contradiction poses problems. As Martha Nussbaum notes, sceptics clearly assent to the principle of non-contradiction. And sceptical thought-progressions, as outlined by Sextus, are indeed entirely rational until the too quick (and perhaps counterintuitive) assumption of *isostheneia* – of the equal persuasiveness of conflicting claims or perceptions.[32] At this point the sceptic engages in an over-eager capitulation. It is not so much that reason's operations are overtly condemned as that the sceptic, through a form of humility, supposes either that no criterion may be isolated to aid in the choice between contraries, or that another chain of reasoning might yield another equally persuasive conclusion. These suppositions, not irrational in themselves, none the less prompt detachment from any of the potential conclusions available, and the sceptic suspends judgement. In short, ancient scepticism, especially Sextus' Pyrrhonism, embodies conflicting assumptions about reason that are routinely revived in early modern Europe. And particularly crucial is a sympathy towards anti-dogmatic humility. As I argue more fully below, a significant change gradually manifests itself as rational enquiry becomes overtly embraced as a sceptical practice; this can be seen, for instance, in the Socinian amalgam of doubt, toleration and respect for reason in religious contexts. Still, a powerful sense of intellectual humility remains central to scepticism, and it is this which should prevent us from too quickly assuming that doubt regarding supernatural intervention resolves easily into flat dismissal of such ideas. Strier's secular readings of *Lear* and *A Midsummer Night's Dream* align scepticism too fully with rational critique and hence fail to register the more elusive character of the sceptical outlook which intrigued Montaigne and his English contemporaries. It may be true to say, as Strier does, that in *Lear* Shakespeare creates 'a thoroughly secular world' where ideas of grace and sin function without 'transcendental guarantee' (189). But if Shakespeare does so, and if he means for us to think that our own world is similarly devoid of mystery, then he is being less a sceptic than a dogmatist, for extended rational doubt in the service of definitive conclusion amounts to a species of dogmatism for Renaissance sceptics. My own suspicion is that Shakespeare is posing questions more than answering them, and thereby preserving the sceptical dialectic between rational interrogation and intellectual modesty.

(7) Also closely informed by classical sources is the sceptical paradigm centred on criteria for judgement. Sometimes the validity of an existing criterion is questioned ironically, as when Gratiana asks, 'by what rule should we square our lives, / But by our betters' actions?' (*Revenger's*, 2.1.147–8). Sometimes specific judgements are exposed as illegitimate due to their derivation from interested parties. In *Richard II*, Gaunt laments that 'correction lieth in those hands / Which made the fault that we cannot correct' (2.1.4–5), and in *The Revenger's Tragedy* the Duke suspends the sentencing of his stepson despite the latter's confession of rape (1.2.82). Sometimes no criterion for judgement appears to be available – or no *untainted* criterion – and subsequent action is predicated on its very absence, as in the treatment of incest in *'Tis Pity She's a Whore*. In almost every instance, Sextus' arguments regarding judgemental criteria emerge as strikingly germane to the discussion (*PH*, 1.59–60, 2.14–21). As Montaigne observes, in paraphrasing Sextus' treatment of conflicting sense-data:

> who will be a proper judge of such differences? It is like saying that we could do with a judge who is not bound to either party in our religious strife, who is dispassionate and without prejudice. Among Christians that cannot be. The same applies here: if the judge is old, he cannot judge the sense-impressions of old age, since he is a party to the dispute; so too if he is young; so too if he is well; so too if he is unwell, asleep, or awake. We would need a man exempt from all these qualities, so that, without preconception, he could judge those propositions as matters indifferent to him. On this reckoning we would need a judge such as never was.

If we are to judge, Montaigne concludes, we require an instrument of judgement. But to ascertain the veracity of that instrument ,'we need practical proof; to test that proof we need an instrument. We are going round in circles' (*Apology*, 185).[33]

Scrutinizing judgemental criteria is by no means limited to Montaigne and his kindred spirits among the playwrights of early modern England. In lyrics such as *The Flea* and *The Indifferent*, Donne comically exploits a libertinistic scepticism through his speakers' facile arguments that promiscuous sexuality is legitimated by the absence, or triviality, of existing standards. As Herschel Baker notes, Donne 'rationalizes sexual license on the ground that moral codes have only the sanction of obsolete convention'.[34] This is *not* genuine Pyrrhonism, and Donne would have known it; conventional morality in fact holds powerful sway over Pyrrhonian conceptions of behaviour due to its status as a *de facto* criterion (*PH*, 1.17–24). But we are dealing here with tendentious appropriations as well as with more balanced deployments of ancient sceptical doubt. The condition of the judge who is 'a party to the dispute' exercises an enduring fascination for English Renaissance writers. Webster's Ferdinand, reacting to Bosola's blunt claim that the Duchess of Malfi was murdered on Ferdinand's own authority, provides a study in prevarication:

> Was I her judge?
> Did any ceremonial form of law
> Doom her to not-being? Did a complete jury
> Deliver her conviction up i'th' court?
> Where shalt thou find this judgement registered
> Unless in hell? See: like a bloody fool
> Thou'st forfeited thy life, and thou shalt die for't.

To which Bosola icily replies, 'The office of justice is perverted quite / When one thief hangs another' (4.2.291–9). The sceptical abyss into which Bosola subsequently descends derives no small part of its vertiginous nature from the doubts regarding judgemental criteria generated by the earlier action of the play.

* * *

These, then, are the principal paradigms of scepticism's literary reception in early modern Britain: the most common forms in which the philosophical scepticism of antiquity revives itself in literary contexts. The paradigms are anything but mutually exclusive; they overlap and interpenetrate a good deal. It is none the less useful to delineate them so as to make clear their relative emphases. And lest we think it solely in dramatic works that these paradigms routinely surface, let me provide one final poetic example before offering a few closing remarks about the practical applications and implicit values emerging from scepticism's literary embodiment.

Early in Book One of *The Faerie Queene*, the Redcross Knight and Fidessa pause to rest beneath 'two goodly trees'.[35] Unaware that his companion is actually the 'cruell witch' Duessa, Redcross plucks a bough and begins to weave a garland for her. But the bough is spotted with drops of blood, and the tree from which it came suddenly shrieks, urging Redcross to flee if he hopes to avoid misfortune. Redcross, 'doubting much his sence', demands an explanation. The talking tree then reveals that his name is Fradubio ('in doubt' or 'brother doubt') and that he was once a knight but has been metamorphosed by a sorceress. In a narrative closely mirroring the recent adventures of Redcross, Fradubio explains that long ago he and his 'gentle Lady' Fraelissa encountered another knight and lady; that, upon being challenged, he slew his opposite and acquired the second lady as a martial prize; and that he then, 'in doubt', compared the women to determine which 'in beauties glorie did exceede'. At first they appeared equally lovely. But Duessa (the second lady), observing the 'doubtfull ballaunce equally to sway', used magic to raise a fog and dim Fraelissa's 'shining ray'. Fradubio succumbed to the illusion: viewing Fraelissa's 'loathly visage' with disdain, he decided to kill her, but Duessa stayed his 'wrathfull hand'. He thus left Fraelissa alone and forlorn, and she 'turnd to treen mould'.

Later, of course, Fradubio recognized his errors. He discovered that his new companion was in fact the 'divelish hag' Duessa, and for his pains he was transformed into the tree with whom Redcross now converses. For his part – and true to form – Redcross fails to note any resemblances between Fradubio's story and his own. Accompanied by the same false beauty who ruined Fradubio's life, blithely trusting appearances just as Fradubio did, he has abandoned Una as readily as Fradubio abandoned Fraelissa, and he is thus exposed as Fradubio's brother in doubt. For Spenser, the central emphasis here lies on doubt as faltering of faith: neither Redcross nor Fradubio should have wavered in their trust and commitment. But inseparable from such condemnation is praise of more localized doubt. Redcross has yet to learn that seeming is not always being, that appearances sometimes deceive, that part of knowing is knowing *when* to doubt. And the poetic sequence by which Spenser makes this evident reveals with startling clarity how thoroughly the paradigms of scepticism's literary reception permeate the discursive habits even of a poet little given to sceptical meditation. Initially emphasizing the ease with which sense-data may mislead, Spenser progresses to the moment of *skepsis*, or involuntary doubt, prompted by conflicting or equally convincing appearances. He then demonstrates how quickly such equipollence, or *isostheneia*, may resolve into what Charron calls 'precipitation of judgement': 'Eftsoones,' says Fradubio, 'I thought her such, as [Duessa] me told.' It is certainly the case that Redcross must learn to recognize truth and never doubt it. But he must also learn when to exercise caution, for Faerie Land has its white devils, just as Jacobean tragedy does.[36] Spenser is no sceptic, but a number of the premises and values associated with ancient scepticism resonate profoundly in his poetry. As he asks, quite rhetorically, elsewhere in *The Faerie Queene*, 'Why then should witlesse man so much misweene / That nothing is, but that which he hath seene?' (2.Prologue.3).

Openness to the *unseen* is central to scepticism, both because what we see may deceive us and because what we do not see may none the less exist. And this brings me to a few concluding observations about scepticism's early modern reception. The first and most important of these, as I have intimated, is that sustained enquiry and truth-seeking play a greater role in Renaissance doubt than they do in its classical precedents. The *zetetic* mode of scepticism is certainly broached by Sextus, but the prevailing impression left by his *Outlines* is that knowledge is probably unattainable, that we should resign ourselves to uncertainty since the method of opposition continually prompts new withholdings of judgement on new matters of dispute. Indeed, Pyrrhonism understood this way seems rather close to Academic scepticism, given the latter's emphasis on *acatalepsia*. Moreover, since Pyrrhonian *ataraxia* is attained through judgemental suspension rather than through continued enquiry, one can see why abandoning the search gradually acquires a privileged, if unofficial, status within the mental outlook of committed Pyrrhonists. This is true both in Sextus' writings and in those of certain critics of scepticism, among them Bacon. Technically, of course, continued enquiry and judgemental suspension are *not* presented as mutually exclusive, though perhaps the one is generally subordinated to the other. Cicero certainly emphasizes the search: he states in the *Academica* that while Stoics and sceptics both value investigation, the former pursue it 'with the intention of believing and affirming', whereas the latter resolve to eschew 'rash opinions' and to think themselves fortunate if they discover 'that which bears a likeness to truth' (2.128). Augustine too offers praise for investigation, allowing Licentius to opine that 'man can reach the happy life with the mere search for truth, even if he never finds it' (*Academicos*, 1.5–11). It is little surprise, then, that in Montaigne the *zetetic* mode emerges so forcefully: 'I am seeking the truth, not laying it down'; 'this world is but a school of inquiry' (*Essays*, 355, 1051).[37] And the example of Socrates powerfully reinforces his point. Continually questioning, Socrates acquires *de facto* status as a sceptic in Montaigne's philosophical genealogy: 'he is never satisfied and never reaches any conclusion' (*Apology*, 77). Constant doubt is thus valorized for Montaigne, and to the extent that doubt is viewed as rational enquiry, rationality itself is tacitly praised through the exercise of doubt. Scepticism's *zetetic* dimension entails a deepening respect for reason even as it retains a sense that reason can also lead to contradiction or reify its creations. And this loose conflation of pro- and anti-rational attitudes – evident, for instance, in scepticism's intersections with Socinian thought – increasingly characterizes the sceptical outlook in early modern Europe. The intellectual movement that has been termed the 'broad Socinian tradition', beginning with Erasmus and extending through Castellio, Acontius, Mornay and Grotius, would have regarded as entirely congenial Thomas Stanley's 1659 translation of the opening of Sextus' *Outlines*. 'The *Sceptick* Institution', writes Stanley, 'is called also *Zetetick* (*Inquisitive*) from the act of enquiring; *Ephectick* (*suspensive*) from the affection rais'd by enquiry after things; *Aporetick* (*dubitative*) either from doubting of, and seeking after all things, or from being in doubt whether to assent or deny; *Pyrrhonian*, in as much as *Pyrrho* delivered it to us more substantially and cleerly than those before him' (7–8).[38]

Montaigne's invocation of Socrates also reminds us that it is Cicero's rather than Sextus' sense of scepticism's genealogy that prevails in Renaissance Europe. The *Academica* tells us that the general obscurity of things 'led Socrates to a confession of ignorance, as also previously his predecessors Democritus, Anaxagoras, Empedocles, and almost all the old philosophers' (1.44). Major pre-Socratic figures are thereby drawn into the fold, and many later thinkers, especially Bacon, are attracted to the resulting historical construction.[39] Indeed, Renaissance writers frequently conjoin Socratic ignorance and Pyrrhonian uncertainty, the consequence being a relatively uncritical synthesis of Academic scepticism and Pyrrhonism. Montaigne knows the difference, but he still finds it useful to declare that 'two out of the three generic schools of Philosophy make an express profession of doubt and ignorance' (*Apology*, 73–4). As for the targets of that doubt, it is worth stressing that while pre-Cartesian thinkers generally restrict themselves to 'property scepticism' – doubts about the *properties* of things rather than about those things' very existence – it is none the less the case that more radical doubt also manifests itself. Montaigne and Mede exhibit flashes of external world scepticism well before Descartes; Mornay reveals in religious polemic, as Aaron and Tamburlaine do in drama, that God's reality may be suspected.[40] And once the operations of doubt extend to pure existence as well as to correspondences between surface and interior, it is no large step to various forms of religious scepticism. What Stephen Greenblatt has termed the 'Machiavellian hypothesis' is frequently sounded in early modern writing. 'I count religion but a childish toy,' asserts Machiavel in *The Jew of Malta* (Prologue); to which Flamineo adds, 'Religion! O how it is commeddled with policy' (*White Devil*, 3.3.34).[41] The idea that religion was introduced to keep humanity in check can also metamorphose into forms of denial, as in Nashe's equation of sceptics and atheists: 'soulebenummed' unbelievers, he says, 'followe the Pironicks, whose position it is that there is no Hel or misery but opinion'.[42] *Lear*'s Edmund also comes to mind. Rejecting the ideological assumptions of his culture, he embraces a brutal naturalism which validates his desires, and in this he is less a sceptic than a dogmatist – a dogmatist whose beliefs stand diametrically opposed to those of his father and king.[43]

The refusal to believe, or the willingness to *disbelieve*, can sometimes generate efforts at recuperation or containment. Hartog has discussed this phenomenon, claiming that Herodotus, by persistently alluding to the Greeks' rejection of certain historical allegations, buttresses his narrative's 'ability to elicit belief'. Greenblatt concentrates on a similar trajectory in his reading of *Lear*, suggesting that the play recuperates what it seems to dismiss, validating 'a hope [for redemption] even while literally rejecting it'.[44] And the notion that disbelief can somehow be redeemed – brought back to its senses, so to speak, through its own extremity or *lack* of sense – seems crucially relevant to the early modern sceptical emphasis on conformity and quietude. With philosophical roots in Sextus (*PH*, 1.17–24, 1.226–37), this tendency surfaces repeatedly in Montaigne, above all in his resistance to legal and social reform: 'There is no system so bad (provided it be old and durable) as not to be better than change and innovation' (*Essays*, 745).[45] From here it is only a short step to the fideistic embrace of the Roman Church. Agrippa and Gianfrancesco Pico are perhaps Montaigne's most interesting forebears in this regard, but with Montaigne the pattern is particularly intriguing due to its transparent ties to sceptical epistemology. Just when Montaigne seems to have practised an exemplary suspension of judgement, he abandons the sceptical mode and construes Christian belief as inscription by divine grace; what appears to be a rush to judgement is reconceived as Pyrrhonian conformity.[46] We thus witness a movement into what Sextus would surely have considered unfounded dogmatism, but at the same time we see clear evidence of intellectual indebtedness to sceptical habits of mind. And a homologous thought structure, if not an identical conclusion, is at times granted stunning fictional transformation. Marlowe's Faustus gluts the longing of his heart's desire (A.5.1.83), but his choice, as I argue in chapter 5, repeatedly presupposes an acute consciousness of corrosive doubt. Faustus hopes to evade this doubt; instead, he continually rediscovers it.

Lars Engle has observed that 'the kind of complex and socially-specific exploration of problems we get in an essay by Montaigne or a play by Shakespeare ceases [by the 1630s] to be a model for intellectually serious investigation'. This may be an exaggeration, relying as it does on Toulmin's emphatic separation of tolerant humanism from hard-nosed rationalism, but it remains a valuable insight.[47] And one of the principal reasons for this is that the essayistic or dramatic exploration of which Engle speaks is routinely informed by the varied paradigms of scepticism that I have outlined. Emerging from these paradigms, though by no means identical with them, is a loose set of sceptical values – values more often implicitly than explicitly endorsed, and, in keeping with the Pyrrhonian ethos, seldom if ever advanced as dogmatic tenets. I conclude this chapter by sketching the chief among these values.

Heuristic or propaedeutic doubt is one of them: the sense, in other words, that it is intellectually respectable, indeed desirable, to commence any investigation by placing in question all authorities, preconceptions and popularly received verities. Such doubt may not be permanent – for Bacon it is expressly conceived as preliminary and instrumental – but its initial value is difficult to overestimate. Coeval with this doubt, and scarcely separable from it, is a judgemental suspension that makes room for, and is often prompted by, an open-minded consideration of opposing perspectives and arguments. Being 'disengaged on either side', as Lucy Cary writes, conduces admirably to a writer's potential for being heard and considered persuasive. 'Too speedy resolvers', on the other hand, are harshly censured, and not only by Cary, but by Montaigne, Bacon and scores of others. As early as 1565 Acontius devotes substantial attention to the condemnation of rash assertion and judgement.[48] Hence affirmation and denial are both placed under scrutiny: not rejected, but carefully distinguished from the withholding of assent *and* dissent that gradually comes to be understood as an invaluable prior stage. 'The Sceptick', we remember, 'doth neither affirm nor deny any position, but doubteth of it' (42).

Still more fundamental as sceptical values are the modesty, diffidence and intellectual humility encouraged by sustained recognition of the limitations of human reason and perception. Reason is by no means utterly condemned, as we have seen with Montaigne; indeed its stock rises sharply as the seventeenth century unfolds. But its operations are none the less questioned and, at times, humiliated within the sceptical outlook. Partly resulting from the mockery of intellectual hubris is an exhilarating though chastened sense of the liberating possibilities of unfettered enquiry. What Schmitt has termed the *'libertas philosophandi* aspect' of Academicism is probably given its most concise expression by Omer Talon in his 1550 commentary on Cicero, which stresses the independence, patience and intellectual modesty of the Academics.[49] A paramount sceptical value, then, and a value thoroughly consonant with ancient scepticism's status not so much as a philosophical position as an *outlook*, a way of life, is freedom of thought and expression: open enquiry unencumbered by authoritative pronouncement or dogmatic presupposition and bias. And such freedom, despite the vagaries of early modern censorship, patronage, printing practice and theatrical collaboration, is frequently apparent in the writings of Shakespeare and his contemporaries. I have attempted in this chapter to direct attention to the specific distortions, appropriations and strategic deployments of Pyrrhonian and Academic scepticism that reveal themselves in such writings. I will close by saying that if scepticism's greatest value lies in its potential for combating dogmatism and fanaticism – in its implicit promotion of tolerance, humility and open-minded enquiry – then the ways in which it was received and granted literary expression in early modern Britain deserve our continued close attention.[50]

# 5
# Casting Doubt in *Doctor Faustus*

> He that casts all doubts shall never be resolved.
> English Renaissance proverb

It will come as news to no one that *Doctor Faustus* can be and has been deemed a sceptical play. More than a century ago, J. R. Green characterized Marlowe's outlook as a 'daring scepticism' and claimed that *Faustus* was 'the first dramatic attempt to touch the great problem of the relations of man to the unseen world, to paint the power of doubt in a temper leavened with superstition'. Fifty years later Una Ellis-Fermor called *Faustus* 'perhaps the most notable Satanic play in literature'.[1] And the varied testimony of Marlowe's contemporaries – Robert Greene, Richard Baines and Thomas Kyd among them – reveals that both the man and his writings could be considered iconoclastic and profoundly irreverent: both susceptible to charges of 'monstruous opinions', 'hereticall conceipts', even 'diabolical atheism'.[2] True, the circumstances in which these allegations were sometimes made force us to question their accuracy. Yet there still exists an extraordinary congruence of contemporary attitude about Marlowe – about what we might call his scepticism. But what are the sceptical paradigms inherent in Marlowe's great tragedy? How can we argue that the play exhibits pervasive engagement with early modern doubt?

As a means of approaching these questions, I would like briefly to examine the enabling premises and methodological strategies of the best-known current commentator on scepticism and English tragedy: Stanley Cavell. While Cavell has not written on Marlowe – indeed, his dramatic criticism has focused almost exclusively on Shakespeare – it is none the less worth our while to attend to his programmatic statements regarding what he calls the 'skeptical problematic'.[3] He claims,

144

for instance, that Shakespeare 'engage[s] the depth of the philosophical preoccupations of his culture', adding that 'the advent of skepticism as manifested in Descartes' *Meditations* is already in full
existence' in Shakespearean tragedy of the early seventeenth century
(2–3). But these two statements would appear to be incompatible, for
while it may be true that Shakespeare anticipates the hyperbolic doubt
of Descartes, it is anachronistic to characterize that doubt as a 'philosophical preoccupation' of the first decade of Britain's seventeenth
century. Not that doubt did not exist or that epistemological questions were not asked – far from it. But, as we have seen, the forms of
philosophical scepticism to which Shakespeare and Marlowe could
have been exposed were principally those derived from the Pyrrhonian and Academic orientations of antiquity. Indeed, Marlowe quotes,
in the 1604 quarto of *Faustus*, a phrase lifted from Sextus Empiricus'
*Against the Mathematicians*, a work readily available at Cambridge
during Marlowe's student days and also circulating in London.[4] And
Montaigne, Sextus' principal champion in the late sixteenth century,
was indisputably read by Shakespeare. Hence Cavell's implicit diminu-
tion of the influence of Montaigne – not to mention his neglect of
many other figures through whose writings classical scepticism
was channelled into early modern intellectual life – is fundamentally
ahistorical.[5]

Cavell claims that the 'skeptical problematic' he envisages 'is given
its philosophical refinement in Descartes' way of raising the questions
of God's existence and the immortality of the soul'. He goes on to
assert that the 'issue' posed in Shakespeare's tragedies is not, 'as with
earlier skepticism, how to conduct oneself best in an uncertain world;
the issue suggested is how to live at all in a groundless world. Our skepticism is a function of our now illimitable desire' (3). Several responses
are in order. First, while Cavell's characterizations of Pyrrhonian and
modern scepticism are essentially accurate, it remains true that
Descartes is ultimately less remarkable for his doubt than for the edifice
of certainty his doubt enables him to build. Descartes embraces 'a
groundless world' only to reject it; his scepticism, however radical, is
always an instrument in the discovery of truth, and, when coupled
with an appropriate method of investigation, allows for the perpetua-
tion of dogmatic philosophy. As Gail Fine observes, we must 'bear
in mind that Descartes is *not* a skeptic. On the contrary, he thinks he
is the first to have offered a satisfactory reply to skepticism.'[6] Second,
Pyrrhonism has the *potential* to be as radical a form of doubt as
that employed by Descartes; witness, for instance, Sextus' trenchant

interrogation of the existence of gods (*PH*, 3.2–12). And while no one in pre-Cartesian Europe fully exploits Pyrrhonism's inherent potential for doubt, this in itself does not invalidate the possibility. Late in his *Apology*, for instance, Montaigne moves briefly beyond property scepticism and lays the groundwork for questioning the existence of the external world – and this despite Cavell's allegation that such questioning in philosophical tracts begins only with Descartes.[7] Moreover, the comments on scepticism in Mornay's *Woorke concerning the trewnesse of the Christian Religion* indicate the extent to which Pyrrhonism's capacity for rendering uncertain the existence of the Judeo-Christian God could trouble late sixteenth-century intellectuals. Mornay writes, in the 1587 translation prepared by Sidney and Golding, that in antiquity '[t]here were indeede a kinde of Philosophers called Scepticks, which did rather suspend their Judgement concerning the Godhead, then call it in question ... . these folke say at a worde for all, how shall wee beleeve that there is a God, sith we see him not?' (12). Mornay attempts to render scepticism innocuous by suggesting that its interrogation of God's existence amounts merely to the doubting Thomas topos: that we forgo belief until we see, demanding 'ocular proof'. But he can do this only by occluding Pyrrhonism's potent considerations of the criteria by which judgements are levelled, considerations widely dispersed through Sextus and sharply noted by Montaigne (*PH*, 1.21–4, 2.14–79; *Apology*, 185–6). And Mornay's frequent reliance, elsewhere in his book, on standard tactics of sceptical argumentation suggests the extent to which his customary habits of thought are inflected by familiarity with Pyrrhonism's basic attitudes (243–8, 256–7). Indeed, Mornay explicitly acknowledges the value of open-minded enquiry when he writes that 'foresetled opinions do bring in bondage the reason of them that have best wits; wheras notwithstanding, it belongeth not to the will to overrule the wit, but to the wit to guide the will' (sig. ***iir).

Mornay's position *vis-à-vis* scepticism is thus complex: like most devout sixteenth-century Christians, Protestant or Catholic, he sees radical Pyrrhonian attitudes as misguided, even laughable, but he is simultaneously conscious of the inherent potency of sceptical objections. Indeed, the time he devotes to rejecting, ridiculing and (occasionally) deploying them indicates their formative power in his outlook as a religious polemicist. And Mornay was widely read in England: the Sidney-Golding translation was reprinted in 1592, 1604 and 1617, and many contemporaries studied it, among them John Florio, Fulke Greville, Sir John Davies, William Chillingworth and

John Earle – each of whom played a role in the history of scepticism's reception in Tudor/Stuart Britain.

In short, allegations such as Cavell's about Pyrrhonism's intrinsic weakness as a means of investigating metaphysical questions have tended towards exaggeration; they have had more to do with explicit early modern deployments of sceptical thought than with the implicit unease about scepticism we may infer from the incessant stream of early modern refutations. From 1562 forward, after all, European intellectuals had ready access – thanks to Henri Estienne's Latin translation of the *Outlines* – to Sextus' concise presentation of Pyrrhonian thought, where scepticism is defined as 'an ability to set out oppositions among things which appear and are thought of in any way at all, an ability by which, because of the equipollence (*isostheneia*) in the opposed objects and accounts, we come first to suspension of judgement (*epochē*) and afterwards to tranquillity (*ataraxia*)'.[8] They had access, in short, to a closely argued treatise offering the position that all mental apprehensions – perceptions, memories, ratiocinations, judgements, beliefs – are subject to doubt, and specifically to the sort of doubt generated by the technique of opposition, which according to Sextus leads to the impasse of equal persuasiveness. Thus, despite Pyrrhonism's advocacy of judgemental suspension and subsequent quietude, the rupture between ancient and modern scepticism is not as severe as it is sometimes made out to be – a fact which indirectly strengthens Cavell's case, though it diminishes his sense of Shakespeare's prescience.[9] But when Cavell adds that 'skepticism is a function of our now illimitable desire', he severs himself irrecoverably from classical scepticism. Desire is presupposed here, functioning as a *given* in this essentially Freudian formulation, and a 'groundless world' – a world deprived of the 'assurance' of God's existence and providential supervision – allows desire to be 'illimitable'. Scepticism, then, becomes a 'function' or 'expression' of desire, a consequence of a prior discovery, and it manifests itself as a 'banishment of the world' (5). Moreover, scepticism for Cavell is not merely doubt, but doubt coupled with denial and disappointment – a supposition of the worst.

Yet if there is anything we can say with accuracy about epistemological discussion in Shakespeare's day, it is that doubt is sharply distinguished from both assent and dissent. 'The Sceptick', after all, 'doth neither affirm nor deny any position, but doubteth of it'; he is thus 'more contentious then eyther the Dogmatique which affirmes, or Academique which denyes'.[10] And in the 1593 testament on Marlowe's 'damnable judgment of religion', Richard Baines claims that Marlowe 'quoted contrarieties out of the Scripture' – an allegation which, even if false, shows that Baines knew the subversive potential of the Pyrrhonian tactic of establishing a clash of authoritative opinion.[11] Clearly, the scepticism which Marlowe and Shakespeare can reasonably be supposed to have encountered – scepticism derivative from Pyrrhonism and its Academic incarnations, thoroughly laid out by Sextus and Cicero, and channelled through Diogenes Laertius, Galen, Augustine, Erasmus, Gianfrancesco Pico, Montaigne and others – was committed not only to suspension of judgement in the face of diverse opinion, but to careful discrimination between various states of cognition. It was an antidote rather than a substitute for dogmatism, and it promoted the avoidance of rash judgement and a heightened sensitivity to epistemological questions, distinctions and anxieties. 'The profession of the Phyrrhonians', writes Montaigne, 'is ever to waver, to doubt and to enquire; never to be assured of anything, nor to take any warrant of himself' (Florio, 449).

Still, in spite of all this, it would seem that Cavell's understanding of scepticism might be remarkably fruitful for a reading of *Doctor Faustus* – more fruitful, perhaps, than for most of Shakespeare's tragedies. For what character in Renaissance drama better exemplifies desire and appetitiveness than Faustus? What character more thoroughly banishes the world in order to replace it with the solipsistic trappings of his fantasy – a fantasy that 'will receive no object', but 'ruminates on necromantic skill' (1.1.106–7)? None the less, I argue that despite this apparent consonance of Marlowe's play and Cavell's scepticism, *Faustus* in fact reveals a more complex interaction of doubt and desire, a paradoxical reciprocity between the two that hints, in my view, at genuine 'philosophical preoccupations' of the culture in which Marlowe and Shakespeare lived. For common to the quartos of 1604 (the 'A-text') and 1616 (the 'B-text'), and despite their significant differences, is a series of cyclical trajectories wherein Faustus' habit of casting doubt is preempted by an experience of euphoric ravishment – ravishment that yields in turn to new casting of doubt.[12] Faustus' desire to be resolved 'of all ambiguities' (1.1.82) is frequently expressed and frequently satisfied during the play, its representation often marked by sexual metaphor. But, appropriately enough, the resolution figured as sexual consummation only engenders new ambiguities.[13] Like the planets about which Faustus enquires, doubt and desire exhibit a 'double motion' (2.3.51); their forward and backward movements serve as a means of depicting Faustus' psychomachia. Indeed, to draw on another of the play's astronomical metaphors, desire and doubt are 'mutually folded in each others' orb' (2.3.39), locked in a symbiotic but incestuous embrace. Marlowe thereby explores both the genesis of doubt and the relation of doubt to belief, two cynosures of epistemological investigation in early modern Europe, and authentic preoccupations of intellectual life in Marlowe and Shakespeare's England.

Consider the ways in which familiar, distinctly Faustian attitudes habitually succeed one another. The cavalier dismissal of conventional truth so prominent early in the play, and embedded in such claims as 'This word "damnation" terrifies not [me]', gives way first to involuntary casting of doubt, as in 'Was not that Lucifer an angel once?', and then to ravished contemplation:

> Now that I have obtained what I desire,
> I'll live in speculation of this art
> Till Mephistopheles return again.
> (1.3.60–6, 1.3.114–16)[14]

Later, when doubts merge more fully with what the *English Faust Book* calls 'godly motions' (112), and when resolution of ambiguity becomes almost indistinguishable from presumption of damnation, Faustus undergoes still more rapid shifts of mind. 'What art thou', he asks himself, 'but a man condemned to die?' Yet within four lines he adds, 'Tush! Christ did call the thief upon the cross; / Then rest thee, Faustus, quiet in conceit' (4.1.139–44). In this latter and astonishingly suggestive line, the 'conceit' to which Faustus proposes to yield is the converse of the 'speculation' to which he earlier inclined, yet still a mental state tinged with sexual innuendo. Indeed, the 'unjust presumption' of which Faustus later accuses himself (5.1.71) is presumption only from the demonic perspective. We thus witness a series of Satanic inversions as the play progresses – inversions which steer our attention towards the sharp distinctions among Faustus' mental dispositions.

If Faustus' cavalier rejection of dogma is concentrated in the play's first two acts, and his presumptuous (though sympathetic) self-condemnation in the last three, his wavering is distributed throughout. Often expressed interrogatively, it serves as the basis for some of the play's most memorable passages: 'What might the staying of my blood portend?' (2.1.64); 'Why streams it not, that I may write afresh?' (2.1.66); 'Be I a devil, yet God may pity me' (2.3.15); 'See, see where Christ's blood streams in the firmament! / One drop would save my soul, half a drop' (5.2.78–9). The very presence of the Good and Evil Angels can be read not only as an externalization of Faustus' cerebral discord, but as a manifestation of the sceptic's experience of opposition – the mutually exclusive testimony so heavily stressed by Sextus, Montaigne and others.[15] And if Faustus' customary response to such opposition is not to suspend judgement in Pyrrhonian fashion, but to 'extinguish clean / These thoughts' and 'glut the longing of [his] heart's desire' (5.1.83–6), he is scarcely alone in early modern Europe.[16] From a strict Pyrrhonian perspective, his choice appears no more aberrant than Montaigne's fideistic embrace of the Roman Church.[17] Fictional character and historical personage both participate in a key vector of the standard Pyrrhonian trajectory, only to abandon it in what serves, during the sixteenth century, as a prominent paradigm in the appropriation of ancient scepticism: a rush to judgement reconfigured as the inevitable outcome of an experience of conflicting opinion.

But perhaps the best example of the succession and interpenetration of characteristic Faustian attitudes may be found in the soliloquy that begins act 2:

> Now, Faustus, must thou needs be damned,
> And canst thou not be saved.
> What boots it then to think of God or heaven?
> Away with such vain fancies and despair!
> Despair in God and trust in Beelzebub.
> Now go not backward. No, Faustus, be resolute.
> Why waverest thou? O, something soundeth in mine ears:
> 'Abjure this magic, turn to God again!'
> Ay, and Faustus will turn to God again.
> To God? He loves thee not.
> The God thou servest is thine own appetite,
> Wherein is fixed the love of Beelzebub.
> To him I'll build an altar and a church,
> And offer lukewarm blood of new-born babes.
>
> (2.1.1–14)

The first six-and-a-half lines of this speech employ the rhetorical technique of second-person self-address, a technique on which Marlowe frequently relies, particularly in speeches where emphasis is placed on Faustus' inner turmoil. And while I agree with David Bevington, Michael Keefer, W. W. Greg and other editors that the question mark

at the end of line 2 in the A-text is probably intended not as an interrogative but as an exclamation point (thereby contributing to the
emphatic statement of Faustus' present condition), even if the mark
indicates interrogation, the resulting rhetorical question only adds to
the development of the speaker's persona.[18] It is a persona characterized by confidence, keen observation, frequent resort to the imperative
mood and, above all, presumption. He presumes to know Faustus' state
of imminent and irrevocable damnation, and thereby constructs a
superficially logical critique of Faustus' tendency to cast doubts, to turn
his thoughts towards heaven: 'What boots it then to think of God?'
This is followed by the peremptory 'Away with such vain fancies and
despair! / Despair in God and trust in Beelzebub' – a command making
it clear that within the implied mental world of this persona, thoughts
of God are mere 'fantasies' when conceived by an abandoned soul and
should be replaced with acts of 'trust': specifically, trust in demonic
beings such as Beelzebub, who, like Mephistopheles and Lucifer – but
unlike God and Christ – do in fact appear during the play.[19] Unstated
but implicit is the understanding that it *does* 'boot' – it does avail – to
think of and trust in demons. Moreover, such thoughts and trust are
metaphorically associated with forward movement, unlike the wavering and potential backsliding associated with the mind that turns
towards God.[20]

Midway through line 7, and responding to the question, a first-
person voice emerges – 'something soundeth in mine ears' – and in
line 8 this 'something' is represented in still another voice, a terse,
disembodied voice cast in the imperative: 'Abjure this magic, turn
to God again!' In line 9 the first-person voice returns, this time
speaking in the future tense: 'Ay, and Faustus will turn to God
again.' As the first indication of resolve and fixed purpose in the
soliloquy, this line stands out dramatically, demanding comparison
with the second such moment of resolve, that found in lines 13–14.
But the line is also tainted. Despite its mood of compliance and
humility, despite its presentation of a 'godly motion', it substitutes
the protagonist's name for the expected first-person pronoun. In
short, the line has been infiltrated by the second-person voice's
habit of self-address, and the stated resolve is subtly undermined.
We have a foreshadowing of disaster.

In line 10 the second-person voice reassumes control and, with characteristic presumption, informs the voice of line 9 that God 'loves thee
not'. Lines 11–12 follow up this assertion by transforming, through
mere allegation, a partial truth into an unqualified truth: 'The God

thou servest is thine own appetite, / Wherein is fixed the love of Beelzebub.' The former admonition to 'trust in Beelzebub' has metamorphosed into an affirmation that the first-person Faustus has a fixed 'love' of this devil. And the affirmation is tacitly assented to in lines 13–14, even though the lines can be read with equal legitimacy as emanating from the first- *or* the second-person Faustus. The use of the first-person pronoun in line 13 suggests the former possibility, and certainly this reading is attractive for the additional reason that, as in line 9, we encounter the future tense, this time in a defiant and grotesque resolution to 'build an altar' and 'offer lukewarm blood of new-born babes'. But it may be that this is rather the second-person Faustus, appropriating the first-person pronoun in an attempt to achieve a rhetorical integration of the self that is so evidently divided throughout the speech. If this is the case, then the pronoun appropriation we witness here mirrors the infiltration of self-address we saw in line 9. Either way, a clear parallel is drawn to line 9, and in retrospect we can see that both resolves might be characterized as 'vain fancies' – fantasies of future action that cannot possibly ensue as long as Faustus endures the inner conflict here depicted. On the one hand, Faustus desires an intimacy with God that can never be achieved in conjunction with the second-person voice's presumption. On the other hand, he seeks a defiant and definitive rejection of God that can never occur as long as the first-person voice is able to conceive the words of line 8: 'Abjure this magic, turn to God again!' Indeed, line 14's gruesome resolve to slaughter infants may serve, additionally, as a metaphorical attempt to bleed out the vitality of such cunning cerebral births as those of lines 8–9. But the attempt is futile, for as the Prologue has informed us, Faustus is 'swoll'n with cunning of a self-conceit': pregnant with such cunning and able to conceive it, and deliver it, time and again.[21]

Faustus, then, cannot help but engender 'godly motions'. And when he assures himself, a moment later, 'Thou art safe; / Cast no more doubts' (2.1.25–6), he merely stipulates a condition of psychic stasis that has already been and will continue to be contradicted by his behaviour. He engages, that is, in magical thinking, assuming a causal relation between speech and reality, hoping thereby to stave off his implicit recognition that from the Satanic point of view, casting doubt is dangerous: it amounts to 'unjust presumption'. But inseparable from this recognition is the idea that doubting – wavering – is valuable, valuable precisely because it functions as temporary detachment from dogmatic positions, thus enabling the possibility of change, and of growth. One of the best expressions of this idea in early modern drama may be found in Elizabeth Cary's *Tragedy of Mariam*, composed perhaps a decade and a half after Marlowe's death. There, in the Chorus concluding act 2, we encounter a sustained critique of partiality in judgement:

> Our ears and hearts are apt to hold for good
> That we ourselves do most desire to be:
> And then we drown objections in the flood
> Of partiality, 'tis that we see
> > That makes false rumours long with credit pass'd,
> > Though they like rumours must conclude at last.
> The greatest part of us, prejudicate,
> With wishing Herod's death do hold it true:
> The being once deluded doth not bate
> The credit to a better likelihood due.
> > Those few that wish it not, the multitude
> > Do carry headlong, so they doubts conclude.
> > > (2.4.413–24)

Desire, in short, curtails doubt; the wavering that can lead to truth, hence to growth, is usually displaced by the precipitous rush to judgement practised by the sort of people that Cary's daughter calls 'too speedy resolvers'.[22] And Faustus, of course, is one of these. But Marlowe makes it clear that the ravishment of resolution is always only temporary. Casting doubt is as fundamental to Faustus as resolving ambiguity; it seems a natural outgrowth or consequence of resolution and perhaps points to the ultimately unsatisfactory stasis of dogmatic conclusion.[23]

Marlowe's tragedy thus offers a sceptical commentary on the human propensity for the static, the preference for *being* over *becoming*. Faustus wants to perform miracles, to do the wondrous, to transcend human frailty and uncertainty; he wants to 'gain a deity' (1.1.65). And all this is associated with resolving ambiguity. But what he learns is that this intransitive desire of his – desire that takes as its object knowledge or sex, music or travel, but never attains satisfaction – this desire not only fails to 'extinguish' his doubts, but breeds them: it cannot exist without them. Hence, despite the anatomy of scepticism offered by Cavell, we cannot confidently say that desire precedes doubt in *Doctor Faustus*. The transgressive dismissal of conventional truth so evident in the play cannot be read simply as a consequence of Faustus' pre-existent desire to engage in the occult. Nor, conversely, can the wish to be a powerful magician, a 'demigod' (B.1.1.61), be read simply as an outcome of doubt – a solipsistic refurnishing of a now vacant space. Rather, the two impulses are reciprocal. In much the same way that fantasies become truths for Faustus even as conventional truths metamorphose into fantasies, Faustian doubt and desire coexist and presuppose one another. And while Marlowe is probably not suggesting that sceptical detachment is the solution to the potentially tragic dilemma of 'forward wits' like Faustus (Epilogue.7), he clearly designs a dramatic scenario wherein his protagonist follows a quasi-Pyrrhonian trajectory in cleansing his mind of dogma only to re-inscribe it, compulsively, with the fast-fading signature of his desire. The trajectory itself – intimately related to the sixth paradigm I have sketched in chapter 4 – constitutes a sceptical appropriation, manifest also in Montaigne, in which the vacuum created through doubt invites its own elimination, thereby initiating an endless cycle of evacuation and substitution. There is no question that this trajectory distorts Pyrrhonian thought as represented by Sextus; equally, there is no question that the Renaissance understands it as a form of scepticism, a basic sceptical paradigm. To contextualize *Doctor Faustus* within early modern scepticism is thus to discover that its eponymous figure experiences a mental life corresponding with remarkable fidelity to one of the major sixteenth-century misconstructions (and subsequent deployments) of Pyrrhonism.

*Faustus* is a sceptical play not in advocacy but in depiction: not in proposing an attitude of *detachment* but in portraying passionate *attachment* and the attendant, enormously sympathetic self-destruction it can bring on. And the brilliant irony is that Faustus' fundamental alternative – the choice he rejects – also constitutes a form of attachment: contentment with a particular shape of resolution, and thus, tacitly, with an abandonment of enquiry. But Faustus recognizes that what modernity might call 'normative behaviour' always demands a closing down of doubt and desire, a consistent tracking of resolution, an acquiescence that in diminishing one diminishes all. Faustus rejects this capitulation, aware both that it amounts to a falling short of human potential and that in so doing he renders his life incompatible with conventional earthly existence. We might say that for Faustus, despite his recurrent emphasis upon the tangible, the logical, and the here-and-now, believing is seeing precisely as often as seeing is believing.

But this is merely the beginning. Elsewhere in the first act we watch the King of Spain grant equal favour to his aristocratic nephew, Lorenzo, and to the non-aristocratic Horatio, even though everyone knows that the latter is solely responsible for Balthazar's defeat. Neither Horatio nor his father Hieronimo balks at this judgement, and indeed the King's decision seems partly defensible, especially given his concern over proper accommodation for a royal captive: the middle-class Horatio lacks the means to house Balthazar and his train. But at the same time there is no question that caste loyalties play a crucial role in the King's 'doom' (1.2.175).[2] Thus Hieronimo's scrupulous concern not to be 'partial' (1.2.167) is tacitly mocked by the King's overt favouritism. And the King himself acts as he perceives the 'heavens' to have acted in the Spanish victory over Portugal: it was, after all, through their 'fair influence' that such 'justice' flowed (1.2.11). What might be attributed to chance is forcibly reconceived as divine intention, with the result that terrestrial outcome is necessarily construed as unbiased desert. Transcendental and monarchical powers move into perfect alignment.[3]

Still more egregious is the breach of justice in the Portuguese court. Convinced that his son has perished in the war, the Viceroy of Portugal ignores the claim of his courtier Alexandro that Balthazar, in fact, has merely been captured. Instead he listens to Villuppo, another courtier, who preposterously alleges that Alexandro murdered Balthazar on the battlefield. Villuppo's appeal to eyewitness authority – 'hear the truth which these mine eyes have seen' (1.3.59) – carries the day against Alexandro's protestations of innocence. Indeed, the very *appearance* of innocence becomes, through Villuppo's clever manipulation, evidence of Alexandro's guilt (1.3.65–6). Meanwhile the Viceroy's only criterion for judgement appears to be the testimony of his 'nightly dreams' (1.3.76). Hence with no further opportunity for self-defence, Alexandro is hustled off to prison and imminent execution. The image of judgement that emerges from the scene is one of absolute royal prerogative, precipitous and arbitrary. And while Alexandro's innocence and Villuppo's villainy are both exposed in due course, their discovery looks so much like the random operation of chance that attributing it to the machinations of divine justice seems as wilful as sharing the King of Spain's self-serving view of his Portuguese triumph.

With such an abundance of adjudications, and such a scarcity of justice, it is perhaps no wonder that *The Spanish Tragedy* has often generated indignant, even hostile, assessment. Harold Bloom has declared that it is 'a dreadful play, hideously written and silly; common readers will determine this for themselves ... . They will not get much past the opening, and will find it hard to credit the notion that this impressed Shakespeare.'[4] But the play is *not* dreadful, although it is laboured at times, and over-indulgently rhetorical, and dramatically slack at the end due to Hieronimo's too easy victory over the once formidable Lorenzo. Still less is it silly. As C. L. Barber notes, Kyd's fascination with the outrage generated by violations of people's deep investment in social and familial piety 'proved congenial to Shakespeare', who exploited the theme both in *Titus Andronicus* and in *Hamlet*.[5] *The Spanish Tragedy* may not have 'impressed' Shakespeare in the narrowly aesthetic sense that Bloom has in mind, but it unquestionably made a strong impression on him: surely his interest in the agonizing obliteration of family bonds was, if not originally prompted, at least further stimulated by Kyd's frequently revived drama. And not only is *The Spanish Tragedy* important for its formative impact on Shakespeare and other playwrights, but also because its explorations of perspective, ignorance and efforts at just resolve demonstrate how central a preoccupation such topics were when Kyd was writing. Original and sensitive despite its clumsiness, *The Spanish Tragedy* reveals a self-conscious, imaginative and highly perceptive mind at work on issues of pressing importance to the surrounding culture.

Engaging the sceptical paradigm of opposition, the play repeatedly stages the resolution of doubt. Early in the second act, Lorenzo and Balthazar puzzle over the perplexing fact that Bel-imperia shows no interest in the Portuguese heir. 'What if my sister love some other knight?' asks Lorenzo, to which Balthazar responds with insipid Petrarchan conceit: 'My summer's day will turn to winter's night' (2.1.33–4). But Lorenzo pursues the matter:

> I have already found a stratagem
> To sound the bottom of this doubtful theme.
> My lord, for once you shall be ruled by me;
> Hinder me not, whate'er you hear or see.
> By force or fair means will I cast about
> To find the truth of all this question out.
>
> (2.1.35–40)

And within fifty lines he does precisely that, brutally eliciting from Pedringano the news that Bel-imperia loves Horatio. It is worth noting that Lorenzo's stratagem might have revealed the same 'information' even if it had not been true, since he was quite prepared to use force to learn what he wanted to hear. But as it happens Lorenzo's suspicion coincides with reality. His sister's love for Hieronimo's son threatens a dynastic marriage, and because that is unacceptable, Horatio must be eliminated. Resolution of doubt is promptly followed by resolution of action, and 'revenge' is the word supplied in facile justification (2.1.111–37).

Similarly, the play's own dramaturgy stages a resolution of doubt in the initially confusing matter of Andrea's death. As Joel Altman has shown, the successive narrations of this event constitute clarifying accounts rather than conflicting testimonies, and the overall impression with which we are left is that a violation of the laws of martial honour did in fact occur: Andrea fully merits the urge towards revenge that Proserpine has conjured.[6] But how this impulse may be squared with the question of Andrea's ultimate 'doom' remains unanswered. Indeed this is one of several unsettling problems raised by the play's insistent focus on the investigation of doubtful matters.

The most notorious such investigation is Hieronimo's enquiry into the gruesome death of his son. As Spain's Knight Marshal and a judge renowned for painstaking 'pursuit of equity' (3.13.51–4), Hieronimo is the polar opposite of the Portuguese Viceroy, whose imagined loss of Balthazar prefigures the genuine loss of Horatio. And Hieronimo's patience and fact-collecting tendencies surface immediately upon the discovery of his son's mutilated corpse. 'To know the author were some ease of grief', he tells his wife Isabella, quickly adding that until the murderer's identity has been exposed she should cease her 'plaints' – or at least 'dissemble them awhile; / So shall we sooner find the practice out' (2.5.40, 60–2). The line between proper judicial inquest and Machiavellian cunning is thus blurred, and this undoubtedly helps to explain Hieronimo's ultimate success as a revenger. But that Hieronimo so quickly embraces the *idea* of revenge, just as Lorenzo, Balthazar, the Viceroy and Andrea have elsewhere done, suggests Kyd's positing of a universal impulse, a human desire to fill any vacuum – loss, uncertainty, indecision – with abrupt resolve to action, usually retributive action. The Pyrrhonian theory of *ataraxia* – of the unanticipated tranquility following judgemental suspension – would seem to be aggressively, even conclusively, refuted.

This is not to deny that Hieronimo can engage in temporary and instrumental withholding of assent.[7] When Bel-imperia's 'bloody writ' drops before him, he instantly cautions himself not to be 'credulous' (3.2.26–39). Like Hamlet, his dramatic descendant, he finds grounds for suspicion in every incident and vows not to 'hazard' himself lightly: 'I therefore will by circumstances try / What I can gather to confirm this writ' (3.2.46–9). And the play apparently supports his decision. Five scenes later, after Lorenzo's surgical removal of Serberine and Pedringano, an undelivered note from the latter comes to Hieronimo's attention – a note (intended for Lorenzo) that fully corroborates Bel-imperia's earlier allegation regarding the identities of Horatio's assassins. Hieronimo's patience is thus rewarded, or so he imagines, and he resolves to approach the King and 'cry aloud for justice through the court' (3.7.70). The scene ends with a sense of relative optimism; the general trajectory moves against Hieronimo's earlier scepticism about heavenly supervision. Isabella's articles of faith – that the 'heavens are just', that 'murder cannot be hid', that 'time will bring this treachery to light' (2.5.57–9) – now command Hieronimo's belief, or at least his fervent desire:

> O sacred heavens, may it come to pass
> That such a monstrous and detested deed,
> So closely smothered and so long concealed,
> Shall thus by this be vengèd and revealed?
> (3.7.45–8)

The universe, for one precarious instant, seems morally responsive, if not benign.

But all this changes with the play's next movement. First Isabella 'runs lunatic', a development suggesting that Christian forbearance counts for little against the ravages of grief and uncertainty.[8] Then Bel-imperia condemns Hieronimo's inaction and resigns herself to the same 'patience' (3.9.13) that ultimately draws Isabella to suicide. In Bel-imperia's case, such patience soon metamorphoses into a habit of temporizing that usefully advances her impulse towards revenge (e.g. 3.10.61–6). But there is no sense that the plight of either woman resonates with Hieronimo's current plan. If anything, their separate paths underscore the futility of his effort to work with existing structures and avoid the temptations of what Bacon calls 'wild justice' (*WFB*, 6:384). And this futility rapidly manifests itself. In the scene with the visiting Portingales, Hieronimo's allegorical fantasy regarding Lorenzo's current whereabouts can only be construed by his interlocutors as lunacy or dotage.[9] And when, after undergoing suicidal longings parallel to those of his wife, Hieronimo finally gains access to the king, his frantic importunity ('O justice! O my son!' [3.12.65]) merely aids Lorenzo's plot to derail his suit. The king, still ignorant of Horatio's death, is easily manipulated into believing that Hieronimo covets the Portuguese ransom. Lorenzo plays Villuppo to the king's viceroy, and the class solidarities earlier implied now emerge in overt display. A monarch once praised by Hieronimo as 'just and wise' (1.2.166) is revealed to be hopelessly out of touch with his subjects, grossly neglectful of his proper cares. His vow to look 'further' into the business of Hieronimo's transformation relegates the play's obsession with resolving doubt to the lip service of *noblesse oblige* (3.12.100).

So it comes as little surprise that in the next scene Hieronimo makes his choice. True to the play's established patterns, the scene begins with a spectacle of indecision. Hieronimo, reading a book, finds himself caught between conflicting admonishments. Precisely *which* book he reads is a question not to be asked, since the proffered textual wisdom derives equally from Senecan tragedy and Pauline epistle.[10] Perhaps the volume is Hieronimo's commonplace book, newly resuscitated from his student days at Toledo. But its quoted pronouncements, being emblems of received authority, merit serious contemplation, and Hieronimo's temporary perplexity serves as a figure of larger-scale societal ambivalence. Like the play's opening conflict between Spain and Portugal – a conflict in which, for many hours, 'victory to neither part inclined' (1.2.64) – Hieronimo's uncertainty hints at the roughly equal persuasiveness (*isostheneia*) of mutually exclusive resolutions, and it gestures more broadly to the dilemma he has endured since Horatio's slaughter. But while his vacillation soon gives way to firm resolve – 'And, to conclude, I will revenge his death!' (3.13.20) – the end of deadlock only marks the birth of new dead ends.

In passing I wish to note that the metaphor of a hanging balance, common enough in classical sources, is frequently appropriated in early modern contexts as an image of more specifically epistemological doubt. We have seen that Primaudaye characterizes doubt as 'a neuter judgement, hanging betweene consent and his contrary, inclining neither to one side nor the other'.[11] Spenser too employs the metaphor, allowing Duessa to watch the 'doubtfull ballaunce equally to sway' as Fradubio contemplates the relative beauties of two fair 'Dames' (*FQ*, 1.2.36–8). Further examples might be adduced from *All's Well That Ends Well*, Wilcox's *Discourse on Doubting*, Tomkis' *Lingua* and Earle's 'Sceptic in Religion', but here it is perhaps most pertinent to stress that just as Duessa resolves Fradubio's crisis through a resort to 'guile', Hieronimo's passage out of doubtful indecision entails not 'open' and 'vulgar' action but a secret 'mean':

> I will rest me in unrest,
> Dissembling quiet in unquietness,

> Not seeming that I know their villainies,
> That my simplicity may make them think
> That ignorantly I will let all slip.
>                                             (3.13.29–33)[12]

Like Bel-imperia, who independently concludes that temporizing is her sole remaining option, Hieronimo now embarks on a journey of no return. His judicial training and humanist educational background prove eminently suited to the ordeal; indeed, their energies flow smoothly into the channels of Machiavellian intrigue and dissimulation. But there is no concealing the brutal immediacy of Hieronimo's decision. The arguments marshalled against *Vindicta mihi* and the theory of divine retribution are in themselves unpersuasive. Rather, the criterion for Hieronimo's choice seems to lie in a set of coercive assumptions (3.13.8–19), assumptions no more intrinsically convincing than the ideological scheme against which they are deployed. Revenge, above all else, offers a fantasy of relief – imminent relief, if not instantaneous – and its potential for inhabiting the lacunae created by anxiety, doubt and sorrow is only matched by the power it possesses to consume its agent.

Hence the viceroy's subsequent announcement to the Spanish king – 'I come not, as thou think'st, / With doubtful followers, unresolvèd men' (3.14.23–4) – works as an external figure of Hieronimo's internal persuasion. But this denigration of doubt, while certainly reinforcing the play's general sense that revenge quells anxiety and confounds sceptical theory, also proves remarkably fragile. In the first place, as the scene with Don Bazulto demonstrates, the commitment to Machiavellian composure is liable to unanticipated moments of collapse. Confronted with a 'lively portrait' of his grief (3.13.85), Hieronimo endures Horatio's death once again and, in Lear-like rantings, exposes his petitioners to the mythicized outline of a scheme better left unspoken:

> Though on this earth justice will not be found,
> I'll down to hell, and in this passion
> Knock at the dismal gates of Pluto's court,
> Getting by force, as once Alcides did,
> A troop of Furies and tormenting hags
> To torture Don Lorenzo and the rest ... .
> Then will I rent and tear them, thus and thus,
> Shivering their limbs in pieces with my teeth.
>                                             (3.13.108–22)[13]

Shredding the legal papers, he makes literal sense of the claim that 'justice is exilèd from the earth' (3.13.139). But beyond this intimation of frailty – an intimation also recognized by Hamlet, and famously mobilized in his testing of Claudius – there is the additional and much larger problem of disparate proportionality, specifically the colossal lack of parity between blood vengeance and the loss it seeks to assuage. The disjuncture can cut both ways, of course, and such instances as Balthazar's 'revenge' on Horatio (2.1.114–16) function partly to contextualize Hieronimo's plan within a trivializing frame. But in the end Hieronimo's resolve succumbs to a diminishment already inherent in its conception. For besides what Katharine Maus has characterized as its pedagogical failure – its inability, that is, to convey to its auditors the sense that Hieronimo's miseries are no less genuine than their own – Hieronimo's prosecution of revenge offers no enduring ease, no tranquillity or calm.[14] The voluntary extinction of terrestrial consciousness that seems invariably tied to 'successful' vengeance is at the same time testimony to its very inability to succeed.

So Hieronimo revives his old tragedy, with Bel-imperia serving as co-director. Mocking providential supervision ('I see that heaven applies our drift'), they joke in coded language as they broach their production plans to Lorenzo and Balthazar:

> *Hieronimo*: Now, my good lord, could you entreat
> Your sister Bel-imperia to make one?
> For what's a play without a woman in it? ...
> *Balthazar*: But which of us is to perform that part?
> *Hieronimo*: O, that will I, my lords, make no doubt of it.
> I'll play the murderer, I warrant you,
> For I already have conceited that ... . [and] because I know
> That Bel-imperia hath practiced the French,
> In courtly French shall all her phrases be.
> *Bel-imperia*: You mean to try my cunning then, Hieronimo?
>
> (4.1.31–173)

Assigning Hieronimo the role of the guilt-ridden murderer (the Bashaw) is a brilliant stroke on Kyd's part: it resonates beautifully with the allegorical imagination already displayed by the Knight Marshal (3.11.12–31), and it buttresses the idea that remorse is still conceivable, still possible even in a world no longer underwritten by just and attentive divinity. Indeed, the theme of *inattentiveness*, comically introduced in Revenge's onstage slumber (3.15), is immediately reactivated in

Bel-imperia's Andrea-like outrage at Hieronimo's apparent lethargy (4.1.1–28). His Machiavellian vigilance – the rest 'in unrest' that Bel-imperia shares, yet fails at first to recognize – powerfully signals the displacement of mindfulness from transcendental to merely human precincts (3.13.29).

Isabella too thinks Hieronimo has given up on Horatio's ghost. Suffering pitiably, and in apparent isolation from her husband, she condemns his 'negligence' and 'delay', going so far as to suggest that he has forgiven the murderers, which would of course be to take her own premise of Christian patience to its prescribed conclusion (4.2.30–3). But her suicide casts doubt on the viability of such patience, as well as offering an apt prelude to the play's bloody catastrophe. Hieronimo, after concealing his son's cadaver behind the curtain and briefly playing the role of frenetic stage-manager ('Our scene is Rhodes. What, is your beard on?' [4.3.15]), joins with Bel-imperia in executing scripted vengeance on Lorenzo and Balthazar. Indeed Bel-imperia follows the script too closely, taking her own life despite Hieronimo's last-minute emendations to the tragedy (4.4.139–44). But her 'resolution' scarcely surprises him, mirroring, as it does, his own: 'Methinks since I grew inward with revenge, / I cannot look with scorn enough on death' (5th Addition). As it happens, Kyd did not write these lines, but they fully accord with the tenor of the play's finale. And while Hieronimo goes on to tell the king that he feels 'eased' with having exacted revenge, the terms in which he continues to describe his loss, combined with the wish that further afflictions be visited on the now-dead murderers (4.4.174–90), give the lie to his calm. Like the Ghost of Andrea, who declares that 'blood and sorrow finish my desires' yet eagerly anticipates chthonic torments for Balthazar and the rest (4.5.2–44), Hieronimo's desires are also unsatisfied, unresolved. Michael Neill has written persuasively about the deferral of closure in *The Spanish Tragedy*, and I merely add that just as the space of Andrea's postmortem consciousness is filled with Prosperine's will, so Hieronimo's dying hope finds elaboration in Andrea's ongoing scheme.[15] The 'endless tragedy' promised by Revenge carries no convincing promise of ease, not even for those who will inhabit the vaguely Elysian fields alluded to by Andrea (4.5.17–48). And if Andrea's 'doom' has finally been determined – decided, in effect, as a judicial by-product of other more consuming narrative interests – its accidental quality points as well to the ultimate triviality of revenge urges, which through their very need to be infinitely reenacted suggest their inherent impotence.

G. K. Hunter argues that one of the principal reasons *The Spanish Tragedy* has been undervalued is that critics have categorized it too narrowly as a revenge drama, failing to appreciate its status as 'the inheritor of a rich tradition of moralizing dramaturgy'.[16] Hunter concentrates on the play's obsessive interest in questions of justice, suggesting that dramatic ironies generated through discrepant levels of awareness invite Kyd's audience to suppose that his characters are not independent agents but 'puppets of a predetermined and omnicompetent justice' (93). Even Hieronimo labours under ignorance and incomprehension, and his madness results from the collision of his own purely human sense of justice with the inscrutable workings of a 'divine justice machine'. In the end, according to Hunter, Hieronimo 'becomes the instrument of Revenge by becoming inhuman'; indeed, humanity is 'sacrificed' so that justice may be enacted (101–4). The result is that, however bizarre or inequitable the play's outcomes may seem – especially when we view them from its own interior perspectives – in fact justice *is* done, and the play's final moment 'places everyone where he morally belongs' (104). Kyd's universe is harsh, even Calvinistic in severity, but for Hunter there is no question that its operations reveal an icy logic of 'perfect recompense' (97).

Hunter is a shrewd observer of dramatic structure, and his commentary on *The Spanish Tragedy* is illuminating, at times compelling. But I am less convinced than he that the 'divine justice machine' is indeed just. Hunter assumes that justice is at work because the outermost frame of the play insists that this is the case, and the play's conclusion does in fact deliver what Revenge promises Andrea: the death of Balthazar at the hands of Bel-imperia. It strikes me, however, that the play's abundant ironies invite ironic interpretation even of this outcome. For one thing, Bel-imperia has given scant thought to Andrea since her tryst with Horatio in his father's 'pleasant bower'. More importantly, the fact that something is predicted and then occurs need not imply causality, let alone coherent cosmic purpose and equity. As Maus observes, Hunter's justice machine at times looks 'all too human'.[17] Moreover, in claiming that Hieronimo becomes God's scourge by 'becoming inhuman', Hunter implies that had the Knight Marshal, like his wife, remained 'human' (and humane), he would *not* have become such an instrument – and this in turn implies agency. But above all else, Hunter's argument fails to reckon adequately with the murder of Horatio. If Horatio must die solely as part of an overarching scheme whose purpose is to grant Andrea justice, we must ask why Andrea's death merits such justice when Horatio's does not. And if Horatio's death is itself just, we must wonder *why*, since Horatio commits no crime and never becomes 'inhuman'. How does Horatio deserve his fate? Unless we invoke Calvinist logic, or resort to the class assumptions repeatedly interrogated by the play, we are forced, I believe, to say that, like Cordelia's death, or Antonio's in *The Duchess of Malfi*, the murder of Horatio remains brutally inexplicable – a just emblem of the prevailing injustice of human existence.

And so Hieronimo's increasing scepticism counts for more than the anguished speculation of a cosmic pawn. His poetry of bereavement, passionately voiced in one soliloquy after another, is grounded in a sense of ferocious indignation with which every listener has the potential to identify. At first, still in shock at Horatio's death, Hieronimo's lament is convention-bound and formal:

> O heavens, why made you night to cover sin?
> By day this deed of darkness had not been.
> O earth, why didst thou not in time devour
> The vile profaner of this sacred bower?
> (2.5.24–7)

But soon his stunned amazement gives way to fervent reproach:

> O sacred heavens! If this unhallowed deed ...
> Shall unrevealed and unrevengèd pass,
> How should we term your dealings to be just,
> If you unjustly deal with those that in your justice trust?
> (3.2.5–11)

Soon after this, reproach evolves into deep suspicion of estrangement. Apostrophes to the 'sacred' heavens cease to seem germane; audience and focus move inward:

> Yet still tormented is my tortured soul
> With broken sighs and restless passions,
> That wingèd mount, and hovering in the air,
> Beat at the windows of the brightest heavens,
> Soliciting for justice and revenge:
> But they are placed in those empyreal heights,
> Where, countermured with walls of diamond,
> I find the place impregnable; and they
> Resist my woes and give my words no way.
> (3.7.10–18)

Finally, the thesis of alienation is embraced with conviction, and Hieronimo abruptly proclaims to others what he earlier entertained only as private hypothesis: 'For here's no justice; gentle boy, begone, / For justice is exilèd from the earth' (3.13.138–9).[18] The play has driven a wedge between 'doom' and the ideological supposition that the 'heavens are just' (2.5.57). Hieronimo's conclusion – an understandable if precipitous verdict – is that the two have no relation. Like many of *The Spanish Tragedy*'s other judgements, the validity of this one is never finally determined. But Kyd grants it coercive power through his play's design and cumulative effect. And if, as Hunter writes, the structure and thematic elaboration of the tragedy imply the presence of 'the unsleeping eye of God' (93), it is a god whose wakefulness is scarcely distinguishable from nonexistence. From Hieronimo's perspective, the latter might indeed be more reassuring.

# 7
# The Plague of Opinion: *Troilus and Cressida*

> All things have two handles and two visages, and there is reason for all, and there is not any that hath not his contrarie.
>
> Charron, *Of Wisdome*

That *Troilus and Cressida* exposes human acts of valuation to relentless sceptical scrutiny is beyond any doubt. When Cressida observes that 'Men prize the thing ungained more than it is' (1.2.280), she initiates a play-long debate on the question of 'prizing' and simultaneously advances two implicit opinions: that the 'thing ungained' has intrinsic, ascertainable value, and that men routinely inflate that value until the 'thing' is no longer 'ungained'.[1] Both opinions are contested in the play. Cressida also informs us that while she loves Troilus deeply, none of that love 'shall from [her] eyes appear' – a remark intimating her skill as a conscious dissembler (1.2.286). Of course, she has legitimate reasons for dissembling, but later, when she insists that she cannot 'temporize' with her affection (4.4.6), we wonder about the truth of her claim, since her earlier behaviour may be construed as a species of temporizing. More generally, though, the pervasive emphasis in *Troilus and Cressida* on the difficulty of judging the worth of a person or an enterprise is profoundly inflected by sceptical considerations regarding the complex interference of internal states of mind upon the human acting as a judge. That such considerations bear as well on the notorious problem of the play's dramatic genre seems ironically appropriate. But while I will not argue that *Troilus* is a tragedy or that it exhibits major structural or generic similarities with *Doctor Faustus* or *The Spanish Tragedy*, I believe that it shares with them, and with other plays I will discuss, a deep imbrication in sceptical matrices as well as a thoroughgoing concern – thematic and linguistic – with paradox, proof, uncertainty and the dramatic fallout from the explosive collision of poorly examined but fiercely held assumptions.

Composed around 1601–2, *Troilus and Cressida* dates, like *Hamlet*, from the final years of Elizabeth's reign, displaying similar indications of imaginative genesis within the *angst* of the Elizabethan end-game. Scholars have not been as insistent with *Troilus* as they have with *Hamlet* that Shakespeare relied on Montaigne in drafting the play; but if he did, the same reasons that make such speculation plausible with *Hamlet* obtain as well with its contemporary. In any case, as Graham Bradshaw has observed, even before Shakespeare encounters Montaigne his plays exhibit traces of a 'radical scepticism' that juxtaposes 'the human need to affirm values against the inherently problematic nature of all acts of valuing'.[2] Bradshaw distinguishes such 'radical' scepticism from an alternative, 'dogmatic' form: the 'terminal, materialistic nihilism of a Thersites, Iago, or Edmund' (39). But while Bradshaw's two scepticisms scarcely do justice to the range of sceptical paradigms available to Shakespeare, his treatment of *Troilus and Cressida* is perceptive and provocative, and I wish to engage it here in order to move towards questions at the heart of the play.

Contending that *Troilus* renders all acts of valuation problematic through its brilliant design and 'long-range ironies', Bradshaw concentrates in particular on the 'Hector-problem', resourcefully arguing that Hector's *volte-face* in the Trojan debate is in fact a reversion to his customary attitudes, attitudes for which we have been well prepared earlier on (132–42). The true anomaly, according to Bradshaw, is Hector's prudential insistence that Helen be returned to the Greeks. Bradshaw acknowledges that understanding Hector the way Achilles understands him has its shortcomings – particularly in shaping our response to the Trojan's ultimate slaughter – but in general he pushes for a consistency of characterization in Hector that works against the grain of his broader thesis that the play subjects such summings-up to 'dizzying perspectivism' (144). Bradshaw is more successful in his treatment of Ulysses; indeed, he links Hector with Ulysses in their common protestations regarding Natural Law and cosmic order. Whereas Agamemnon and Troilus are 'exposed' even as they speak, the utterances of Ulysses and Hector are more puzzling due to 'the uncertainty of the relationship between the seemingly impressive speech and its speaker' (152).

For the most part this is excellent, as is Bradshaw's collateral insistence that Thersites is crucial to the play's design and success. A 'puny performing freak', Thersites functions as a terminally sceptical nihilist whose views demonstrate how humanly diminished a person must be to find pleasure in the reduction of all acts and motives to the basest common denominator (141). According to Bradshaw, Thersites never looks inward, never achieves the self-reflexivity that *Troilus and Cressida* routinely attains through its habitual modes of 'dramatic thinking' (154).[3] Such a view may underestimate Thersites' wit and self-knowledge – displayed, for instance, in the 'bastard' scene with Margareton – but it certainly dispels the power of critical accounts in which Thersites' voice becomes authorial. Bradshaw is right, then, that *Troilus* works interrogatively, incessantly juxtaposing perspectives and, in the process, challenging us to make judgements of our own. Yet his account also undercuts itself through an excessive tendency towards realism. He imposes on the play too strong a desire for consistency and full characterization, as when he says that Troilus 'has never shown much interest in what the real Cressida thinks and feels' (144) – a remark faulting a fictitious being as though he were a disagreeable in-law. The ultimate effect of the Trojan debate is not so much to make us wonder if Hector stays in character as to raise for our consideration the difficult issue of whether, as Hector suggests, we can isolate 'some image of th' affected merit' (2.2.60). In other words, the cautious warrior who proposes sending Helen back both *is* and *is not* Hector.

This begins to explain why emotional involvement is such a problem in the play. Shakespeareans have long debated the question of critical detachment in *Troilus*, some supporting the idea by linking it to the possibility of the work's initial performance in coterie settings such as Cambridge or the Inns of Court, others disputing it on the grounds that the play in fact encourages strong allegiance and identification.[4] 'It is simply not possible', writes Anne Barton, 'to watch this play with unbroken intellectual detachment.'[5] And in the theatre this is probably true more often than not, particularly given the twin imperatives of stage practice (what 'works') and conventional audience expectation. But I suggest that even on stage, let alone in the study, honest and thorough exploration of *Troilus* confounds sustained emotional engagement with its characters and events – and in much the same way that the play continually frustrates the processes of rational deliberation. It is not that we do not care about Troilus or Cressida, but that our caring is intermittent, qualified and intricately framed: it feels entirely different from our involvement, say, with Romeo and Juliet or with Othello and Desdemona. Likewise, the play's frequent resort to intellectual debate, so suggestive of university disputation *in utramque partem*, is accompanied by both a sense of real-world urgency and by prior concession to a rather lethargic distrust of the ultimate adequacy of ratiocination. On the one hand, *Troilus* repeatedly mimics the tropes and argumentative tactics of ancient scepticism as it was received in early modern England, and this partly accounts for the play's generally recognized sense of intellectuality. But it enacts its mimicry even to the extent of casting doubt on the inherent value of persuasion. It says, in effect, that we must extend a courteous hearing to the deliberations of reason, but that since such deliberations typically preface *non sequitur* and contrary resolution, we need not abide by their outcomes. Indeed, we may conscript reason into the service of appetite and will – and with a sceptically tranquil conscience.

But this is to jump ahead. Let me first offer a few instances of *Troilus'* participation in the paradigms of Renaissance scepticism. I have already hinted at some of these in chapter 4: the play's obsessive interest in conflicting appearances and evaluations; its fascination with false generalization and involuntary judgemental suspension; and its deployment of 'doubting Thomas' variants, as when Thersites asks whether Troilus will 'swagger himself out on's own eyes' (5.2.142). But there is more, and indeed Thersites' allusion to visual testimony taps into the play's deep current of debate over relations between seeing and knowing, a debate that often surfaces in comic forms. 'Do you know a man if you see him?' Pandarus asks Cressida, to which she replies, with bawdy innuendo, 'Ay, if I ever saw him before and knew him' (1.2.63–4). Setting aside the joke and the Shakespearean penchant for antimetabole, the sober suggestion here is that knowing is contingent on *prior* knowing; perception itself leads nowhere. The idea is picked up again soon afterwards, when Aeneas issues Hector's challenge. Seeking the Greek leader Agamemnon, Aeneas resorts to his courtliest style in posing the unavoidable preliminary question:

> How may
> A stranger to those most imperial looks
> Know them from the eyes of other mortals?
> (1.3.223–5)

The astonished Agamemnon can only grunt a monosyllabic 'How?' Critics debate whether Aeneas is mocking the Greeks or expressing genuine uncertainty – there are plausible reasons for taking either position – but what is beyond doubt is that Aeneas transforms epistemological possibility into coercive force. In essence, he says that even though the Greeks have camped for seven years on the Dardan plain, it is still possible that a Trojan might *not* know their commander by sight; they must therefore admit such a possibility and stoop to the indignity of introducing him. The play is replete with such moments of serio-comic deflation – Cressida even feigns ignorance of her own city's heroes – but this one is particularly inflected by its presence within the ongoing meditation on seeing and knowing.

If Aeneas seeks to learn another's identity, several figures in *Troilus* avoid seeking their own. Achilles and Ajax loom prominently in this respect, and Ulysses' character-sketch of the former provides details for both. Speaking to Agamemnon, but at the same time shamelessly manipulating Ajax, Ulysses describes Achilles as so 'plaguy proud' that he

> never suffers matter of the world
> Enter his thoughts, save such as doth revolve
> And ruminate himself.
>                           (2.3.174–85)

Reminiscent of Marlowe's Faustus, whose 'fantasy' receives 'no object' but 'ruminates' on its own desires, Achilles by this account is a solipsist, a man whose 'imagined worth' bears no firm relation to the level at which his comrades prize him (2.3.169). Agamemnon in fact observes that Achilles' 'self-assumption' exceeds 'the note of judgement' (2.3.122–3), a remark implying agreement with the earlier opinions of Hector and Cressida that people and things may be properly estimated. Diomedes too participates in this tradition, brutally informing Troilus that he will treat Cressida as he sees fit: 'To her own worth / She shall be prized' (4.4.132–3). But the same Diomedes, only moments before, has been asked by Paris whether Helen's husband or her current lover 'merits' her the most. This is his reply:

> Both alike.
> He merits well to have her that doth seek her,
> Not making any scruple of her soilure,
> With such a hell of pain and world of charge;
> And you as well to keep her that defend her,
> Not palating the taste of her dishonour,
> With such a costly loss of wealth and friends … .
> Both merits poised, each weighs nor less nor more,
> But he as he. Which heavier for a whore?
>                           (4.1.56–68)

Laced with bitter irony, Diomedes' answer embodies to a remarkable degree the Pyrrhonian concept of *isostheneia*: the essentially equal persuasiveness of opposed claims or arguments.[6] And certainly it appears that Diomedes exhibits sceptical indifference to the entire question, though of course he is quite preoccupied with other matters. We are perhaps reminded of Troilus at the play's outset – the Troilus who exclaims 'Fools on both sides!' and asserts that he 'cannot fight upon this argument; / It is too starved a subject for my sword' (1.1.86–9). This is *not* the Troilus we witness at the play's end, but his exclamations none the less give voice to the simultaneously absurd and passionate inflection the play imparts to its repeated expressions of paradox: 'all eyes and no sight' (1.2.30), 'brown and not brown ... true and not true' (1.2.93–4), 'what is or is not' (1.3.183), 'abundant scarce' (2.3.14), 'hateful love' (4.1.35), 'so true to him / To be false to him' (4.2.57–8), 'This is and is not Cressid' (5.2.153), 'proof is called impossibility' (5.5.29), and so on. No Shakespearean play relies more heavily on oxymoron.[7]

The presentation of a multiplicity of views, especially mutually incompatible views, raises the issue of contradiction in an acute way, and scepticism clearly relies on logic and common sense to the extent that it admits that contradiction poses problems. But scepticism's time-honoured tactic is to *exploit* those problems, and in so doing it deflects potential allegations that the sceptic tacitly assents to the principle of non-contradiction: that A and not-A cannot both be true. Such allegations, however, are relatively unlikely to arise outside the realm of formal logic, and thus when sceptical attitudes animate dramatic imagination, as in *Troilus*, their effect is typically powerful and disorienting. This, I believe, goes some way towards explaining why the debates in the play have attracted so much interest and prompted so many attempts at sifting and assessing their constituent claims. But even beyond the level of overt pronouncement, these debates expose and probe various enabling assumptions, and here too, as elsewhere with the interchanges between Troilus and Cressida, we witness something of the play's meta-dramatic aloofness from faith in the operations of reason.

I have mentioned Bradshaw's contention that Hector ultimately agrees with Troilus because he never truly disagrees with him. Many critics dispute this. One insists that Hector, after 'having argued against making an idol of market valuation as advocated by Troilus ... succumbs to the alluring notion of "our joint and several dignities".'[8] Another adds that Hector, being the 'tragic hero' in a non-tragic play, is a man who 'chooses what is destined', and what he chooses is honour: 'Life every man holds dear', he tells Andromache, 'but the dear man / Holds honour far more precious-dear than life' (5.3.27–8).[9] By these accounts, different as they are, Hector's arguments for relinquishing Helen are neither shallow nor duplicitous, but heartfelt and persuasive. Indeed, Hector speaks of them as 'the way of truth' immediately before announcing his 'resolution' to 'keep Helen still' (2.2.189–91). There is no sense of retraction here, no embarrassment or disavowal. Rather, Hector's lines bespeak a capitulation to dividedness, to a suspicion that the sphere of human behaviour inevitably entails more than rationally justified conduct. And the very calmness of it all is reminiscent of the theory of 'double truth': reconciliation to a sharp split between realms, to an idea that belief and action may be riven 'more wider than the sky and earth' (5.2.156).[10]

Hence there are traces of the early modern Pyrrhonist in Hector, and they give the lie to claims such as that of Rolf Soellner that the Hector/Troilus interchange depicts 'philosophical orthodoxy versus skepticism'.[11] It is true that Hector speaks of Natural Law and understands value in ways more sophisticated and conventionally defensible than those advanced by Troilus, but it is also clear that he characterizes himself as temperamentally uncertain and cautious: no one is 'more ready to cry out "Who knows what follows?"' (2.2.13). He believes that 'surety' – overconfidence – is the 'wound of peace', and in its place recommends 'modest doubt' as the 'beacon of the wise' (2.2.14–16; cp. 5.2.62). He also attacks 'partial indulgence' to 'benumbed wills', in effect launching a critique of rash conclusion and unconsidered judgement (2.2.178–9). And, in an intriguing and highly rhetorical sleight of hand, he equates Helen's low value with the merit of any 'reason' offered against yielding her up (2.2.21–5). Objective worth here conditions the genesis and evaluation of argument.[12]

So Hector's position is not precisely 'philosophical orthodoxy', nor can Troilus' strategies be summed up as merely 'sceptical'. The labelling of specific characters as 'sceptics' has in fact constituted a minor plague in Shakespearean criticism, and it would be well to replace it by awareness of the manifold ways in which sceptical paradigms infiltrate and shape dramatic representation.[13] Soellner moves in this direction when he recognizes how little Shakespeare owes to Caxton and Lydgate in fashioning the 'philosophical dialectic' of the Trojan debate, a recognition that in itself hints at the sceptical orientations of late Elizabethan thought. But he undercuts this insight by attempting to be over-precise about Shakespeare's philosophical knowledge, insisting that the Hector/Troilus dispute yields 'proof' that Shakespeare knew the distinction between Academic and Pyrrhonian scepticism. Hector, he claims, takes the milder Ciceronian stance, while Troilus is a Pyrrhonist because his initial question – 'What's aught but as 'tis valued?' (2.2.52) – casts doubt on Hector's theory of objective worth.[14] One might equally maintain that if Shakespeare knew the difference between Academics and Pyrrhonians he would recognize that Troilus' remark implies a negative dogmatism, since Troilus seems assured that value is *only* relative. Indeed Soellner confuses relativism and scepticism more than once, often leaning towards a loose conflation of the two.[15] He is right to understand the Trojan debate as deeply resonant with sceptical concerns of the period, but what he overlooks is that *Troilus* itself interrogates the assumptions and opinions of its characters in a manner that exposes them all as inadequate in their sceptical inclinations. Troilus' view that no criterion exists by which inherent value may be determined is only one among many such assumptions.

We have seen that Hector's speeches belie the notion that he is devoted exclusively to rational calculation. Troilus, meanwhile, deploys many reasons in addition to his passion, above all the idea of constancy. We *chose* to steal Helen, he argues, and we must therefore never choose to give her back. Had Hector been reading Montaigne he might have stressed to his brother that people change their minds, that they sometimes know more later than they did earlier – or at least something different. He might have brought up Sextus' fourth mode of doubt, which concentrates on the ways in which our perceptions vary depending on circumstances and conditions: 'We perceive objects to be like this or that', writes Montaigne, 'in accordance with our own state and how they seem to us' (*Apology*, 183). But Hector does *not* bring up such objections, and this is probably just as well, since they could be mobilized with equal effect against him. Despite his voicing of an entire constellation of sceptical values, Hector repeatedly begs questions – and not only questions about intrinsic value. As critics have variously shown, Hector's faith in Natural Law invites instant suspicion, as does his facile claim that 'moral philosophy' aids 'free determination / 'Twixt right and wrong' (2.2.167–71).[16] If Troilus transmutes mere stubborn consistency into dignity and honour, Hector displays his own 'partial indulgence' by invoking 'moral laws / Of nature and of nations' (2.2.184–5) – laws whose degree of reality may be only that of reified desire.

Dogmatic assumptions, then, plague both sides in the Trojan debate, and the play itself, not the professed behaviour of any of its characters, functions as the 'tent that searches / To th' bottom of the worst' (2.2.16–17). *Troilus* brings with it its own tools and tactics of analysis; it plays anatomist to its own exquisite corpse, and it does so through complex dramatic orchestration, through juxtaposition and ironic framing, through repetition, variation, linguistic extravagance and tonal shift. When Hector asks 'What merit's in that reason' (2.2.24), his words presage the 'merit' talk of Troilus and Diomedes later on (3.2.89, 4.1.57–68, 4.4.84). And in a similar mode of call-and-response, Cressida's choice of the word 'achievement' finds a double echo: once when Ulysses glorifies Greek ability in disparaging Patroclus' pageants, and again when Troilus reacts to the abrupt news of Cressida's exchange: 'How my achievements mock me!' (1.2.284, 1.3.181, 4.2.71). That 'achievement is command' may be true in one respect, but *Troilus* also asks whether we may 'achieve' anything in life without inviting derisive commentary on the very nature of accomplishment.

Cressida denies that any woman 'ever knew / Love got so sweet as when desire did sue' (1.2.281–2). Troilus offers a displaced rebuttal to her fear when he asserts in council that to relinquish Helen would be to 'Beggar the estimation' of that which the Trojans have 'prized / Richer than sea and land' (2.2.91–2). Of course, this is typical of the pair: Cressida taking such shifts in valuation as a fact of life, Troilus railing against their very potential for manifestation. But the juxtaposition also raises the question of sympathy again, and it serves to draw our attention to the 'plague of opinion' (3.3.265) that infects the discourse not only of war, but of love. Bound by myth and tradition, Troilus and Cressida are trapped in their future; their speeches and actions are always contextualized by what they later say and do. Not surprisingly, many critics have followed this interpretive cue, and it is thus understandable, if unfortunate, that a writer as astute as A. P. Rossiter has called Cressida 'a chatty, vulgar little piece'.[17] More recent studies have considerably reduced the potential for this kind of assessment; Janet Adelman's commentaries in particular have redirected our attention to the ways in which characterization and plot development may be conditioned by deep-seated engagement with fantasies of sexual union and separation. I agree with Adelman that *Troilus* invites us to perceive Cressida, until her departure from Troy, as possessing a developed and attractive inwardness, and it seems clear too that this apparently knowable subjectivity recedes near the drama's end.[18] But I am less convinced that the play is as consistently harsh towards Troilus as many recent critics maintain. Both lovers, I think, are presented in radically disjointed fashion, by turns inspiring

perception: 'let my lady apprehend no fear'. Even in the act of as-
suaging anxiety, Troilus exacerbates it through his well-meant displacement of agency.

We have, then, two lovers united in common apprehension, though
they certainly exhibit identifiable differences in position and response.
And this is crucial to bear in mind as we trace their subsequent interaction. Adelman remarks that 'one can hardly imagine a speech more
calculated to create infidelity' than Troilus' 'O, that I thought it could
be in a woman ... To keep her constancy' (3.2.153–65). It is difficult
to disagree with her, especially given Troilus' later iteration of the con-
descending 'Be thou but true' (4.4.57ff). At the same time, there is an
immense gulf between creating infidelity through desire and prompting it inadvertently through fear; I am not certain that Adelman is
right in claiming that 'Troilus needs to imagine a Cressida who betrays
him' (57). If we turn back to the speech in the war council where
Troilus illustrates his argument by fictive example (2.2.61–8), we discover not that he expects to 'distaste' his hypothetical wife – not that
he wishes to 'blench' from her – but that he cannot avoid imagining
such *possibilities*. The emphasis lies on distasteful potential, not on
desire or need. Troilus' imagination, understandably coloured by the
world he inhabits, cannot help but rush forward in envisaging what
Hector and Cressida both call 'the worst'.

So the dregs that Cressida spies are matched by the infidelity Troilus
fears, and both attain displaced corroboration in the vows that conclude the scene – vows in which each lover protests too much. Then
Pandarus dismisses the two, sending them to bed, and thirty lines later
we learn that Cressida will be deported from Troy. Perhaps this is a case
of the plot coming to Troilus' rescue, as Adelman proposes, but
perhaps it is a belated and partial explanation for the very doubts both
lovers experience. In any case, I stress that these doubts are reciprocal,
and that in each instance they embody a rush to judgement, a degree
of dogmatic assumption. For Cressida, the 'partial indulgence' lies primarily in the expectation that men's valuation of women will always
decrease after sexual consummation, a view that, however worldly-
wise, is not true by internal necessity, and is explicitly contested by the
protestations of Troilus and the actions of Paris. For his part, Troilus is
dogmatic in the misogynistic assumption of women's proneness
to betrayal, an assumption reinforced by Helen but discouraged by
Cressida's overt pronouncements.[19] Both lovers' understanding of love
carries with it a fear of inadequacy – inadequacy of the self *and* the
other – and in both cases this fear hardens into presumption, which in

turn conditions speech. We wonder if Troilus could have been a constant valuer of Cressida had she not thought that he, like every other man, was incapable of unwavering devotion; we wonder whether Cressida might have proved faithful had Troilus not proclaimed that 'persuasion' itself could not convince him that his own 'integrity and truth ... Might be affronted with the match and weight / Of such a winnowed purity' (3.2.159–62). 'Affronted', with its suggestion of insult as well as equal presentation, seems the perfect word in light of our sense that Troilus' view of women would have imploded had Cressida proven true. But the lovers, despite their desperate desire for permanence, exhibit a common inability to imagine their way beyond the expectations induced by a world of flux and unfulfilled potential. That 'something may be done that we will not' (4.4.93) is a premise with which both would instantly concur.

In her grief, Cressida tells Pandarus that she cannot 'temporize' with her affection, that her 'love admits no qualifying dross; / No more my grief, in such a precious loss' (4.4.6–10). 'Loss' is crucial here, as it inflects the present with a sense of finality that can in fact be conferred only by the future (e.g. 5.2.152). Similarly, Troilus' remark to Ulysses demonstrates the cognitive invasion of negative possibility: 'She was beloved, she loved; she is, she doth; / But still sweet love is food for Fortune's tooth' (4.5.292–3). We hear in 'still' not merely 'often' or 'routinely' but 'always' and 'forever', and we witness the displacement of human fickleness onto an abstract principle of arbitrary event: 'Something may be done'. Thus we are well prepared for the play's climactic scene. But we underestimate the power of that scene if we do not also imagine that Troilus and Cressida fully believe in their grief. They feel, that is, the unallayed anguish of sundered, disillusioned love, even though they themselves contribute immeasurably – through mutual 'maculation' and 'qualifying dross' – to that love's demise (4.4.63, 4.4.9).

Sense-data discussion quickly surfaces in the scene of Cressida's betrayal. Just after she exits to fetch a token for Diomedes, Troilus informs Ulysses that 'I will not be myself, nor have cognition / Of what I feel' (5.2.62–6). He reassures his guide, in other words, that he will sever perception from mentation in his effort to remain calm, although he simultaneously acknowledges that such division entails divorce from the self. Moments later, after Diomedes has departed with Troilus' sleeve, Cressida utters her second soliloquy:

> Troilus, farewell! One eye yet looks on thee,
> But with my heart the other eye doth see.

> Ah, poor our sex! This fault in us I find:
> The error of our eye directs our mind.
> What error leads must err. O, then conclude,
> Minds swayed by eyes are full of turpitude.
>                                   (5.2.113–18)

Gesturing broadly towards perceptual infirmity, this speech genders such infirmity in a way that most critics find problematic; Jonathan Dollimore, for instance, exculpates Cressida by arguing that she 'makes ideological "sense" of sudden dislocation' by concurring with the 'dominant myth of female frailty'.[20] It is worth adding, however, that the specific frailty Cressida emphasizes is not 'the error of our eye' but the fact that such error possesses undue power of mental direction. Visual unreliability in itself applies equally to both sexes. Cressida thus offers a displaced response to Troilus' earlier remark about the separation of cognition and sensation; the play, in effect, examines the ways that humans exploit their awareness of this difference. Cressida's account of her betrayal is confused and perhaps incoherent, but what is clear is that a profound recognition of the *power* of perceptual frailty infiltrates and shapes her explanation – a recognition that simultaneously challenges Troilus' effort to isolate himself from the world of sense.

But of course he cannot do so, and one of his self-preservative tactics is to mobilize Cressida's very awareness of 'the error of our eye'. As he insists to Ulysses, his belief in Cressida's fidelity 'doth invert th' attest of eyes and ears, / As if those organs had deceptious functions, / Created only to calumniate' (5.2.128–30). Ulysses counters that this is nonsense – that Cressida was indeed present, that she said and did what Troilus heard and saw. And Thersites, looking on, concurs: 'Will 'a swagger himself out on's own eyes?' (5.2.142). But Troilus persists, resorting next to the desperate measure of creating mutually exclusive Cressidas:

> This she? No, this is Diomed's Cressida.
> If beauty have a soul, this is not she;
> If souls guide vows, if vows be sanctimonies,
> If sanctimony be the gods' delight,
> If there be rule in unity itself,
> This is not she. O, madness of discourse,
> That cause sets up with and against itself!
> Bifold authority, where reason can revolt

> Without perdition, and loss assume all reason
> Without revolt! This is and is not Cressid.
>
> (5.2.144–53)

Troilus thereby admits 'th' attest of eyes and ears' even while disputing it; he experiences 'a moment of acute and paralysing doubt' in which all bases for judgement dissolve.[21] His paralysis and pain of course belie Pyrrhonian theory – he achieves no calming *ataraxia* – but so, too, do the very assumptions embedded in his argument. If there is rule in unity, as he apparently believes, then this cannot be Cressida. But if this *is* Cressida – if sense perceptions are what they seem – then, by *modus tollens*, there can be no rule in unity. This is a formal argument, and even if Shakespeare wrote *Troilus* for an Inns of Court audience, he would not have expected them to analyse it in this fashion, but he certainly would have anticipated their ready grasp of Troilus' cognitive dilemma. Troilus claims, first of all, that reason can doubt sense-evidence and still be itself ('revolt / Without perdition'), a claim well enough justified by the notorious unreliability of perception. He then adds that 'loss [can] assume all reason without revolt', a phrase considerably more difficult to interpret. It may mean, as Barton suggests, that 'loss of reason (inability to trust the senses) can, without revolt against reason, arrogate to itself the appearance of the highest reason'.[22] But since this train of thought leads to the same conclusion reached by the former clause – that 'this is not Cressida' – it fails to suggest the full force of the 'Bifold authority' about which Troilus has just exclaimed. So 'loss' may mean, or also mean, 'loss of Cressida', a loss now verified by 'th' attest of eyes and ears' and prepared for by the 'precious loss' which Cressida has earlier bemoaned (4.4.10). Hence the self-evident betrayal that Troilus observes carries with it a substantial degree of the reasonable: this *is* Cressida. Troilus' own dogmatic assumptions are allowed to play themselves out, the madness/reason binary remains intact, and the entire passage achieves an even fuller sense of utter, absolute contradiction.

It is scarcely surprising, then, that Troilus continues by alluding to internal conflict:

> Within my soul there doth conduce a fight
> Of this strange nature, that a thing inseparate
> Divides more wider than the sky and earth,
> And yet the spacious breadth of this division
> Admits no orifex for a point as subtle

As Ariachne's broken woof to enter.
Instance, O instance, strong as Pluto's gates,
Cressid is mine, tied with the bonds of heaven;
Instance, O instance, strong as heaven itself,
The bonds of heaven are slipped, dissolved, and loosed.
                                                    (5.2.154–63)

Appropriately suffused with sexual innuendo – 'thing', 'orifex', 'point', 'enter' – this speech perpetuates the overwhelming impression of equipollence established by the earlier 'Bifold authority'. At the same time it moves into false generalization; Troilus transforms his confusion into a law of universal chaos.[23] If the bonds of heaven are dissolved, there *is* no rule in unity. Of course we are prepared for Troilus to make this kind of claim, since we have already heard him suggest that Cressida's apparent betrayal soils 'womanhood' itself: 'stubborn critics' will now 'square the general sex / By Cressid's rule' (5.2.135–9). But the localized combination of paradigms – strong emphasis on *isostheneia* conjoined with precisely the rash judgement that scepticism condemns – underlines Shakespeare's continued dramatic exploitation of the lineaments of sceptical thinking. Troilus' perplexity and anguish are conveyed with ferocious intensity by the language and tropes of early modern doubt.

   And then Troilus recedes. He does not vanish, as Cressida does, but becomes a vengeful automaton, channelling his now confirmed sense of loverly betrayal into the brute mechanics of slaughter. Few auditors, I suspect, take interest in the metamorphosis, perhaps regarding the very conversion of energy as a feeble stratagem of identity preservation. This is Troilus, yes, but not the Troilus we have known. Yet precisely here we witness something crucial to the play's full design, a meta-dramatic dimension wherein irreconcilable oppositions between opinions and values find replication in the oppositions within people. George Bernard Shaw once wrote that 'Shakespeare made exactly one attempt, in *Troilus*, to hold the mirror up to nature ... and he nearly ruined himself by it'. The latter claim is pure speculation, but I agree in essence with the former, adding only that while a critic like Rossiter sees in the play a determined 'refusal to engage our sympathies', I see repeated attempts to engage them – and repeated undermining of that engagement.[24] *Troilus* is cruel in this regard, or, if not cruel, at least inclining towards the inhuman. Even *King Lear* offers more in the way of consolation: terror that ceases, loss that is recognized, pity, tears. But *Troilus* shies away from the kind of fictional shaping in which human longings are satisfied at the expense of agreed-upon simplifications. It does so, I would argue, substantially through its embodiment of sceptical thinking.

'There is every possibility of speaking for and against anything', writes Montaigne; 'no one characteristic clasps us purely and universally in its embrace' (*Essays*, 314, 264). For Montaigne, moments of resolution and belief are almost always contextualized by uncertainty – hedged round with doubt. They carry with them a sense of oppositional potential, and they are all the more striking precisely because they eschew unconsidered affirmation. Moreover, because sceptical resolution of this Montaignian sort comprehends not only acts of belief and disbelief but extensions of emotional investment, its structure is available for appropriation in a range of discursive realms outside that principally concerned with epistemological enquiry. It is readily discernable in *Troilus*, though I do not insist upon specific Montaignian influence. The play, as I see it, is structured by opposition and permeated by doubt. And much of this doubt is dogmatic: that which is most desired is none the less subject to suspicion, and then denial. This is nowhere more apparent than in the central love scenes and in the twin depictions of grief. The protestations of Troilus and Cressida are sincere, but they are infiltrated by a doubt that constantly threatens to harden into expectation, into conviction. So the mutual vulnerability of the lovers is qualified by a mutual tendency to succumb. Yet this vulnerability is at the same time beautiful, attractive in itself, and perhaps all the more so due to its very propensity for self-cancellation.

The play-world of *Troilus and Cressida* bears remarkable affinities with the world into which the play is received. In terms of external events and internal conflicts, *Troilus* seems characterized by inscrutable tendencies of opposition and entropy that are perhaps best captured by Ulysses' reference to planetary retrogression:

> But when the planets
> In evil mixture to disorder wander,
> What plagues and what portents, what mutiny,
> What raging of the sea, shaking of earth,
> Commotion in the winds, frights, changes, horrors,
> Divert and crack, rend and deracinate
> The unity and married calm of states
> Quite from their fixture!
>
> (1.3.94–101)

The rhetorical sweep of Ulysses' speech is, of course, calculated to imply that 'plagues' and 'horrors' are avoidable; it lies within our power to observe degree. But readers have always known that plagues are inevitable in the universe Ulysses inhabits – and in our own as well. What I have suggested is that the plagues of *Troilus and Cressida* are often – and sometimes most insidiously – those associated with opinion and unyielding assumption. Troilus calls explicit attention to this when he exclaims that persuasion itself cannot change his mind. Indeed, persuasion seems terminally ineffectual in this play: repeatedly staged, it none the less occupies no privileged position in the determination of human choice and action. Hence it is extremely difficult, perhaps impossible, to fashion rational explanation for the events that unfold in *Troilus,* and difficult in particular to exculpate the play's young lovers from their mutual betrayal. Still, it is less difficult if we think simultaneously of ourselves.

# 8
# Temporizing as Pyrrhonizing in *The Malcontent*

> It had beene to Pyrrhonize a thousand yeares ago, had any
> man gone about to make a question of the opinions that have
> been received.
>
> Montaigne, *Essays*

Critics often allude to the scepticism of John Marston's drama. Robert
Ornstein calls Marston 'the first Jacobean to exploit dramatically
the skepticism about Stoic self-sufficiency expressed by Erasmus and
Montaigne and implicit in the moral philosophy of the age'. Jonathan
Dollimore interprets the close of *Antonio's Revenge* (1600–1) as 'a sub-
version of providentialist orthodoxy'. And Keith Sturgess argues that
*The Dutch Courtesan* (1605) is informed by 'Montaigne's skepticism and moral realism', thereby encouraging Marston 'to explode any
simple moral structures ... by engaging with the genuine complexity
of human experience'.[1] *The Malcontent* (1603), however, despite its
status as Marston's best-known play, has received virtually no attention along these lines; rather, critics have generally focused on its brilliant exploration of role-play and its closely related doubleness of
theme, mood and structure.[2] Yet given the intellectual milieu in which
the play was composed, not to mention Marston's evident familiarity with Pyrrhonism, it seems worthwhile to ask what relations may
obtain between, on the one hand, *The Malcontent*'s examination of
role-play and duality and, on the other, its participation in the various
sceptical paradigms available to an intellectually curious poet or
playwright at the outset of the seventeenth century.

That Marston had been exposed to the sceptical lexicon and to
common sceptical ideas is clear. Both at Oxford, where epistemological
*quaestiones* were routinely posed for disputation, and at London's Inns

of Court, notorious in the 1590s for the cultivation of radical ideas in philosophy and art,[3] Marston would have had access to the Latin translations of Sextus published in the 1560s, as well as to other works which summarized, applauded, countered or lampooned sceptical arguments with varying degrees of accuracy and persuasiveness. He would in addition, during his dozen-year tenure at the Middle Temple (1595–1606), have been acquainted with Sir John Davies, John Webster, John Ford and possibly Fulke Greville and Walter Ralegh, each of whom played a part in the English dissemination of sceptical thought.[4] And he may well have read *The Sceptick*. It thus comes as little surprise that in his satirical *Scourge of Villanie* (1598), Marston chastises a fictional interlocutor: 'Fye *Gallus*, what, a skeptick *Pyrrhomist?*'[5] Besides offering the earliest known instance of the word 'Pyrrhonist' in English, this speech, in context, demonstrates a relatively accurate understanding of a central Pyrrhonian idea: Marston's satiric persona refuses to withhold belief in the fashion advocated by sceptics. Rather, he assures Gallus that he is a plain speaker – and that he intends to stay that way. In contrast, then, to a writer such as Nashe, who also alludes to Sextus and 'Pironiks' in various works from the 1590s, Marston demonstrates a sharper understanding of Pyrrhonism, an understanding closer to that evinced by Donne (another Inns of Court student), who asserts that 'the Sceptique which doubts all is more contentious then eyther the Dogmatique which affirmes, or Academique which denyes'.[6] Unlike Donne, however, Marston did not read Montaigne until after the 1603 publication of Florio's translation, and thus his initial understanding of Pyrrhonism depends on knowledge of sources other than the *Essays*.[7]

Yet Marston's acquaintance with elements of the sceptical lexicon is only part of the story. He is also familiar, as are many of his contemporaries, with commonplaces of ancient philosophy closely tied to scepticism, among them the Socratic *nihil scio* and the tactic of arguing *in utramque partem*. His plays are laced with aphorisms such as 'I know I know naught but I naught do know' (*What You Will*, 2.2.193) and 'There's naught that's safe and sweet but ignorance' (*Malcontent*, 3.1.32).[8] And his cognizance of the Ciceronian strategy of examining questions from both sides is evident, for instance, in the attitudes of *What You Will*'s Lampatho, a malcontent who, like Vindice, Flamineo and Bosola of later Jacobean tragedy, laments his endeavours at study:

> I was a scholar: seven useful springs
> Did I deflower in quotations

Of cross'd opinions 'bout the soul of man.
The more I learnt the more I learnt to doubt:
Knowledge and wit, faith's foes, turn faith about.
(2.2.151–5)

That 'cross'd opinions' can lead to terminal doubt is not only the standard conclusion of Pyrrhonian thought with respect to the juxtaposition of opposed beliefs or perceptions, but also a common trajectory of the 'vanity of learning' topos so prominent in English philosophical poetry at the turn of the seventeenth century.[9] Finally, it is worth noting one last bit of evidence suggesting Marston's direct acquaintance with the works of Sextus. Late in *The Malcontent*, when Maquerelle and Malevole debate whether Maria will succumb to Mendoza's marital advances, Maquerelle queries Malevole about the current sign of the zodiac. Malevole mockingly responds by exclaiming, 'Sign! Why, is there any moment in that?' To which Maquerelle earnestly replies:

O, believe me, a most secret power. Look ye, a Chaldean or an Assyrian (I am sure 'twas a most sweet Jew) told me, court any woman in the right sign, you shall not miss. But you must take her in the right vein then; as, when the sign is in Pisces, a fishmonger's wife is very sociable; in Cancer, a precisian's wife is very flexible; in Capricorn, a merchant's wife hardly holds out; ... only in Scorpio 'tis very dangerous meddling. (5.1.108–17)

The conjunction of 'Chaldean' with ridicule of astrological determinism strongly suggests Marston's familiarity either with Sextus' parallel conjunction in *Adversus astrologos* (*M*, 5.21), or with recent allusions to Sextus and Chaldean belief in the dispute over judicial astrology carried out by Chamber and Heydon.[10] Directly or indirectly, then, Marston knows Sextus; more significantly, however, he is poised to experiment with sceptical paradigms derived from contemporary English understanding, misunderstanding, appropriation and deployment of ancient sceptical ideas.

But how do the sceptical paradigms available to Marston relate to *The Malcontent*'s fascination with role-play, disguise and dissimulation? One way to approach this question is to examine the assumptions embedded within a recent summary of critical stances towards the play's exploration of whether and how far the adoption of the mask of malcontent/revenger corrupts the adopting subject. Responding to

critical pronouncements by Arthur Kirsch and Alvin Kernan, Joan Lord
Hall writes that

> If Altofronto/Malevole is felt to be a composite and controlled char-
> acter, the 'central intelligence' whose 'supreme and dominating role-
> playing crystallizes the whole of the play', then the play's happy
> ending is an optimistic comment on man's ability to manipulate
> roles creatively rather than becoming 'intrapped' in them, to use
> Montaigne's term. But if the audience loses this sense of the control-
> ling consciousness behind the scurrilous Malevole, then it will regis-
> ter the malcontent role mainly as an insidious manifestation of a
> warped character in a corrupt society.[11]

The first and most obvious response to this summary is that neither
readers nor playgoers are likely to lose their sense of a 'controlling consciousness' behind Malevole's presence. More than a dozen times we
are reminded of such a consciousness through Marston's deployment
of soliloquies and asides, not to mention his emphasis on intimate
conversations between Altofronto and Celso – conversations reminiscent of those between Hamlet and Horatio. In only one of these
moments does Altofronto register explicit reluctance to play the part
of Malevole – 'O God, how loathsome this toying is to me! That a duke
should be forced to fool it!' (5.2.41–4) – and thus Sturgess's claim
that Altofronto must 'keep himself insulated from the spoiling, pruri-
ent, corruption-loving Malevole' seems extreme in emphasis.[12] On the
contrary, Altofronto generally appears to relish the role of malcontent:

> Well, this disguise doth yet afford me that
> Which kings do seldom hear, or great men use –
> Free speech. And though my state's usurped,
> Yet this affected strain gives me a tongue
> As fetterless as is an emperor's.
> 
> (1.3.154–8)

He clearly values the freedom of expression granted by his disguise.
Hence there are unquestionably continuities between the inward
thought of Altofronto and the outward speech of Malevole: the latter
may say what the former can only think. Moreover, to the extent that
Altofronto's delight in 'free speech' is consonant with the praise for
poetic liberty proffered both in the play's Induction and in its preliminary ode, such delight constitutes a normative attitude within

the play and thus validates the Thersites-like speech of Malevole.[13] To 'bespurtle' (1.2.11), 'tent' (4.5.64) or exercise a 'home-thrusting tongue' (3.5.23) is to indulge in the 'tartness' appropriate to the 'freedom of a satire' ('To the Reader'). And if Altofronto's identity, like the dyer's hand, is subdued to what it works in, the subduing is not a corruption but a necessary, creative, even desired, evolution. Tempting as it may seem – and despite G. K. Hunter's claim that Marston's malcontent is 'eaten into by the evil he beholds' – Malevole's Altofronto cannot be viewed in quite the same way as Piato's Vindice.[14]

Returning to Hall's summary, I believe the next assumption worthy of interrogation is that the play's ending is 'happy' and 'optimistic', and that this optimism is inextricably tied to a sense that Altofronto is never 'intrapped' in the role of Malevole. First, as I have argued, Altofronto enjoys his role as Malevole, and thus appears to *be* Malevole in some sense worth considering; it follows from this that if he is not precisely 'intrapped' in the role, the role none the less functions as a part of him – an extension or development, perhaps – much in the way that we view Hamlet's 'antic disposition' as having been adopted with comparative ease. Second, the play's ending strikes me less as happy or optimistic than as perfunctorily generic – rather like the close of *Measure for Measure*. Conventional with a vengeance, it foregrounds genre expectations to an almost ludicrous degree, thereby drawing them powerfully into question.[15] Moreover, the providential optimism embedded in several of Altofronto's late-play speeches hangs in curious suspension with the vehement pessimism expressed by Malevole: if the world is morally responsive, averse to allowing one to sink 'that close can temporise', it is none the less a world in which temporizing is necessary – a world where 'Mature discretion is the life of state' (4.5.144–8). Thus Malevole's estimate of earth and its inhabitants – offered to Pietro just prior to the revelation of Malevole's 'true' identity – amounts in effect to Altofronto's estimate as well:

> this earth is the only grave and Golgotha wherein all things that live must rot; 'tis but the draught wherein the heavenly bodies discharge their corruption, the very muckhill on which the sublunary orbs cast their excrements. Man is the slime of this dung-pit, and princes are the governors of these men. (4.5.107–12)

The play offers no sense that the explicit resumption of Altofronto's ducal role negates or dissipates any of the claims Malevole has made. On the contrary, the world still seems a 'dung-pit', and if it is a providential world, it is providential in a way somehow consonant with thoroughgoing corruption, depravity and Golgotha-like death-stress.[16] One might object that Malevole's pronouncements merely ring a Protestant variation on early modern strains of the *contemptus mundi* attitude. Erasmus, after all, had claimed that if viewed from the moon, human activity would seem the commotion of 'a swarm of flies or gnats', all quarreling and betraying one another (*CWE*, 27:122); Montaigne had wondered whether it was 'possible to imagine anything more laughable' than that humanity, buried amidst 'the mire and shit of the world', should none the less consider itself 'Emperor of the universe' (*Apology*, 13–16). But the vehemence of Malevole's remarks, combined with their comic corroboration in the play's narrowly averted violence and in Ferneze's cony-catching antics during the climactic masque (5.4.83–99), renders thoroughly problematic their easy subsumption within the ideal of a morally responsive cosmos.[17] Like the Calvinist impasse generated through dual emphasis on divine benevolence and human depravity, *The Malcontent*'s doubleness presents us with a forceful paradox. But whereas Calvin resorts to Pauline pronouncements, stipulating that it is wicked for humans to question God's will, *The Malcontent* offers no moral guidance in the face of its paradox.[18]

In short, the collective professions of Altofronto/Malevole constitute a simultaneous assertion of what *The Sceptick* calls 'contrarieties' (49); they amount to a violation of the Aristotelian principle of non-contradiction inasmuch as they insist upon both A and not-A. To be sure, the professions are not as precisely oppositional as Troilus' 'This is, and is not, Cressid' (5.2.143), or even Vindice's 'I'm in doubt / Whether I'm myself or no' (4.4.24–5); but to demand such precision is less germane than to note the clear emphasis on contraposition. Rather than eschewing choice among opposites and thus suspending judgement in Pyrrhonian fashion, Altofronto/Malevole practises *in utramque partem* argumentation but concludes that *both* sides are true. He thus follows a sceptical trajectory to the extent that he entertains 'cross'd opinions' and refuses to choose between them, but he abandons the trajectory in departing from the Pyrrhonian principle of non-assertion. Instead of 'A, but not-A, therefore neither', he presents us with 'A, but not-A, therefore both'. And this subscription to 'double truth' – to what Troilus terms 'bifold authority' – is one of several sceptical 'conclusions' available to Elizabethan and Jacobean intellectuals living amidst the flurry of Pyrrhonian speculation in the wake of the Sextus trans-lations.[19] A variant of the second paradigm outlined in chapter 4, this thought-progression allows for the toleration of apparent contradiction without suggesting that we cease our search into vexing metaphysical issues. It promotes provisional acquiescence to inscrutability even while encouraging ongoing investigation (scepticism's *zetetic* mode) into the paradoxes of divine providence, earthly corruption and God's alleged alignment with virtuous action. As readers or playgoers, then, we are asked both to see ourselves as the 'slime' of the world's 'muck-hill' and to assent without hesitation to the implied answer to Altofronto's rhetorical question: 'Who doubts of providence, that sees this change?' (4.5.138–9). We are asked to contemplate the simultaneous truth and falsity of Malevole's remark to Pietro: 'I would not trust heaven with my vengeance anything' (1.3.144–5). More generally, we are invited to reflect on Montaigne's observation that 'I may perhaps gaine-say myself, but truth I never gaine-say: Were my mind settled, I would not essay, but resolve myself' (Florio, 726).

Indeed, a habit of never gainsaying truth seems woven into the verbal fabric of *The Malcontent*. It manifests itself in Malevole's delight in oxymoron: he refers to himself as 'an honest villain' (1.3.84) and 'an excellent pander' (4.3.88); he addresses Mendoza as 'friendly damnation' (2.5.135). Other characters participate as well in this verbal corroboration of pervasive dual authority. Maria calls Mendoza a 'gracious devil' (5.4.38) and Bilioso praises Maquerelle's self-promotion strategies as 'excellent policy' (5.1.32). But in addition to sharp verbal oppositions, Marston clearly favours paradoxical expression as a rhetorical strategy particularly suited to *The Malcontent*. Bilioso, according to Malevole, is 'half a man, half a goat, all a beast' (1.3.34–5), and Malevole, in turn, is 'a man, or rather a monster', whose 'soul is at variance within herself' and whose 'highest delight is to procure others' vexation' (1.2.18–27). Maquerelle, swearing by her 'maidenhead' (5.3.113), advises Bianca and Emilia to 'Cherish anything saving your husband' (2.4.34); elsewhere she argues that 'Honesty is but an art to seem so' (5.2.12). And to the extent that Mendoza believes that 'vengeance makes men wise' (1.7.80) and Bilioso testifies that he 'had rather stand with wrong, than fall with right' (4.5.90), it is scarcely surprising that Malevole implores God to 'deliver me from my friends!' (4.4.19–20).

But the paradoxes exposed by the simultaneous representation of 'two tugging factions' (3.3.12) are even more evident in *The Malcontent*'s sceptical generalizations about human nature. Railing against women, Mendoza avers that 'these monsters in nature' are 'only constant in unconstancy' (1.6.82–8); and his misogyny is more subtly perpetuated by Pietro, who requests that his entertainers 'Sing of the nature of women, and then the song shall be surely full of variety, old crotchets and most sweet closes; it shall be humorous, grave, fantastic, amorous, melancholy, sprightly, one in all, and all in one' (3.4.29–32). Probably the best instance, however, of that allegation of human all-inclusiveness that refuses, in essence, to choose between a given claim and its opposite, lies in another observation by Pietro. Despondent in the aftermath of the supposed murder of Ferneze, Pietro exclaims, with clear Faustian overtones,

> Good God, that men should desire
> To search out that, which being found, kills all
> Their joy of life! To taste the tree of knowledge,
> And then be driven from out paradise.
>                                    (3.1.15–18)

Though not as intensely bitter in tone as Shakespeare's more famous expression of the same fundamental sentiment – that 'Desire is death' and that we long for 'that which longer nurseth the disease, / Feeding on that which doth preserve the ill' (Sonnet 147) – Pietro's exclamation none the less captures a sense of the simultaneous exhilaration and peril of human desire; it serves too as an indirect indictment of God's choice thus to constitute the human psyche. Perhaps most significant of all, given *The Malcontent*'s cast of characters and the various oscillations of Altofronto/Malevole, the remark adds nuance and complexity to our assessments not only of Pietro, but of Mendoza, Bianca, Maquerelle and even Bilioso.

In one respect, the sceptical orientation I have outlined here seems unremarkable inasmuch as it resonates thoroughly with the fundamental premise of the theatrical milieu in which it takes its life. Just as one actor plays both Altofronto and Malevole, thereby effectively engaging in the portrayal both of not-Malevole and not-Altofronto, so the combined Altofronto/Malevole asserts 'cross'd opinions' whose reconciliation demands some degree of assent to mystery. But beyond this we must consider that Altofronto is not merely dissembling as Malevole, and thus not merely playing the Machiavel, but 'temporizing' in the role, as he twice observes (1.4.28, 4.5.144). An example from Shakespeare may clarify the distinction. When Cressida exclaims that she cannot 'temporize with [her] affections', she understands temporizing as moderating; she argues that since her love 'admits no qualifying dross, / No more my grief, in such a

precious loss' (4.4.6–10). To temporize with her affections would be
to ascribe impurity to them, and to the extent that she sees herself
as incapable of doing this, she similarly eschews the possibility of
moderating her grief and thus acting according to the time. But the
transparent illogic of Cressida's argument – her unfounded assumption that alteration of outward appearance necessarily depends on
alteration of inward feeling – throws light on Altofronto's conception of temporizing. For to 'temporise', as he suggests to Celso, while
indeed to play a role and thus in a broad sense to dissemble, is more
specifically to acknowledge that while behaviour must often change
with circumstance, such change does *not* imply discontinuity of
interior feeling or purpose. Consequently, characterizing Altofronto's behaviour as 'virtuous Machiavellianism' or claiming that
his temporizing amounts to a 'Machiavellian compromise with ideal-
ism' are both slightly misleading.[20] Mendoza, not Altofronto, is the
Machiavel of this play: his methods secretive, his ends self-serving,
his confidence overweening, his imagination enfeebled by its divorce from human community (4.3.134–41, 5.3.72–9). Altofronto,
by contrast, confides first in Celso and then in Ferneze, Pietro and
his wife Maria, thereby suggesting that the ducal restoration he seeks
depends on solidarity and truth-telling, hence upon vulnerability.
The very potential for failure here – the inherent dimension of risk –
again resonates with the yoking of contraries constitutive of the
sceptical paradigm I have presented. Temporizing, for Altofronto,
ineluctably amounts to hoping:

> Climb not a falling tower, Celso,
> 'Tis well held desperation, no zeal,
> Hopeless to strive with fate. Peace! Temporise.
> Hope, hope, that never forsak'st the wretched'st man,
> Yet bidd'st me live, and lurk in this disguise ... .
> Some way t' will work – Phewt! I'll not shrink.
> He's resolute who can no longer sink.
>
> (1.4.26–42)

It amounts, in short, to the assumption of a degree of humility entirely
alien to the standard Machiavellian dissimulation with which we are
familiar from Marlowe's Barabas and Ferneze, or, better still, Kyd's
Lorenzo. It thus equates with Pyrrhonizing inasmuch as it reflects the
structural form of the quasi-Pyrrhonian sceptical paradigm I have
described, as also in its rejection of dogmatic stances generally.

As one final instance of *The Malcontent's* underlining of its dual-protagonist's complex form of role-playing, we may consider the play's emphatic but seldom-remarked spotlighting of religious affiliation. Beginning with Malevole's ironic 'I'll go to church' (1.2.11) and followed by Pietro's bemused 'I wonder what religion thou art of?' (1.3.7), this line of interrogation evolves into a dramatic refrain; the play is punctuated with queries about religious status that accentuate the radical shifts in commitment and belief exhibited by such characters as Pietro and Bilioso:

> What religion wilt thou be of next? (2.3.12)
> What, art an infidel still? (4.4.5)
> Of what faith art now? (4.4.15)
> What religion will you be of now? (4.5.91)

It is not that Malevole feels genuine curiosity about these characters' religious affiliations, but that the possibility of shifting religious alliance serves metaphorically to underscore the difference between these characters' role-playing and the temporizing practised by Altofronto. In a world where, as Marston well knows, the conventional answer to the question of what 'makes most infidels now?' is 'Sects, sects' (1.3.9–11), the employment of pointed queries about religious affiliation serves admirably as a means of stressing the potential for easy drift among mutually exclusive commitments and alliances. And the punning on sexual infidelity, thoroughly appropriate given the double cuckolding of Pietro by Mendoza and Ferneze, only heightens our attention to questions of loyalty, betrayal and adulteration.

*The Malcontent*, then, juxtaposes Mendoza's Machiavellian dissembling with Altofronto's temporizing: both are forms of role-play, but they are meant to be distinguished from one another, as well as from Aurelia's brazen counterfeiting and Bilioso's mindless following of favour. If Mendoza is accurately characterized as one who hypocritically 'snibs filth in other men and retains it in himself' (3.3.28–9), we are perhaps justified in understanding Altofronto/Malevole as one who also 'snibs filth' as part of his role, but does not 'retain' it so much as apprehend it with constant imaginative intensity. His is a 'hideous imagination' (1.3.133), as Pietro astutely observes. Like Vincentio in *Measure for Measure*, Altofronto/Malevole adheres to the formula 'Craft against vice I must apply' (3.2.280), temporizing in a manner that demonstrates both his profound experiential understanding of vice and his acknowledgement of the paradox that pervasive human viciousness coexists with pervasive providential supervision. If the world, as Thomas Beard had claimed in 1597, is the theatre of God's judgements, it is a theatre where actors write substantial portions of the script. And while *The Malcontent* undoubtedly offers moments of the subversive examination of providentialist orthodoxy that Dollimore, for instance, might seize upon (e.g. 3.3.119–23), the larger movement of the play suggests that its scepticism lies rather in its participation in that sceptical paradigm which assents simultaneously to the need for human temporizing in response to the world's undeniable depravity, and to a vision of the world as ultimately overseen and governed by a just, benign power in whom 'all' should invest their 'hearty faith' (4.5.139). To the extent that this dual assent both rehearses and interrogates early modern disputes between activity and passivity, works and faith, and the world as 'sterile promontory' versus 'goodly frame', its manifestation in *The Malcontent* resonates profoundly with Pyrrhonism's entry into and shaping of the *fin de siècle* Elizabethan preoccupation with the mystery of opinions both 'cross'd' and 'true'.

# 9
## *Mariam* and the Critique of Pure Reason

> But men may construe things after their fashion,
> Clean from the purpose of the things themselves.
>
> Cicero, in *Julius Caesar*

The young Elizabeth Tanfield was a voracious reader. Linguistically gifted, she mastered Latin, French and Italian as a girl, studied Hebrew and, according to her daughter Lucy, read 'very exceeding much'. Poetry, theology, classical history and English chronicle all figured significantly in this reading, as did books 'treating of moral virtue or wisdom (such as Seneca, Plutarch ... French Mountaine, and English Bacon)'. Indeed, the future Elizabeth Cary not only translated Seneca's *Epistles*, but thoroughly immersed herself in the realm of wisdom literature – and 'not without making her profit'.[1] What that profit was and how it manifested itself are questions one might well desire to ask Cary's daughter, as are the related matters of precisely when, and in what circumstances and intellectual context, Cary encountered Montaigne and Bacon – and, in the case of the former, whether she read his *Essays* in French or in Florio's recent English version. But that Montaigne in particular had a perceptible impact on Cary's habits of contemplating 'moral virtue' seems beyond dispute. *The Tragedy of Mariam*, published in 1613 but composed between 1602 and 1609, illustrates in varied ways not only that Cary was indebted to Montaigne, but that like the French essayist and many contemporary intellectuals she was intrigued by the complex epistemological relations among knowing, perceiving, seeming and believing. More precisely, her play interrogates the facile distinction between reason and feeling that several of its characters – and especially the Chorus – routinely assume, and which contributes significantly to the protagonist's death.

Drawing on her familiarity with the time-honoured sceptical tendency to question Stoic sententiousness – a tendency frequently displayed by Montaigne – Cary schools her audience to scrutinize the Chorus's habits of judgement and to cast doubt on its self-assured verdicts.[2] The claims of the Chorus become, in effect, necessary antecedents rather than final adjudications, and *Mariam*'s auditors emerge as active participants in an ongoing dialectic of judicial assessment.

Recent editions of *Mariam* have noted Cary's likely reliance on Montaigne in the title character's opening soliloquy. Reacting to the report of her husband Herod's death, Mariam acknowledges the intricacy of her emotional response and chastises herself for her earlier censure of Julius Caesar, who had wept at the news of Pompey's demise. In an apostrophe to the now-dead 'Roman lord', Mariam asks for leniency:

> Excuse too rash a judgment in a woman:
> My sex pleads pardon, pardon then afford,
> Mistaking is with us but too too common.
> Now do I find, by self-experience taught,
> One object yields both grief and joy:
> You wept indeed, when on his worth you thought,
> But joy'd that slaughter did your foe destroy.
> So at his death your eyes true drops did rain,
> Whom dead, you did not wish alive again.
>
> (1.1.6–14)

As Marta Straznicky and Richard Rowland have observed, Cary seems indebted here to the chapter entitled 'How we weepe and laugh at one selfe-same thing', which illustrates how thoroughly Montaigne's sense of human mutability infiltrates even his earlier and more Stoically inclined meditations.[3] Not only does he stress that 'our mindes are agitated by divers passions', but he foregrounds the story of Caesar and Pompey, remarking, as Mariam does in different words, that it is not particularly strange 'to mourne for him dead, whom a man by no meanes would have alive again' (Florio, 185–7). Unquestionably agitated by 'divers passions', Mariam sets the stage here for Herod's later psychomachia, where 'love and hate do fight' (4.4.244). Cary's debt to Montaigne thus seems probable almost to the point of certainty.

But the interest of the passage far exceeds this debt. The 'mistaking' of which Mariam speaks, and whose prevalence she pre-emptively ascribes to her sex, is the 'rash' judgement that Caesar was a dissembler and hypocrite – a judgement that, as Montaigne notes, no less a writer than Lucan had levelled (186). Hence the gender binary proposed by Mariam is immediately destabilized by source examination, just as it is textually imperiled by the tacit equation of the complex emotional reactions of Mariam and Caesar. But beyond this, the passage opens proleptically upon the play's thoroughgoing concern with the human tendency to rush to judgement, a tendency excoriated in the play's second Chorus and ironically displayed in Mariam's very confidence that the rumour of her husband's death is true. Cary seems fascinated by this phenomenon, presenting it not as an isolated facet of Mariam's behaviour but as a universal proclivity, no more female than male in character. The false belief that Herod is dead is the engine that powers the first half of *Mariam*, and as such it commands Cary's attention as a representative instance of an intrinsically compelling feature of cognition. And when Alexandra chides Mariam by telling Salome that her daughter laments 'with more than reason' at being 'freed from such a sad annoy' (1.3.215–16), Cary suggests both how shallow is Alexandra's understanding of Mariam's inward life and how inadequate is that stipulative definition of 'reason' that excludes what lies behind, or beyond, strict ratiocination.

Most of the critical commentary on *Mariam* in the past fifteen years has concentrated on the play's explorations of women's 'public voice', female resistance to patriarchal tyranny and contradictions within prevailing gender and political discourses. Studies by such scholars as Margaret Ferguson, Barbara Lewalski, Elaine Beilin, Betty Travitsky, Maureen Quilligan and Laurie Shannon have raised the profile of this once obscure closet drama by drawing attention to the manifold ways in which Cary 'challenges patriarchal control within marriage' by depicting a heroine who 'claims a wife's right to self-definition and the integrity of her own emotional life'. But as Diane Purkiss observes, *Mariam* also participates in 'humanist and intellectual projects usually believed to be wholly masculine by modern critics'; the play's fluency with Stoic ideas and Senecan drama exemplify its connection 'with the realm of letters and the circulation of ideas, discourses, and writings'. Shari Zimmerman further elaborates *Mariam*'s discursive embeddedness by examining its exploration of 'counterfeit performance' in conjunction with John Milton's assumptions about wifely dissembling. For Zimmerman, the motto 'be and seem' (inscribed by Cary in her daughter Catherine's wedding ring) takes on new and complex significance, and *Mariam* begins to resonate not only with Shakespeare's meditations on appearance in *Hamlet* but with deep-seated cultural ambivalences regarding duplicity and dissimulation.[4] Given all this – and given as well the reliance on Montaigne – it seems appropriate to turn to *Mariam*'s focus, at times bordering obsession, on epistemological concerns demonstrably important to Cary and her contemporaries.

Indeed, the play will not let them rest. In the 'Argument', for instance, Cary goes out of her way to explain why the report of Herod's execution was so quickly embraced by Jerusalem's inhabitants: it was 'their willingness it should be so, together with the likelihood', that gave the rumor such 'good credit' (67). Standing out conspicuously in a narration otherwise devoted to facts, this explanation broaches Cary's interest in the phenomenon of desire conditioning belief, and it also serves, almost apologetically, as a way of accounting to ostensibly sceptical readers why the Judeans acted as they did. In other words, Cary shapes her audience, constructing them as cautious and self-restrained rationalists who construe as immediately implausible the same rumour the Judeans find so plausible as to construe as truth. And this readerly construction, as I suggest below, contributes importantly to the ways in which the play's notoriously puzzling choral commentaries acquire and generate meaning.

Or, to take another example, consider Constabarus' debate with the sons of Babas. Like Mariam, Alexandra, Pheroras, Graphina and Sohemus, all of whom readily accept the claim that Herod is dead, Constabarus acts confidently in the assumed truth of the news. But Babas' First Son thinks otherwise. Capable of suspending judgement on the matter and imagining that the 'tale' of Herod's demise may 'prove a very tale indeed' (2.2.147–8), he proposes that he and his brother remain in hiding until the 'truth' of Herod's state is known. Constabarus explodes at this suggestion, accusing the Son of cowardice and, in an interchange where the word 'doubt' appears five times in a dozen lines, defending the 'undoubted truth' of the tyrant's death with arguments grounded in probability (2.2.156). But it is clear that Babas' First Son is no coward, and thus this passage, besides foreshadowing Herod's imminent return, concentrates our attention on the distinction between doubt as fear and as withholding of assent. The former view, often characteristic of those inclined to rush to judgement, comes easily to Constabarus and complicates his portrayal considerably. Cary makes him attractive as a loyal friend to Babas' sons and a victim of Salome's intrigues, but his later misogynistic tirade is among the most vehement in all Renaissance drama (4.6.309–50), and he is also alleged, as is Herod, to exhibit a stifling and jealous love for his wife – though of course the allegation comes from Salome herself (1.6.418). A subtle alignment is thus established between Constabarus and Herod, and the play's second Chorus, with its explicit denunciation of 'rash' and 'heady' conclusion, resonates significantly beyond the specific circumstance of 'this tale of Herod's end' (2.4.405–26).[5]

In short, *Mariam* insists on foregrounding a dimension of its play-world that we, as readers four centuries later, may be tempted to marginalize: a constellation of cognitive phenomena including precipitous judgement, suspension of belief, false generalization, deluded perception, assent conditioned by desire, and 'reason' constituted as more than mere logic. Yes, we may think, the play's unfolding depends on a radically mistaken belief, but surely the machinations of Salome and the principled decisions of Mariam hold more dramatic interest than this belief; hence they gather and concentrate a far greater degree of the play's internal reflection. Yet Cary draws out parallels between Judea's conclusion of Herod's death and Herod's conclusion of Mariam's infidelity that ultimately defy any marginalization of epistemological concerns (2.4.406–12, 5.1.109). Like John Davies of Hereford, her childhood tutor and writing master, Cary exhibits sustained interest in questions of doubt and credulity. And they are questions that return uncannily to haunt her nearly three decades later, when William Chillingworth attempts to lure her daughters away from their professed Catholicism.

\* \* \*

Davies, who in 1612 refers with pride to Cary as his former 'Pupill', places considerable emphasis in various philosophical poems on the intrinsic frailties of reason and sense-perception. In *Mirum in Modum* (1602) he relates anecdotal information about Pyrrho of Elis, and in *Microcosmos* (1603) he claims that

> the state of things is so vnstay'd
> That *humane wisedome* stands it wotts not howe;
> Unsure in all; for *Judgment's* oft betrai'd
> In that which *proofe* before had well assai'd.

Davies buttresses this assertion with a marginal note lifted almost verbatim from the Elizabethan translation of Agrippa's *Vanitie*. 'Every knowledge', he writes, 'hath its beginning of the senses, which are often deceiu'd. Therefore all sciences which are deriu'd & fast rooted in the senses are vncertaine, & deceiptfull.'[6] Davies thus displays clear acquaintance with ancient scepticism as it was channelled into sixteenth-century Europe through such writers as Agrippa and Bartas, and through such translations as Traversari's rendition of Laertius and perhaps Estienne's version of Sextus.

As for Chillingworth, Lucy Cary's biography of her mother depicts him as a quasi-demonic figure in his subtle self-presentation to Lucy and her sisters as 'a long waverer', a man deeply worried that they, in their conversion to the Roman Church, may have been 'too speedy resolvers' (*Life*, 233). Always 'professing himself a Catholic' during his visits to Cary's London house in the early 1630s, Chillingworth attempted to lead the daughters through a cautious and rational re-valuation of their decision. Quoting St Peter's precept that 'everyone ought to be able to give a reason of his faith', he argued that 'it was not enough to believe the right, unless they could defend the reasonable-ness of it' (234–6). Eventually, he was exposed as a 'willful deceiver and seducer'; he was 'forbid the house' and prevented from further efforts at eroding the daughters' confidence in their Catholic profession (241–3). But what emerges clearly from Lucy's admittedly tendentious narration is that the intellectual climate in which Cary and her chil-dren existed – and which Chillingworth and other members of the Great Tew circle overtly promoted – saw epistemological doubt as a virtue and gave positive valence to the state of being 'disengaged on either side' (238).[7] Chillingworth's very effort at undermining Cary's daughters' faith was premised on their respect for his perceived status, like that of their elder brother Lucius, as a doubter and cautious student, an ongoing 'inquirer' rather than 'an absolute defender of anything' (244). Their own respect for the sceptical outlook, in other words, was craftily deployed against them.

To be sure, the eclectic combination of enquiry, disengagement and Socinian rationalism exhibited by Chillingworth represents an idio-syncratic manifestation of scepticism's early modern reception rather than a rigorous replication of Pyrrhonism; it represents, in short, a sceptical paradigm. But there is no question that Chillingworth was thoroughly conversant with the Pyrrhonian tradition. Aubrey tells us that as a student at Oxford he 'much delighted in Sextus', and Clarendon adds that he was so skilful in disputation as to develop, ulti-mately, 'such an irresolution and habit of doubting, that by degrees he grew confident of nothing, and a sceptic, at least, in the greatest mys-teries of faith'.[8] Not long after the episode with Cary's daughters, more-over, Chillingworth published his *Religion of Protestants* (1638), a treatise profoundly concerned with problems of certainty in religious profession and intimately acquainted with Pyrrhonian tactics of argumentation. Chillingworth's scepticism, eclectic but real, thus instantiates a paradigm of the early modern reception of Pyrrhonism; it is closely tied in particular to the emphasis on continual enquiry (Sextus' *zetetic* mode) so crucial to Montaigne and Charron.[9]

Cary, who might easily have read Davies' poems in manuscript or in their initial printed versions, was very likely familiar with the Socinian writings important to her eldest son. And being a woman who 'loved good company so much that the contrary was almost insupportable', she would have known from frequent conversational experience that sceptical arguments were constantly appropriated and deployed in contemporary theological dispute (225). Indeed, as someone who challenged Calvin's theses at the age of twelve (188), she would have known this decades before her unpleasant encounter with Chillingworth – an encounter I emphasize because it strikingly illustrates sceptical tactics in action. It may be true that Pyrrhonian-style disputation had 'growne out of fashion' by the late seventeenth century – Aubrey terms it 'an Epidemick evill', 'unmannerly and boyish' – but in the century's earlier years, as in the latter part of Elizabeth's reign, sceptical arguments still mattered, still were taken seriously and perceived as having potentially eternal consequences for the people utilizing them. What might strike twenty-first-century ears as arid or unnecessary questions are crucial to Cary and her imagined readers, and indeed she inflects those readers as already astutely conscious of the importance of such matters. So if the balances of *Mariam* seem slightly off-kilter by present-day aesthetic standards, they none the less reflect genuine intellectual concerns of its author and her audience.

One thing this means, in practical terms, is that a person in whom there seems 'a kind of impossibility of agreement between his heart and his tongue' is equally susceptible of appearance in Cary's life as in her tragedy (227). Notwithstanding differences of sex and intention, let alone ontological status, Chillingworth and Salome share a fundamental position, in Cary's outlook and that of her daughter, as embodiments of the familiar archetype of the white devil or 'painted sepulchre' (2.4.325–8, 4.6.321–4). It is an archetype to which Mariam is also at times assimilated (4.4.175–8, 4.7.429–30), and with which English playwrights were endlessly fascinated – especially playwrights like Marston, Shakespeare and Webster, who were also readers of Montaigne.[10] 'The greatest number of our actions', writes the essayist, are 'masked and painted over with dissimulation' (Florio, 186). And the vigilance Mariam displays in attempting *not* to be other than she seems is further evidence of Cary's concern with such dissimulation (3.3.163–70, 4.3.91–2, 4.3.145–6), though the disjunction between being and seeming generated by the impossibility of controlling the perceptions of others leads quickly to the recognition that self-protective feigning may at times emerge as the shrewdest way to 'be and seem'.[11] In any event, because the impulse to unite seeming and being stems from the experiential knowledge that appearance and reality often conflict, *Mariam*'s treatment of the theme – and especially of the ease with which humans may be deceived – becomes, in effect, an allegorical representation of the perceptual frailty emphasized by Montaigne and Davies of Hereford, and central to sceptical accounts of cognition. Hence it is that *Hamlet* intrudes almost imperceptibly into the discussion.

'Seems, madam?' asks the prince of his mother; 'Nay, it is. I know not seems' (1.2.76). Like Mariam, Hamlet is acutely conscious of the potential fissure between surface and interior. As Katharine Maus writes, his clothes and behaviour 'fail to denote him truly not because they are false – Hamlet's sorrow for his father is sincere – but because they *might* be false, because some other person might conceivably employ them deceitfully'.[12] For Hamlet, who asserts that he has 'that within which passeth show', the possibility exists not merely that seeming and being may diverge, but that surfaces may at times be intrinsically incapable of accurately signifying interiors. Even sincere seeming will often fall short or deceive through inadequacy. And behaviour such as that of *The Faerie Queene*'s Una – who 'did seeme such, as she was' (1.12.8) – will always, even to the most generous in spirit, be open to doubt. This is a crisis indeed, and while Cary does not explore the issue as deeply as does Shakespeare, she none the less exposes her thorough familiarity with its central questions. Moreover, as Ferguson notes, Mariam's soliloquies, 'like Hamlet's, work to dissolve binary oppositions'.[13] They penetrate facile assumptions such as those deployed by Alexandra, Herod and even Salome, and in so doing they depend for their success on the sharp attentiveness of readers likewise familiar with contemporary epistemological debates.

\* \* \*

Nowhere in the play do readership issues come to the fore more strikingly than in the five choral odes. As Ferguson and Barry Weller observe, these 'gnomic, conventional utterances seem somewhat off the mark, not only capricious and volatile in the application of general precepts but also inadequate to the psychological, spiritual, or even practical situation of the protagonist' (35). Most critics of *Mariam*, moreover, have exhibited broad agreement with the idea that the Chorus, as Lewalski writes, 'speaks from a limited rather than an authorized vantage point', and hence invites investigation of what such an authorized view might be.[14] But precisely *how* the Choruses are to be interpreted – how we are to make meaning from their often in-apposite and heavy-handed claims – is a question that, thus far, has been only skirted in *Mariam*'s critical history. I propose that, given the evidence of what we might call reader-inflection elsewhere in the play, the choral odes engage our critical attention precisely because of their obtuse or even incoherent judgements. Like the 'contrarieties' seized on by Montaigne and Charron as the raw material of scepticism, the disparities between those conclusions pronounced by the Chorus and those intimated by *Mariam*'s action effectively serve the function of the sceptical technique of opposition, thereby suggesting a suspension of assent.[15] And inasmuch as the odes themselves embody not only sen-tentious utterance but precipitous and dogmatic judgement, I think Cary can expect her readers to act as they presumably wish Herod himself had acted: by 'trying' before 'trusting' (2.4.406, 5.1.109).

Consider the third Chorus, the most frequently discussed of the five.[16] Opening with the assertion that a wife must not only keep herself 'spotless' but also 'free her life' from the 'suspicion' of those around her, it goes on to imply that controlling the suspicion of others may be achieved through wifely self-restraint, and especially through strict avoidance of 'public language'. When a wife gives 'private word to any second ear' she 'wounds her honour'. We naturally think of Mariam when this ode begins – she has just been on stage and Sohemus has claimed that 'Unbridled speech is Mariam's worst dis-grace' – but at the same time we are reminded of Salome, who has spoken to a 'second ear' (that of Silleus) more extensively than has Mariam (to Sohemus), and whom Constabarus has counselled to be 'both chaste and chastely deem'd' (1.6.394). Consequently, when the Chorus reveals that Mariam is its sole target (3.3.249), we are inclined to question the validity of its allegations – especially the notion that Mariam has acted 'out of glory', desiring to walk 'on the ridge' when she had 'spacious ground' on which to tread. Still more importantly, given the aggressive presence of Salome, we are sceptical that Mariam could have been 'free from fear' if only she had refrained from speak-ing so openly. It is true that Salome uses Mariam's speech with

Sohemus as evidence against her, and true as well that Herod construes this speech as proof of unchastity (4.7.433–4), but Mariam has the power to counter Salome's claim with still further speech, leading Herod 'captive with a gentle word' (3.3.164). In short, Mariam's refusal to feign – her unwillingness 'other speech than meaning to afford' – is more potent than Salome's exploitation of her 'public language'. Hence the Chorus' precept is rendered at once absurd and inadequate: absurd because the power of forming judgements lies ultimately not in the judged but in the judge, and inadequate because, in Mariam's case, honest speech 'to her lord alone' weighs more heavily than speech to 'any second ear'. It is in fact precisely that which precipitates her execution.[17]

Or take the first and fourth Choruses, remarkably similar to one another in structure and also strongly reminiscent of the third. As Weller and Ferguson note, 'the Chorus of act 1 runs against the grain of a reader's expectations in a particularly striking way', preparing us to condemn Salome when, all along, Mariam is the character under discussion (35–6). The Chorus says that 'no content attends a wavering mind'; Constabarus has just chastised Salome for 'wavering thoughts' (1.6.474). The Chorus castigates the human desire for 'change'; Salome has twice used that word in immediately-preceding scenes (1.4.322, 1.5.362). Thus the Chorus's announcement of Mariam as its subject seems comically inapposite (1.6.517): she is the least likely character in the play to 'dote upon delight', and while she certainly desires freedom from Herod, this is scarcely due to 'expectation of variety'. Like Alexandra, moreover, the Chorus cannot fathom Mariam's grief for Herod, reducing its Montaignian complexity to further evidence of a perverse and capricious nature – a nature incapable of guiding its 'wishes' (1.6.519–26). The Chorus's Stoic moralizing seems grotesquely inapropos, and Cary presumably expects her readers to discern the mismatch, then wrestle with the formation of a more adequate response.

Essentially the same patterns are at work in the choral commentary concluding act 4. Since Doris has just left the stage after imploring God to take revenge on Mariam for stealing Herod's affection (4.8.575–624), we assume that the Chorus's injunction to forgive – to scorn 'to revenge an injury' – applies to Herod's former wife. We quickly learn, however, that the Chorus once again has Mariam in mind (4.8.659), even though Herod and Salome both seem more likely candidates for such reproof. To construe Mariam as bent on revenge is harsh indeed: all she has done is remember Herod's heinous crimes against her family, inform Sohemus that she will not be 'reconcil'd' to Herod's love, and reproach her husband directly – and then only mildly (4.3.111–16). It is certainly true that she has not forgiven Herod, but in light of the Chorus's suggestion that forgiveness is 'vengeance of the noblest kind', her behaviour seems as much open to praise as to censure. As Travitsky notes, Mariam's overall demeanour is far less aggressive than that, say, of Doris, and most of the Chorus's disapproval revolves around the allegation that she is 'by sullen passion sway'd'.[18] Yet given *Mariam*'s persistent interrogation of the reason/passion binary – in particular, Cary's suggestion that through passion and feeling we have the potential to approach truth more nearly than through adherence to reason alone – what emerges is that Mariam is perhaps to be commended for her emotional honesty and 'froward humour' (4.3.140). Herod, for instance, never comes closer to recognizing his wife's innocence and his sister's malignity than when he succumbs to the evidence of his feelings (4.7.457–68), but Salome cunningly counters his progress by mocking its basis: 'I'll leave you to your passion' (4.7.517). As earlier in the same scene, when she tells Herod to 'speak of reason more, of Mariam less' (4.7.456), she establishes a false opposition, equating Mariam with passion and implying that it would be foolish, even irrational, not to execute her for infidelity. The fourth choral ode thus offers a radically reductive account of what Mariam has done, felt and thought up to this point in the play, and Cary underlines its fragile claim to interpretive validity by exposing its methodological confidence: 'Truth's school for certain', it avers, 'doth this same allow, / High-heartedness doth sometimes teach to bow' (4.8.645–6). Aligning itself with schoolmasters who derive their truths from experience, the Chorus blandly mouths its unobjectionable axiom without once questioning that axiom's relevance to Mariam – especially given the context and complexity of her present situation. The questioning, in other words, is left to us.

As for the second and fifth Choruses, the judgements they proffer tend to be less glaringly inapposite and their concerns still more explicitly epistemological. The former begins by asserting that 'To hear a tale with ears prejudicate, / It spoils the judgment, and corrupts the sense'. Possibly echoing Charron's claim that when a judge 'heares a cause with prejudicate opinion' he cannot be 'just, upright, and true' (*Wisdome*, 244), this choral assertion simultaneously directs us back to Babas' First Son's concern about 'this tale of Herod's death' (2.2.147–8) and forward to Pheroras' remark, on learning of the tyrant's return, that 'A heavier tale did never pierce mine ear' (3.2.52). Indeed, Pheroras' interchange with Salome vigorously foregrounds the ease with which the distinction between 'tale' as fiction and 'tale' as true account may be blurred (3.2.77–80). And Cary continues to tease out this theme as she assimilates Mariam's supposed infidelity to the status of a 'tale' (4.5.261). The Chorus, in short, alludes both to Judea's present belief that Herod is dead and to Herod's future belief that Mariam is unchaste, and it may additionally hint at Mariam's later surprise that her beauty and innocence are insufficient to save her (4.8.525–8). All three beliefs constitute 'rash' conclusions, 'unjust' presumptions. And the source of this cerebral corruption – this 'human error' common to 'every state' – is of course desire.[19] As Bacon later puts it, 'what a man had rather were true he more readily believes' (*WFB*, 4:57). 'Our ears and hearts are apt to hold for good / That we ourselves do most desire to be,' says the Chorus. Being 'prejudicate', we take the false rumour of Herod's demise for certain truth; we 'drown objections in the flood / Of partiality'. And 'partialitie', as Charron notes, is always 'an enemie to libertie' (244).

But Cary does not stop here. Ever faithful in her concern for what her daughter Lucy calls 'too speedy resolvers' (233), she allows the Chorus to take an explicit interest in their opposites, the sceptics. Those 'few' that have no desire for Herod's death, it claims, are swept 'headlong' by the 'multitude'. Well aware of the 'weak uncertain ground' on which the death's 'tale' is 'built', they none the less concede their 'doubts'; fully capable of weighing 'the circumstance our ear receives' – of trying before trusting – they forfeit the possibility and thus, along with the majority, 'pawn their lives and fortunes'. And Cary makes this claim even more pointed by presenting the play's most outspoken doubter, Babas' First Son, not as an impartial observer but as a man who stands to profit if the rumour holds true. But she also subtly qualifies the Chorus's assertion. For when it censoriously concludes that if the majority's actions 'do rightly hit, / Let them commend their fortune, not their wit', it advocates prudential doubt while simultaneously activating the reason/passion binary already explored by Cary through the blinkered speech of Alexandra. It is witless, the Chorus implies, to abandon pure, strict reason, but it is also entirely human to do so. Perpetually subject to desire, people are 'apt' to think wishfully and thus be 'deluded' even in the face of 'better likelihood'. So the Chorus betrays its recognition of human frailty even while castigating it, and the result is that its reprimand takes on a jejune, sophomoric quality. We are reminded, perhaps, of Salome's earlier rejoinder to Constabarus:

> If once I lov'd you, greater is your debt:
> For certain 'tis that you deserved it not.
> And undeservèd love we soon forget,
> And therefore that to me can be no blot.
> (1.6.465–8)

Brutally facile in logic, eschewing all emotional complexity, this self-serving jab conjures an apparently syllogistic legitimacy for a thought demanding far greater nuance. And much the same could be said of the conclusion to the second choral ode. Despite the epistemological acuity of the first five stanzas, the Chorus's final pronouncement depends on a tidy segregation of reason and emotion that *Mariam*, as a whole, refuses to countenance.

The fifth Chorus drives this home:

> Whoever hath beheld with steadfast eye,
> The strange events of this one only day:
> How many were deceiv'd, how many die,
> That once today did grounds of safety lay!
> It will from them all certainty bereave,
> Since twice six hours so many can deceive.
> (5.1.259–64)

The heavy emphasis on deception gives the lie to ideas about the ease with which humans may, through rational deliberation, avert disaster. And while the Chorus goes on to wonder what might have happened had Herod 'with wisdom now [Mariam's] death delay'd', its conclusion nevertheless stresses the likelihood that he would have found reason to kill her: 'He at his pleasure might command her death.' The weighing of circumstance and the trying before trusting so adamantly enjoined by other voices in the play (2.4.406–10, 4.7.489, 5.1.109) are cast to the wind. The day's events are subsumed within a larger pattern of certain ordination – cautionary and providential – and we are informed that 'sagest Hebrews' will later refer to them as 'the school of wisdom'. Precisely what 'warning to posterity' the day's events produce has been debated by critics; Shannon, for instance, argues that there are two dimensions to the caution: 'a conventional, choral wisdom of socially-embedded response and a feminist or reforming wisdom that exceeds the chorus' perspective'.[20] I agree with this, adding only that whereas at the opening of the Chorus wisdom is equated with deliberation and delay, at the end it is transformed into thoughtful reflection on what we might call *necessary* experience. The implication is that if humanity, as a whole, is to become wise, individual humans must undergo such wrenching trials as those depicted in the play. The 'admirably strange variety' (5.1.292) of the dramatic action constitutes a Montaignian distillation of the world's mutability, and careful attention to this pageant of deception and change bereaves us of any certain knowledge. We are left, in short, with a dogmatic claim about the need to be undogmatic in belief and expectation. Nothing could be more fitting given the events and investigations of the play.

*Mariam*'s five Choruses, then, engage through inadequacy. They are not so much ironic as purposely inept, and they capitalize on a streak of wary, judicious scepticism that Cary encourages in her readers and auditors. Like Mariam herself, who asks 'Is this a dream?' after hearing Herod move impressionistically from an accurate judgement of Sohemus' falsity to a false conclusion of her own 'impurity' (4.4.171–93), we too are struck by the dreamlike incompleteness of the choral pronouncements. Indeed we may say, as Hermione does to Leontes, that we 'stand in the level of [their] dreams' (*Winter's Tale*, 3.2.78–80). But nowhere does Cary more thoroughly reap the profits of her readerly inflection than in her Montaignian exploration of the facile oppositions of feeling and reason. Here the continuities between choral utterance and dramatic action are sustained throughout. Whether we think of Herod's upbraiding of Pheroras (4.2.59–62), Pheroras' self-scrutiny in the combined presence of Graphina's 'hot' love and the rumor of a cold tyrant's death (2.1.9–12), or Alexandra's reprimand to Mariam – 'Then send those tears away that are not sent / To thee by reason, but by passion's power' (1.2.151–2) – we see that Cary's play insistently demands our questioning of any too sharp demarcation between the rational and affective realms. Mariam herself comes closest to acknowledging the intricate overlap; in a reprise of her opening soliloquy's consideration of hypocrisy, she speculates that her judgement was accurate after all:

> Oh, now I see I was an hypocrite:
> I did this morning for his death complain,
> And yet do mourn, because he lives, ere night.
> When I his death believ'd, compassion wrought,
> And was the stickler 'twixt my heart and him:

But now that curtain's drawn from off my thought,
Hate doth appear again with visage grim.

(3.3.152–8)

But Mariam is anything but a hypocrite. When she says she complained for Herod's death, she momentarily succumbs to the very tendency, so pronounced in the play, to simplify essentially irreducible complexities. In fact what she learned was that one object may yield 'both grief and joy'. What is truer, and more impressive, about Mariam than the self-allegation of hypocrisy is her sustained emotional honesty, her willingness to observe internal states and reflect on them, her readiness to struggle with and chastise herself. If compassion serves as the 'stickler' between Mariam's heart and Herod, Mariam serves the same mediating function in the play's larger negotiation of the claims of reason and affection.

'I think with more than reason she laments,' says Alexandra to Salome, at once berating Mariam and initiating a play-long meditation on the meaning of reasonable conduct: 'Who is 't will weep to part from discontent?' (1.3.215–17). But Mariam senses, as Pascal later writes, that the heart has reasons that reason cannot know. Montaigne would surely have agreed, and Pascal, despite his frustrations with the *Essays'* author, was certainly aware how unceasingly his predecessor had explored this intricate terrain. Cary explores it too. Her *Tragedy of Mariam*, besides offering a powerful exposé of the potentially disastrous consequences of patriarchal structures and assumptions, suggests through a complex web of action, speech, and choral response that the sceptic's suspicion of pervasive human frailty may be parabolically displayed through Judea's collective deception, and that human desire and judgement, notwithstanding persistent claims to the contrary, ground themselves relentlessly on something more than reason.

# 10
# False Fire: Providence and Violence in Webster's Tragedies

> When will this fearful slumber have an end?
>
> *Titus Andronicus*

When Rosencrantz informs Gertrude and Claudius that 'certain players' have come to Elsinore, he adds that Hamlet, learning of their arrival, has exhibited 'a kind of joy / To hear of it'.[1] And little wonder. The players, in Hamlet's view, are instruments of providence, lingering manifestations of a morally responsive universe in which 'murder, though it have no tongue, will speak / With most miraculous organ' (2.2.570–1). More precisely, they provide him with the occasion to oppose one form of feigning against another: what we might call imitating truth against imitating falsehood. And Hamlet's operating premise – deeply suspect, to be sure – is that the players' illusion of violence will 'unkennel' the guilt currently 'occulted' behind Claudius' illusion of innocence (3.2.73–4).[2] Hamlet assumes, in short, that a core of vulnerability exists in all humans, and that sufficiently cunning art can expose 'that within which passeth show' – at least if 'that within' constitutes a truth or state of being that has been deliberately withheld from the world.[3] It is crucial to note, however, that it is precisely because a spectacle of violence is recognized as fictional that it can serve a purpose that authentic violence could never be trusted to serve: unkenneling guilt. Faced with a genuine act of poisoning, Claudius would be obliged to respond, to react in some way to the perpetration of violence – or else, as when Gertrude drinks the wine, to assume a façade of ignorance. But faced with an elaborately ritualized illusion of poisoning, he is free to disengage himself from potential action (or potential dissembling) and thus to adopt a posture of receptivity that, paradoxically, positions him to betray himself. Such, at any rate, appears to be Hamlet's assumption. And it is an assumption not far removed from the more general claim, advanced for example by Sidney in his *Defense of Poesy*, that tragedy promotes moral growth, making 'tyrants manifest their tyrannical humours'. The ancient despot who 'was not ashamed to make matters for tragedies' none the less 'could not resist the sweet violence' of tragic spectacle: a well-chosen drama 'drew abundance of tears' from his eyes.[4] In the pages that follow, while referring occasionally to *Hamlet*, I wish to turn principally to John Webster's two great tragedies, exploring the structures of assumption that underlie their recurrent reliance on illusory violence, and perhaps thereby better understanding both their fascination with violence itself and their attitude towards the hypothesis of a providential cosmos.

Webster, as I have noted, is generally thought to have spent several years as a student at London's Middle Temple, matriculating in 1598. If this is the case, he would have met and conversed with such men as Marston, Sir John Davies and possibly Ralegh, Henry Wotton and John Ford. He would also have had access to the Middle Temple's library, which held a copy of the 1569 edition of Sextus, along with scores of other relevant books. But even if the author of *The Duchess of Malfi* is not the 'John Webster of London' listed in the Temple's *Register of Admissions*, he was clearly a man of wide reading, as R. W. Dent demonstrates in his study of Webster's borrowing. And Montaigne appears to have been one of his favourite writers. About forty passages in Webster's plays may be traced to Florio's translation of the *Essays*, with chapters such as 'Of presumption', 'Of judging of others' death', 'Upon some verses of Virgil' and the *Apology of Raymond Sebond* emerging with particular frequency.[5] It is true, as Dent points out, that Webster sometimes draws on Montaignian observations previously isolated by Marston; indeed, Webster may have had access to Marston's copy of Florio, and, in any case, since he revised *The Malcontent* and composed its induction, he and Marston probably had opportunities to discuss their common interest in the essayist's meditations. Charron, too, figures occasionally in Webster's borrowing, as do Lucian, Erasmus, Rabelais, Donne and others whose thought tends, now and again, towards sceptical imaginings.[6] Thus while Robert Ornstein may be correct in claiming that Webster has no interest in philosophical issues, his insistence that the playwright was uninfluenced 'by Montaigne's view of life' seems overstated.[7] Webster does not replicate the *Essays'* fideistic Pyrrhonism, but he exhibits consistent engagement with doubt, showing interest in the tropes of epistemological scepticism, casting a wary eye on metaphysical suppositions, and demonstrating a distinct lack of confidence in any human ability to find moral coherence on earth through the exercise of reason or the testimony of experience.

In *The White Devil*, for instance, Flamineo's discourse on the frailties of eyesight (1.2.95–106) is entirely consonant with early modern commentaries on sense-perception; his remark that people afflicted with 'yellow jaundice think all objects they look on to be yellow' is taken directly from Montaigne, and thus derives from Sextus (Florio, 541; *PH*, 1.44–7).[8] Bracciano's observation that 'quails feed on poison' (5.3.90) may likewise originate with Sextus and reach Webster via *The Sceptick*, where we read that 'cicuta feedeth quails' (44). But beyond such verbal parallels we also encounter sceptical habits of mind in Flamineo's repeated exclamations about religion. 'Pray, sir, resolve me, what religion's best / For a man to die in?' he demands of Bracciano's ghost (5.4.125–6); and earlier, marvelling at the temerity of Cardinal Monticelso, he voices a sentiment with which malcontents from Barabas to Giovanni might vehemently concur: 'Religion! O how it is commeddled with policy. The first bloodshed in the world happened about religion' (3.3.34–6). Proleptically signalling his own future status as a Cain figure, Flamineo suggests here that religious practice is and always has been bound up with politics and violence – a suggestion confirmed in both Monticelso's subsequent excommunication of Vittoria and in the revenge machinations of Francisco and Lodovico. Francisco himself, one of the few Jacobean revengers to survive his schemes, utters a sceptical sentiment directly counter to the Montaignian conservatism of *All's Well*'s Lafeu: observing the ghost of his sister Isabella, he concludes that 'Thought, as a subtle juggler, makes us deem / Things supernatural which have cause / Common as sickness' (4.1.104–6; cp. *Duchess*, 5.3.8–9). And Flamineo ends his life exclaiming that 'While we look up to heaven we confound / Knowledge with knowledge' (5.6.258–9), a remark implying that we delude ourselves when we posit truths beyond experience: what we know is in fact radically limited, circumscribed by our own infirm capacity and perception. Flamineo never denies that 'Knowledge' might exist, but he strongly suspects that he has no reliable access to it.

Nor does his sister have access to justice. Critics have commented that Webster presents Vittoria in such a way as to 'baffle ordinary moral judgment', but none, to my knowledge, have noted that in her trial

Webster in effect dramatizes the criterion argument from classical scepticism.[9] Mounting a spirited defense against Monticelso's allegation of her adultery, Vittoria takes the following argumentative tack:

> If you be my accuser
> Pray cease to be my judge; come from the bench,
> Give in your evidence 'gainst me, and let these
> Be moderators.
>
> (3.2.225–8)

Sextus' incessant stress on the apparent impossibility of unbiased judgement is clearly reflected here (*PH*, 1.112–23, 2.14–21), though transposed from the rarefied epistemological precincts of sense-data disputation to the practical arena of legal proceeding. Yet Webster need not have consulted Sextus to make his case: the same section of Montaigne's *Apology* from which he took the jaundice example also offers an incisive discussion of the implicated judge – the judge who is himself 'a party in this controversie' (Florio, 544; *PH*, 1.59–60). And if there is any doubt that the paradigm of compromised judgement fascinated Webster, one need only turn to *The Duchess of Malfi*, where Bosola scornfully dismisses Ferdinand's attempt to dissociate himself from his sister's murder: 'The office of justice is perverted quite / When one thief hangs another' (4.2.298–9). As so often with Bosola, we sense a vestigial faith in the existence of moral absolutes, but a faith profoundly qualified by acute awareness of *realpolitik* and worldly corruption.

Similar sentiments emerge earlier when Bosola deploys his caustic wit at the expense of Castruccio, the Old Lady and Antonio. We are not surprised to learn from Dent that Webster draws on Montaigne seven times in 100 lines; Michael Neill goes so far as to say that Bosola transforms the *Essays* into 'a bible of degraded scepticism'.[10] Later, in the aftermath of his accidental slaughter of Antonio, Bosola slips permanently into the sceptical morass from which he had begun to emerge at his moral awakening upon the Duchess's death. 'Other sins only speak; murder shrieks out' he had declared to Ferdinand, showing a trace of Hamlet's providential confidence (4.2.253). But now, asked how Antonio came to die, he mutters merely this: 'In a mist: I know not how; / Such a mistake as I have often seen / In a play' (5.5.93–5). Echoing his earlier sentiment that life is 'a general mist of error' (4.2.179) – and indeed recapitulating Flamineo's dying gasp – Bosola's remark functions microcosmically to characterize the widespread uncertainty evoked by the play's closing scenes: there may be forms of goodness and justice, but they appear to be inapprehensible – and all the more so when desperately sought. Like Flamineo, Bosola ultimately renounces experiential mimesis: he will imitate neither 'things glorious' nor 'base', but simply stand as his own example (5.4.80–1; cp. *Devil*, 5.6.255–7). The solipsism to which he is thus reduced accurately reflects his sense that terrestrial virtue is a chimera, a dream. What experience appears to confirm, by contrast, is the outlook embedded in the haunting metaphor of the Duchess's final claim. When she is dead, she says, her brothers may at last 'feed in quiet', like hyenas in the night (4.2.229).

Bosola's glance at the theatre also serves to reinforce a recurrent concern in *The Duchess* with the illusory violence to which I have earlier alluded. Granted, the waxworks episode would seem at first to bear little relation to *Hamlet*'s 'Mousetrap' and its accompanying dumb show. For one thing – and despite Ferdinand's obsessively held opinion – the Duchess is not a 'guilty creature' as Claudius is, and both the Duchess's reference to Antonio's 'lifeless trunk' and Ferdinand's claim that his sister takes the wax figures for 'true substantial bodies' suggest that Webster wants us to think the Duchess believes she sees the corpses of her husband and children (4.1.68). There seems little doubt, moreover, that most stage productions, Jacobean and later, have opted for motionless actors rather than elaborate dummies or painted wax effigies to fill the discovery space. Yet Webster, as he so often does, blurs the distinction between illusion and reality. The stage direction in the 1623 quarto reads as follows: '*Here is discover'd, (behind a Travers) the artificiall figures of* Antonio, *and his children; appearing as if they were dead.*'[11] Not only does Webster resort to his habitual employment of the traverse, but he insists on 'artificiall' figures, thus very possibly revealing his own conception of the scene's ideal staging.[12] And combined with Bosola's allusions to 'the piece' and 'this sad spectacle' – not to mention the Duchess's extended remark on how the sight 'wastes me more / Than were't my picture, fashioned out of wax' – the stress on artifice contributes to a strong case for theatrical staging in which the Duchess recognizes that what lies before her amounts to a fiction representing truth rather than truth itself (4.1.56–63).[13] In other words, as in *Hamlet*'s play-within-a-play, we have an instance of illusory violence – ritualized fiction depicting recent or imminent murder – and the potential for emotional penetration would seem to stand in direct proportion to the fictionality. As Ferdinand observes, the Duchess is 'plagued in art' (4.1.111), and indeed it strikes me as readily conceivable that her despair would be all the more intense in response to a macabre display of artificial bodies than to genuine flesh and blood.[14] Nor would this merely be a consequence of the uncertainty thereby introduced, for Webster makes it clear that the Duchess believes her family is gone. Rather, Ferdinand's 'spectacle' reveals his sadistic obsessiveness, his desire to multiply images of horror exponentially, so that not only the theme but its elaborate and voyeuristic variations may reverberate through his own and his sister's imaginings. And, I might add, through ours as well.

It may be, however, that Webster's most consuming interest along these lines is precisely the border between representation and reality. On several occasions, after all, his dramatic spectacles, consistently ritualized, leave us uncertain as to the exact nature of what we see. Later in *The Duchess*, for instance, Bosola *'Shewes the children strangled'* to Ferdinand (4.2.244), and since nothing thus far has indicated that bodies have been transported on stage, we are left to wonder whether what Ferdinand actually views is another set of effigies. That Bosola accompanies his demonstration with the remark, 'But here begin your pity' (4.2.249), further suggests that even if the bodies are real, their ritualized presentation – mediated by Bosola and possibly conjoined with another act of curtain drawing – may have the potential to work providentially on Ferdinand, affecting him 'with most miraculous organ'. As it happens, Webster leaves this possibility undetermined, allowing directors and readers to choose for themselves whether Ferdinand will 'blench' at the sight – or, on the contrary, experience further delectation.

A similar spectacle occurs late in *The White Devil*, when Flamineo, informed by Francisco that his mother and her waiting-women are grieving over the corpse of Marcello, decides that he will observe them: 'They are behind the traverse. I'll discover / Their superstitious howling' (5.4.60–1). He then opens the curtain and, for a time, watches unnoticed while Cornelia undergoes an Ophelia-like passage into distraction. As Dena Goldberg notes, 'the women form a tableau which is clearly, like the dumb show, a kind of entertainment, something related to pageantry and masque'.[15] And indeed, nothing in the play necessitates that what Flamineo see here take place within the same dimension of time as that in which he sees it. The frame is broken, however, when Zanche the Moor discovers the presence of Flamineo and Francisco; at this point the spectators merge with the spectacle, and the titillations of Flamineo's voyeurism instantly vanish: 'I would I were from hence' (5.4.87). Moments later Cornelia and her retinue leave the stage – again suggesting that their presence was as much a miming of reality as reality itself – and between that instant and the convenient, almost perfunctory arrival of Bracciano's ghost, Flamineo uncharacteristically remarks to himself,

> I have a strange thing in me, to th' which
> I cannot give a name, without it be
> Compassion ... . I have lived
> Riotously ill, like some that live in court;
> And sometimes, when my face was full of smiles
> Have felt the maze of conscience in my breast.
> Oft gay and honoured robes those tortures try;
> We think caged birds sing, when indeed they cry.
> (5.4.109–19)

The miraculous organ appears to be speaking.[16]

But unhappily for providential imaginings of the sort that Hamlet entertains, Webster also offers substantial counter-evidence, the best examples surfacing in *The White Devil*. Consider the pair of dumb shows wherein Bracciano observes how the murders of Isabella and Camillo 'grow to action' (2.2.4). Mediated by the Conjurer, accompanied by music, witnessed by the seated duke wearing a 'charmed' night-cap (2.2.21) and thoroughly vexed in their mimetic status, these pantomimes bear roughly the same relation to Bracciano that the dumb show and 'The Mousetrap' bear to Claudius. They are, moreover, similarly contextualized by conventional and elaborate ritual. But the on-stage audience response could scarcely be more different. Whereas Claudius rises from his chair and thus, at the very minimum, displays an unwillingness to watch any more of the play, Bracciano remains seated and attends carefully to both shows, responding with language appropriate to aesthetic display: 'Excellent, then she's dead ... . 'Twas quaintly done, but yet each circumstance / I taste not fully' (2.2.24–39). In short, far from being emotionally penetrated by 'the very cunning of the scene', Bracciano attains emotional distance from his murders through their transformation into 'art'.[17] It is true that Bracciano's situation differs from that of Claudius inasmuch as the latter possesses no foreknowledge that the illusory violence he is about to witness bears directly on his own past behaviour. It is true as well that Claudius himself is the immediate agent of his brother's death, while Bracciano, like countless other Jacobean villains, employs 'instruments' in his crimes. And it may be that these differences are aii-important, outweighing any similarities. But from the perspective of the *off-stage* audiences observing these scenes, I suspect that structural parallels tend to diminish otherwise important variances in character knowledge and motivation, so that, as Christina Luckyj remarks about this moment in *The White Devil*, Webster's interest lies less in villainy itself than in 'different responses to villainy'.[18] Webster invites us, that is, to compare our reactions to those of Bracciano, just as Shakespeare, aligning us with Hamlet, asks us to observe Gertrude and especially Claudius. And what we note, given these invitations, is that while we are indeed distanced from the victims' deaths – which register only faintly on our sympathies compared, say, to the butchery of Horatio in *The Spanish Tragedy* – we are at the same time brought more intensely into dramatic engagement with the varied onstage observers. We experience a simultaneous diminishing and heightening of emotional response, and when we test our reactions against those of Bracciano and Claudius, we test Hamlet's theory, interrogating what Alvin Kernan has called 'the great Renaissance dream of a universe sympathetic with man and moving parallel to his moral laws'.[19] We thus examine perhaps the most urgent of all metaphysical questions, and Webster's answer in this instance, clearly less ambiguous than Shakespeare's, none the less resonates powerfully with *The White Devil*'s general sense of fractured or dubious cosmic responsiveness. If we characterize Bracciano's reaction as callous or inhuman, we instantly place a burden of proof on ourselves – a burden that, like Bosola's claim that he suffers death 'for what is just' (*Duchess*, 5.5.103), may permanently defy demonstration. *Hamlet*, in short, while never decisively confirming its hero's providential imagination, none the less aligns us with an overwhelming desire that the universe both sanction and buttress humanity's moral theorizing; and it is this, perhaps, that prompts most readers to agree with Hamlet that Claudius winces like a 'gallèd jade' in reaction to the murder of Gonzago. Both *The Duchess* and especially *The White Devil*, however, present a world in which, from the outset, we are more sceptical of the providential dream because we recognize its potency as inextricably tied to its mildly comic improbability.

A final and particularly complex example of Webster's illusory violence may be found in Flamineo's feigned death near the close of *The White Devil*. Squarely in the tradition of other such feignings in Elizabethan drama – 'deaths' like those enacted by Barabas, Faustus, Malevole and Vindice – Flamineo's none the less inflects the convention anew through its clever manipulation of discrepant awareness.

Not only Vittoria and Zanche, but readers and viewers as well are asked to believe that Flamineo has been fatally shot (5.6.119–49). The violent spectacle is thus illusory, but not recognized as such until Flamineo's 'resurrection', a dramatic *volte-face* that must inevitably strike audiences as comical. Prior to this resurrection, however, Webster directs our focus sharply on the responses of Vittoria and Zanche, and to the extent that they exhibit neither shock nor remorse for Flamineo's impending expiration, they, like Bracciano earlier in the play, diminish in our eyes as candidates for sympathy and well-rounded humanity even as they challenge us to make good the standards by which we level such judgements. It is true that our ignorance of Flamineo's device tends to diminish our sympathy for him as well – the laughter at his rising proves that the joke is partly on us – but, concomitantly, the well-established dramatic convention of allowable moral testing restores to Flamineo a roughly equal degree of audience respect.[20] Like Hamlet – indeed more convincingly – he learns here what he wants to know.

Webster's tragedies thus throw into profound confusion many of the most habitual moral assumptions allied with providential imagining. Though his characters may often be hypocritical and generate little of the powerful audience sympathy typically associated with Shakespearean tragic figures, their very lack of 'appropriate' response forces us to question our own basis for the tacit acceptance of such appropriateness. And while the Duchess of Malfi may constitute an exception to this rule, she simultaneously proves it in so far as her power to command our quick and perhaps unreflecting sympathy can itself become a matter for reflection. Webster also helps us – perhaps not altogether anachronistically – to interrogate Shakespeare, particularly Shakespeare's portrayals of violence and the habits of audience response thereby conjured. It may be instructive, for instance, to consider our reactions to the blinding of Gloucester or the slaughter of Macduff's young son in light of the more complex and mediated spectacles of violent action depicted in *The White Devil* and *The Duchess*. And Hamlet's providential supposition, dependent as it is on the satisfaction of so many precise conditions (fictionality, resemblance, surprise, cunning, and so on), may begin to seem rather precious when juxtaposed against roughly parallel spectacles in Webster – a preciosity perhaps only faintly suggested by Shakespeare through the inscrutability of Claudius' immediate response, and further occluded by the fact that Claudius, as we learn later but always suspect, is guilty of the crime Hamlet attributes to him. Webster, in short, immensely complicates the idea of being 'frighted with false fire' (*Hamlet*, 3.2.244); the suggestions of conscience we witness in Flamineo, Bosola and perhaps Ferdinand and the Cardinal are rendered mildly absurd – even mildly irritating – by the conjoined pathos and comic perfunctoriness of their presentation. And the detachment that enables such perception seems a direct function of a dramaturgic tactic, clearly cultivated by the playwright, in which genuine and illusory violence constantly contextualize one another. The effect, I think, is not so much to sensationalize violence or to throw its malevolence into terminal doubt as to suggest that its status as 'evil' can only be the result of an act of faith we must constantly acknowledge as both necessary and coterminous with engaged human consciousness. Flamineo, at the play's closing, claims that he will 'not look / Who went before, nor who shall follow me; / No, at myself I will begin and end' (5.6.255–7). The inhumanity of violence, and in particular its propensity to stir providential dreaming, likewise begins and ends, Webster implies, only with contemplation.

# 11
## *The Changeling*: Blood, Will and Intellectual Eyesight

> It is our blood to err, though hell gap'd loud.
> *The Revenger's Tragedy*

*The Changeling*, collaboratively written by Thomas Middleton and William Rowley around 1621, may seem an unlikely candidate for discussion in this book, since its engagements with doubt are less wide-ranging than those in other plays I consider. It conveys a far stronger sense of ethical mooring than, say, *Troilus and Cressida, The White Devil* or even *The Spanish Tragedy*; it suggests the existence of a morally responsive universe through its repeated allusions to foreboding, instinct and conscience; it raises the spectre of private vengeance only to intimate that revenge is superfluous in the world inhabited by its characters; and it gives its heroine, Beatrice-Joanna, a final speech of such thorough self-condemnation that the social status quo of Alicante seems absolutely reaffirmed. It is true that the play's conclusion is so perfunctory and complacent that its moralizing appears tainted by the very artificiality of its presentation. But patriarchal structures and conventional cosmological assumptions are ultimately reinforced by *The Changeling*'s brilliant double plot and the consequent character-mirroring this plot establishes, particularly that of Isabella and Beatrice-Joanna.[1] So if the play strikes us as less ideologically conservative than Tourneur's *Atheist's Tragedy*, or if it astonishes us through the psychological intensity of its interchanges between Beatrice-Joanna and De Flores, it none the less carries with it a sense of diminishment – of capitulation to the existing order – that seems out of keeping with the fictions it powerfully stages.

This is not to deny that *The Changeling* offers much in the way of social critique. The madhouse scenes in particular mock class hierarchy and the offensive pretensions of gentility. When Lollio learns that Antonio, the newly-arrived 'idiot', is in fact a gentleman, his response travesties the conventional trope of gentle blood's self-disclosure: 'Nay, there's nobody doubted that; at first sight I knew him for a gentleman – he looks no other yet' (1.2.109–10). With its ironic conjunction of doubting, seeing and knowing, this speech echoes key moments in the main-plot dialogue between Beatrice-Joanna and Alsemero, and in its mildly ominous use of 'yet' it foreshadows not only Antonio's fall but those, more spectacularly, of De Flores and Beatrice-Joanna. Lollio goes on to ridicule the levels of 'wit' normally exhibited by constables and justices; he boasts that his new pupil will be 'fit to bear office in five weeks' (1.2.118). And later he suggests that 'honour' is 'but a caper': it 'rises as fast and high, has a knee or two, and falls to th' ground again' (4.3.86–7). The sexual innuendo here, along with the bantering deflation, contribute significantly to a broader impression that the madhouse scenes exist above all else to enforce a sense of social levelling.[2] The frailties on display in Alibius' asylum are not far removed from those we witness inside Vermandero's citadel.

This is corroborated by another dimension of the play's social commentary. Diaphanta, emerging at last from her bed-trick tryst with Alsemero, passes Beatrice-Joanna in the corridor and blithely excuses her tardiness: 'Pardon frailty, madam; / In troth I was so well, I ev'n forgot myself' (5.1.76–7). Her frailty may, of course, be traced to her blood, that putative source of sexual desire which circulates throughout *The Changeling*. It is blood that needs taming, curing, letting, easing or cooling, according to the play's various metaphors.[3] And it is blood – or the promptings of blood – that ultimately accounts for Alsemero's venture into pseudo-medical practice. Armed with his copy of 'The Book of Experiment, / Call'd *Secrets in Nature*', Alsemero feels confident that he can discern realities beyond appearance: 'whether a woman be with child or no', 'whether a woman be a maid or not' (4.1.24–40).[4] The specific *kinds* of knowledge he seeks help to preserve patriarchal control, and they presuppose female duplicity; his is a knowledge-project thoroughly conditioned by misogyny. But the misogyny itself is informed by a stipulative understanding of the operations and effects of blood. Hence the entire project is ludicrous. Not only does it depend on a double standard and imply a fantasy of instantaneous certainty in matters that admit of no such facile determination, but it is easily circumvented through cunning: Beatrice-Joanna's mimicry of the virginal response to 'Glass M' comically underscores the point (4.2.141–50). It may be, then, that the frailty of women, ostensibly urged by the blood, initially propels Alsemero into amateur science, but it is his own thoroughly human frailty that allows his investigations to be so readily subverted.[5]

If we return to the play's opening, however, we find that frailty does not in every instance pass without self-recognition. That this is true is best exemplified in Beatrice-Joanna's cautionary dialogue with Alsemero:

> *Beatrice:*          Be better advis'd, sir:
> Our eyes are sentinels unto our judgments
> And should give certain judgment what they see;
> But they are rash sometimes, and tell us wonders
> Of common things, which when our judgments find,
> They can then check the eyes, and call them blind.
> *Alsemero:*   But I am further, lady; yesterday
> Was mine eyes' employment, and hither now
> They brought my judgment, where are both agreed.
> Both houses then consenting, 'tis agreed,
> Only there wants the confirmation
> By the hand royal, that's your part, lady.
> *Beatrice:*   O there's one above me, sir. [*Aside*] For five days past
> To be recall'd! Sure, mine eyes were mistaken,
> This was the man was meant me.
>
>                                              (1.1.69–83)

Perhaps Beatrice's finest moment before her dying speech, this warning to Alsemero is premised on a general acknowledgement of sense-deception combined with a specific recognition of error: 'mine eyes were mistaken'. She speaks, in short, from experience, and although she may be marshalling sceptical sentiments to justify a new and potentially ephemeral passion, she none the less provides Alsemero with the conventional materials for prudent choice. The eyes *are* rash at times; they forget their status as watchmen, 'sentinels' to the mind. But Alsemero, with truly Baconian optimism, replies that his eyes and judgement have already conferred: the epistemic checks and balances have been carried out, and the 'houses' are in full bicameral agreement. Beatrice-Joanna's single gesture in the interests of caution is peremptorily brushed aside.

But before the headlong rush into passionate action depicted in acts 2 and 3, one last moment passes when human frailty becomes the object of explicit discussion. De Flores has entered the room, and Alsemero notes a change in Beatrice-Joanna: she seems suddenly 'displeas'd'. Beatrice accounts for this by confessing her 'infirmity', even acknowledging its apparently irrational nature; De Flores, in her view, is 'a deadly poison, / Which to a thousand other tastes were wholesome'. But Alsemero reassures her that such reactions, however inexplicable, are common:

> This is a frequent frailty in our nature.
> There's scarce a man amongst a thousand sound
> But hath his imperfection: one distastes
> The scent of roses, which to infinites
> Most pleasing is, and odoriferous;
> One oil, the enemy of poison;
> Another wine, the cheerer of the heart
> And lively refresher of the countenance.
> Indeed this fault (if so it be) is general,
> There's scarce a thing but is both lov'd and loath'd.
> Myself (I must confess) have the same frailty.
>
> (1.1.105–23)

These lines have generated considerable commentary, much of it swirling around the question of whether Beatrice-Joanna already feels some degree of sexual attraction to De Flores, however repressed or unconscious.[6] But I wish to add that Alsemero's maxim – 'There's scarce a thing but is both lov'd and loath'd' – perfectly captures the essence of Sextus' second mode of doubt, that dealing with conflicting perceptions among different people (*PH*, 1.79–90). Indeed, despite the commonplace nature of his claim, two of Alsemero's examples – wine and poison – are deployed as well by Sextus, and a broader sense of the currency of his remark is conveyed by *The Sceptick*'s explanatory gloss that 'if one hate and another love the very same thing, it must needs be that their fantasies differ, else all would love it or all would hate it' (49).[7] De Flores is of course the 'poison' in Alsemero's unwitting illustration, and there is no question that he strikes the 'fantasies' of Beatrice-Joanna and her father in radically opposing ways: he is 'a gentleman / In good respect' with the latter, while the former can scarcely endure his sight (1.1.131–2). More insidiously though, given subsequent events in the play, Alsemero's remark suggests that the same thing may be loved and loathed by the same person at different times (cp. 2.2.76–7, 2.2.136, 3.4.170–1, 5.2.38–9, 5.3.49–52).[8] And this in turn, as it applies to Beatrice-Joanna or Alsemero, grants further resonance to the title of the play: humans are often changelings in their shifts of affection, their innate frailties exposed to common view.

Perhaps 'frailty' is too harsh a word in this context, though Alsemero uses it twice. As reflective readers we know that our opinions and preferences sometimes change. Typically, we account for this by invoking experience, maturity, wisdom, and so on, but I suspect that few people are immune to the force of Montaigne's remark that 'No single characteristic clasps us purely and universally in its embrace' (*Essays*, 264). Our later choices, Montaigne implies, may be just as contaminated by ignorance or folly as those which preceded them; we lack an absolute guarantee of our judgement's progressive perfection. So when Jasperino exclaims to Alsemero, 'Lover I'm sure y' are none, the stoic / Was found in you long ago', his words carry a potent undercurrent of irony. Ostensibly praising Stoic aversion to emotional entanglement, Jasperino in fact believes that Alsemero's metamorphosis into an adoring *amant* would be 'better news at Valencia than if he had ransom'd half Greece from the Turk' (1.1.36–61). But through ironies unavailable to either character, the notion that Alsemero's love should be inspired by Beatrice-Joanna throws us back on the doubts proposed by Montaigne. Indeed, *The Changeling* gives the sceptical lie to Alsemero's characterization as a Stoic. And through its pervasive interest in matters of perception, knowledge, judgement, proof and certainty, it raises intriguing and at times disturbing questions about the human propensity simultaneously to acknowledge and disown the frailties of cognition and feeling.

Conventional wisdom has it that Rowley rather than Middleton composed *The Changeling*'s opening and closing scenes – not to mention the subplot – so it is of little use to suggest that the play's possible reliance on Sextus and its evident interest in sceptical themes derive from Middleton's tenure at Oxford, where he studied intermittently between 1598 and 1601 at Queen's College.[9] It is true that the authorial collaboration in the play is remarkably tight; Middleton might well have proposed details for the first scene which Rowley subsequently adopted. But such a supposition, besides depriving Rowley of what may justly be his, suffers from the more fundamental flaw of assuming that even in the third decade of the seventeenth century English writers required advanced formal education in order to attain familiarity with the lineaments of scepticism. As I trust my earlier chapters have demonstrated, this would *not* have been the case in the 1620s. The tropes and arguments of the Pyrrhonists would have been common knowledge by then, at least to anyone with modest intellectual curiosity and access to books and conversation; university exposure was no longer a prerequisite. So Rowley, mysterious though he is, should not be denied responsibility for the sceptical colouring of *The Changeling*'s opening scene. And later variations of that colouring, in scenes attributed to Middleton, succeed in part due to both writers' familiarity with scepticism's literary paradigms.

Probably the best example lies near the outset of act 2, where Beatrice-Joanna muses on the compliance and efficiency of Alsemero's companion Jasperino:

> How wise is Alsemero in his friend!
> It is a sign he makes his choice with judgment.
> Then I appear in nothing more approv'd
> Than making choice of him;
> For 'tis a principle, he that can choose
> That bosom well, who of his thoughts partakes,
> Proves most discreet in every choice he makes.
> Methinks I love now with the eyes of judgment
> And see the way to merit, clearly see it.
> A true deserver like a diamond sparkles,
> In darkness you may see him, that's in absence,
> Which is the greatest darkness falls on love;
> Yet is he best discern'd then
> With intellectual eyesight.
>
> (2.1.6–19)

Echoing the eyes/judgement interchange between Beatrice and Alsemero in act 1, this speech none the less reveals a singular shift in attitude. Beatrice knows next to nothing about Jasperino, but because he seems discreet and helpful she concludes that Alsemero 'makes his choice with judgement' – a conclusion that of course reflects well on her. She then reasons that Alsemero's good sense justifies *her* choice of *him*. Obviously, there is a whiff of circularity in this argument, but the real problem lies with the initial premise, for it is far from clear that Alsemero's judgement is as good as Beatrice imagines. Nevertheless she cites a corroborating 'principle' drawn, apparently, from her experience of the world, a principle whose expression in rhyme only emphasizes the artificiality of its falsely induced conclusion.

But this is not all. Beatrice flatters herself that she now loves 'with the eyes of judgement', which is to say that she is no longer subject to the rash conclusions of vision. Her remark also carries a tacit acknowledgement that her attraction to Alonzo de Piracquo – and perhaps to Alsemero too, at least in the beginning – was based purely on looks. But now she possesses 'intellectual eyesight': Alsemero is a 'true deserver', a man of genuine merit, and she can discern his merit even in his absence, a 'darkness' where ordinary vision would in any case be useless. It is unfortunate for Alsemero that he possesses no intellectual eyesight of his own, for this would allow him, on his wedding night, to recognize that the supposed body of his bride is in fact that of her eager understudy, Diaphanta. But such discernment, at least in the world of *The Changeling*, is too much to expect.

So Beatrice-Joanna's entire speech is self-serving and specious; it relies on a dubious premise, a false generalization and patently skewed reasoning. She is far more persuasive earlier, when she urges caution on Alsemero. Like Imogen, who notes that 'Our very eyes / Are sometimes like our judgments, blind' (*Cymbeline*, 4.2.303–4), Beatrice has the potential to recognize sense-corruption and avoid precipitous action, but she fails to put that potential into practice. One can scarcely blame her: she is young, her father is adamant about the marriage to Piracquo, and Alsemero exhibits no distinction in intelligence or understanding – nothing that would provide a helpful standard of behaviour. She is entirely on her own.[10] Still, despite mitigating factors, there seems little doubt that Middleton and Rowley expect us to find that the problem with Beatrice-Joanna lies mainly within. As Thomas Wright observes in his *Passions of the Mind*, humans

> are not very good judges in their own causes, specially for the Passion of Love, which blindeth their judgement ... indeed the Passions may be compared to green spectacles, which make all things resemble the colour of green ... so he that loveth, hateth, or by any other passion is vehemently possessed, judgeth all things that occur in favour of that passion to be good and agreeable with reason. (126–7)

Beatrice-Joanna is just such a person: she builds a 'rational' case for her love on a foundation incapable of supporting its arguments. Her very praise of Jasperino is ironically sabotaged by the fact that his final role is to be the shrewd suspecter of her duplicity. Beatrice looks at Alsemero through 'green spectacles', and while this in itself is scarcely unusual, the play has established that she is conscious of the perils of such gazing. The eyes *are* 'rash' sometimes; they 'tell us wonders / Of common things', and judgement calls them 'blind' (1.1.73–5).

Thus when Beatrice next sees Alsemero, it is small wonder that her first words are these: 'I have within mine eyes all my desires' (2.2.8). Her metaphor literalizes her cognitive state, and within minutes she plunges into the twin realms of violence and dissimulation, realms whose close relatedness *The Changeling* powerfully stresses (2.2.66–9). 'Blood-guiltiness becomes a fouler visage', she muses, and then, in an aside, she castigates herself for marring 'so good a market with my scorn' (2.2.40–2). The reference is to De Flores, and although Beatrice's spontaneously generated plan is to use 'his dog-face' to destroy Piracquo – one poison expelling another (2.2.147) – the structure of the scene suggests a different reality: De Flores will replace Alsemero. Even Beatrice's grotesquely false compliment re-inforces this view: 'How lovely now dost thou appear to me!' (2.2.136). Does desire inhabit her eyes here too? Middleton and Rowley achieve a great deal in this brief scene, not only establishing Beatrice's primary responsibility for the murder of Piracquo but demonstrating that while she is quick-witted when her immediate interests are threatened, her 'intellectual eyesight' is, in other respects, remarkably myopic. The very disparities in her foresight suggest that the authors wish us to consider the debilitating con-sequences of her infatuation.

Meanwhile, in the 'pinfold' of Alibius' asylum, other forms of infa-tuation play themselves out. The 'lunatic' Franciscus, Antonio's brother in folly, exclaims that his master's beautiful wife Isabella has 'a wrinkle in her brow as deep as philosophy' (3.3.36–7). Little know-ing how prophetic this remark will prove, he goes on, in a missive of trite Petrarchan conceits, to make sexual advances to his mistress (3.3.108–75, 4.3.1–25). Isabella seems curious about these offers, if not particularly receptive to them, but more than anything else she marvels at the ease with which sexual transgression presents itself for the taking:

> Here the restrained current might make a breach,
> Spite of the watchful bankers; would a woman stray,
> She need not gad abroad to seek her sin,
> It would be brought home one ways or other:
> The needle's point will to the fixed north,
> Such drawing arctics women's beauties are.
>
> (3.3.195–200)

Less interested in scrutinizing the ostensibly transformative power of female beauty than in developing a pragmatic response to male sexual aggression, Isabella resorts in the end to 'practise', and her ingenious duping of Antonio shows that he is anything but a 'quick-sighted lover' (4.3.121). Still, the very resonance of Isabella's action with the conventional idea that vice necessitates cunning suggests that Franciscus and Antonio are scarcely as innocent as they protest. The 'magic' of Isabella's beauty, according to Antonio, has transformed him to his present 'shape of folly'; Franciscus adds that her 'perfections' have made him 'imperfect' (3.3.110–12, 4.3.15–16). But the frailties displayed by the 'madmen' find their genesis less in external victimization than in internal displacements of the will. Both men exhibit a 'weak part of nature' (1.2.84), yet neither recognizes that such 'deformity' admits no such easy 'cure' as that which they propose to Isabella (3.3.172, 4.3.25–7, 4.3.170–1).

In this respect De Flores is much their superior. His deformity is of course literal as well as moral, and through the chiastic structural patterns so endemic to Renaissance drama Middleton and Rowley imply that, unlike the feigned madmen, he undergoes an elevation in self-assurance as the play wears on. He is, moreover, explicitly contrasted with Beatrice-Joanna in the matter of 'intellectual eyesight', for when he murders Piracquo his vision serves him splendidly:

> Ha! What's that
> Threw sparkles in my eye? O 'tis a diamond
> He wears upon his finger.
>
> (3.2.21–3)

Beatrice had claimed that a truly deserving man sparkles 'like a diamond' (2.1.15), but she was speaking of Alsemero, and the context of her remark thoroughly undercut her pretensions to sharp discernment. De Flores, on the other hand, repeatedly shows that his moral understanding, if not his behaviour, is impeccable, and his discovery of the ring partly symbolizes this. He possesses the intellectual eyesight that Beatrice conspicuously lacks. It is thus no wonder that notions of desert surface once again in her later exclamations: 'How rare is that man's speed! ... Here's a man worth loving! ... A wondrous necessary man' (5.1.68–90).

But De Flores is not immune to *The Changeling's* prevailing malady: the attribution of male desire to the compulsions of female beauty. Early on he declares that he 'cannot choose but love' Beatrice-Joanna, that he can 'as well be hang'd as refrain seeing her', that he will experience another 'mad qualm' within the hour (1.1.231, 2.1.28, 2.1.79). And in the play's great central scene he confirms that her 'love-shooting eye' is the source of his 'pain' – a pain that she alone can ease.[11] Indeed he asserts that justice 'invites' her 'blood' to understand him (3.4.97–100). Within fifty brilliant lines Middleton and Rowley bring into tight proximity all the meanings of 'blood' they have thus far deployed: caste, consanguinity, merit, violence, life-force, sexual drive. Beatrice is now a woman 'dipp'd in blood', and when she attempts to sever herself from De Flores on the grounds of superior rank, his response is immediate, blunt, and irrefutable:

> Look but into your conscience, read me there,
> 'Tis a true book, you'll find me there your equal.
> Push! Fly not to your birth, but settle you
> In what the act has made you, y' are no more now;
> You must forget your parentage to me:
> Y' are the deed's creature; by that name
> You lost your first condition, and I challenge you,
> As peace and innocency has turn'd you out,
> And made you one with me.
> (3.4.132–40)

His allusion to 'conscience', in fact, is one of three in this scene – none of them uttered by Beatrice – so it seems evident that however much De Flores subscribes to the theory of lust-as-victimization, he is also acutely aware of choice and moral consequence.[12] This sets him in explicit opposition to his new lover, whose talk of 'choice' (2.1.7–12) serves mainly to demonstrate how little discretion she possesses, and whose remark about her mother's 'curs'd' womb merely perpetuates her evasion of responsibility (3.4.165). But for De Flores the discourse of victimization is always nuanced: he ascribes the promptings of blood to profound external influence, but never in a manner suggesting internal delusion. And though he speaks of being 'eased', he harbours no hope of 'cure'.

As if to complement this extensive meditation on frailty, the final scenes of *The Changeling* stage a series of inconclusive inquests. To begin with we have the private investigation of Tomazo de Piracquo, Alonzo's brother, and a 'doubting Thomas' from the play's early moments. Tomazo had informed Alonzo that he saw 'small welcome' in Beatrice's 'eye', but Alonzo dismissed his warning as 'exceptious' – the interference of a well-meaning but sceptical 'censurer' (2.1.106–25). In light of Alonzo's disappearance, however, Tomazo emerges as a potential revenger. The problem is that his action is forestalled by ignorance. *The Changeling*'s forces of doubt concentrate centripetally in Tomazo – perceptive observation, justified suspicion, rational hypothesis – but they are none the less frustrated, and frustrated in a manner that hints at the likely triumph of murderous cunning. Tomazo is reduced to supposing *all* men his enemies: 'league with mankind I renounce for ever / Till I find this murderer' (5.2.43–4). The play does not mock his resolution – indeed treating it less as a false generalization than as a prudent suspension of judgement – but when Tomazo's pursuit of truth collides with Vermandero's independent enquiry, the result is a travesty of forensic caution. Again, we see how easily appearances may deceive: the apprehension of Antonio and Franciscus for the murder of Alonzo constitutes an absurd rush to judgement, the very violence of which mirrors the actions it seeks to address. Yet for the formerly sceptical Tomazo it is a 'blest revelation' (5.2.78).

Hence we are thoroughly prepared for the opening lines of the closing scene: Jasperino's allusion to 'proof' of Beatrice-Joanna's infidelity. Ironically, Jasperino's investigations, unlike those of Tomazo and Vermandero, began by accident, and in fact were temporarily quashed by Alsemero's counter-enquiry into Beatrice's virginity – the episode of the 'treble-qualitied' seizure (4.2.89–150).[13] But now Jasperino possesses further evidence, and in language reminiscent of *Troilus and Cressida* he speaks of slicing to the core:

> 'Tis not a shallow probe
> Can search this ulcer soundly; I fear you'll find it
> Full of corruption.
>
> (5.3.7–9)

For his part, Alsemero finally acknowledges that his 'doubts are strong upon [him]'; he intends to 'seek out truth' in Beatrice-Joanna's heart (5.3.23–36). None the less, the play makes clear that his case is far from conclusive: his star witness, for example, is dead. So when Alsemero confronts his wife it seems at first strange that she volunteers an apparently gratuitous confession. But of course the confession is partial – and pre-emptively so. Beatrice provides one last magnificent display of her lack of moral imagination, supposing that admitting Piracquo's murder while insisting on her chastity will absolve her of transgression, and perhaps impress her husband too. But not even Alsemero's conception of honour is quite this flexible. The confession backfires, De Flores tells the rest of the story, and between them the murderers resolve the mystery that none of the play's investigators could decipher. Vermandero's comical appearance with 'suspicion near as proof' is silenced by Alsemero's 'proof / Beyond suspicion' (5.3.123–5).

Is patience, then, the honest man's revenge? Tomazo thinks so; he assures the gathered assembly that he is 'satisfied'. Alsemero is more insistent: 'Justice hath so right / The guilty hit, that innocence is quit / By proclamation' (5.3.185–90). The world is morally responsive after all. And to the question of how 'blind men' should know 'cunning devils' from 'fair-faced saints', Alsemero's answer can only be that time itself will tell (5.3.108–9). Beatrice-Joanna, however, offers a qualifying perspective to such complacent moralizing. Her last substantial speech is addressed to her father:

> come not near me, sir, I shall defile you:
> I am that of your blood was taken from you
> For your better health; look no more upon't,
> But cast it to the ground regardlessly,
> Let the common sewer take it from distinction.
> Beneath the stars, upon yon meteor
> Ever hung my fate, 'mongst things corruptible;
> I ne'er could pluck it from him: my loathing
> Was prophet to the rest, but ne'er believ'd;
> Mine honour fell with him, and now my life.
> (5.3.149–58)

Demonstrating 'unmitigated repentance', as Lisa Hopkins puts it, these lines represent Beatrice's apogee in self-knowledge.[14] She appropriates the play's pervasive interest in blood-letting as a cure and imagines herself as *nothing but blood*: defiled blood from her father's veins. But her very metaphor implies illness on her father's part. And despite Alsemero's optimism, it is far from evident that Vermandero's malady will vanish with his daughter's death.

As for Beatrice's allegation that her fate always 'hung' with De Flores, here we see a reversion to the determinism so frequently voiced in *The Changeling*. But the movement from 'ne'er could pluck' to 'ne'er believ'd' at least intimates the possibility of choice, while the idea of prophetic 'loathing' recalls the providential 'instinct' discussed by Tomazo and De Flores (4.2.46, 5.2.40). Indeed, the play confines the scope of human freedom to precisely the extent to which Beatrice can hold herself accountable for failing to heed her foreboding. People *can* be 'read' (3.4.132, 5.3.16), but the reading demands vigilance; it requires an alertness and sensitivity which only 'intellectual eyesight' can provide. The play's best exemplars of such vision are De Flores and Isabella: the former with his persistent faith in conscience, the latter with her astute resort to 'practise'. De Flores in particular *sees* with such acuity that his wilful capitulation to the urgings of blood becomes a perverse act of courage. In this he differs remarkably from Iago, Edmund or even Bosola. The world of *The Changeling* is one of radically circumscribed perception – and in this respect the sceptical currents of Jacobean thought are fully represented – but the play's authors counter this circumscription by positing a parallel realm of intuitive moral understanding. We are left to wonder, however, whether Beatrice-Joanna's apprehension of that realm has any more lasting reality than that of a fitfully recollected dream.

# 12
## Criterion Anxiety in 'Tis Pity She's a Whore

> [Custom] conquereth nature: for hence it is that the most
> beautifull daughters of men draw not unto love their naturall
> parents; nor brethren, though excellent in beautie, winne not
> the love of their sisters. This kind of chastitie is not properly of
> nature, but of the use of lawes and customes, which forbid
> them, and make of incest a great sinne.
>
> Charron, Of Wisdome

It is fitting in many ways to close this book with a discussion of John
Ford's *'Tis Pity She's a Whore*. Technically a work of the Caroline
period, the play is still very much a Jacobean tragedy in its intellectuality, its boldness, its contrariety, its 'horrid laughter'.[1] Like
*Mariam* and *The Duchess of Malfi*, *'Tis Pity* concerns itself with sexuality in exogamous and endogamous contexts; like *The Spanish
Tragedy*, *The Malcontent*, *The White Devil* and *The Changeling*, it is
enmeshed in revenge-play conventions; like *The Duchess* and *The
White Devil* it displays strong interest in malevolence and gratuitous
cruelty; and like *Doctor Faustus* it is fascinated with issues of aspira-
tion and forbidden knowledge. Indeed, many critics have emphasized *'Tis Pity*'s epistemological orientation. Cyrus Hoy noted long
ago that Giovanni is 'an eminently rational protagonist whose very
powers of reason make him, paradoxically, at once the more vulnerable to sin and the more culpable in sinning'. And recently Lisa
Hopkins has observed that certainty, uncertainty, blindness and
ignorance 'form an important part of the play's thematic structure':
despite the evident dangers of knowledge, *'Tis Pity* 'never ceases to
remind us that we are always already implicated in it'.[2] Like dramatic
predecessors such as Faustus, Mariam and Webster's Duchess,

Giovanni and Annabella travel 'into a wilderness' (*Duchess*, 1.1.350). And though, in the end, they die for it, the play's efforts both to justify and to condemn their transgression raise the sceptical problem of the criterion with extraordinary persistence and subtlety, indeed drawing deeply on several of the basic paradigms of scepticism's English reception.[3]

The details of Ford's life are notoriously vague. A younger son from a landed family in Devon, he is probably the same 'John Ford' who matriculated at Oxford's Exeter College in 1601. If so, however, his stay was brief, for in 1602 he entered the Middle Temple in London, where he resided almost continuously until 1617. At the Temple he would have known Marston, Sir John Davies, Thomas Overbury and probably Greville, Webster and Francis Beaumont, though of course Webster's tenure there is a matter of dispute.[4] In addition, Ford may have been acquainted with Charles Blount and Henry Percy–the earls, respectively, of Devonshire and Northumberland – and he collaborated with Thomas Dekker and William Rowley on *The Witch of Edmonton* (1621) before proceeding to write the handful of plays for which he is now remembered.[5] He died in obscurity sometime around 1640.

I mention Blount and Percy because both owned copies of Sextus – a fact which, though scarcely remarkable in itself, assumes greater significance when viewed in the context of the literary and philosophical environment in which both men circulated and with which Ford, as a poet and Inns of Court student, was naturally affiliated. We know as well that the Middle Temple's library possessed a copy of the 1569 edition of Sextus, a copy in which Ford could easily have run across Sextus' discussion of consanguinal incest in his treatment of Pyrrhonism's tenth mode of doubt (*PH*, 1.145–63). Demonstrating how customs and laws may be opposed to one another in the interests of inducing *epochē*, Sextus writes that

> among us it is forbidden to have sex with your mother, while in Persia it is the custom to favour such marriages; and in Egypt they marry their sisters, which among us is forbidden by law ... . [Consequently] since so much anomaly has been shown in objects by this [tenth] mode too, we shall not be able to say what each existing object is like in its nature, but only how it appears relative to a given persuasion, law, or custom. Because of this mode too, therefore, it is necessary for us to suspend judgement on the nature of external existing objects. (*PH*, 1.152)[6]

The 'external object' in question here is the moral status of incest, and it is intriguing that Sextus returns to this issue when he ponders whether there exists 'an expertise in living' (*PH*, 3.239). The subtext of his remarks is an assault on Stoic dogmatism, but on the surface he quotes both Zeno's *Discourses* and Chrysippus' *Republic* in support of the view that there was 'nothing dreadful' about the incest of Oedipus and Jocasta. Chrysippus, for instance, claims that 'one should arrange these matters in the way which is in fact the custom – and no bad thing – among some peoples: let mothers have children by their sons, fathers by their daughters, brothers by their sisters'. For his part, Sextus concludes that since we cannot apprehend whether there is indeed an expertise in living, we must suspend judgement on Chrysippus' specific prescriptions (*PH*, 3.245–9). But it is difficult not to suspect that incest functions for Sextus as an especially potent example – a flashpoint where conflicting social ideologies expose themselves in unusually sharp profile.

The same might be said of Montaigne. In his chapter 'On custom' he alludes to incest and mentions that Chrysippus held no objection to incestuous alliance (*Essays*, 128–31). And in the *Apology*, midway through a critique of Natural Law, he comments that 'Nothing in the world has greater variety than law and custom. What is abominable in one place is laudable somewhere else ... . Marriages between close relations are capital offences with us: elsewhere they are much honoured.' Natural laws, he concludes, may exist for some creatures, but 'we have lost them: that fine human reason of ours is always interfering, seeking dominance, confounding the face of everything according to its own vanity and inconstancy' (161–2). No doubt Montaigne would have argued that in European cultures incestuous unions should be avoided; perhaps he would have speculated that were it not for the chaotic interposition of reason we might have discovered their prohibition by Natural Law. My guess, however, is that on this matter Montaigne suspends judgement as thoroughly as does Sextus: the intrinsic moral status of incest, if such a thing exists at all, appears to be beyond our apprehension, though we can obviously formulate pragmatic policies based on cultural precedent. Indeed, since Montaigne clearly relies on the *Outlines* for his examples and discussion, the supposition seems strong that Sextus' arguments carry the day.

It is within this intellectual milieu that Ford would have found himself when he wrote *'Tis Pity*. And even if he had not read Sextus or Montaigne, he undoubtedly had been exposed to fictional considerations of incest in plays ranging from *Hamlet*, *Pericles* and *The*

*Revenger's Tragedy* to *The Duchess of Malfi*, *The Atheist's Tragedy* and *Women Beware Women*. Granted, the difference between incest by affinity and by consanguinity is sufficiently great that the former scarcely seems to merit the outrage it provokes among the characters whose lives it affects. But this merely underscores Montaigne's prevailing theme. And in any event the incest Ford elects to dramatize is the latter variety. It may be true that Ford pits such incest against 'accepted standards of religion and morality' not because he approves of it but because it is 'the most shocking challenge to traditional values of which he can conceive'.[7] But it may also be that while Ford disapproves of incest, he cannot muster conclusive arguments against it; certainly the members of Parmesan society falter in their efforts to justify their horror. One of *'Tis Pity*'s most original departures, then, may be that it explores a human choice whose power to shock far exceeds the susceptibility of that shock to rational modes of explanation.

From the play's outset we experience a sense of impasse. Friar Bonaventura and Giovanni have been debating, but the Friar now urges his young friend to cease the dispute:

> These are no school-points; nice philosophy
> May tolerate unlikely arguments,
> But Heaven admits no jest: wits that presumed
> On wit too much, by striving how to prove
> There was no God, with foolish grounds of art,
> Discovered first the nearest way to hell,
> And filled the world with devilish atheism.
> Such questions, youth, are fond; for better 'tis
> To bless the sun than reason why it shines.
>
> (1.1.2–10)

The Friar, in short, posits a category distinction, separating 'nice philosophy' from heavenly concerns, implying that university-style disputation has no place in the realm of moral absolutes. But while he goes on to assert the superiority of grateful acceptance to inquisitive ratiocination, he none the less volunteers a 'reason' in support of his claim that 'Heaven admits no jest', and it is a reason whose truth-status he cannot possibly ascertain. He thus exhibits a trace of the very presumption he condemns both in his interlocutor and in atheists more generally. So the blurring of categories for which he chastises Giovanni is an offence he simultaneously commits.

But if the Friar begs questions, Giovanni does too. Critical accounts of *'Tis Pity* emphasize the habitual speciousness with which he defends his desires.[8] Annabella's beauty, he claims, is such that the gods themselves should adore her; he and she were conceived in the same womb by the same sire and thus are 'bound' to one another both by 'nature' and by the links of blood, reason and religion (1.1.20–33, 1.2.230–6). Even in his attack on the peevishness of 'customary form' – probably his shrewdest argumentative tactic – he spoils his advantage by asserting that his own 'perpetual happiness' depends on the shattering of convention (1.1.24–7). That this remark will be perceived as anything but grotesque, self-serving hyperbole is undermined by its absolute presumption of certainty and its absolute subordination of Annabella's will to that of her blustering admirer. So when the Friar urges Giovanni to cleanse his 'leprosy of lust' and acknowledge what he is – 'A wretch, a worm, a nothing' – it seems difficult not to agree with him (1.1.74–6). We remember Malevole calling 'man' the 'slime of this dung-pit' (4.5.111); we recollect that when Montaigne contemplates humanity 'unprovided' of God, he wonders whether it is possible 'to imagine anything so ridiculous as this miserable and wretched creature' (Florio, 396). Nor does the Friar exempt himself from the Montaignian estimate he encourages Giovanni to adopt. At the scene's close, then, one character has offered weak reasons for his desire while the other, rejecting that desire, has offered no reasons at all. We have a standoff between inchoate rebellion, passionately but ineffectively justified, and fideistic submission to authority bolstered by broad assent to the thesis of human depravity. It is a dilemma suffused with the preoccupations of early modern scepticism.

And it is a dilemma revisited near the end of act 2, though with one colossal difference: Giovanni and Annabella have now consummated their love. The Friar, horrified, warns Giovanni that 'Heaven is angry' and that divine vengeance will overtake him unless he leaves his sister and seeks the 'throne of mercy' (2.5.9–65). But Giovanni attempts to 'prove' that his incest is 'fit and good': using Neoplatonic commonplaces of the sort mocked by Sidney in *Astrophil and Stella*, he asserts with puerile solemnity that Annabella's beauty guarantees her virtue, and that her virtue, in turn, guarantees his. The speech is a tissue of empty syllogisms, and the Friar rebukes the effort, characterizing it as 'Ignorance in knowledge':

> if we were sure there were no deity,
> Nor Heaven nor hell, then to be led alone
> By nature's light (as were philosophers

> Of elder times), might instance some defence.
> But 'tis not so; then, madman, thou wilt find
> That nature is in Heaven's positions blind.
>
> (2.5.13–34)

Not surprisingly, this response presupposes the existence of an omnipotent divine being and a well-developed metaphysical infrastructure, complete with 'positions'. Hence from the sceptical standpoint, Giovanni's failure to examine his assumptions is matched by a parallel failure on the Friar's part. Both men engage in precipitous judgement, the principal difference being that one does so with the full sanction of 'customary form'. It is intriguing, however, that the Friar's allusion to philosophers of 'elder times' invites a perspective whereby Giovanni's reasoning garners 'some defence'. The slippage, moreover, between being led by 'nature's light' in ratiocination alone, and, more insidiously, in sexual behaviour as well, suggests that Ford may have in mind such contemporary arguments as those of Pierre Charron. Going beyond the judgemental suspension of Montaigne, Charron proposes that the incest taboo is a function not of nature but of custom.[9] I have already discussed Charron's partial reliance on the Stoic criterion of natural reason – a reliance that Sextus would have found deeply problematic – so I merely add here that the Friar's reference to ancient philosophers carries ironic reverberations of which he can scarcely conceive.

On balance, then, I find it difficult to credit such assessments of Giovanni as that offered by Irving Ribner, who speaks of the young man's 'searching rational spirit' and views him, heroically, as one who cannot practise blind acceptance of social prohibition. Robert Ornstein seems closer to the mark in observing that Giovanni is 'hardly a dangerous opponent of morality': his rebellion is 'more emotional than intellectual', his arguments far weaker than those of Edmund or D'Amville in their attempt to justify desire on the basis of naturalistic premises. By the same token, however, I find unconvincing those critical efforts which seek to link Friar Bonaventura with the Good Angel and the Old Man in *Doctor Faustus*, thereby implying that Ford weaves into his tragedy an unproblematic criterion, a standard of moral judgement by which we may gauge the play's varied transgressions. The Friar seems far too ambiguous to embody such a role – and far too *human*, compared to his supposed Marlovian precedents. He is, moreover, a man committed to 'saving the appearances', as he clearly reveals when he urges Annabella to marry Soranzo (3.6.34–56).[10] So the explicit debates of the play, carried out for the most part by the Friar and Giovanni, repeatedly end in stalemate, and as a consequence *'Tis Pity*'s exploratory energies are channelled elsewhere: into action, subplot commentary and exemplification of the ambient moral climate.

The play's second scene provides an excellent example. Beginning with Vasques' provocation of Grimaldi and ending with the extraordinary vows of Annabella and Giovanni, the scene's trajectory is from the margins to the interior, from the indisputably ugly to the debatably pure. In Vasques' insolent brutality we find a concise introduction to the social realities of Parma. And the very structure of the scene – 'lovers rejected [followed by] a lover chosen' – encourages the audience 'to accept Annabella's choice despite the danger of incest'.[11] Grimaldi, after all, is a coward, Soranzo a perjuring bully and Bergetto an imbecile, so at the level of explicit contrast it is small wonder that Giovanni wins his sister's favour. But beyond this there is Giovanni's own charisma, a blend of honesty and earnest passion which never again manifests itself quite the same way, and which ultimately devolves into bravado, jealousy, and maniacal self-delusion. Telling Annabella that he has 'Reasoned against the reasons' of his love, Giovanni demonstrates that he has attempted to avoid precipitation and has subjected himself to a Pyrrhonian-style examination of counter-arguments prior to reaching his current resolve (1.2.222). The resolve itself is of course profoundly anti-sceptical, but to the extent that it assimilates traces of a more narrowly rational doubt, it participates in the larger sceptical tradition. Like Faustus, who proclaims that he is not so 'fond / To imagine that after this life there is any pain ... these are trifles and mere old wives' tales' (A.2.1.136–8), Giovanni refers to religious precepts as 'dreams and old men's tales / To fright unsteady youth' (1.2.151–2, 5.3.1–21). Indeed, he resembles the conventional stage-Machiavel, if only momentarily, in his implication that religion is 'but a childish toy' (*Jew of Malta*, Prologue.14).[12] On the whole, however, Giovanni is presented as a sympathetic figure in this scene, and if he engages in emotional manipulation, at the same time he gives every indication that he truly believes it is irresistible destiny rather than lust which presses him forward (1.2.221–5). Only later do his references to 'fate' take on the quality of evasion.[13]

I thus largely agree with the assessment that *'Tis Pity* depicts society as 'corrupt' and incestuous love as 'capable of deep and fragile beauty'.[14] The key word, however, is 'capable', since the play offers no certain means by which such love may be sustained. Throughout its middle scenes it stages minor epistemological disputes which keep before us the question of *how* we know what we think we know, and these disputes in turn prompt us to reflect on the relative degrees of certainty with which Annabella and Giovanni endow the validity of their affection. 'How do you know that, simplicity?' demands Donado of Bergetto; Giovanni echoes the question when Putana informs him that his sister is 'quick': 'With child? How dost thou know't?' (2.6.98, 3.3.9–10). Florio, meanwhile, brings in Richardetto to examine Annabella, but the man is unable to detect what Putana has instantly perceived, and we wonder about the probability of his success as an avenger (3.4.2–9). In short, the mid-play subplots, often maligned by critics, serve not only to display repulsive suitors and failed relationships but to raise the more abstract problem of the standards to which we inevitably refer in making determinations of moral validity or likely truth.[15] It is beyond question that the subplot world of *'Tis Pity* consists largely of lust, cretinism and revenge intrigue, but at the same time these very preoccupations impinge on our sense of how Giovanni and Annabella justify their love – and how, indeed, they can scarcely *avoid* justifying it, given their alternatives.

Yet it is precisely to the extent that the underworld of *'Tis Pity* erupts into the main story that we feel the precariousness of incestuous love's survival. As early as the close of act 2 we see that Giovanni is infected by jealousy, and by the middle of the following act Annabella has exhibited a breathtaking failure to question the morally dubious counsel proffered by the Friar (3.6.34–42). These capitulations serve as an index of the degree to which the lovers are inhabitants of their world, and perhaps the culminating instance of this trend is Giovanni's adoption of the revenger's motives and language. Presumably aware of Grimaldi's bungled attempt to slay Soranzo, Giovanni is subsequently present throughout Hippolita's elaborate effort to poison her former lover (4.1.35–110). But by denying him a single word during the spectacle, Ford leaves to our imaginations the question of precisely *how* Giovanni responds to the display of foiled vengeance. The Friar warns him to 'mark' the event: 'that marriage seldom's good, / Where the bride-banquet so begins in blood' (4.1.108–10). But the very absurdity of this admonition merely buttresses the likelihood that Giovanni will ignore it – unlike the simple-minded Richardetto, who formally renounces private vengeance in the following scene. Giovanni is unaffected by these ambiguous intimations of providential surveillance, and as late as the middle of act 5 we still find him dismissing religious opinion as idle fear (5.3.1–29,

5.5.32–5). Suddenly, however, he learns that he and his sister have been 'discovered', a fact confirmed by the abrupt entry of Vasques with an invitation to Soranzo's birthday feast. Recognizing that he will be targeted for assassination, Giovanni's instant resolution is 'To strike as deep in slaughter' as his murderous brother-in-law (5.3.35–62).

So the genesis of Giovanni's revenge lies in his society's deeper assent to an ethos of vengeance. He is in fact the last of *'Tis Pity's* characters to embrace revenge – Richardetto, Hippolita, Grimaldi, Soranzo and Vasques all precede him – and the nature of his vindictive action sharply distinguishes it from that of his fellow criminals. Fredson Bowers once remarked that 'It is difficult at first to understand why Giovanni should call his deed a revenge', and certainly this is true if we believe, as Bowers did, that 'Ford is entirely in accord with the ethical spirit of the tragedy of his time'.[16] But Giovanni's revenge consists of more than one 'deed', and while it undoubtedly comprehends the punishment of both Annabella and Soranzo – the one for her 'revolt' (5.5.8), the other for his discovery of incestuous union – at a more fundamental level it constitutes a symbolic slaying of the world: a world which denounces Giovanni's behaviour yet offers no decisive arguments against it, no arguments at all apart from the dogmatic 'curse / Of old prescription' (5.3.74–5). The very authorities who condemn Giovanni and Annabella, in particular the Cardinal, are depicted as condoning and indeed promoting injustice in Parma. Even the Pope is implicated in the shameless protection of Grimaldi (3.9.51–60). And while Nicholas Brooke usefully observes that the play's 'proper moral comments are weakened by being uttered since they are uttered by doubtful voices', the fact is that even if they were uttered by undoubtful voices they would still be weak since their status is only that of propriety.[17] Giovanni takes revenge against a world that coerces conformity while displaying hypocritical allegiance to standards it proclaims but never defends. And, as if there were any lingering doubt about the matter, Parma's corruption and moral shabbiness are once again emphasized when Florio arrives at Soranzo's party in the company of the Cardinal: the same man regarding whose behaviour he had earlier exclaimed, in Hieronimo-like tones, 'Justice is fled to Heaven and comes no nearer' (3.9.62). Institutions familial and divine seem united in an exhibition of blithely amnesiac authority.

If the love of Giovanni and Annabella is destroyed by societal convention, it is also defeated by nature – the same nature that aided its creation. Ford makes this abundantly clear. Had Annabella not become pregnant, she would not have fainted in Soranzo's presence; she would

Our loves, that love will wipe away that rigour
Which would in other incests be abhorred.

(5.5.68–73)

The criterion of incest's moral validity apparently lies in the strength and constancy of the lovers' mutual affection. And while Hopkins has stressed that no one else can 'know' the love of Giovanni and Annabella since 'such knowledge can only be directly experiential, not vicarious', by the same token no one can conclusively demonstrate that their love merits the 'rigour' which Parma summons against it.[19] As so often elsewhere in the play, debates lead only to impasse; the prevailing intellectual impression is one of sceptical paralysis.

But paralysis at one level can stimulate spectacular action at another, and the finale of *'Tis Pity* exhibits precisely such spectacle. Retrospectively indulging the fantasy that a collective act of will on his and Annabella's part might have controlled destiny and shielded them from the malice of others, Giovanni makes the following remarkable announcement to his sister:

why, I hold fate
Clasped in my fist, and could command the course
Of time's eternal motion, hadst thou been
One thought more steady than an ebbing sea.

(5.5.11–14)

And then he stabs her, pre-empting Soranzo's machinations and removing her from the scrutiny both of those who would damn her, like Vasques and the Cardinal, and those who would view her as contrite and thus forgiven, like the Friar and perhaps her father. The bleeding heart he subsequently displays to the amassed banqueters – a heart in which his own lies metaphorically 'entombed' (5.6.28) – becomes simultaneously the receptacle where the truth of his love's validity finally rests. But like the identity of the literal organ, unrecognized as Annabella's despite Giovanni's repeated asseverations, the heart's symbolic status seems equally beyond comprehension; indeed, the suitability of 'fast-knit affections' as a legitimizing standard can never be any more apprehensible to outsiders than can the figurative presence of Giovanni's 'heart' within that of his butchered sister. Both are doomed to solipsistic isolation.

The ultimate inaccessibility of validating criteria is thus emphasized down to the close of *'Tis Pity*, and the play's very title recapitulates the

Parmesan tendency to trivialize that which it cannot understand (5.6.159–60). Of course, as Ford makes clear, Parma may well be in the right, and certainly Giovanni's brutal monomania works directly against his cause. But neither can we neglect the initial love scene between brother and sister: its sense of innocence and purity, its evident superiority to subsequent displays of 'love', its implicit challenge to Parmesan society to provide more wholesome models of sexual affection. By what convincing criterion, the play insistently asks, may consanguinal incest be deemed abhorrent or immoral? If the answer lies only in custom and dogmatic prohibition, then the revolt of Giovanni and Annabella acquires *de facto* justification: the justification provisionally extended to acts which challenge authority even while relying on presumptions of their own as they probe social boundaries. The daring with which sister and brother transgress the moral regulations of their world – particularly the contempt shown by Giovanni for that mindless arrogation of unargued ethical convention into universal common sense – cannot help but inspire sympathy even among auditors who simultaneously experience revulsion at the choice the siblings make. Their pursuit of love, however much it may also be a pursuit of desire, none the less constitutes a metaphorical version of the *zetetic* mode of Pyrrhonism, the ongoing search so central to scepticism's early modern configuration. And while such behaviour is certainly in conflict with the nescience and social conformity advocated both by Sextus and by Parma, it is by no means at odds with the ways in which scepticism was routinely received in the sixteenth and seventeenth centuries: by Montaigne, by Charron and by countless English writers.

\* \* \*

'Whatsoever seemeth strange unto us, and we understand not, we blame and condemne.' So declares Montaigne in Florio's rendition of the *Apology* (413–14). And so concur a number of English playwrights, in varied ways and degrees, in tragedies ranging from *Doctor Faustus* and *Mariam* to *The Duchess of Malfi* and *'Tis Pity She's a Whore*. For Montaigne, the genesis of sexual regulation is a complex and problematic issue: what custom forbids is not necessarily vicious, nor, by implication, is what nature urges necessarily desirable. And the criteria by which the moral validity of human actions may be judged are always open to dispute, since their very existence is subject to the problem of infinitely regressing demonstration. The same problem afflicts the religious quarrels of the Reformation, as writers like Erasmus, Castellio and Donne fully recognize. But if the tolerant attitudes of 'nice philosophy' are not typically encountered in the world at large, the sceptical outlook none the less encourages the question of why this should be so. What is there about incest, Giovanni asks, that should prevent it from being debated as a 'school-point'? What is there, indeed, that should prevent it from being explored? Scepticism never insists that a given action or belief is universally right or wrong, and while it always holds out the possibility that decisive arguments may be found, it also, and more fundamentally, implies that until such arguments appear, continued investigation of opinions and issues is entirely appropriate as an operant habit of mind. And perhaps as a habit of body too.

Hence the immense frustration with sceptical attitudes exhibited by Renaissance counter-sceptics from Luther and Mornay to Bacon, Herbert and Descartes. For them, as for many others, the elusiveness of scepticism was maddening, its protean ability to surface in new forms and guises merely exacerbating its already vexatious nature. In particular, tendentious appropriations and partial deployments of Pyrrhonian theory rendered scepticism immune to most strategies of hostile critique. And because various instrumentalizations of doubt proved useful even to opponents, scepticism not only conserved but promoted its intellectual vitality during the early modern period. Sextus' ten modes of Pyrrhonian doubt, for instance, acquired wide recognition as valuable trajectories of interrogation, and in general the energies of scepticism diffused themselves across vast discursive territory. So it is really no surprise that *'Tis Pity* stages competing forms of Renaissance scepticism: Giovanni's rationalist orientation versus Friar Bonaventura's fideism, Annabella's difficulty with resolve versus her brother's over-confident conviction. Nor is it strange that the tragedies of Marlowe, Shakespeare, Cary, Webster and Middleton likewise exhibit sustained engagement with doubt.

It would indeed have been strange had they *not* done so. The dialogic impulses of drama drew strength from scepticism's habitual tactics, and whether we focus on the Pyrrhonian critique of sense-perception and ratiocination or on allegations regarding the therapeutic and clarifying virtues of doubt, we find that English tragedy repeatedly takes up the basic questions of sceptical epistemology. Thus in the plays I have treated, as in many of the non-dramatic works I have discussed, the early modern reception of scepticism manifests itself by widespread impatience with Pyrrhonian irresolution conjoined with widespread assent to the sceptics' foundational premises: that the

# Notes

## Introduction

1. Sidney, 244. Discussions of dialectic, opposition, paradox and 'complementarity' in early modern literature may be found in *KLG*; Colie, *Paradoxia*; Rabkin, 67–9; Grudin, 1–50; Rozett, 35–40; Bradshaw, 1–49.
2. Popkin (*HS*) and Schmitt (*CS*; *Gianfrancesco*) are principal authorities.
3. Altman, 1–11, 31–106. For *in utramque partem* argumentation: Jardine, 'Valla', 259–65; Schiffman, *Threshold*, 12, 54–66; Kahn, 115–19; Greenblatt, *Self-Fashioning*, 230–1; Sloane, *Contrary*, 39–40, 62.
4. Long, 75–106; *HS*, xvii–xxiv; Stough; *PH*, 1.220–35.
5. *Selected*, 362–4; Toulmin, 1–69. For scepticism as diffidence and secular agnosticism: *CS*, 84, 143, 158.
6. *KLG*, 3–62; Dollimore, 9–21; Cavell, *Disowning*, 1–18; Bradshaw, ix–xii, 1–49; Cave, 'Imagining'. Also Allen, 1–27, 75–110; Wiley, *Subtle*, 59; Strathmann, 7; *HS*, xvii–xxiv, 3–43; Engle, *Pragmatism*, 8–10; Nauert, *Humanism*, 198–9; Martin, 13–22.
7. Friedrich, 56–7.
8. Cave, 205. Carey likewise speaks of the 'onrush of scepticism which was to transform, within half a century, the intellectual orientation of the Western world' (217; cp. 244–5).
9. *CS*, 88; cp. Kristeller, *Greek*, 47–8.
10. For example, Bodin's *Colloquium Heptaplomeres* (*c.* 1588); Bruno's London writings; Le Vayer's *Quatre Dialogues* (1606). On Bodin, see Kuntz; on Bruno, Gatti, 31, 69.
11. *IMD*, 15.
12. *Works*, 4:221.
13. On late Elizabethan social unrest: Archer; Guy; Sommerville; Stone, *Crisis*.
14. Gatti, 31.
15. *Patterns*, 195–214; *KLG*, 171–265. Bradshaw usefully distinguishes between *radical* and *dogmatic* scepticism (39), but downplays historical context and Shakespeare's contemporaries.

## Chapter 1

1. *CS*, 13, 45–52; *SE*, 26–35; *HS*, 19; Schmitt, 'Rediscovery', 'Unstudied'; *RP*, 241; Bolgar, 489; Kristeller, *Renaissance*, 27–31, *Iter*, 6:530a–b; Floridi, 'Diffusion', 76–8; Jardine, 'Valla'; Panizza; Haydn, 77–82; Seigel, 57–94, 246–8; Kraye, 160; Annas and Barnes, 6. The first use of 'scepticus' in English appears to occur in Nicholas Udall's translation of Erasmus' *Apophthegmes* (1542): Aristo is characterized as a 'Scepticus, because he was altogether occupied in consydering & serchyng the state of humain thynges' (64r). Cp. Bucer's *Gratulation* (1549), where the Bishop of

Winchester is characterized as 'a Scepticus' and 'an uncertain sceptical coniecturar' (sigs. Gr, Giiir).

2. Kinney, 32, 323–5; Kristeller, 'Humanism', 280.
3. Walker, 58–62; *HS*, 3–7, 19–27.
4. Schmitt, 'Rediscovery', 236; *Theaetetus*, 152–4; *Metaphysics*, 1010–63. Augustine's *Contra Academicos* (386 CE) grapples with Academic scepticism and probabilism, conceding the frailty of human perception but arguing that some truths are known with certainty.
5. *CWE*, 27:118; also 24:429–38, 3:125. *Folly* was translated into English in 1549.
6. Lucian, 3:140–1; Altman, 121–2; Robinson, *Lucian*; Duncan, 82–96; *KLG*, 48. Erasmus had translated *Icaromenippus* by 1511.
7. Lucian, 1:204–6; also 2:41–90. For 'negative dogmatism': *HS*, xx; *PH*, 1.220–35. Cicero does not make the distinction, nor does Augustine. Schmitt notes that Renaissance thinkers 'did not seem to distinguish [Pyrrhonism and Academicism] any more clearly than they distinguished "Platonism" from "Neoplatonism"' (*CS*, 8).
8. *CWE*, 29:240–4; Durling; Nauert, *Agrippa*, 142–3; Gilbert, 15–16, 157; Sanches, *Nothing*, 64, 184. Sanches never mentions Sextus, but may have encountered Galen in one of the Sextus editions.
9. *Works*, 18.
10. Hankinson, *Galen*, xxiv, 93; Frede, 68–72; Celsus, 6; Viotti, 17–27; Pittion, 105–7, 130; *CWE*, 29:220–3.
11. Screech, 255; *CS*, 57; *HS*, 31; *SE*, 36. Budé relied on both *LP* and *Academica*.
12. Nauert, *Agrippa*, 293, 122–4, 139–50; *HS*, 29–30; *SE*, 37–8.
13. Villey (*HS*, 312); Strathmann, 228; Kaiser, 144.
14. *Vanitie*, 16, 163–6; *Agrippa*, 142.
15. *HS*, 29; Haydn, 101–19; Mebane; Dooley, 119; *IMD*, 29; Brush, 25–7; Nauert, *Agrippa*, 314; Keefer, 615–16; Wiley, *Subtle*, 47; Buckley, 117–18; *SR*, 56; Bullough, 14. Sanford's trans. was published in 1569.
16. *CWE*, 76:7, 7:77–9; Ozment, 294–8.
17. *Works*, 33:20–4; Haydn, 103; *SE*, 38.
18. Rummel, 173; *CS*, 59–62; Armstrong, 44; Jardine, 'Forging', 147–9.
19. *CS*, 2; Ronquist.
20. Ong, 239–40, 362; Ficino, 2:986, 2:1008; Schmitt, 'Rediscovery'; *CS*, 52. Bernardi also relies on Ficino for scepticism (*Seminarium*, 2:810–11); Lipsius divides philosophers into 'Dogmaticam, Academicam, Scepticam', but he had read Sextus (*Manuductionis*, 69–76).
21. Schmitt, *Gianfrancesco*; *RP*, 245–7; *HS*, 19–27; Haydn, 101; Garin, 133–5; *IMD*, 28–9; Brush, 24–5; Cave, 197–9; *SE*, 32–4; Larmore, 1150; Pumfrey, 52; Kristeller, *Renaissance*, 203.
22. *RP*, 246; *CS*, 59.
23. Schmitt, *Gianfrancesco*, 27, 239; Rice, *Epistles*, 416–18; Loyer, *Spectres*, 1:113ff; Bernardi, 2:810–11; *Apology*, xxiii; Green, *Rainolds*, 355, 447; Roberts and Watson.
24. Grafton, 'Higher', 159–60; *SE*, 7. Gesner used the 1544 ed. of the *Suda*, Montaigne the 1564 *Suidae Historica* (*Essays*, 234).
25. Floridi, 'Diffusion', 68–9; cp. *SE*, 70–2.
26. Schmitt, 'Wolley'; *SE*, 84–5. Wolley translated *Adversus logicos*, 1:27–446 (Bodleian MS Sancroft 17).

27. *CS*, 69–71; *SE*, 31, 115.
28. *HS*, 30–1; Nauert, *Agrippa*, 147–8; Kristeller, *Medieval*, 71.
29. *Donne*, 89; Seigel, 16–17, 29, 246–8; Armstrong; Jardine, 'Valla'; Kristeller, *Renaissance*, 252; Schmitt, 'Rediscovery'; Dear, 28–37; Skinner, 8–9, 299–301.
30. *CS*, 55–77; Limbrick, 'Was Montaigne', 70.
31. *CS*, 62–6; *HS*, 11–16; Ginzburg, *Cheese*, 51, 152; Armstrong, 46; Giggisberg; Castellio, *Heretics*, 287–305; Haydn, 104; Wade, 141–2.
32. Green, *Spain*, 3:303–4, 2:186; *Academica*, 2.122; Armstrong, 42–50. Cp. Petrarch, 125; *Apology*, 111.
33. Rummel, 166–7; Vives, 212.
34. Sanches, *Nothing*, 28–36; Green, *Rainolds*, 48–9, *passim*; Bradshaw, 145. On humanist critiques of scholasticism: Perreiah; Nauert, 'Humanism'.
35. Rummel, 26–7.
36. Bakhtin, 69; Screech, 8–10; Chaudhuri, 13–18; *SE*, 35–6; Rabelais, 367–8; Cave, 195–7.
37. *LP*, 9.69; Schwartz, 121. Sextus also offers synonyms for Pyrrhonism (*PH*, 1.7), though they appear in different order.
38. Rabelais, 391.
39. *RP*, 244–5; *CS*, 128; Busson, 94–106; Bredvold, 'Naturalism', 481–5.
40. *HS*, 31; *CS*, 57–8.
41. *CS*, 111–29, 7, 168; Schmitt, 'Castellani'; Popkin, 'Role', 505–6; Brush, 160–4.
42. *RP*, 227–39; *CS*, 79–81; Brués, 298; Ramus, *Scholae dialecticae*, 1:4, cols. 9–13; *LP*, 9.79–88.
43. *CS*, 82–4, 89–91, 101–8.
44. *CS*, 92–102; Armstrong, 44–5; *HS*, 31–3.
45. *CS*, 103; Brués, 5–6, 88, 112–13, 144–78, 211; Brush, 28–30; *Apology*, xxiii, 115, 123. Brués' order of synonyms is identical to *LP*, 9.69–70.
46. Gilbert, 145–63; Rabelais, 428.
47. Jacobus, 17; Hardin, 'Marlowe', 388–9; Hutton, 52; Roberts and Watson; Feingold, *Apprenticeship*, 99; Farrington, 64; Howell, ch. 4; Porter, 51, 225, 290; Feingold, 'Ramism'; Dent, 'Ramist'; Jones, 39–40.
48. Jardine, 'Humanism'; Mullinger, 89. Important translations of Cicero were published in 1556 (*Three bokes*) and 1561 (*Fyve Questions*), with references to 'Sceptikes', 'Academiks' and 'Pyrrhonians' (3v, 65; lviiv, Div).
49. Acontius, 52–5 (against rash assertion); Trevor-Roper, *Catholics*, 190; Cooper also mentions Carneades, Arcesilaus, 'Novi Academici'.

# Chapter 2

1. Heywood, 125; *Histriomastix*, 1.1.76; *What You Will*, 2.2.193.
2. Tilley, N276, D571, N268; Cotgrave, Aaaaiv; Florio, 140.
3. Anglo, 112, 139; Maus, 18–19; Guy, 414; Shumaker, 79; Clark, 211–12; Greenblatt, *Hamlet*, 195–6; Strier, 'Shakespeare', 176–80. James VI of Scotland, in his *Daemonologie* (1597), attacks Scot in an effort 'to resolve the doubting harts of many' (xi).
4. *Discoverie*, xxvii; *Demonomanie*, sig. Iv.

5. *Nothing*, 70–1; *HS*, 42; Brush, 32–4.
6. *Demonomanie*, sig. Iv. Bodin's reference to 'Ariston, Pirrhon, Herile' may indicate familiarity with Cicero's *Tusculan Disputations*, which alludes to the same figures (5.85). See also Horowitz, *Seeds*, 190; Clark, 176, 212–13.
7. *Pyrrhoniarum*, 2; Spolsky, 13–15; Brush, 31–2; Cave, 199–202; *SE*, 73–7.
8. Legros, 54–8; *HS*, 35–7; Wade, 142; *SE*, 39.
9. Wykeham's heavily annotated copy, now at the Bodleian, is signed and dated: 'Guli. Wyckhamus xvi Junii 1562'. The book is also signed by Edward Cobham (matriculated Trinity College, Cambridge, 1563).
10. *BCI*, 1:408, 1:463, 2:702; Adams, S1026; Roger Lovatt (correspondence).
11. Leedham-Green and McKitterick, 195.
12. Adams, S1026.
13. Suzanne Eward (correspondence).
14. James Anthony (correspondence).
15. Savile also purchased a manuscript of *Adversus mathematicos* in Italy (*Merton College Register*, 1.3.150).
16. DeMolen, 327–34, 400.
17. Feingold, *Apprenticeship*, 58; Bodleian MS Wood D.10.
18. Sion's copy of 1569 bears this label: 'Nathaniel Torporley Mathematicus ... donavit MDCXXXIII'.
19. *Registrum Benefactorum*, 1.26; James, *First*, 317.
20. *Catalogus*, 177.
21. Sparrow.
22. Roberts and Watson; the volume is signed 'Nich: Saunder'.
23. Mortimer.
24. The date of Jennings' death is unknown; the book is held at St. Bonaventure University.
25. British Library, Harley MS 3267, fol. 14; Paget took a BA at Christ Church, Oxford, in 1589/90.
26. McKitterick.
27. Stuart Adams (correspondence).
28. *CLC*: 1562 (Ripon, Salisbury); 1621 (Ely, Exeter, Canterbury, Chester, St. Paul's, Worcester, Gloucester, St. George's Chapel [Windsor]).
29. Germaine Warkentin (correspondence).
30. British Library, Royal MS Appendix 86, fol. 47; *Catalogus Petworthianae*, fol. 30.
31. *Registrum*, 1:248; one of the Bodleian's copies of 1621 derives from the 'Bibliotheca Saviliana'; Miles, rector of Meline, received degrees from Jesus College, Oxford (1601–4). Thomas Gataker and Kenelm Digby both owned 1621, as did John Selden, who donated his copy to the Bodleian.
32. Ralegh's library held the *Sceptick* manuscript now at Dr Williams' Library; Ussher's *Sceptick* is now at Trinity College, Dublin. Stillingfleet owned the copy of 1562 now residing at Marsh's Library, Dublin. For Vossius, whose father, Gerhard, was an Arminian and friend of Grotius: Bernard, 2:60; Sloane MS 1783, fols. 29, 52v.
33. *IMD*, 15; Valencia, 9–19, 27–33; *HS*, 38; *CS*, 74–6. Continental owners of printed Sextus editions included Montaigne, Estienne, Hervet, Jacques-August de Thou, Theodore Canter, Adolphus Vorstius, Philips van Marnix and probably Valencia, Isaac Casaubon and Justus Lipsius.

34. A.1.1.12 (the quotation, *On kai me on*, is from *Adversus logicos*, 1.66); Chamber, 23, paraphrasing *Adversus astrologos*, 15–22; *HS*, 77.
35. *Essayes*, 121, 163; *Apology*, 171–2.
36. Hadfield; *SE*, 76–7; Pattison, 33–5. Casaubon's response to Thomson (7 May 1594) indicates that he is unable to acquire Estienne's permission to loan the manuscript (*Epistolae*, 8).
37. *Paradoxes*, 5–6; *PH*, 1.1–4; *Apology*, 69–70; the distinction does not appear in Cicero's *Academica*. For Donne's knowledge of Montaigne: Bredvold, 'Religious'; Gosse, 1:122.
38. *Donne*, 30; Carey, 217–46.
39. Heydon, 134, 127–48 *passim*.
40. *Second*, B1v; *Bartas*, 593.
41. *KLG*, 40; Trevor-Roper, *Catholics*, 190–1, 166–7; Davies, 326–8.
42. *Woorke*, 'Preface'; Colie, *Paradoxia*, 400–1.
43. *SR*, 55; Wiley, *Subtle*, 101–19; Calvin, 1:619; *HS*, 70–5.
44. *Spectres*, 46, 110–13; Loyer's mirror and apple examples (126–30) appear to be drawn from *PH*, 1.48, 1.94–9. See Clark for more on Loyer.
45. *Spectres*, 192, 106, book 3, ch. 7.
46. Besides Brués, Mornay, Sanches, Montaigne, etc., see Viotti (Gilbert, 152–7); Jacotius (374); Clavius (Jardine, 'Forging', 142); Piccolomini; Cagnati (*Variarum*, 3:6.203–7); Lambin (Lucretius, 2.307–11).
47. *Thesaurus*, 1:a.iiii.v; *Virtutum*, Pviir, PPvir; Scaliger, 10–11; Devaris, 20, 53, 76; Erasmus, *Adagiorum*, col. 903; Sanches, *Nothing*, 20, 37–9.
48. Bucer, Gr. *OED* gives 1639 for the first appearance.
49. Gascoigne, 2:68–9, 2:223; Knowles, 1050–1; for black snow, *PH*, 1.33.
50. Bullough, 6.
51. *Supper*, 97; *Opere*, 2:266–70; Gatti, 2–3; *RP*, 290–303; *HS*, 37; Farrington, 27–8.
52. *Logike*, 'To the Learned Lawyers'; Sloane, *Donne*, 138–41.
53. Willet, 155–70; Binns, 209.
54. For example, 'tranquillatur' (156), 'verisimillimas probabilitates' (159), 'dubitandi' (169), 'ignorantiae' (170).
55. Green, *Rainolds*, *passim*.
56. 'Philosophy', 501, 513; Kristeller, *Greek*, 41–2; Curtis offers further examples of disputation topics (233).
57. Finkelpearl, 3–44, 261–7; Forker, 40–56; Prest; Baker, *Third*; Davies, xxviii–xxxi; Bradbrook, *Webster*, 28–46; Rebholz, 15.
58. *Poems*, 105.
59. Hotson, 44–50; Whitfield; Elton, *Troilus*, 4–13.
60. *Works*, 3:332–3.
61. *Works*, 1:254–6, 2:302, 1:173–4, 1:185–9, 1:206; Kinney, *Continental*, 353.
62. *Sceptick*, 34–41.
63. *Examen*, book 2, chs. 21–9; Bernardi, 2:810–11. For later discussion of the modes: Mersenne, 130–56; Brush, 13; Annas and Barnes; Mates, 233–52.
64. *SR*, 52–4; Shapiro, *Probability*, 22; *SE*, 37.
65. Sprott, 175; Hill, *Intellectual*, 166–71, 183; Bradbrook, *Themes*, 58–60; Haydn, 124, 399; Strathmann, 12, 42, 216; Wiley, *Subtle*, 55–6; *SR*, 58; Carey, 220; Maus, 7–8.
66. *Ralegh*, 66–7, 48–50, 427; Beal considers the attribution 'spurious' (1.2.368).

67. *Bacon*, 66.
68. 'Bacon', 19.
69. Farrington, 62–71; *WFB*, 3:537–8.
70. Wormald, 322–4.
71. Marston, satire 4; Parry, ch. 7; Broughton, 17–28; Hall, *Virgidemiarum*, 2.2, 3.3; Guilpin, satire 6; *Poetaster*, 1.2.39; Davies, 1:14; Bullough, 6; Morton, 1–34; Bush, *English*, 278; Haydn, 93, 125; Forker, 53.
72. Wright, 303–9; Kocher finds Wright's questions 'decidedly skeptical' (*SR*, 53).
73. *Donne*, 86; Carey, 220.
74. Nashe, 3:332; *LP*, 9.101. Also *FQ*, 6.9.30; *What You Will*, 1.1.18; Tilley, M254, O68; Ellrodt, 41; Jenkins' *Hamlet*, 109, 467–8. And see Montaigne's commentary on Stoic *adiaphora*, the view that things are neither good nor bad in themselves, but indifferent (*Essays*, 692, 800; *PH*, 1.27–30, 3.179–96).
75. Calvin, 1:78–81; *HS*, 10–14, 69–70; Sloane, *Donne*, 110.
76. *Wisdome*, 169; for Pyrrhonian *propeteia*, *PH*, 1.20, 1.177–86, 1.205–12.
77. *HS*, 51; Hiley, 12–19; *Apology*, 72, 160.
78. *Poems*, 326–8; Haydn, 111, 534–5.
79. *SR*, 57; Colie, *Paradoxia*, 406–9; Bush, *Science*, 16–18.
80. Dollimore, 15–21, 39–40, 97; Dent, *Borrowing*, 41, 85; Forker, 35–52; Yates, 213–14.
81. Knowles, 1053–4; Burke, *Montaigne*, 68–9.
82. *Hamlet*, 110. Also Kirsch, *Shakespeare*, 'Sexuality'; Engle, '*Measure*'; Knowles, 1052–7.
83. Yates, 213–14, 242; Pooley, 173–9; Lee, 605–7.
84. *Lear* (ed. Foakes), 104, 279; *Essais*, 18, 214, 1056, 335; Salingar, 107–33, Muir, *Sources*. *OED* lists Blount's *Glossographia* (1670) as offering the first instance of 'Pyrrhonism'.
85. For Democritus' axiom: *Academica*, 1.44–5, 2.32; *LP*, 9.72; *WFB*, 6:749; Haydn, 534–5.
86. Hamlin, *Image*, 46–68.
87. Hamlin, 'Continuities', 376–9.
88. Brush, 40–7; Streuver, 190–1; *Academica*, 1.45, 2.66–8.
89. Larmore, 1149; for 'Epechistes', *PH*, 1.7; *LP*, 9.69–70.
90. Limbrick, 'Was Montaigne', 80.
91. Neto; Schiffman, *Threshold*, 84–6.
92. *City of God*, 11.26. Montaigne derives the purgation metaphor from *PH*, 1.206–7, 2.188; also *LP*, 9.76.
93. *SR*, 50–4.

## Chapter 3

1. Bush, *English*, 2–4; Wilson, *Elizabethan*, 18–19; Hill, *Intellectual*, 8–12; McAlindon, 5–8.
2. *English*, 207; *IMD*, 15.
3. Finkelpearl, 198–9; Caputi, 58; Aggeler, 75; Yates, 241; Bredvold, 'Religious', 198, 226; cp. Bredvold, 'Naturalism', 495–8; Gosse, 1:122; Colie, *Paradoxia*, 415–18; Carey, 220–3.

4. *WFB*, 6:379, 5:64; *Revenger's*, 3.5.71–2; Forker, 35, 52, 446–7; Neill, *Issues*, 35; Dollimore, 149; Dent, *Borrowing*, 41–2, 81–5; Prosser; Cotgrave, Giii, Iiiiii, Biiiv.
5. Lennard's translation gives no date, but references in Hakewill's *Vanitie* (1608) reveal that *Wisdome* had been printed by the time Hakewill was writing.
6. Rice, *Renaissance*, 178, 190–7; Larmore, 1152–5; Gregory; *HS*, 59–61, 80–102; *IMD*, 35–7; Brush, 160–6; Lennon, 298.
7. Schiffman, *Threshold*, 81–6; Horowitz, 'View'; Horowitz, *Seeds*, 223–30.
8. Larmore, 1152; Gregory, 88.
9. *Sagesse*, 333; *Essais*, 527.
10. Larmore, 1154–5; Rice, *Renaissance*, 184.
11. Mornay's *Woorke* (3rd edn.) was prepared by Thomas Wilcox in 1604; Sylvester's complete translation of Bartas appeared in 1605, as did Jones' translation of Loyer.
12. *HS*, 38; Frisius, 23r; Mazzoni, 99–129; Spach, 9; Jardine, 'Forging'.
13. *HS*, 62; Villey, *Devant*, 202; Boase, 114–34.
14. *Manuductionis*, 2:69–76; Tuck, 'Scepticism'; Levi; Hutton.
15. Lancre, 369, 436, 521–2, 748.
16. *Registrum*, 1:248, 1:160–3, 1:138; James, *Catalogus*, 8, 177, 335.
17. Jayne and Johnson; McKitterick; *Catalogus Medii Templi*.
18. Aubrey, 64; Norwood, 44; my thanks to Charles Whitney for this reference.
19. Brownlow, 277–8, 35–66; Tyacke, 'Arminianism', 101; Greenblatt, *Negotiations*, 94–128; Strier, 'Shakespeare', 184. See Cox for qualification.
20. Chew, 1136; *SR* 50–1; Hall, *Heaven*, 190–1.
21. *Works*, iii; *HS*, 64–5; Trevor-Roper, *Catholics*, 201; Feingold, *Apprenticeship*, 96–8; Larmore, 1148.
22. *Works*, vii; *HS*, 65.
23. Goodman, 7, 32, 65; Dollimore, 99–103; Bush, *English*, 278; Crooke, 48.
24. Bodleian (G.Pamph.1688 [6, fol. 31]); the *Bodleian Pre-1920 Catalogue* gives a date of *c.* 1605; *STC* gives 1600–7. I thank Drew Jones for this translation.
25. *HS*, 84.
26. Popkin says relatively little about Bacon (*HS*, 110–11); Schmitt makes no mention of him in *CS* but alludes to him in *Gianfrancesco* (10, 56).
27. Villey, *Montaigne et Bacon*, 30–7; *WFB*, 5:64; *Bacon*, 655, 718.
28. Bacon alludes to a saying of Heraclitus found in *Adversus logicos* (*Advancement*, 146; *WFB*, 1:164); he may rely on Sextus for information on astrology (*WFB*, 4:351).
29. For early discussions of induction: *Advancement*, 177–8, 221–7; *WFB*, 3:606–17.
30. Farrington, 111–16, 84; *WFB*, 6:749.
31. Farrington, 89, 127; *Bacon*, 599, 635–6; *SR*, 54.
32. Larmore says, 'Bacon made no distinction between Academic and Pyrrhonian scepticism' (1184); Bacon also merges the Second Academy, headed by Arcesilaus, with the Third, headed by Carneades; Augustine does the same (*Academicos*, 2.13–15). But see *WFB*, 3:244.
33. *Academica*, 2.18; *PH*, 1.2, 1.200; Schmitt translates *acatalepsia* as 'the failure to grasp' (*CS*, 71); Vickers glosses it as a term used by sceptics 'to argue that reality is "non-apprehensible"' (*Bacon*, 636).

34. *Works* (Montagu, ed.), 3:519.
35. Wormald (*Bacon*, 364) claims that *Ladder* deals 'exclusively' with Pyrr-honians, which is not true, since, as elsewhere in Bacon, Academics and Pyrrhonians are conflated. But Wormald is right that the *Ladder's* presentation of scepticism is unusually enthusiastic. Cp. Anderson, 279–80.
36. Zagorin, *Bacon*, 36.
37. *HS*, 78, 110–11, 117; *Sceptick*, 42.
38. Rebholz, 107; Greville, 52–5; Dollimore, 127–8; Wilkes, 326–8; *Treatie*, stanzas 38, 11–12, 75.
39. Wiley, *Subtle*, 47; Buckley, 117; Waswo, 15.
40. *SR*, 56.
41. *Microcosmos*, 1:23; *SR*, 56–7; Colie, *Paradoxia*, 409–10; *Vanitie*, 49.
42. Florio, 207; *LP*, 9.68; Hamlin, 'Borrowing'.
43. *SR*, 53; Soellner, *Patterns*, 198–9; Maus, 5–12.
44. Guiney, 335; Wright, 61–2; Knoll.
45. *IMD*, 25–7; *Academica*, 1.44–5; *Advancement*, 193; *WFB*, 6:749; Farrington, 84, 110–13.
46. Ribner, xi–4.
47. *Vanitie*, 52; Maus, 5–8.
48. British Library, Additional MSS 6789, fol. 460; Clucas, 129–35; Hill, *World*, 174.
49. Oakeshott; Buckley, 137–52; Strathmann, 17–52; Thomas, 167.
50. *Intellectual*, 166–7; Strathmann, 230–53.
51. Nashe, 2:37; *Sceptick*, 48.
52. Wilson, *Elizabethan*, 11.
53. Book 8 of 1569 corresponds to *Against Physicists*, 1.13–194 (*M*, 9.13–194).
54. *Paradoxes*, 5–6; *Ten Sermons*, 115.
55. *Sermons*, 1:278; also *Fifty*, 190.
56. *Paradoxia*, 119; Carey, 222; Scodel, 52–7; Strier, *Resistant*, 118–64.
57. Tyacke, 'Arminianism', 105–6.
58. *Paradoxia*, 429; Tyacke, 'Arminianism', 106; Haydn, 111–16.
59. *Anti-Calvinists*, 245; Tyacke, 'Rise'; Ginzburg, 'High', 39–41.
60. Porter, 376–90; Lake, 201–42; Pinciss, 252–4.
61. Tyacke, 'Arminianism'; Wolfe, 4–7; *Paradise Lost*, 12.581–7.
62. Mullan, 164–5.
63. Trevor-Roper, *Catholics*, 189–92, *Religion*, 193–236; Wormald, *Clarendon*, 261–6; Burckhardt, 350; McLachan, 11, 66–9.
64. *Lady Falkland*, 225; Aubrey, 56; Trevor-Roper, *Catholics*, 187; McLachan, 97.
65. Trevor-Roper, *Catholics*, 196–7; Castellio, *Heretics*, 115.
66. *HS*, 65–6, 112, 173; Jordan, 378–400; Trevor-Roper, *Catholics*, 193–4, 294; Chillingworth, I.Preface.8, I.vi.38.356; Larmore, 1163.
67. Van Leeuwen, *Problem*, 20–2; Orr, 79–99; Popkin, 'Religious', 398–400; Van Leeuwen, 'Certainty', 307–8.
68. Steadman, 13–14.
69. *HS*, 105, 56; Van Leeuwen, 'Certainty', 304–8; Larmore, 1145–55.
70. *HS*, 112–27, 172–3; Clark, 265; Jardine, 'Forging', 146; Berr, 105–8; Dear, 23–47; Brush, 164–6; Larmore, 1155–64.
71. *HS*, 78, 91–6, 103, 112–27; Dear, 46–7; Larmore, 1155–8; Gottlieb, 427–8.

72. Van Leeuwen, *Problem*; Larmore, 1158–63; Shapiro, *Wilkins*; *IMD*, 58–65; Wiley, *Subtle*, 197–226.
73. Southgate; Van Leeuwen, *Problem*, 74, 81–9.
74. *HS*, 128–36; Brush, 166; Tyacke, 'Arminianism', 109; Harth, 75–6.
75. Butler, 138; Carey, 218.
76. *HS*, 122–3, 132–6.
77. *HS*, 132–6.
78. At his death Herbert gave Jesus College books including Charron's *Sagesse* (Fordyce).
79. *Lady Falkland*, 244; *Pagan*, 145.
80. Popkin, 'Religious', 412; Locke, 67–8.
81. Tuck, 'Scepticism', 33; *IMD*, 15, 61.
82. Trevor-Roper, *Catholics*, 201–2; *IMD*, 47–72; Harth, 11–12; Van Leeuwen, *Problem*, 42.
83. Pascal, 78–80, 101–6, 119–24; Larmore, 1177–8; *IMD*, 37–40; Brush, 172–3.
84. Larmore, 1179; Brush, 179–327, Neto, 215–16; *HS*, 73–4; *Dictionnaire*, 3:174; Annas and Barnes, 6.
85. Browne, 79; Wiley, *Subtle*, 137–60; *IMD*, 14–15, 40–6, 71; Trevor-Roper, *Catholics*, 202; Missner; Tuck, intro. to *Leviathan*, ix–xxvi; Kahn, 154, 181; Larmore, 1162–4; Hill, *World*, 180; Skinner, 8–9, 299–301; Harth, 5–7.
86. George, 44; Stillingfleet, 35; Wiley, *Subtle*, 161–96; *IMD*, 64–5; Hill, *World*, 172; Thomas, 167.
87. More, *Poems*, xv; Cudworth, 692–6. For Comenius, Hartlib, Dury and others: Popkin, 'Religious', 395–406; Turnbull. The CD-ROM *Hartlib Papers* provides many references to scepticism.
88. Dickens, 12–13; Thomas, 166–73; Hill, *World*, 88–9, 151–83; Hill, *Intellectual*, 166–7, 328–38; Burckhardt, 344–51; Stone, *Causes*, 108–9; Barber, *Festive*, 470–1; Ginzburg, *Cheese*.
89. Briggs, 250; *KLG*.

# Chapter 4

1. *HS*, 55; Steadman, 1; *IMD*, 16–17; Brush, 19–20.
2. Rice, *Renaissance*, 124–5; Chaudhuri, 47; Hoopes, 322–7; Hamlin, 'Solipsism', 6–9.
3. *IMD*, 16; *SR*, 51; Baker, *Wars*, 144–54.
4. Lennon, 301; *CWE*, 27:147–53; *Apology*, 53–4; *HS*, 29; Dooley, 119.
5. Dickens, 12–13; Thomas, 166–73; Hill, *Intellectual*, 166–7, 328–38; *World*, 88–9, 151–83; Nauert, *Humanism*, 198–9.
6. *Sixe*, 113–14, 123; Dzelzainis, 106–15; Burke, 'Tacitism'; Tuck, *Philosophy*, 45–64, 105–8; Sidney, 220.
7. Dooley, 3–4, 114–23; Bouwsma, 60–2; Woolf, 194–5; Shapiro, *Culture*, 34–62; *HS*, 71–2, 96–7; Franklin, 89–102; Geller; Tinkler; *SE*, 31; Bayle, 3:174.
8. The literature on Renaissance atheism is vast; I sketch here only the broadest outlines of the debate. Febvre (335–53, 455–64) argues that 'atheist' is a 'smear word' and that no atheists existed, or could exist, in the period; Kristeller ('Myth'), Walker (*Ancient*, 136) and Popkin ('Religious', 415)

largely agree. But Buckley finds evidence for denials of God and providence that Dollimore and Davidson approvingly cite; also in this tradition are Elton (*KLG*) and Hill (*World*). Other discussions include Allen (*Boundless*), Aylmer, Clucas, Edwards and Sommerville, Ginzburg ('High'), Greenblatt (*Negotiations*, 21–39), Hunter ('Problem'), Hunter and Wootton, Kocher ('Backgrounds'), Mandelbrote, McCabe (214–39), Pfister, Strier ('Shakespeare'), Thomas, Walker ('Ways'), Watson (*Rest*), Wootton. Atheists in drama include Shakespeare's Aaron and Edmund, Marlowe's Machevill, Marston's Malheureux, Tourneur's D'Amville, Ford's Giovanni.

9. Also *Duchess*, 3.5.69–71; *Hamlet*, 5.1.83; Dent, *Borrowing*, 209.
10. *Apology*, 13–16, 55, 85, 119; Brush, 116–21; Miles, 18–26, 83–109; Aggeler, 40–2.
11. *Sceptick*, 51; *Essays*, 145, 711, 911, 1144.
12. *Nosce*, lines 57–60; *Treatie*, stanzas 54–5; *Passions*, 312–17; *Vanitie*, 10, 386–9; *Woorke*, ch. 16; Wilson, *Rule*, sig. B2v; Nauert, *Agrippa*, 298; *SR*, 32; Buckley, 107–20; *HS*, 29–30; Hoopes, 322; Chaudhuri, 9–10, 35–6; Park and Kessler, 460; Hamlin, 'Solipsism', 6–7.
13. *HS*, 78, 110–17.
14. *CWE*, 3:125, 27:107; Primaudaye, *French*, 160; *Essays*, 178–9; Hamlin, 'Continuities', 374–6.
15. Pierce, 148–50; *PH*, 1.79–90; also Greenblatt, *Hamlet*, 240; *Tempest*, 2.1.45–55; *CWE*, 27:118–19; Sanches, *Nothing*, 222–3; Browne, 76.
16. *RP*, 103–12, 255; *IMD*, 21–2; Friedrich, 97; Baker, *Wars*, 146; Haydn, 100–2; Brush, 21; Burke, *Montaigne*, 25–6; McCabe, 215; Dear, 24.
17. Mullaney, 26–87.
18. Also *Faustus*, 2.1.79; *Errors*, 2.2.181–216; *Troilus*, 4.1.42–3; *Hamlet*, 1.2.13; *Macbeth*, 1.3.81–3; *Mariam*, 1.2.171–86.
19. Also *Atheist's Tragedy*, 1.2.207–14.
20. *Essais*, 505; Brush, 140–5; *PH*, 1.8–10, 1.31–5, 1.196; *Academica*, 1.44–6, 2.59, 2.108.
21. *Satire 3*; Scodel, 63; Wiley, *Creative*, 21–46.
22. For variations: *Merchant*, 2.5.1; *Shrew*, 4.5.72; *1H4*, 5.4.123; *Lear*, 1.2.27–117.
23. Spolsky, 28–44; Hillman, 'Visceral', 85.
24. Marchitello, 100; Hartog, 260–71; Hamlin, 'Continuities', 366–74.
25. *Apology*, 12–16, 51, 81, 116; *Essays*, 204, 487, 1115, 1169, 1220; Wiley, *Creative*, 23.
26. Maus, 8. For comparable examples: Loyer, *Treatise*, 111r; *Sceptick*, 43, 50.
27. Cp. *Titus*, 5.2.65–6; *1H4*, 5.4.131–3; *Changeling*, 1.1.70–5.
28. Cp. *Spanish Tragedy*, 3.1.18; *Titus*, 2.3.266–7; *Troilus*, 1.3.84; *Duchess*, 1.1.227–8; *Changeling*, 5.3.108–9. Cf. Hillman, 'Visceral', 82ff.
29. Cp. *Cymbeline*, 2.5.1–35; *Winter's*, 2.1.139–41.
30. Cp. *Rape of Lucrece*, 1534–40.
31. Strier, 'Shakespeare', 171.
32. Nussbaum, 307–8; Hamlin, 'Continuities', 366–9.
33. The passage relies on *PH*, 1.114–17 (also covered by *Sceptick*, 45).
34. *Wars*, 147.
35. The Fradubio episode occupies stanzas 28–45.
36. *Wisdome*, 169. Una's 'hastie trust' of Archimago is criticized at 1.6.12. For sceptical motifs elsewhere: 1.7.1, 1.9.11, 3.12.6–15.

37. Also *Apology*, 69–77; *Essays*, 392; *WFB*, 2:688–9, 4:261–2, 6:378; *Advancement*, 177; Erasmus, *Apophthegmes*, 64r.
38. Trevor-Roper, *Catholics*, 186–93; Ginzbury, 'High'.
39. *WFB*, 3:565–9, 4:72–3, 4:108–9; Montaigne, *Essays*, 337–40, 1051; *Apology*, 55, 69, 77–8, 130, 169.
40. Fine, 196; Larmore, 1148; *Apology*, 185; Mede, iii; Mornay, *Woorke*, 12; *Tamburlaine II*, 5.1.199; *Titus*, 5.1.71–85.
41. *Negotiations*, 26–7; *KLG*, 42–3; Kocher, *Marlowe*, 49–50; Hamlin, 'Imagined', 413–16; *Apology*, 160; Primaudaye, *Second*, 579; Burton, 3:347–50.
42. *Works*, 2:115–16, 1:172; also Hamlin, 'Continuities', 361–3. Nashe's stress on opinion is tied to Stoic *adiaphora*, which in turn contributes to early modern expressions of relativism. Cp. *Hamlet*, 2.2.245–6; *Essays*, 126, 231, 331, 1115, 1227; *Apology*, 17, 136.
43. *Lear*, 1.2.1–22, 1.2.118–33; Greenblatt, *Negotiations*, 121; Bradshaw, 39.
44. *Mirror*, 294; *Negotiations*, 120–8; Strier, 'Shakespeare', 187.
45. Also *Apology*, 72–3; *Essays*, 135–7, 302, 1180.
46. Hamlin, 'Continuities', 374–9; *Apology*, 85; Baker, *Wars*, 148–53.
47. *Pragmatism*, 8; *Cosmopolis*, 22–56.
48. *Lady Falkland*, 238, 233; Acontius, 52–6.
49. *CS*, 84; cp. *Apology*, 114.
50. Estienne's preface to Sextus (1562) stresses anti-dogmatic functions of scepticism, endorsing moderate doubt compatible with faith.

# Chapter 5

1. *History*, 2:863–4; *Frontiers*, 142. Quotations from *Faustus* are drawn from the 1993 Revels edition; unless otherwise noted I use the 'A-text' of 1604.
2. Cole, 155–8; Nicholl, 42–7, 277–9; Davidson.
3. *Disowning*, 1–3.
4. A.1.1.12; *On kai me on* ('being and not-being'), attributed by Sextus to Gorgias of Leontini, derives from *Adversus logicos*, 1.66 (*M*, 7.66). For implications of the phrase: Hankinson, *Sceptics*, 51. The phrase also appears in Richardson's *Logicians School-Master*, which discusses scepticism (318); Richardson was Marlowe's contemporary at Cambridge (Dent, 'Ramist').
5. Cavell's suggestion that Pyrrhonism never considers how to live 'in a groundless world' assumes that Pyrrhonism in early modern Europe may be equated with one of Montaigne's routine deployments of Pyrrhonism – essentially a Christian appropriation of scepticism. See also Vickers, 308–20.
6. Fine, 198; Larmore, 1164–5.
7. *Disowning*, 3–4; Larmore, 1148; *Apology*, 180–6, 114.
8. *PH*, 1.8. Nussbaum stresses that Sextus' modes of scepticism 'contain no restriction of subject matter, but range widely over many areas' in which people hold beliefs (288); cp. Barnes, 2, 12; Hamlin, 'Continuities'.
9. Popkin and Schmitt both discuss commonalities between ancient and modern scepticism; Schmitt claims that 'the recovery and reassimilation of the ancient writings were the primary factor in the evolution of the modern skeptical attitude' ('Rediscovery', 228).
10. *Sceptick*, 42; Donne, *Paradoxes*, 5–6.

11. Cole, 158.
12. For example, 1.1.6–12; cp. *English Faust Book*, 100, 119.
13. 2.3.62–6, 3.Chorus.2–7, 4.Chorus.9–10.
14. Cp. 2.1.130–8. The *Faust Book* informs us that Faustus was called 'the Speculator' (92), signing himself 'Faustus the insatiable speculator' (129).
15. *PH*, 1.8–10, 1.31–4; *Apology*, 70, 113–36. Sanches, who does not seem to have read Sextus or Montaigne before publishing *That Nothing Is Known* (1581), none the less emphasizes diversity of opinion as a prologue to doubt (213, 222–3).
16. See Pro.23–5, 1.1.80, 5.2.10–11 and B.3.1.58–9 for further images of over-consumption.
17. Montaigne might disagree, since he chooses to do that which is customary in his society, while Faustus does not. But Montaigne's embrace is not merely a passive following but an active endorsing of custom, therefore an abandonment of Pyrrhonism.
18. Greg (1950 edn.), 320–1; Keefer (1991 edn.), 29; Bevington/Rasmussen, 138n.
19. Cp. Mephistopheles at B.5.2.13–15 (not in A-text).
20. *Faustus* establishes an association between forward motion, magic and re-solution, and between backward motion and conventional religious belief. Being resolute, resolving ambiguities, living voluptuously, etc., are connect-ed to being a 'forward wit', moving forward and engaging in magic (1.1.76, Epilogue.7, B.2.1.14). Wavering and acknowledging uncertainty, fear and doubt are connected to moving backward (2.1.6–7, 1.3.14, 2.1.26).
21. Hamlin, 'Swolne'.
22. *Lady Falkland*, 233.
23. Davies' *Nosce Teipsum* likewise considers the soul's tendency to seek static resolution.

## Chapter 6

1. For perspectivism in the play: Baines; Hamilton; Hill, 'Senecan'.
2. Maus, 55–71; Hunter, ignoring class issues, praises the Spanish king for displaying 'Solomon-like wisdom in making a just decision' ('Ironies', 94).
3. Cp. 3.14.97, 4.4.10–11.
4. Bloom, 398.
5. *Creating*, 133, 143; also Braden, 215–23; Watson, 'Tragedy', 323.
6. Altman, 271–3.
7. Aggeler, 66.
8. It also tends to belie Charlemont's claim that 'patience is the honest man's revenge' (*Atheist's Tragedy*, 5.2.276).
9. The Portingales' quest to find Lorenzo merges, in Hieronimo's mind, with the more abstract and apparently endless quest for truth and justice.
10. Specifically, Romans 12:19 ('Vindicta mihi'), Seneca's *Agamemnon*, 115 ('Per scelus'), and Seneca's *Troades*, 511–12 ('Fata si miseros').
11. *Second*, 185.
12. *All's Well*, 1.3.107–9; Wilcox, 186; *Lingua*, sig. H3v; Earle, 74.
13. See also 4th Addition ('Painter Scene'), lines 79–163.
14. *Inwardness*, 69–70.

15. *Issues*, 201–15.
16. 'Ironies', 91–2.
17. *Inwardness*, 65; Aggeler, 71.
18. Cp. *Titus Andronicus*, 4.3.4–5.

# Chapter 7

1. Quotations derive from Bevington's Arden3 edition. For variations on 'prizing': 2.2.56, 2.2.91, 4.4.133, 4.5.75.
2. Bradshaw, 39; cp. 140–2; Pierce, 158; Soellner, *Patterns*, 141.
3. For other views of Thersites: Hillman, 'Visceral', 88; Colie, *Living*, 349; Grady, 70–4.
4. Bevington summarizes the Inns of Court theory, 88–9; see also Rossiter, 129–30, 142–50; Grady, 61; Elton, *Shakespeare's Troilus, passim*.
5. Intro., *Troilus* (*Riverside*, 444); contrast Colie, *Living*, 339; Rossiter, 147–8; Girard, 208.
6. Cp. 5.2.151–67. For similar instances: *All's Well* 1.2.107–9; *FQ*, 1.2.38; Earle, 74–6.
7. See Colie for discussion of the paradoxical encomium (*Living*, 343–7).
8. Barfoot, 49; Rossiter, 141–3; Soellner, 'Prudence', 259.
9. Bevington, intro., *Troilus*, 33–4.
10. For earlier images of rift: 1.1.32–49, 1.3.316.
11. 'Prudence', 264.
12. 'Reason' appears eleven times in the first fifty lines of 2.2, and frequently elsewhere. It is used variably to designate the faculty of ratiocination as well as the specific premises and components of argument; there seems little doubt that Shakespeare asks us to reflect on our understandings of the word.
13. Soellner sees not only Troilus but Ulysses and Thersites as sceptics (*Patterns*, 196–214); Elton classifies Lear as a sceptic (*KLG*, 55–7); Greenblatt calls Iago a 'Renaissance skeptic' (*Self-Fashioning*, 246); Hillman says Thersites best 'embodies' *Troilus'* 'skeptical impulse', also finding Leontes a sceptic ('Visceral', 88–94).
14. 'Prudence', 255; *Patterns*, 141–2.
15. 'Prudence', 259; cp. Hillman, 'Gastric', 312. For distinctions between scepticism and relativism: *Apology*, 38–40; Morphos; Pierce, 146; Hankinson, *Sceptics*, 15, 262; Hamlin, 'Continuities', 371–2.
16. Bradshaw, 133, 159; Dollimore, 42–4.
17. Rossiter, 132; Ellis-Fermor, *Frontiers*, 59, 70; Ornstein, 240–5; Soellner, *Patterns*, 210; Colie, *Living*, 329.
18. Adelman, 46–52.
19. I cannot agree with Girard, who claims that the possibility of Cressida's infidelity never enters Troilus' mind until *after* Cressida imagines herself a woeful figure among the 'merry Greeks' (194–5). Girard's treatment of 'mimetic desire' in *Troilus* relies too heavily on essentialist premises and too little on the play's language and temporal unfolding.
20. Dollimore, 48.
21. Levine, *Men*, 26.
22. *Riverside Shakespeare*, 486.

23. Ornstein, 249; Rossiter, 134–5.
24. Shaw, 261; Rossiter, 150.


## Chapter 8

1. Ornstein, 158; Dollimore, 38; Sturgess, xxii; cp. Aggeler, 92–6; Forker, 52–3; Bradbrook, *Webster*, 41; *CWE*, 27:90–7, 27:109–10.
2. Eliot, *Elizabethan*, 177–95; Caputi, 193–9.
3. Sturgess, vii; Haydn, 81–93, 107–10; Rossiter, 129–30.
4. Davies, *Poems*, xxviii–xxxi; Finkelpearl, 261–7; Forker, 40–56; Bradbrook, *Webster*, 28–46; Webster, *Works*, 1:5–6.
5. *Poems*, 105.
6. Nashe, 2:116, 2:302, 3:254, 3:332–3, 4:428–9, 5:120; *Paradoxes*, 5–6; *PH*, 1.1–4; *Apology*, 70. The distinction does not appear in Cicero's *Academica*.
7. Marston's reliance on Florio is evident in *The Dutch Courtesan*, which contains 45 borrowings from Montaigne; see Finkelpearl, 198–9; Caputi, 58; Ellrodt, 41; Aggeler, 75.
8. Quotations from *The Malcontent* follow Harris' edition; quotations from other plays are drawn from Bullen's *Works*; cp. Davies' *Nosce Teipsum*, line 76.
9. For example, Davies' *Nosce*; Davies of Hereford's *Mirum* and *Microcosmos*; Greville's *Treatie*; also *Antonio's Revenge*, 4.1.38–60. Cf. Haydn, 93, 125; Forker, 52–3.
10. Chamber, 23; Heydon, 127–48.
11. 'To play', 177.
12. Sturgess, xxi.
13. Induction, 63–4; ode, 15–16. Webster wrote the Induction, but the ode is Marston's, as is the preface, which approves the 'freedom' of satire (26). Cp. 1.2.11, 1.3.2, 1.4.31.
14. Hunter, 'English', 101. From the very outset Vindice views his transformation into the 'knave' Piato as a form of corruption: 'For to be honest is not to be i' th' world' (1.1.93–6). Hippolito's remark about Piato, 'This our age swims within him' (1.3.24), serves not only as a way of enticing Lussurioso, but also foreshadows a genuine transformation in Vindice – a transformation never witnessed in Altofronto, since his temporizing is a calculated response that preserves his integrity. Vindice, meanwhile, will 'forget [his] nature' (1.3.177).
15. Bliss, 'Pastiche', 246; Hunter, *Drama*, 65, 286, 309–10.
16. Sextus juxtaposes arguments for and against providence (*PH*, 1.32, 1.151).
17. Eliot concludes that Ferneze's words to Bianca in the final scene 'indicate that Marston had forgotten' that Bianca was Bilioso's wife (187). Even Aggeler, despite a tidy reading, admits that Ferneze's attempt to seduce Bianca suggests that Altofronto/Malevole's penchant for character reformation is 'not entirely successful' (99).
18. *Institutes*, 3.23.2–7. For paradox and drama: Neill, 'Defence'.
19. Cp. Eusebius on Pyrrho, who said that 'of everything it can be affirmed with equal validity that it is, that it is not, that it is and is not at the same time, and that it neither is nor is not' (Kristeller, *Greek*, 43–4).

20. Finkelpearl, 178; Sturgess, 329; cp. Aggeler, 97–8. For less complex examples of temporizing: D'Amville (*Atheist's*, 3.4.32); Guise (*Revenge of Bussy*, 4.4.25); cp. *Spanish Tragedy*, 3.9.13; *Macbeth*, 1.5.61–2.

## Chapter 9

1. *The Lady Falkland: Her Life*, in *Mariam* (Weller and Ferguson, eds.), 186, 268–9. Quotations from biography and play are drawn from this edition.
2. For Montaigne's sceptical critique of Stoicism, see, e.g., *Apology*, 14, 56, 60, 101, 104, 119, 164, 171, 176, 178, 190.
3. *Mariam* (Dunstan, ed., 1992), xxv. 'How we weepe' is conventionally dated to 1572–74, though Montaigne continued to work on the essay, making several post-1588 additions. Rowland and Straznicky state that several of *Mariam*'s choruses 'also suggest the influence of Montaigne' (xxv), though they do not elaborate. See Defaux, 148–51, for arguments against the Villey-Strowski thesis of a 'crise sceptique'.
4. Lewalski, 'Writing', 808; *Mariam* (Purkiss, ed.), ix–xix; Zimmerman, 555–60. For other discussions of 'be and seem': Ferguson, 'Running', 49–50; Lewalski, *Writing*, 184.
5. See the Argument's comment on Herod's 'rashness'; cp. Bacon, *Advancement* (147, 164, 176) for discussions of precipitous judgement.
6. *Works*, 1:23–7; *Vanitie*, 49; *SR*, 56–7; Lewalksi, *Writing*, 181–3.
7. Trevor-Roper, *Catholics*, 166–230.
8. Aubrey, 64; Hyde, 42.
9. *Religion*, 356; *HS*, 14, 65–6; *PH*, 1.7–10; Florio, 273, 448–51, 838; *Wisdome*, 231–8. That Chillingworth read Montaigne is clear (*Religion*, 1:41).
10. Matthew 23:27 characterizes Pharisees as hypocrites, 'like unto whited sepulchres.' Cp. Dent, *Shakespeare's*, F29; *Revenger's Tragedy*, 3.5.144.
11. Zimmerman, 553–60.
12. Maus, 1; Quilligan, 226.
13. 'Running', 47.
14. Lewalski, *Writing*, 191; Shannon, 139, 147; Zimmerman, 554; Beilin, 159; Belsey, 173.
15. *Sceptick*, 49; *PH*, 1.12, 1.31–4.
16. Ferguson, 'Running', 50–3; Beilin, 170; Travitsky, 189–90; Belsey, 173–4; Quilligan, 225; Kegl, 149.
17. Cp. Belsey, 173.
18. Travitsky, 188–9.
19. On this chorus see Lewalski, *Writing*, 196; Zimmerman, 557–60.
20. Shannon, 147; Kegl, 142–3.

## Chapter 10

1. *Hamlet*, 3.1.17–20. Quotations from Webster follow Weis's edition.
2. 'Unkennel', suggesting enfranchisement, may imply that guilt's normative state is not hidden but open to public view, its kenneling merely temporary. A different form of unkenneling is posited by Lear during the storm; he expects the 'dreadful pother' to expose 'undivulgèd crimes' and

'close pent-up guilts' (*Lear*, 3.2.47–58). But whether or not the storm may be construed as the gods' art, its providential efficacy is dubious.

3. Hamlet's woe passes show not because he tries to conceal it but because it is incapable of being exhibited to the world in its true intensity. Claudius' guilt, on the other hand, may include such woe, but principally involves recognition of a hidden reality: the murder of his brother. Outward signs thus cannot denote Hamlet truly, while outward signs succeed in denoting Claudius falsely. Though we have distinctly different situations, there is still a degree of overlap.

4. Sidney, 230.

5. *Borrowing*, 41–2; Forker, 35, 52.

6. *White Devil*, 5.6.108–13; *Duchess*, 3.2.245–9; Dent, *passim*.

7. Ornstein, 134.

8. Cp. *Sceptick*, 43; Dent, *Borrowing*, 81.

9. Bogard, 97; Dollimore, 231–46.

10. *Issues*, 349. See also 4.2.119–26; Bosola's stress on the contemptible frailty of humans accords not only with Montaigne and Erasmus, but with *The Malcontent* (4.5.104–15) and *The Revenger's Tragedy* (3.5.68–81).

11. 4.1.54 (Gunby, ed.).

12. Weis deletes 'artificial' from the stage direction, though he suspects it 'may not only derive from Webster's first draft, but might in fact have been a last-minute addition by the dramatist during press-correction, in which case it would carry additional authority' (397). See also Bosola to the dying Duchess at 4.2.343: 'The dead bodies you saw were but feigned statues'.

13. This was the case in the July 2003 production at the Cambridge Arts Theatre; images of Antonio and the children were projected on a screen in an eerie holograph.

14. See Forker, 309. For an alternative reaction to the matter of beholding the 'picture' versus the 'lively body', see *Titus Andronicus*, 3.1.103–5.

15. Goldberg, 74.

16. Forker, 274–5; Ewbank, 163–4.

17. On the distancing effects produced by these dumb shows: Mulryne, 203; Ewbank, 168; Bliss, *Perspective*, 110–11.

18. Luckyj, 111.

19. Kernan, 400.

20. By 'moral testing' I mean such incidents as Vincentio's testing of Angelo, Vindice's of Gratiana, and Malcolm's of Macduff; cp. the Cardinal in *Duchess*, 5.4.1–15. One archetype for these actions lies in the Book of Job.

## Chapter 11

1. On the double plot: Empson, 46–50; Bradbrook, *Themes*, 206–17; Levin, 34–48. Hopkins discusses the 'reformation of homosocial bonding after disruption by threatening women' ('Beguiling', 158); Neill observes that *The Changeling* makes an 'un-Websterian assault on the principle of tragic distinction' (*Issues*, 169); cp. Belsey, 165.

2. Cp. Vindice (*Revenger's*, 3.5.79–81); also Brooke, 83.

3. See Ricks on multiple meanings of such words as blood, will, deed, service.

4. Antonius Mizaldus' *De arcanis naturae* (1558) does not in fact describe experiments for pregnancy and virginity; *The Changeling* thus assimilates such specific concerns to the more general fascination with forbidden knowledge.
5. Hopkins (150–2) discusses Alsemero's virginity test within the context of prevailing misogynistic attitudes.
6. Daalder, 502–8.
7. Also *CWE*, 27:118–19. See Martin (39–57) for Middleton and scepticism more generally.
8. See Sextus' fourth mode (*PH*, 1.100–17).
9. Yachnin, 55–8; it is unclear whether Middleton took a degree. Schmitt discusses sceptical *quaestiones* used for disputation at Oxford in the 1580s/1590s ('Philosophy', 501).
10. Heinemann treats the profound social pressures contributing to the corruption of Middleton's protagonists (174, 191–9).
11. Note the possible allusion here to an alternate meaning of 'eye' – that suggested at 3.3.69–70. Shakespeare too exploits the eye/vagina parallel: *Merchant* (2.5.44), *Troilus* (2.1.78), *Measure* (1.2.90).
12. Cp. 3.4.44, 3.4.70, 4.2.56, 5.1.60. De Flores' talk of conscience begins well before Piracquo's ghost appears.
13. Beatrice stages two investigations of her own: the genuine enquiry into whether Diaphanta is a virgin, and the feigned enquiry (undertaken with Diaphanta's complicity) designed to 'try' her fears about loss of maidenhead (4.1.66–117).
14. 'Beguiling', 156.

# Chapter 12

1. Brooke, 114–15; Ornstein, 200–13; Ellis-Fermor, *Jacobean*, 227.
2. Hoy, 153; Hopkins, 'Knowing', 1, 18; Ribner, 173; Boehrer, 363–71; Wilks, 254–64; McCabe, 229–31.
3. For foundational discussions of the problem of the criterion: *PH*, 1.21, 1.59–60, 1.112–17, 1.166, 2.14–79.
4. Finkelpearl, 261–2; Hopkins, *Ford*, 3; Boehrer, 369; Barbour, 'Ford', 349. Beaumont was a member of the adjacent Inner Temple.
5. Ford wrote an elegy on Blount's death in 1606; the anonymous *Golden Mean* (1613), dedicated to Northumberland, is also widely regarded as Ford's. Wilks emphasizes the 'epistemological uncertainty' of the latter work (254).
6. For discussions of Sextus' tenth mode: Annas and Barnes, 160; Hankinson, *Sceptics*, 156, 262–72; Hamlin, 'Continuities', 366–9; Mates, 250–2.
7. Ribner, 170; Ornstein, 203.
8. Ornstein, 205–7; Hoy, 147–54; Hopkins, *Ford*, 100–3.
9. *Wisdome*, 310–11. Ornstein (206–7) and McCabe (132, 216) both discuss Charron. See Boehrer for Giovanni's divorce of the books of nature and scripture. For ideological functions of the incest taboo: Whigham, 167–71.
10. Ribner, 173; Ornstein, 207–9; Hoy, 146–9; Ellis-Fermor comments on the Friar's 'moral obliquity' (*Jacobean*, 244); Ribner treats the absurdity of his counsel to Annabella (164–8).

11. McLuskie, 129–30.
12. For the topos of religion's introduction as means of keeping people in awe: Greenblatt, *Negotiations*, 26–7; Nashe, *Works*, 1:172, 2:115–16; Hamlin, 'Imagined', 413–16.
13. Hopkins, 'Knowing', 4; Hoy, 149; Brooke, 127; Boehrer, 363.
14. Morris, intro., xxvii.
15. Brooke, 127–8; see also the knowledge-problem staged in 4.3 regarding the 'author' of Annabella's pregnancy.
16. Bowers, 209–11. For other perspectives on Giovanni's revenge: Boehrer, 367–9; Ornstein, 211.
17. Brooke, 120; McCabe, 229.
18. 'Ford', 350.
19. 'Knowing', 4.

# Select Bibliography

## Abbreviations

BHR: *Bibliothèque d'Humanisme et Renaissance*
CompD: *Comparative Drama*
ELH: *English Literary History*
ELR: *English Literary Renaissance*
EMLS: *Early Modern Literary Studies*
HLQ: *Huntington Library Quarterly*
JHI: *Journal of the History of Ideas*
JHP: *Journal of the History of Philosophy*
JWCI: *Journal of the Warburg and Courtauld Institutes*
MRTS: *Medieval and Renaissance Texts and Studies*
N&Q: *Notes and Queries*
P&P: *Past and Present*
PMLA: *Publication of the Modern Language Association*
PQ: *Philological Quarterly*
R&L: *Religion and Literature*
RenD: *Renaissance Drama*
RES: *Review of English Studies*
RORD: *Research Opportunities in Renaissance Drama*
RQ: *Renaissance Quarterly*
SCJ: *Sixteenth Century Journal*
SEL: *Studies in English Literature, 1500–1900*
ShakS: *Shakespeare Studies*
ShS: *Shakespeare Survey*
SQ: *Shakespeare Quarterly*

## Manuscript sources

### Bodleian Library, Oxford University

Chamber, John, *A Confutation of Astrologicall Daemonologie* (1603–4), MS Savile 42.
*Registrum Benefactorum.*
Sextus Empiricus, *Adversus logicos* 1.27–466, tr. John Wolley, MS Sancroft 17.
——— *Adversus mathematicos* and *Dissoi Logoi* (anonymous), MS Savile 1.
——— *Pyrrhoniarum hypotyposeon*, MS Savile 11.

### British Library, London

Anonymous, miscellaneous catalogues of the Royal Library (1661–66), Royal MS Appendix 86.
Anonymous, catalogue of manuscripts owned by Isaac Vossius, Sloane MS 1783, fols. 17–53.

Canter, Theodore, miscellaneous notes, Burney MS 367, fol. 194.
Harriot, Thomas, miscellaneous notes, Additional MS 6789, fols. 460, 464.
Hassall, John, catalogue of the Paget Library (1617), Harley MS 3267, fols. 1–29.
*The Sceptick*, Lansdowne MS 254, fols. 308r–21v.
*The Sceptique*, Harley MS 7017, fols. 25r–33r.
Sextus Empiricus, *Pyrrhoniae Hypotyposes*, Royal MS 16 D XIII.
Thomson, Richard, miscellaneous correspondence, Burney MS 366, fols. 234–5.

### Corpus Christi College, Oxford

Sextus Empiricus, *Ex Sexto Empirico adversus mathematicos*, MS 263, fols. 149b–64b.

### Dr Williams' Library, London

*Sir Walter Raleigh's Sceptick*, Jones MS B 60, fols. 151–68.

### Merton College, Oxford

Sextus Empiricus, *Adversus mathematicos*, MS 304.

### Petworth House Archives, West Sussex Record Office, Chichester

*Catalogus Librorum Bibliothecae Petworthianae*, PHA MS 5377.

### Trinity College, Dublin

*The Scepticke*, TCD MS 532, fols. 129r–45r.

## Printed works

Acontius, Jacobus, *Darkness Discovered (Satan's Strategems)*, intro. R. Field. Delmar, NY: Scholars' Facsimiles, 1978.
Adams, H. M., *Catalogue of Books Printed on the Continent of Europe 1501–1600 in Cambridge Libraries*, 2 vols. Cambridge: Cambridge University Press, 1967.
Adelman, Janet, *Suffocating Mothers*. New York: Routledge, 1992.
Aggeler, Geoffrey, *Nobler in the Mind: The Stoic-Skeptic Dialectic in English Renaissance Tragedy*. Newark: University of Delaware Press, 1998.
Agrippa von Nettesheim, Henry Cornelius, *Of the Vanitie and Uncertaintie of Artes and Sciences*, tr. James Sanford (London, 1569), ed. Catherine Dunn. Northridge: California State University Press, 1974.
Allen, Don Cameron, *Doubt's Boundless Sea: Skepticism and Faith in the Renaissance*. Baltimore: Johns Hopkins University Press, 1964.
Altman, Joel, *The Tudor Play of Mind*. Berkeley: University of California Press, 1978.
Anderson, Fulton, *Philosophy of Francis Bacon*. Chicago: University of Chicago Press, 1948.
Anglo, Sydney, 'Scot's *Discoverie of Witchcraft*: Scepticism and Sadduceeism', in Sydney Anglo, ed., *The Damned Art* (London: Routledge, 1977), 106–39.
Annas, Julia, and Jonathan Barnes, *Modes of Scepticism: Ancient Texts and Modern Interpretations*. Cambridge: Cambridge University Press, 1985.
Archer, Ian, *The Pursuit of Stability*. Cambridge: Cambridge University Press, 1991.

Armstrong, C., 'Dialectical Road to Truth', in P. Sharratt, ed., *French Renaissance Studies* (Edinburgh: Edinburgh University Press, 1976), 36–51.

Ascham, Roger, *The Scholemaster*, ed. J. Mayor. London, 1863.

Aubrey, John, *Brief Lives*, ed. O. Dick. Ann Arbor: University of Michigan Press, 1962.

Augustine, Bishop of Hippo, *Against the Academicians*, tr. P. King. Indianapolis: Hackett, 1995.

Aylmer, G., 'Unbelief in Seventeenth-Century England', in D. Pennington and K. Thomas, eds., *Puritans and Revolutionaries* (Oxford: Clarendon, 1978), 22–46.

Bacon, Francis, *Francis Bacon: A Critical Edition of the Major Works*, ed. Brian Vickers. Oxford: Oxford University Press, 1996.

—— *Works of Francis Bacon*, ed. James Spedding, Robert L. Ellis, Douglas D. Heath, 14 vols. London, 1857–74; Stuttgart, 1963.

—— *Works*, ed. Basil Montagu, 3 vols. Philadelphia, 1881.

Baines, Barbara, 'Kyd's Silenus Box', *Journal of Medieval and Renaissance Studies*, 10 (1980): 41–51.

Baker, Herschel, *Wars of Truth*. Cambridge: Harvard University Press, 1952.

Baker, John, *Third University of England*. London: Selden Society, 1990.

Bakhtin, Mikhail, *Rabelais and His World*, tr. H. Iswolsky. Bloomington: Indiana University Press, 1984.

Barber, C. L., *Creating Elizabethan Tragedy*, ed. Richard Wheeler. Chicago: University of Chicago Press, 1988.

—— *Shakespeare's Festive Comedy*. Princeton: Princeton University Press, 1959.

Barbour, Reid, *English Epicures and Stoics*. Amherst: University of Massachusetts Press, 1998.

—— 'John Ford and Resolve', *Studies in Philology*, 86 (1989): 341–66.

Barfoot, C. C., '*Troilus and Cressida*: "Praise us as we are tasted"', *SQ*, 39:1 (1988): 45–57.

Barnes, Jonathan, 'The Beliefs of a Pyrrhonist', *Proceedings of the Cambridge Philological Society*, 29 (1982): 1–29.

Bayle, Pierre, *Dictionnaire Historique et Critique*, 16 vols. Paris, 1820.

Beal, Peter, *Index of English Literary Manuscripts*. London: Mansell, 1980–93.

Beaumont, John, *The Metamorphosis of Tabacco*. London, 1602.

Beilin, Elaine, *Redeeming Eve*. Princeton: Princeton University Press, 1987.

Belsey, Catherine, *The Subject of Tragedy*. New York: Methuen, 1985.

Bernard, Edward, *Catalogi Librorum Manuscriptorum*. Oxford, 1697.

Bernardi, Giovanni, *Seminarium Totius Philosophiae Aristotelicae et Platonicae*. Lyon, 1599.

Berr, Henri, *Du Scepticisme de Gassendi*, ed. Bernard Rochot. Paris: Albin Michel, 1960.

Binns, J. W., *Intellectual Culture in Elizabethan and Jacobean England*. Leeds: Cairns, 1990.

Bliss, Lee, 'Pastiche, Burlesque, Tragicomedy', in *Cambridge Companion to English Renaissance Drama*, 237–61.

—— *The World's Perspective: Webster and the Jacobean Drama*. New Brunswick: Rutgers University Press, 1983.

Bloom, Harold, *Shakespeare*. New York: Riverhead, 1998.

Boase, Alan, *The Fortunes of Montaigne*. London, 1935.

Bodin, Jean, *De la Demonomanie des Sorciers*. Paris, 1580.

—— *On the Demon-Mania of Witches*, tr. R. Scott and J. Pearl. Toronto: CRRS, 1995.

Boehrer, Bruce, 'Nice Philosophy: '*Tis Pity She's a Whore* and the Two Books of God', *SEL*, 24:2 (1984): 355–71.

Bogard, Travis, *Tragic Satire of John Webster*. Berkeley: University of California Press, 1955.

Bolgar, R. R., *The Classical Heritage*. Cambridge: Cambridge University Press, 1954.

Bouwsma, William, *The Waning of the Renaissance*. New Haven: Yale University Press, 2000.

Bowers, Fredson, *Elizabethan Revenge Tragedy*. Princeton: Princeton University Press, 1940.

Bradbrook, M. C., *Themes and Conventions of Elizabethan Tragedy*. Cambridge: Cambridge University Press, 1980.

—— *John Webster*. London: Weidenfeld & Nicolson, 1980.

Braden, Gordon, *Renaissance Tragedy and the Senecan Tradition*. New Haven: Yale University Press, 1985.

Bradshaw, Graham, *Shakespeare's Scepticism*. New York: St. Martin's Press, 1987.

Brathwaite, Richard, *A Strappado for the Divell*, ed. J. Ebsworth. Boston, Lincolnshire, 1828.

Bredvold, Louis, *The Intellectual Milieu of John Dryden*. Ann Arbor: University of Michigan Press, 1934.

—— 'Naturalism of Donne', *Journal of English and Germanic Philology*, 22 (1923): 471–502.

—— 'Religious Thought of Donne', in Louis Bredvold, ed., *Studies in Shakespeare, Milton, and Donne* (New York: Macmillan, 1925), 193–232.

Briggs, Julia, *This Stage-Play World*. Oxford: Oxford University Press, 1997.

Brooke, Nicholas, *Horrid Laughter in Jacobean Tragedy*. London: Barnes & Noble, 1979.

Broughton, Richard, *First Part of the Resolution of Religion*. London, 1603.

Brown, John Russell and Bernard Harris, eds., *Jacobean Theatre*. New York: St. Martin's Press, 1960.

Browne, Thomas, *Selected Writings*, ed. Geoffrey Keynes. Chicago: University of Chicago Press, 1968.

Brownlow, F. W., *Shakespeare, Harsnett, and the Devils of Denham*. Newark: University of Delaware Press, 1993.

Brués, Guy de, *Dialogues contre les Nouveaux Academiciens*, ed. P. Morphos. Baltimore: Johns Hopkins University Press, 1953.

Bruno, Giordano, *The Ash Wednesday Supper*, tr. E. Gosselin and L. Lerner. Hamden, CT: Archon, 1977.

—— *Cabala del Cavallo Pegaseo*. London, 1585.

—— *Opere Italiane*, 2 vols. Bari, 1907.

Brush, Craig, *Montaigne and Bayle: Variations of the Theme of Skepticism*. The Hague: Martinus Nijhoff, 1966.

Bucer, Martin, *The Gratulation of Martin Bucer*. London, 1549.

Buchanan, George, *Vernacular Writings*, ed. P. Brown. Edinburgh: Blackwood, 1892.

Buckley, George, *Atheism in the English Renaissance*. Chicago: University of Chicago Press, 1932.

Bullough, Geoffrey, 'Bacon and the Defence of Learning', in *Seventeenth Century Studies* (Oxford: Clarendon, 1938), 1–20.

Burckhardt, Jacob, *The Civilization of the Renaissance in Italy*, tr. S. Middlemore. Harmondsworth: Penguin, 1990.

Burke, Peter, *Montaigne*. Oxford: Oxford University Press, 1981.

—— 'Tacitism, Scepticism, and Reason of State', in J. Burns, ed., *Cambridge History of Political Thought* (Cambridge: Cambridge University Press, 1991), 479–98.

Burnyeat, Myles, ed., *The Skeptical Tradition*. Berkeley: University of California Press, 1983.

—— and Michael Frede, eds., *The Original Sceptics*. Indianapolis: Hackett, 1997.

Burton, Robert, *The Anatomy of Melancholy*, ed. Thomas Faulkner, et al., 5 vols. Oxford: Clarendon, 1989–2000.

Bush, Douglas, *English Literature in the Earlier Seventeenth Century*. Oxford: Clarendon, 1945.

—— *Science and English Poetry*. New York: Oxford University Press, 1950.

Busson, Henri, *Le Rationalisme dans la littérature française de la Renaissance*. Paris: Vrin, 1957.

Butler, John, *Lord Herbert of Chirbury: An Intellectual Biography*. Lewiston, ME: Mellen, 1990.

Cagnati, Marsilio, 'De Sexto, quem Empiricum aliqui vocant', *Acta Eruditorum*, 3:580–1.

—— *Variarum Observationum*. Rome, 1587.

Calvin, Jean, *Institutes of the Christian Religion*, tr. John Allen, 2 vols. Philadelphia: Presbyterian Board, 1936.

*Cambridge Companion to English Renaissance Drama*, ed. A. Braunmuller and M. Hattaway. Cambridge: CUP, 1990.

*Cambridge Companion to Renaissance Humanism*, ed. Jill Kraye. Cambridge: Cambridge University Press, 1996.

*Cambridge History of Renaissance Philosophy*, ed. Charles Schmitt, et al. Cambridge: Cambridge University Press, 1988.

*Cambridge History of Seventeenth-Century Philosophy*, ed. D. Garber and M. Ayers, 2 vols. Cambridge: Cambridge University Press, 1998.

Caputi, Anthony, *John Marston, Satirist*. Ithaca: Cornell University Press, 1961.

Carey, John, *John Donne: Life, Mind and Art*. London: Faber, 1981

Cary, Elizabeth, *The Tragedy of Mariam*, ed. Diane Purkiss. London, 1994.

—— *The Tragedy of Mariam*, ed. Barry Weller and Margaret Ferguson. Berkeley: University of California Press, 1994.

Casaubon, Isaac, *Isaaci Casauboni Epistolae*. Rotterdam, 1709.

Castellani, Giulio, *Adversus Marci Tullii Ciceronis academicas quaestiones*. Bologna, 1558.

Castellio, Sebastian, *Concerning Heretics*, tr. Roland Bainton. New York: Columbia University Press, 1935.

—— *De haereticis an sint persequendi*. Magdeburg, 1554.

*Catalogus Librorum Bibliothecae Medii Templi*. London, 1734.

Cave, Terence, 'Imagining Scepticism in the Sixteenth Century', *Journal of the Institute of Romance Studies*, 1 (1992): 193–205.

Cavell, Stanley, *The Claim of Reason*. Oxford: Clarendon, 1979.

—— *Disowning Knowledge in Six Plays of Shakespeare*. Cambridge: Cambridge University Press, 1987.

Celsus, Cornelius, *De Re Medica*. Lyons, 1542.

Chamber, John, *Treatise Against Iudicial Astrologie*. London, 1601.

Chapman, George, *Bussy D'Ambois*, ed. N. Brooke. Manchester: Manchester University Press, 1964.

Charron, Pierre, *De la sagesse*. Bordeaux, 1601; Paris, 1604.

—— *Les trois verités*. Bordeaux, 1593; Paris, 1595.

—— *Of Wisdome*, tr. Samson Lennard. London, *c*. 1608; New York, 1971.

Chaudhuri, Sukanta, *Infirm Glory*. Oxford: Clarendon, 1981.

Chew, Audrey, 'Joseph Hall and Neo-Stoicism', *PMLA*, 65 (1950): 1130–45.

Chillingworth, William, *The Religion of Protestants a Safe Way to Salvation*. Oxford, 1638.

Cicero, *Academica*, tr. H. Rackham. Cambridge: Harvard University Press, 1951.

—— *Ciceroes three bokes of duties*, tr. Nicolas Grimalde. London, 1556.

—— *Those fyve Questions disputed in his Manor of Tusculanum*, tr. John Dolman. London, 1561.

—— *Tusculan Disputations II & V*, ed. A. E. Douglas. Warminster: Aris & Phillips, 1990.

Clark, Stuart, *Thinking with Demons*. Oxford: Oxford University Press, 1999.

Clucas, Stephen. 'Thomas Harriot and the Field of Knowledge in the English Renaissance', in Fox, 93–136.

Cole, Douglas, *Christopher Marlowe and the Renaissance of Tragedy*. Westport, CT: Praeger, 1995.

Colie, Rosalie, *Paradoxia Epidemica*. Princeton: Princeton University Press, 1966.

—— *Shakespeare's Living Art*. Princeton: Princeton University Press, 1974.

Cooper, Thomas, *Thesaurus Linguae Romanae et Britannicae*. London, 1565.

Copenhaver, Brian, and Charles Schmitt, *Renaissance Philosophy*. Oxford: Oxford University Press, 1992.

Cornwallis, Sir William, *Essayes*, ed. Don Cameron Allen. Baltimore: Johns Hopkins University Press, 1946.

Cotgrave, Randle, *Dictionarie of the French and English Tongues*. London, 1611; Amsterdam, 1971.

Cox, John, 'Shakespeare's Religious and Moral Thinking: Skepticism or Suspicion?', *R&L*, 36:1 (2004): 39–66.

Crooke, Helkiah, *Mikrokosmographia, A Description of the Body of Man*. London, 1615.

Cudworth, Ralph, *True Intellectual System of the Universe*. London, 1678.

Curtis, Mark, *Oxford and Cambridge in Transition*. Oxford: Clarendon, 1959.

Daalder, Joost, and A. Moore, '"There's scarce a thing but is both loved and loathed"', *English Studies*, 80:6 (1999): 499–508.

Daneau, Lambert, *Wonderfull Woorkmanship of the World*, tr. Thomas Twyne. London, 1578.

Davidson, Nicholas, 'Marlowe and Atheism', in D. Grantley and P. Roberts, eds., *Christopher Marlowe and English Renaissance Culture* (Aldershot: Ashgate, 1996), 129–47.

Davies, Sir John, *Poems*, ed. Robert Krueger. Oxford: Clarendon, 1975.

Davies of Hereford, John, *Works*, ed. Alexander Grosart, 2 vols. Edinburgh, 1878.

Dear, Peter, *Mersenne and the Learning of the Schools*. Ithaca: Cornell University Press, 1988.

Defaux, Gérard, 'Montaigne chez les sceptiques', *French Forum*, 23:2 (1998): 147–66.

DeMolen, Richard, 'Library of William Camden', *Proceedings of the American Philosophical Society*, 128:4 (1984): 327–409.

Dent, R. W., *John Webster's Borrowing*. Berkeley: University of California Press, 1960.

—— *Proverbial Language in English Drama Exclusive of Shakespeare*. Berkeley: University of California Press, 1984.

—— 'Ramist Faustus or Ramist Marlowe?', *Neuphilologische Mitteilungen*, 73 (1972): 63–74.

—— *Shakespeare's Proverbial Language*. Berkeley: University of California Press, 1981.

Descartes, René, *Philosophical Writings*, tr. and ed. E. Anscombe and P. Geach. Indianapolis: Bobbs-Merrill, 1971.

Devaris, Matthew, *Liber de Graecae Linguae*. Rome, 1588.

Dickens, A. G., *Lollards and Protestants*. London: Oxford University Press, 1959.

Diogenes Laertius, *Diogenous Laertiou peri bion, dogmaton kai aposthegmaton*, ed. Henri Estienne. Geneva, 1570.

—— *Lives of Eminent Philosophers*, tr. R. D. Hicks, 2 vols. London: Heinemann, 1925.

—— *De vitis, dogmatis & apophthegmatis clarorum Philosophorum*, ed. Isaac Casaubon. Geneva, 1593.

Dollimore, Jonathan, *Radical Tragedy*. Durham, NC: Duke University Press, 1993.

Donne, John, *Essays in Divinity*, ed. Augustus Jessopp. London, 1855.

—— *Essays in Divinity*, ed. Evelyn Simpson. Oxford: Clarendon, 1952.

—— *Fifty Sermons*. London, 1649.

—— *John Donne*, ed. John Carey. Oxford: Oxford University Press, 1990.

—— *Paradoxes and Problems*, ed. Helen Peters. Oxford: Clarendon, 1980.

—— *Sermons*, ed. George Potter and Evelyn Simpson, 10 vols. Berkeley: University of California Press, 1953.

—— *Ten Sermons*, ed. Geoffrey Keynes. London, 1923.

Dooley, Brendan, *The Social History of Skepticism*. Baltimore: Johns Hopkins University Press, 1999.

Du Bartas, Guillaume, *Bartas: His Devine Weekes*, tr. Joshua Sylvester. London, 1605.

—— *The Second Weeke*, tr. Joshua Sylvester. London, 1598.

—— *Triumph of Faith*, tr. Joshua Sylvester. London, 1592.

Duncan, Douglas, *Ben Jonson and the Lucianic Tradition*. Cambridge: Cambridge University Press, 1979.

Durling, Richard, 'Census of Renaissance Editions of Galen', *JWCI*, 24 (1961): 230–305.

Dzelzainis, Martin, 'Shakespeare and Political Thought', in Kastan, *Companion*, 100–16.

Earle, John, *Microcosmography*, ed. Harold Osborne. London: Tutorial Press, 1972.

Edwards, John, and C. J. Sommerville, 'Debate: Religious Faith, Doubt and Atheism', *P&P*, 128 (1990): 155–61.

Eliot, T. S., *Elizabethan Essays*. London: Faber, 1934.

—— '*Pensées* of Pascal', in *Selected Essays* (New York: Harcourt Brace, 1950), 355–68.

Ellis-Fermor, Una, *Frontiers of Drama*. London: Methuen, 1964.

—— *Jacobean Drama*. London: Methuen, 1958.

Ellrodt, Robert, 'Self-Consciousness in Montaigne and Shakespeare', *ShS*, 28 (1975): 37–50.

Elton, Willam, *King Lear and the Gods*. San Marino: Huntington Library, 1966.

—— *Shakespeare's Troilus and Cressida and the Inns of Court Revels*. Brookfield: Ashgate, 2000.

—— 'Shakespeare's Ulysses and the Problem of Value', *ShakS*, 2 (1966): 95–111.

Empson, William, *Some Versions of Pastoral*. London: Chatto & Windus, 1935.

Engle, Lars, '*Measure for Measure* and Modernity: The Problem of the Sceptic's Authority', in Hugh Grady, ed., *Shakespeare and Modernity* (London: Routledge, 2000), 84–104.

—— *Shakespearean Pragmatism*. Chicago: University of Chicago Press, 1993.

*The English Faust Book: A Critical Edition*, ed. John Henry Jones. Cambridge: Cambridge University Press, 1994.

Erasmus, Desiderius, *Adagiorum Chiliades Iuxta Locos Communes*. Frankfurt am Main, 1599.

—— *Apophthegmes*, tr. Nicholas Udall. London, 1542.

—— *The Collected Works of Erasmus*, ed. J. McConica, et al. Toronto: University of Toronto Press, 1974–.

Estienne, Henri, *Thesaurus Graecae Lingua*, 5 vols. Paris, 1572.

—— *Virtutum encomia*. Geneva, 1573.

Evans, Lewis, *The Abridgement of Logique*. London, 1568.

Ewbank, Inga-Stina, 'Webster's Realism', in B. Morris, ed., *John Webster* (London: Benn, 1970), 159–78.

Farrington, Benjamin, *The Philosophy of Francis Bacon*. Chicago: University of Chicago Press, 1964.

Febvre, Lucien, *The Problem of Unbelief in the Sixteenth Century*, tr. Beatrice Gottlieb. Cambridge: Harvard University Press, 1982.

Fehrenbach, Robert, and Elisabeth Leedham-Green, eds., *Private Libraries in Renaissance England*. Binghamton: MRTS, 1992–.

Feingold, Mordechai, 'English Ramism', in M. Feingold, et al., eds., *The Influence of Petrus Ramus* (Basel: Schwabe, 2001), 127–76.

—— *The Mathematicians' Apprenticeship*. Cambridge: Cambridge University Press, 1984.

—— 'Science as a Calling?', *Science in Context*, 15:1 (2002): 79–119.

Ferguson, Margaret, 'Running On with Almost Public Voice', in F. Howe, ed., *Tradition and the Talents of Women* (Urbana: University of Illinois Press, 1991), 37–67.

—— 'The Spectre of Resistance', in Kastan and Stallybrass, 235–50.

Ficino, Marsilio, *Opera Omnia*, 2 vols. Basel, 1576; Turino, 1959.

Fine, Gail, 'Descartes and Ancient Skepticism: Reheated Cabbage?', *Philosophical Review*, 109:2 (2000): 195–234.

Finkelpearl, Philip, *John Marston of the Middle Temple*. Cambridge: Harvard University Press, 1969.

Fitzherbert, Thomas, *A Treatise Concerning Policy and Religion*. Douai, 1606.

Floridi, Luciano, 'Diffusion of Sextus Empiricus's Works in the Renaissance', *JHI*, 56:1 (1995): 63–85.

—— *Sextus Empiricus: The Transmission and Recovery of Pyrrhonism*. New York: Oxford University Press, 2002.

Ford, John, *'Tis Pity She's a Whore*, ed. Brian Morris. New York: Norton, 1990.

Fordyce, C., and T. Knox, *Library of Jesus College, Oxford*. Oxford: Oxford University Press, 1937.

Forker, Charles, *Skull Beneath the Skin: The Achievement of John Webster*. Carbondale: Southern Illinois University Press, 1986.

Fox, Robert, ed., *Thomas Harriot: An Elizabethan Man of Science*. Aldershot: Ashgate, 2000.

Franklin, Julian, *Jean Bodin and the Sixteenth-Century Revolution in the Methodology of Law and History*. New York: Columbia University Press, 1963.

Fraunce, Abraham, *The Arcadian Rhetorike*, ed. Ethel Seaton. Oxford: Blackwell, 1950.

—— *The Lawiers Logike*. London, 1588.

Frede, Michael, 'On Galen's Epistemology', in Vivian Nutton, ed., *Galen* (London: Wellcome Institute, 1981), 65–86.

Friedrich, Hugo, *Montaigne*, tr. Dawn Eng, ed. Philippe Desan. Berkeley: University of California Press, 1991.

Frisius, Johann, *Bibliotheca Philosophorum Classicorum Authorum*. Zurich, 1592.

Galen, *Selected Works*, tr. P. Singer. Oxford: Oxford University Press, 1997.

Galland, Pierre, *Pro schola Parisiensi contra novam academiam Petri Rami*. Paris, 1551.

Garin, Eugenio, *Italian Humanism*, tr. Peter Munz. New York: Harper & Row, 1965.

Gascoigne, George, *Complete Works*, ed. John Cunliffe, 2 vols. Cambridge: Cambridge University Press, 1907.

Gatti, Hilary, *The Renaissance Drama of Knowledge: Giordano Bruno in England*. New York: Routledge, 1989.

Geller, Sherri, 'Historical Pyrrhonism in *A Mirror for Magistrates*', in Peter Herman, ed., *Opening the Borders* (Newark: University of Delaware Press, 1999), 150–84.

George, Edward, *Seventeenth Century Men of Latitude*. New York: Scribner's, 1908.

Gesner, Konrad, *Bibliotheca universalis*. Zurich, 1545.

Giggisberg, Hans, 'Castellio: Problems of Writing a New Biography', in C. Berkvens-Stevelinck, ed., *The Emergence of Tolerance in the Dutch Republic* (Leiden: Brill, 1997), 75–89.

Gilbert, N. W., *Renaissance Concepts of Method*. New York: Columbia University Press, 1960.

Ginzburg, Carlo, *The Cheese and the Worms*, tr. John and Anne Tedeschi. New York: Penguin, 1982.

—— 'High and Low: Forbidden Knowledge in the Sixteenth and Seventeenth Centuries', *P&P*, 73 (1976): 28–41.

Girard, René, 'The Politics of Desire in *Troilus and Cressida*', in P. Parker and G. Hartman, eds., *Shakespeare and the Question of Theory* (London: Methuen, 1985), 188–209.

Glanvill, Joseph, *The Vanity of Dogmatizing*. London, 1661.

Goldberg, Dena, '"By Report": The Spectator as Voyeur in Webster's *White Devil*', *ELR*, 17:1 (1987): 67–84.

Goodman, Godfrey, *The Fall of Man*. London, 1616.

Gosse, Edmund, *Life and Letters of Donne*, 2 vols. London, 1899.

Gosson, Stephen, *The Ephemerides of Phialo*. London, 1579.

Gottlieb, Anthony, *The Dream of Reason*. New York: Norton, 2000.

Grady, Hugh, *Shakespeare's Universal Wolf*. Oxford: Clarendon, 1996.

Grafton, Anthony, 'Availability of Ancient Works', in *Cambridge History of Renaissance Philosophy*, 767–91.

—— 'Higher Criticism Ancient and Modern', in A. Dionisotti, ed., *Uses of Greek and Latin* (London: Warburg Institute, 1988), 155–70.

—— *Joseph Scaliger*, 2 vols. Oxford: Clarendon, 1983.

Green, J. R., *A Short History of the English People*, 4 vols. New York, 1895.

Green, Lawrence, ed., *John Rainolds's Oxford Lectures on Aristotle's Rhetoric*. Newark: University of Delaware Press, 1986.

Green, Otis, *Spain and the Western Tradition*, 4 vols. Madison: University of Wisconsin Press, 1968.

Greenblatt, Stephen, *Hamlet in Purgatory*. Princeton: Princeton University Press, 2001.

—— *Renaissance Self-Fashioning*. Chicago: University of Chicago Press, 1980.

—— *Shakespearean Negotiations*. Berkeley: University of California Press, 1988.

Gregory, Tullio, 'Charron's "Scandalous Book"', in Hunter and Wootton, 87–109.

Greville, Fulke, *Poems and Dramas*, ed. Geoffrey Bullough, 2 vols. New York: Oxford University Press, 1945.

Grotius, Hugo, *Briefwisseling*, ed. P. Molhuysen and B. Meulenbroek, 10 vols. The Hague, 1928–76.

Grudin, Robert, *Mighty Opposites*. Berkeley: University of California Press, 1979.

Guiney, Imogen, *Recusant Poets*. New York: Sheed & Ward, 1938.

Guy, John, *Tudor England*. Oxford: Oxford University Press, 1988.

Hadfield, Andrew, 'The Name "Eudoxus" in Spenser's *View*', *N&Q*, 44:4 (1997): 477–8.

Hakewill, George, *The Vanitie of the Eye*. Oxford, 1608.

Hall, Joan Lord, '"To play the man well and duely": Role-playing in Montaigne and Jacobean Drama', *Comparative Literature Studies*, 22:2 (1985): 173–86.

Hall, Joseph, *Another World and Yet the Same: Mundus Alter et Idem*, tr. J. Wands. New Haven, CT: Yale University Press, 1981.

—— *The Discovery of a New World*, tr. John Healey, ed. H. Brown. Cambridge, MA: Harvard University Press, 1937.

—— *Heaven upon Earth and Characters of Vertues and Vices*, ed. Rudolf Kirk. New Brunswick: Rutgers University Press, 1948.

—— *Works*, ed. Josiah Pratt, 10 vols. London, 1808.

Hamilton, Donna, '*The Spanish Tragedy*: A Speaking Picture', *ELR*, 4:2 (1974): 203–17.

Hamlin, William M., 'A Borrowing from Nashe in *Bussy D'Ambois*', *N&Q*, 48:3 (2001): 264–5.

—— 'Casting Doubt in Marlowe's *Doctor Faustus*', *SEL*, 41:2 (2001): 257–75.

—— 'Elizabeth Cary's *Mariam* and the Critique of Pure Reason', *EMLS*, 9:1 (2003): 2:1–22.

—— 'What Did Montaigne's Skepticism Mean to Shakespeare and His Contemporaries?', *Montaigne Studies*, 17 (2005): 197–212.

—— *The Image of America in Montaigne, Spenser, and Shakespeare*. New York: St. Martin's Press, 1995.

—— 'Imagined Apotheoses: Drake, Harriot and Ralegh in the Americas', *JHI*, 57:3 (1996): 405–28.

—— 'A Lost Translation Found? An Edition of *The Sceptick* (*c.* 1590) Based on Extant Manuscripts', *ELR*, 31:1 (2001): 34–51.

—— 'On Continuities between Skepticism and Early Ethnography', *SCJ*, 31:2 (2000): 361–79.

—— 'Skepticism and Solipsism in *Doctor Faustus*', *RORD*, 36 (1997): 1–22.

—— 'Temporizing as Pyrrhonizing in Marston's *Malcontent*', *CompD*, 34:3 (2000): 305–20.

Hankinson, R. J., *Galen*. Oxford: Clarendon, 1991.

—— 'A Purely Verbal Dispute? Galen on Stoic and Academic Epistemology', *Revue Internationale de Philosophie*, 178 (1991): 267–300.

—— *The Sceptics*. London: Routledge, 1995.

Hardin, Richard, 'Marlowe and the Fruits of Scholarism', *PQ*, 63 (1984): 387–400.

Harth, Philip, *Contexts of Dryden's Thought*. Chicago: University of Chicago Press, 1968.

Hartlib, Samuel, et al., *The Hartlib Papers*, ed. J. Crawford, 2 CD-ROMs. Ann Arbor: University Microfilms, 1996.

Hartog, François, *The Mirror of Herodotus*, tr. Janet Lloyd. Berkeley: University of California Press, 1988.

Hattaway, Michael, ed., *A Companion to English Renaissance Literature and Culture*. Oxford: Blackwell, 2000.

Haydn, Hiram, *The Counter-Renaissance*. New York: Scribner's, 1950.

Heinemann, Margot, *Puritanism and Theatre*. Cambridge: Cambridge University Press, 1980.

Herbert, Edward, *De Veritate*, tr. Meyrick Carré. Bristol: University of Bristol Press, 1937.

—— *Pagan Religion*, tr. John Butler. Binghamton: MRTS, 1996.

Heydon, Christopher, *A Defence of Iudiciall Astrologie, in answer to A Treatise by John Chamber*. Cambridge, 1603.

Heywood, John, *A Dialogue of Proverbs*, ed. Rudolph Habenicht. Berkeley: University of California Press, 1963.

Hiley, David, *Philosophy in Question: Essays on a Pyrrhonian Theme*. Chicago: University of Chicago Press, 1988.

Hill, Christopher, *Intellectual Origins of the English Revolution Revisited*. Oxford: Clarendon, 1997.

—— *The World Turned Upside Down: Radical Ideas During the English Revolution*. New York: Viking, 1972.

Hill, Eugene, 'Senecan and Virgilian Perspectives in *The Spanish Tragedy*', *ELR*, 15:2 (1985): 143–65.

Hillman, David, 'The Gastric Epic: *Troilus and Cressida*', *SQ*, 48:3 (1997): 295–313.

—— 'Visceral Knowledge', in D. Hillman and C. Mazzio, eds., *The Body in Parts* (New York: Routledge, 1997), 81–105.

Hoopes, Robert, 'Fideism and Skepticism during the Renaissance', *HLQ*, 14:4 (1951): 319–47.

Hopkins, Lisa, 'Beguiling the Master of the Mystery: Form and Power in *The Changeling*', *Medieval and Renaissance Drama in England*, 9 (1997): 149–61.

—— *John Ford's Political Theatre*. Manchester: Manchester University Press, 1994.

—— 'Knowing Their Loves: Knowledge, Ignorance, and Blindness in *'Tis Pity She's a Whore'*, *Renaissance Forum*, 3:1 (1998): 1–18.

Horowitz, Maryanne, 'Charron's View of the Source of Wisdom', *JHP*, 9:4 (1971): 443–57.

—— *Seeds of Virtue and Knowledge*. Princeton: Princeton University Press, 1998.

Hotson, Leslie, *Shakespeare's Sonnets Dated*. London: Hart-Davis, 1949.

Howell, Wilbur, *Logic and Rhetoric in England, 1500–1700*. Princeton: Princeton University Press, 1956.

Hoy, Cyrus, '"Ignorance in Knowledge": Marlowe's Faustus and Ford's Giovanni', *Modern Philology*, 57 (1960): 145–54.

Hunter, G. K., *English Drama, 1586–1642*. Oxford: Clarendon, 1997.

—— 'English Folly and Italian Vice: The Moral Landscape of Marston', in Brown and Harris, 85–111.

—— 'Ironies of Justice in *The Spanish Tragedy*', *RenD*, 8 (1965): 89–104.

Hunter, Michael, 'The Problem of "Atheism" in Early Modern England', *Transactions of the Royal Historical Society*, 35 (1985): 135–57.

—— and David Wootton, eds., *Atheism from the Reformation to the Enlightenment*. Oxford: Clarendon, 1992.

Hutton, Sarah, 'Platonism, Stoicism, Scepticism and Classical Imitation', in Hattaway, 44–57.

Hyde, Edward, *Selections from The History of the Rebellion*, ed. Hugh Trevor-Roper. Oxford: Oxford University Press, 1978.

Jacobus, Lee, *Shakespeare and the Dialectic of Certainty*. New York: St. Martin's Press, 1992.

Jacotius, Desiderius, *Tabula Compendiosa de origine, successione, aetate, et doctrina veterum philosophorum*. Basel, 1580.

James VI/I, *Daemonologie*. Edinburgh, 1597; London, 1924.

James, Thomas, *Catalogus Universalis Librorum in Bibliotheca Bodleiana*. Oxford, 1620.

—— *First Printed Catalogue of the Bodleian Library, 1605*. Oxford: Clarendon, 1986.

Jardine, Lisa, 'Humanism and the Sixteenth-Century Cambridge Arts Course', *History of Education*, 4 (1975): 16–31.

—— 'Lorenzo Valla: Academic Skepticism and the New Humanist Dialectic', in Burnyeat, *Skeptical Tradition*, 253–86.

Jardine, Nicholas, 'The Forging of Modern Realism: Clavius and Kepler Against the Sceptics', *Studies in History and Philosophy of Science*, 10 (1979): 141–73.

—— 'Scepticism in Renaissance Astronomy', in Popkin and Schmitt, 83–102.

Jayne, Sears, and Francis Johnson, eds., *The Lumley Library: Catalogue of 1609*. London: British Museum, 1956.

Johnson, Robert, *Essaies, or rather imperfect offers*. London, 1601.

Jones, Norman, 'Shakespeare's England', in Kastan, *Companion*, 25–42.

Jonson, Ben, *Ben Jonson*, ed. Ian Donaldson. Oxford: Oxford University Press, 1985.

Jordan, W. K., *The Development of Religious Toleration in England, 1603–1640*. Cambridge: Cambridge University Press, 1936.

Kahn, Victoria, *Rhetoric, Prudence, and Skepticism in the Renaissance*. Ithaca: Cornell University Press, 1985.

Kaiser, Walter, *Praisers of Folly*. Cambridge: Harvard University Press, 1963.

Kastan, David Scott, ed., *Companion to Shakespeare*. Oxford: Blackwell, 1999.

—— and Peter Stallybrass, eds., *Staging the Renaissance*. New York: Routledge, 1991.

Keefer, Michael, 'Agrippa's Dilemma', *RQ,* 41:4 (1988): 614–53.

Kegl, Rosemary, 'Theaters, Households, and a "Kind of History"', in V. Comensoli and A. Russell, eds., *Enacting Gender* (Urbana: University of Illinois Press, 1999), 135–53.

Kernan, Alvin, '"Banisht!": The Dark World of Jacobean Tragedy', in Leeds Barroll, et al., eds., *Revels History of Drama in English*, 8 vols. (London: Methuen, 1975) 3:384–403.

Kerrigan, John, *Revenge Tragedy*. Oxford: Clarendon, 1996.

Kiessling, Nicolas, *Library of Robert Burton*. Oxford: Oxford Bibliographical Society, 1988.

Kinney, Arthur F., *Continental Humanist Poetics*. Amherst: University of Massachusetts Press, 1989.

Kirsch, Arthur, 'Sexuality and Marriage in Montaigne and *All's Well That Ends Well'*, *Montaigne Studies*, 9 (1997): 187–202.

—— *Shakespeare and the Experience of Love*. Cambridge: Cambridge University Press, 1981.

Knoll, Robert, *Ben Jonson's Plays*. Lincoln: University of Nebraska Press, 1964.

Knowles, Ronald, '*Hamlet* and Counter-Humanism', *RQ,* 51:4 (1999): 1046–69.

Kocher, Paul, 'Backgrounds for Marlowe's Atheist Lecture', *PQ,* 20 (1941): 304–24.

—— *Christopher Marlowe*. Chapel Hill: University of North Carolina Press, 1946.

—— *Science and Religion in Elizabethan England*. San Marino: Huntington Library, 1953.

Kraye, Jill, 'Philologists and Philosophers', in *Cambridge Companion to Renaissance Humanism*, 142–60.

Kristeller, Paul O., *Greek Philosophers of the Hellenistic Age*, tr. Gregory Woods. New York: Columbia University Press, 1993.

—— 'Humanism and Moral Philosophy', in Rabil, 3:271–309.

—— *Iter Italicum*, 7 vols. London: Warburg Institute, 1963–97.

—— *Medieval Aspects of Renaissance Learning*, ed. Edward Mahoney. Durham, NC: Duke University Press, 1974.

—— 'The Myth of Renaissance Atheism and the French Tradition of Free Thought', *JHP*, 6 (1968): 233–43.

—— 'Renaissance Humanism and Classical Antiquity', in Rabil, 1:5–16.

—— *Renaissance Thought and Its Sources*, ed. Michael Mooney. New York: Columbia University Press, 1979.

Kuntz, Marion, 'The Concept of Toleration in *Colloquium Heptaplomeres'*, in J. Laursen and C. Nederman, eds., *Beyond the Persecuting Society* (Philadelphia: University of Pennsylvania Press, 1998), 125–44.

Kyd, Thomas, *The Spanish Tragedy*, ed. J. R. Mulryne. New York: Norton, 1989.

Lake, Peter, *Moderate Puritans and the Elizabethan Church*. Cambridge: Cambridge University Press, 1982.

La Mothe Le Vayer, François (pseud. Orasius Tubero), *Quatre dialogues faits a l'imitation des anciens*. Frankfurt, 1606.

Lancre, Pierre de. *Tableau de l'inconstance et instabilité de toutes choses: ou il est monstré, qu'en Dieu seul gist la vraye constance, à laquelle l'homme sage doit viser.* Paris, 1607.

Larmore, Charles, 'Scepticism', in *Cambridge History of Seventeenth-Century Philosophy*, 2:1145–92.

Laursen, John, *The Politics of Skepticism in the Ancients, Montaigne, Hume, and Kant.* Leiden: Brill, 1992.

Lee, John, 'The English Renaissance Essay', in Hattaway, 600–8.

Leedham-Green, Elisabeth, *Books in Cambridge Inventories: Book-Lists from the Vice-Chancellor's Court Probate Inventories in the Tudor and Stuart Periods*, 2 vols. Cambridge: Cambridge University Press, 1986.

—— and David McKitterick, 'Catalogue of Cambridge University Library, 1583', in J. Carley and C. Tite, eds., *Books and Collectors 1200–1700* (London: British Library, 1997), 153–235.

Lefranc, Pierre, *Sir Walter Ralegh Ecrivain.* Paris: Armand Colin, 1968.

Legros, Alain, 'La Dédicace de l'*Adversus Mathematicos*', *Bulletin de la Société des Amis de Montaigne*, 8th series, 15–16 (1999): 51–72.

Le Loyer, Pierre, *IIII Livres des Spectres.* Angers, 1586.

—— *A treatise of specters*, tr. Zachary Jones. London, 1605.

Lennon, Thomas, 'Jansenism and the *Crise Pyrrhonienne*', *JHI*, 38 (1977): 297–306.

Levi, A. H., 'The Relationship of Stoicism and Scepticism: Justus Lipsius', in Jill Kraye and M. Stone, eds., *Humanism and Early Modern Philosophy* (New York: Routledge, 2000), 91–106.

Levin, Richard, *The Multiple Plot in English Renaissance Drama.* Chicago: University of Chicago Press, 1971.

Levine, Laura. *Men in Women's Clothing.* Cambridge: Cambridge University Press, 1994.

Lewalski, Barbara, 'Writing Women and Reading the Renaissance', *RQ*, 44:4 (1991): 792–821.

—— *Writing Women in Jacobean England.* Cambridge: Harvard University Press, 1993.

Limbrick, Elaine, 'Franciscus Sanchez, "Scepticus"', *Renaissance & Reformation*, 6:4 (1982): 264–72.

—— 'Montaigne et le spectre du pyrrhonisme', in C. Blum, ed., *Montaigne* (Paris: Champion, 1990), 143–55.

—— 'Was Montaigne Really a Pyrrhonian?', *BHR*, 39 (1977): 67–80.

Lipsius, Justus, *Manuductionis ad Stoicam Philosophiam.* Antwerp, 1610.

—— *Sixe Bookes of Politickes or Civil Doctrine*, tr. William Jones. London, 1594.

Locke, John, *An Essay Concerning Human Understanding.* New York: New American Library, 1964.

Long, A. A. *Hellenistic Philosophy*, 2nd edn. Berkeley: University of California Press, 1986.

—— and D. Sedley, eds., *The Hellenistic Philosophers*, 2 vols. Cambridge: Cambridge University Press, 1987.

Lucian, *Works*, tr. H. W. Fowler, 4 vols. Oxford: Clarendon, 1905.

Luckyj, Christina, *A Winter's Snake: Dramatic Form in the Tragedies of John Webster.* Athens: University of Georgia Press, 1989.

Lucretius, *De Rerum Natura*, ed. Denys Lambin. Paris, 1563.

Luther, Martin, *Works*, ed. Helmut Lehman, 55 vols. Philadelphia: Fortress, 1972.

Lyly, John, *Campaspe*, ed. G. K. Hunter. Manchester: Manchester University Press, 1991.

Mandelbrote, Scott, 'The Religion of Thomas Harriot,' in Fox, 246–79.

Marchitello, Howard, *Narrative and Meaning in Early Modern England*. Cambridge: Cambridge University Press, 1997.

Marlowe, Christopher, *Doctor Faustus: A- and B-Texts*, ed. David Bevington and Eric Rasmussen. Manchester: Manchester University Press, 1993.

Marston, John, *The Malcontent*, ed. Bernard Harris. New York: Norton, 1967.

—— *The Malcontent and Other Plays*, ed. Keith Sturgess. Oxford: Oxford University Press, 1997.

—— *Poems*, ed. Arnold Davenport. Liverpool: Liverpool University Press, 1961.

—— *Works*, ed. A. Bullen, 3 vols. New York: Olms, 1970.

Martin, Mathew, *Between Theater and Philosophy: Skepticism in the Major City Comedies of Ben Jonson and Thomas Middleton*. Newark: University of Delaware Press, 2001.

Mates, Benson, *The Skeptic Way*. Oxford: Oxford University Press, 1996.

Maus, Katharine Eisaman, *Inwardness and Theater in the English Renaissance*. Chicago: University of Chicago Press, 1995.

Mazzoni, Jacopo, *Universam Platonis et Aristotelis Philosophiam*. Venice, 1597.

McAlindon, T., *English Renaissance Tragedy*. London: Macmillan, 1986.

McCabe, Richard, *Incest, Drama, and Nature's Law*. Cambridge: Cambridge University Press, 1993.

McKitterick, D., *Library of Thomas Knyvett*. Cambridge: Cambridge University Press, 1978.

McLachan, John, *Socinianism in Seventeenth-Century England*. Oxford: Oxford University Press, 1951.

McLuskie, Kathleen, *Renaissance Dramatists*. Atlantic Highlands, NJ: Humanities Press, 1989.

Mebane, John, 'Skepticism and Radical Reform in Agrippa's *Uncertainty*', *Renaissance Papers*, 32 (1987): 1–10.

Mede, Joseph, *Works*, ed. John Worthington. London, 1664.

Mersenne, Marin, *La verité des sciences, contre les septiques ou pyrrhoniens*. Paris, 1625.

Middleton, Thomas, *Five Plays*, ed. B. Loughrey and N. Taylor. Harmondsworth: Penguin, 1988.

Miles, Geoffrey, *Shakespeare and the Constant Romans*. Oxford: Clarendon, 1996.

Missner, Marshall, 'Skepticism and Hobbes's Political Philosophy', *JHI*, 44:3 (1983): 407–27.

Montaigne, Michel de, *An Apology for Raymond Sebond*, tr. M. A. Screech. Harmondsworth: Penguin, 1987.

—— *Complete Essays*, tr. M. A. Screech. Harmondsworth: Penguin, 1991.

—— *Les Essais*, ed. Pierre Villey, rev. V.-L. Saulnier, 3 vols. Paris: Presses Universitaires de France, 1992.

—— *Essayes of Montaigne*, tr. John Florio. London, 1603; New York: Modern Library, 1933.

More, Henry, *Poems*, ed. Alexander Grosart. London, 1878; New York, 1967.

More, Sir Thomas, *Complete Works*, ed. L. Martz, et al., 15 vols. New Haven: Yale University Press, 1963–86.

Mornay, Philippe du Plessis, *De la Verité de la religion chrestienne*. Anvers, 1581.

—— *A Woorke concerning the trewnesse of the Christian Religion*, tr. Philip Sidney and Arthur Golding, ed. F. Sypher. Delmar, NY: Scholars' Facsimiles, 1976.

Morphos, Panos, 'An Aspect of Renaissance Scepticism and Relativism', in Brués, 3–84.

Mortimer, Jean, 'Library of Anthony Higgin', *Leeds Philosophical Society*, 10:1 (1962): 1–75.

Morton, Thomas, *Treatise of the Nature of God*. London, 1599.

Muir, Kenneth, *Shakespeare's Sources*. London: Methuen, 1957.

Mullan, David, 'Masked Popery and Pyrrhonian Uncertainty', *Journal of Religious History*, 21:2 (1997): 159–77.

Mullaney, Steven, *The Place of the Stage*. Chicago: University of Chicago Press, 1988.

Mullinger, James, *The University of Cambridge*. Cambridge: Cambridge University Press, 1884.

Mulryne, J. R., '*The White Devil* and *The Duchess of Malfi*', in Brown and Harris, 201–25.

Nashe, Thomas, *Works*, ed. R. B. McKerrow, 5 vols. London, 1904–10; Oxford, 1958.

Nauert, Charles, *Agrippa and the Crisis of Renaissance Thought*. Urbana: University of Illinois Press, 1965.

—— *Humanism and the Culture of Renaissance Europe*. Cambridge: Cambridge University Press, 1995.

—— 'Humanism as Method', *SCJ*, 29:2 (1998): 427–38.

Neill, Michael, 'The Defence of Contraries', *SEL*, 21:2 (1981): 319–32.

—— *Issues of Death: Mortality and Identity in English Renaissance Tragedy*. Oxford: Clarendon, 1997.

Neto, José, 'Academic Skepticism in Early Modern Philosophy', *JHI*, 58:2 (1997): 199–220.

Nicholas of Cusa, *Of Learned Ignorance*, tr. G. Heron. New Haven: Yale University Press, 1954.

Nicholl, Charles, *The Reckoning*. London: Cape, 1992.

Norden, John, *Vicissitudo Rerum*. London, 1600.

Norwood, Richard, *Journal*, ed. Wesley Craven. New York: Scholars' Facsimiles, 1935.

Nussbaum, Martha, *The Therapy of Desire: Theory and Practice in Hellenistic Ethics*. Princeton: Princeton University Press, 1994.

Oakeshott, Walter, 'Ralegh's Library', *The Library*, 5th series, 23:4 (1968): 285–327.

Ong, Walter, *Ramus, Method, and the Decay of Dialogue*. Cambridge, MA: Harvard University Press, 1958.

Ornstein, Robert, *The Moral Vision of Jacobean Tragedy*. Madison: University of Wisconsin Press, 1960.

Orr, Robert, *Reason and Authority: The Thought of William Chillingworth*. Oxford: Clarendon, 1967.

Osler, Margaret, 'Skepticism', *Encyclopedia of the Renaissance*, 6 vols. (New York: Scribner's, 1999), 6:36–8.

Ozment, Steven, *The Age of Reform, 1250–1550*. New Haven, CT: Yale University Press, 1980.

Panizza, Letizia, 'Lorenzo Valla, Lactantius, and Oratorical Scepticism', *JWCI*, 41 (1978): 76–107.

Park, Katharine, and Eckhard Kessler, 'The Concept of Psychology', in *Cambridge History of Renaissance Philosophy*, 455–63.

Pascal, Blaise, *Pensées*, tr. W. Trotter, intro. T. S. Eliot. New York: Dutton, 1958.

Pattison, Mark, *Isaac Casaubon*. London, 1875.

Peltonen, Markku, ed., *Cambridge Companion to Bacon*. Cambridge: Cambridge University Press, 1996.

Penelhum, Terence, 'Skepticism and Fideism', in Burnyeat, *Skeptical Tradition*, 287–316.

Perreiah, Alan, 'Humanistic Critiques of Scholastic Dialectic', *SCJ*, 13:3 (1982): 3–22.

Petrarch, Francesco, *On His Own Ignorance*, in Ernst Cassirer, ed., *The Renaissance Philosophy of Man*. Chicago: University of Chicago Press, 1948, 49–133.

Pfister, Manfred, 'Elizabethan Atheism: Discourse without Subject', *Shakespeare Jahrbuch*, 127 (1991): 59–81.

Piccolomini, Francesco, *Universa Philosophia de moribus*. Geneva, 1596.

Pico della Mirandola, Gianfrancesco, *Examen vanitatis doctrinae gentium et veritatis Christianae disciplinae*. Mirandola, 1520.

Pierce, Robert, 'Shakespeare and the Ten Modes of Scepticism', *ShS*, 46 (1994): 145–58.

Pinciss, G. M., 'Marlowe's Cambridge Years', *SEL*, 33:2 (1993): 249–64.

Pittion, J.-P., 'Scepticism and Medicine in the Renaissance', in Popkin and Schmitt, 103–32.

Plutarch, *Adversus colotem*, in Long and Sedley, 1:440–1, 1:450.

—— *The Philosophie, commonlie called the Morals*, tr. Philemond Holland. London, 1603.

Pooley, Roger, *English Prose of the Seventeenth Century*. London: Longman, 1992.

Popkin, Richard, 'Charron and Descartes', *Journal of Philosophy*, 51 (1954): 831–7.

—— *The History of Scepticism from Savonarola to Bayle*. Oxford: Oxford University Press, 2003.

—— 'The Religious Background of Seventeenth-Century Philosophy', in *Cambridge History of Seventeenth-Century Philosophy*, 1:393–422.

—— 'The Role of Scepticism in Modern Philosophy Reconsidered', *JHP*, 31:4 (1993): 501–17.

—— 'Scepticism and Modernity', in Tom Sorell, ed., *The Rise of Modern Philosophy* (Oxford: Clarendon, 1993), 15–32.

—— 'Skepticism and the Counter-Reformation in France', *Archiv für Reformationsgeschichte*, 51 (1960): 58–87.

—— 'Theories of Knowledge', in *Cambridge History of Renaissance Philosophy*, 668–84.

—— and Charles Schmitt, eds., *Scepticism from the Reformation to the Enlightenment*. Wiesbaden: Harrassowitz, 1987.

Porter, H. C., *Reformation and Reaction in Tudor Cambridge*. Cambridge: Cambridge University Press, 1958.

Prest, Wilfrid, *The Inns of Court Under Elizabeth and the Early Stuarts*. Totowa: Rowman & Littlefield, 1972.

Primaudaye, Pierre de la, *The French Academie*, tr. T. B. London, 1586.

—— *Second Part of the French Academie*, tr. T. B. London, 1594.

Prosser, Eleanor, 'Shakespeare, Montaigne, and the Rarer Action', *ShakS*, 1 (1965): 261–4.

Pumfrey, Stephen, 'The History of Science and the Renaissance Science of History', in S. Pumfrey, et al., eds., *Science, Culture and Popular Belief* (Manchester: Manchester University Press, 1991), 48–70.

Quilligan, Maureen, 'Staging Gender: William Shakespeare and Elizabeth Cary', in J. Turner, ed., *Sexuality and Gender in Early Modern Europe* (Cambridge: Cambridge University Press, 1993), 208–32.

Rabelais, François, *Complete Works*, tr. Donald Frame. Berkeley: University of California Press, 1991.

Rabil, Albert, ed., *Renaissance Humanism*, 3 vols. Philadelphia: University of Pennsylvania Press, 1988.

Rabkin, Norman, *Shakespeare and the Common Understanding*. New York: Free Press, 1967.

Ralegh, Sir Walter, *The History of the World*, ed. C. A. Patrides. Philadelphia: Temple University Press, 1971.

Ramus, Peter, *Scholae in liberales artes*. Basel, 1569; New York, 1970.

Rebholz, Ronald, *Life of Fulke Greville*. Oxford: Clarendon, 1971.

Ribner, Irving, *Jacobean Tragedy: The Quest for Moral Order*. New York: Barnes & Noble, 1962.

Rice, Eugene, *Prefatory Epistles of Jacques Lefèvre d'Etaples*. New York: Columbia University Press, 1972.

—— *The Renaissance Idea of Wisdom*. Cambridge, MA: Harvard University Press, 1958.

Richardson, Alexander, *The Logicians School-Master: Or, A Comment Upon Ramus Logicke*. London, 1629.

Ricks, Christopher, 'Moral and Poetic Structure of *The Changeling*'. *Essays in Criticism*, 10 (1960): 290–306.

Rider, John, *Bibliotheca Scholastica*. London, 1589.

Roberts, Julian, and Andrew Watson, eds., *John Dee's Library Catalogue*. London: Bibliographical Society, 1990.

Robinson, Christopher, *Lucian and His Influence*. Chapel Hill: University of North Carolina Press, 1979.

Robinson, T. M., *Contrasting Arguments: An Edition of the Dissoi Logoi*. New York: Arno, 1979.

Ronquist, Eyvind, 'Rhetoric and Early Modern Skepticism', *Canadian Journal of Rhetorical Studies*, 5 (1995): 49–75.

Rossiter, A. P., *Angel with Horns*. London: Longman, 1961.

Rowlands, Samuel, *Greene's Ghost Haunting Coniecatchers*. London, 1602; Glasgow, 1872.

Rozett, Martha, *The Doctrine of Election and the Emergence of Elizabethan Tragedy*. Princeton: Princeton University Press, 1984.

Rummel, Erika, *The Humanist-Scholastic Debate in the Renaissance and Reformation*. Cambridge, MA: Harvard University Press, 1995.

Salingar, Leo, *Dramatic Form in Shakespeare and the Jacobeans*. Cambridge: Cambridge University Press, 1986.

Sanches, Francisco, *Quod nihil scitur*. Lyons, 1581.

—— *That Nothing Is Known*, tr. Douglas Thomson, intro. Elaine Limbrick. Cambridge: Cambridge University Press, 1988.

Scaliger, Joseph, *In Manili Quinque Libros Astronomicon, Commentarius et Castigationes*. Paris, 1578.

*Scepticorum Epochē, est retinenda*, Bodleian Library, G.Pamph,1688, 6, fol. 31.

Schiffman, Zachary, 'Montaigne and the Rise of Skepticism', *JHI*, 45 (1984): 499–516.

—— *On the Threshold of Modernity: Relativism in the French Renaissance*. Baltimore: Johns Hopkins University Press, 1991.

Schmitt, Charles B., *Cicero Scepticus: A Study of the Influence of the Academica in the Renaissance*. The Hague: Martinus Nijhoff, 1972.

—— *Gianfrancesco Pico della Mirandola and His Critique of Aristotle*. The Hague: Martinus Nijhoff, 1967.

—— 'Giulio Castellani', *JHP*, 5 (1967): 15–39.

—— 'John Wolley and the first Latin translation of Sextus Empiricus, adversus logicos I', in Watson and Force, 61–70.

—— 'Philosophy and Science in Sixteenth-Century Universities', in J. Murdoch and E. Sylla, eds., *The Cultural Context of Medieval Learning* (Dordrecht: Reidel, 1975), 485–537.

—— 'The Recovery and Assimilation of Ancient Scepticism', *Rivista Critica di Storia della Filosofia*, 4 (1972): 363–84.

—— 'The Rediscovery of Ancient Skepticism in Modern Times', in Burnyeat, *Skeptical Tradition*, 225–51.

—— 'An Unstudied Fifteenth-Century Latin Translation of Sextus by Giovanni Lorenzi', in C. Clough, ed., *Cultural Aspects of the Italian Renaissance* (Manchester: Manchester University Press, 1976), 244–61.

Schwartz, Jerome, *Irony and Ideology in Rabelais*. Cambridge: Cambridge University Press, 1990.

Scodel, Joshua, 'John Donne and the Religious Politics of the Mean', in R. Frontain and F. Malpezzi, eds., *John Donne's Religious Imagination*. Conway: University of Central Arkansas Press, 1995, 45–80.

Scot, Reginald, *The Discoverie of Witchcraft*, ed. Brinsley Nicholson. Totowa: Rowman & Littlefield, 1973.

Screech, M. A., *Rabelais*. Ithaca: Cornell University Press, 1979.

Sedley, David, 'Sublimity and Skepticism in Montaigne', *PMLA*, 113:5 (1998): 1079–92.

Seigel, Jerrold, *Rhetoric and Philosophy in Renaissance Humanism*. Princeton: Princeton University Press, 1968.

Sextus Empiricus, *Oeuvres Choisies*, tr. Jean Grenier and Geneviève Goron. Paris: Aubier, 1948.

—— *Outlines of Scepticism*, tr. Julia Annas and Jonathan Barnes. Cambridge: Cambridge University Press, 1994.

—— *Sexti Empirici Adversus mathematicos*, tr. Gentian Hervet. Paris, 1569.

—— *Sexti Empirici Opera quae extant*, ed. Pierre and Jacob Chouet. Paris and Geneva, 1621.

—— *Sexti Philosophi Pyrrhoniarum hypotyposeon libri III*, tr. Henri Estienne. Geneva, 1562.

—— *Sextus Empiricus*, tr. R. G. Bury, 4 vols. Cambridge: Harvard University Press, 1955.

Shakespeare, William, *Hamlet*, ed. Harold Jenkins. London: Methuen, 1982.
—— *The Norton Shakespeare*, ed. Stephen Greenblatt, et al. New York: Norton, 1997.
—— *The Riverside Shakespeare*, ed. G. Blakemore Evans. Boston: Houghton Mifflin, 1974.
—— *Troilus and Cressida*, ed. David Bevington. Walton-on-Thames: Thomas Nelson, 1998.
Shannon, Laurie, '*The Tragedie of Mariam*: Cary's Critique of the Terms of Founding Social Discourses', *ELR*, 24:1 (1994): 135–53.
Shapiro, Barbara, *A Culture of Fact: England, 1550–1720*. Ithaca: Cornell University Press, 2000.
—— *John Wilkins*. Berkeley: University of California Press, 1969.
—— *Probability and Certainty in Seventeenth-Century England*. Princeton: Princeton University Press, 1983.
Shaw, David, ed., *Cathedral Libraries Catalogue*, 2 vols. London: British Library, 1998.
Shaw, George Bernard, *Shaw on Shakespeare*, ed. Edwin Wilson. New York: Dutton, 1961.
Shirley, John, *Thomas Harriot*. Oxford: Clarendon, 1983.
Shumaker, Wayne, *Occult Sciences in the Renaissance*. Berkeley: University of California Press, 1972.
Sidney, Sir Philip, *Sidney: A Critical Edition*, ed. Katherine Duncan-Jones. Oxford: Oxford University Press, 1989.
*Sir Walter Raleigh's SCEPTICK*, in *Raleigh's Sceptick, or Speculations* (London, 1651), 1–31.
Skinner, Quentin, *Reason and Rhetoric in the Philosophy of Hobbes*. Cambridge: Cambridge University Press, 1996.
Sloane, Thomas, *Donne, Milton, and the End of Humanist Rhetoric*. Berkeley: University of California Press, 1985.
—— *On the Contrary: The Protocol of Traditional Rhetoric*. Washington: Catholic University of America Press, 1997.
Smith, William, *Classical Dictionary of Biography, Mythology, and Geography*. London, 1889.
Soellner, Rolf, 'Prudence and the Price of Helen', *SQ*, 20 (1969): 255–63.
—— *Shakespeare's Patterns of Self-Knowledge*. Columbus: Ohio State University Press, 1972.
Sommerville, J. P., *Politics and Ideology in England, 1603–1640*. London: Longman, 1986.
Southgate, Beverley, 'Excluding sceptics', in Watson and Force, 71–86.
Spach, Israel, *Nomenclator Scriptorum Philosophicorum*. Strasbourg, 1598.
Sparrow, John, 'Earlier Owners of Books in Selden's Library', *Bodleian Quarterly Record*, 6 (1931): 263–74.
Spenser, Edmund, *The Faerie Queene*, ed. A. C. Hamilton, 2nd edn. London: Longman, 2001.
Spolsky, Ellen, *Satisfying Skepticism*. Aldershot: Ashgate, 2001.
Sprott, S. E., 'Ralegh's "Sceptic" and the Elizabethan Translation of Sextus', *PQ*, 42 (1963): 166–75.
Stanley, Thomas, *A Summary of Scepticism*, in Thomas Stanley, *The History of Philosophy, Fourth Part: Containing the Sceptick Sect* (London, 1659), 1–104.

Steadman, John, *The Hill and the Labyrinth*. Berkeley: University of California Press, 1984.

Stillingfleet, Edward, *Discourse Concerning the Nature and Grounds of the Certainty of Faith*. London, 1688.

Stone, Lawrence, *The Causes of the English Revolution, 1529–1642*. New York: Harper & Row, 1972.

—— *The Crisis of the Aristocracy, 1558–1641*. Oxford: Clarendon, 1965.

Stough, Charlotte, *Greek Skepticism*. Berkeley: University of California Press, 1969.

Strathmann, Ernest, *Sir Walter Ralegh: A Study in Elizabethan Skepticism*. New York: Columbia University Press, 1951.

Straznicky, Marta, '"Profane Stoical Paradoxes": *The Tragedie of Mariam* and Sidnean Closet Drama', *ELR*, 24:1 (1994): 104–34.

Strier, Richard, *Resistant Structures: Particularity, Radicalism, and Renaissance Texts*. Berkeley: University of California Press, 1995.

—— 'Shakespeare and the Skeptics', *R&L*, 32:2 (2000): 171–96.

Struever, Nancy, *Theory as Practice: Ethical Inquiry in the Renaissance*. Chicago: University of Chicago Press, 1992.

*Suidae Historica, caeterique omnia que ulla ex parte ad cognitionem rerum spectant*. Basel, 1564.

Thomas, Keith, *Religion and the Decline of Magic*. London: Weidenfeld & Nicolson, 1971.

Thomson, Richard, *Diatriba de amissione et intercisione gratiae et iustificationis*. Leiden, 1616.

Tilley, Morris P., *Dictionary of the Proverbs in England in the Sixteenth and Seventeenth Centuries*. Ann Arbor: University of Michigan Press, 1950.

Tilney, Edmond, *The Flower of Friendship*, ed. Valerie Wayne. Ithaca, NY: Cornell University Press, 1992.

Tinkler, John, 'Bacon and History', in Peltonen, 232–59.

Toulmin, Stephen, *Cosmopolis: The Hidden Agenda of Modernity*. Chicago: University of Chicago Press, 1990.

Travitsky, Betty, 'The *Feme Covert* in Cary's *Mariam*', in C. Levin and J. Watson, eds., *Ambiguous Realities*. Detroit: Wayne State University Press, 1987, 184–96.

Trevor-Roper, Hugh, *Catholics, Anglicans and Puritans*. Chicago: University of Chicago Press, 1988.

—— *Religion, the Reformation, and Social Change*. London: Macmillan, 1967.

Tuck, Richard, intro. to Thomas Hobbes, *Leviathan*. Cambridge: Cambridge University Press, 1991, ix–xxvi.

—— *Philosophy and Government, 1572–1651*. Cambridge: Cambridge University Press, 1993.

—— 'Scepticism and Toleration in the Seventeenth Century', in S. Mendus, ed., *Justifying Toleration*. Cambridge: Cambridge University Press, 1988, 21–35.

Turnbull, G., *Hartlib, Dury and Comenius*. Liverpool: Liverpool University Press, 1947.

Tyacke, Nicholas, *Anti-Calvinists: The Rise of English Arminianism*. Oxford: Clarendon, 1987.

—— 'Arminianism and English Culture', in A. Duke and C. Tamse, eds., *Britain and the Netherlands*. The Hague: Martinus Nijhoff, 1981, 7:94–117.

—— 'The Rise of Arminianism Reconsidered', *P&P*, 115 (1987): 201–16.

Valencia, Pedro de, *Academica sive de Iudicio erga verum*. Antwerp, 1596.

Van Leeuwen, Henry, 'Certainty in Seventeenth-Century Thought', in P. Wiener, ed., *Dictionary of the History of Ideas*, 5 vols. New York: Scribner's, 1973–74, 1:304–11.

—— *The Problem of Certainty in English Thought, 1630–1690*. The Hague: Martinus Nijhoff, 1970.

Vickers, Brian, *Appropriating Shakespeare: Contemporary Critical Quarrels*. New Haven, CT: Yale University Press, 1993.

Villey, Pierre, *Montaigne devant la Postérité*. Paris, 1935.

—— *Montaigne et François Bacon*. Paris, 1913; Geneva, 1973.

—— *Les Sources et l'Évolution des Essais de Montaigne*, 2nd edn., 2 vols. Paris: Hachette, 1933.

Viotti, Bartolomeo, *De Demonstratione*. Paris, 1560.

Vives, Juan Luis, *On Education: A Translation of the De Tradendis Disciplinis*, tr. Foster Watson. Cambridge: Cambridge University Press, 1913.

Wade, Ira, *Intellectual Origins of the French Enlightenment*. Princeton: Princeton University Press, 1971.

Walker, D. P., *The Ancient Theology*. Ithaca, NY: Cornell University Press, 1972.

—— 'Ways of Dealing with Atheists', *BHR*, 17 (1955): 252–77.

Waswo, Richard, *The Fatal Mirror: Themes and Techniques in the Poetry of Fulke Greville*. Charlottesville: University Press of Virginia, 1972.

Watson, Richard, and James Force, eds., *The Sceptical Mode in Modern Philosophy*. Dordrecht: Martinus Nijhoff, 1988.

Watson, Robert, *The Rest is Silence: Death and Annihilation in the English Renaissance*. Berkeley: University of California Press, 1994.

—— 'Tragedy', in *Cambridge Companion to English Renaissance Drama*, 301–51.

Webster, John, *The Duchess of Malfi and Other Plays*, ed. René Weis. Oxford: Oxford University Press, 1996.

—— *Works*, ed. David Gunby, et al. Cambridge: Cambridge University Press, 1995–.

Whigham, Frank, 'Sexual and Social Mobility in *The Duchess of Malfi*', *PMLA*, 100:2 (1985): 167–86.

White, Thomas, *An Exclusion of Scepticks from all Title to Dispute*. London, 1665.

Whitfield, Christopher, 'Some of Shakespeare's Contemporaries at the Middle Temple', *N&Q*, 13:12 (1966): 122–5, 283–7, 363–9, 443–8.

Whitlock, Richard, *Zootomia*. London, 1654.

Wilcox, Thomas, *A Discourse Touching the Doctrine of Doubting*. Cambridge, 1598.

Wiley, Margaret, *Creative Sceptics*. London: Allen & Unwin, 1966.

—— *The Subtle Knot: Creative Skepticism in Seventeenth-Century England*. Cambridge, MA: Harvard University Press, 1952.

Wilkes, G., 'The Chorus Sacerdotum in Greville's *Mustapha*', *RES*, 49 (1998): 326–8.

Wilks, John, *The Idea of Conscience in Renaissance Tragedy*. London: Routledge, 1990.

Willet, Andrew, *De animae natura et viribus quaestiones quaedem*. Cambridge, 1585.

Wilson, F. P., *Elizabethan and Jacobean*. Oxford: Clarendon, 1945.

Wilson, Thomas, *The Rule of Reason*. London, 1551.

Wolfe, Heather, ed., *Elizabeth Cary, Lady Falkland: Life and Letters*. Tempe: MRTS, 2001.

Woolf, D. R., 'The Shapes of History', in Kastan, *Companion*, 186–205.

Wootton, David, 'Unbelief in Early-Modern Europe', *History Workshop*, 20 (1985): 82–100.

Wormald, B. H. G., *Clarendon*. Cambridge: Cambridge University Press, 1951.

—— *Francis Bacon*. Cambridge: Cambridge University Press, 1993.

Wright, Thomas, *The Passions of the Mind in General*, ed. William Newbold. New York: Garland, 1986.

Yachnin, Paul, *Stage-Wrights: Shakespeare, Jonson, Middleton, and the Making of Theatrical Value*. Philadelphia: University of Pennsylvania Press, 1997.

Yates, Frances, *John Florio*. Cambridge: Cambridge University Press, 1934.

Zagorin, Perez, *Francis Bacon*. Princeton: Princeton University Press, 1998.

—— *Ways of Lying*. Cambridge, MA: Harvard University Press, 1990.

Zimmerman, Shari, 'Disaffection, Dissimulation, and the Uncertain Ground of Silent Dismission: Juxtaposing John Milton and Elizabeth Cary', *ELH*, 66 (1999): 553–89.

# Index

Printed in the United States
153120LV00001B/4/A

9 781403 945983